MOMENTS OF MEETING

SUNY series in Communication Studies
Dudley D. Cahn, editor

Moments of Meeting

*Buber, Rogers, and the Potential
for Public Dialogue*

Kenneth N. Cissna
and
Rob Anderson

STATE UNIVERSITY OF NEW YORK PRESS

Published by
State University of New York Press, Albany

The photograph of Martin Buber was provided by his granddaughter, Judith Buber Agassi, and is reproduced with her permission. Photo credit: M. Huttman. The Carl Rogers photograph was provided by his daughter, Natalie Rogers, and is used with her permission. Photo credit: Louise Barker.

For information, address State University of New York Press,
90 State Street, Suite 700, Albany, NY 12207

Production by Cathleen Collins
Marketing by Anne Valentine

Library of Congress Cataloging in Publication Data

Cissna, Kenneth N.
    Moments of meeting: Buber, Rogers, and the potential for public
  dialogue / Kenneth N. Cissna and Rob Anderson.
        p. cm.—(SUNY series in communication studies)
    Includes bibliographical references (p.) and index.
    ISBN 0-7914-5283-2 (alk. paper)—ISBN 0-7914-5284-0 (pbk. : alk. paper)
      1. Buber, Martin, 1878–1965.   2. Rogers, Carl R. (Carl Ransom), 1902–
  3. Dialogue.   I. Anderson, Rob, 1945– II. Title.   III. Series.

B3213.B84 C57 2002
150'.92'2—dc21   2001031354

10 9 8 7 6 5 4 3 2 1

Contents

Foreword   vii
Barnett Pearce

Introduction   xv

1. Dialogue in Public Space   1

2. A Rhetorical Approach to Dialogue   15

3. Buber and the Philosophy of Dialogue   35

4. Rogers and the Praxis of Dialogue   59

5. Historical Context and the Buber–Rogers Meeting   99

6. Interhuman Meeting   123

7. Theorizing Dialogic Moments   173

8. Conversations of Democracy   209

9. The Next Voices   243

Notes   267

References   277

About the Authors   309

Author Index   311

Subject Index   317

Foreword

Barnett Pearce

Moments of Meeting: Buber, Rogers, and the Potential for Public Dialogue addresses an important topic; it is a work of serious scholarship; it makes a useful contribution for practitioners; and—perhaps surprisingly, given the characteristics just cited—it tells a good story and tells it well.

I want to start with that enigmatic, oxymoronic phrase with which their title ends: "public dialogue." As the founding member of a nonprofit organization called the Public Dialogue Consortium, I do not come to this issue without certain commitments. But just that experience sensitizes me to questions like these: What is "dialogue" anyway? Is dialogue-in-public the same thing as "public dialogue"? When and for whom and for whose purposes is dialogue desirable?

At one level, the questions above seem naïve. Conventional wisdom has developed remarkable sophistication in recent years about the importance of forms of communication and the need to institutionalize better forms of communication as the way of doing democracy, conflict resolution, management, and interpersonal relations. For example, Tannen's (1998) *The Argument Culture: Moving from Debate to Dialogue* demonstrates convincingly that confrontational, adversarial communication practices are the standard operating procedure throughout our culture, and that this has deleterious effects. A book describing how to improve "difficult conversations" has been surprisingly successful (Stone, Patton, & Heen, 1999).

The preferable alternative is often termed "dialogue" (see Arnett & Arneson, 1999; Bohm, 1996; Ellinor & Gerard, 1998; Flick, 1998; Isaacs, 1999; Saunders, 1999; Tannen, 1998; and Yankelovich, 1999). However, a close reading of these books and, to the extent possible, an observation of the practices of those working in these traditions, reveals that there are some important differences in what counts as "dialogue"; when, where, and how one would go about bringing it into being; and what functions one would hope to achieve by it (see Pearce & Pearce, 2000). As I unpack the apparently naïve questions above, these become some of the most interesting and socially important questions that we might ask:

- How should we understand "dialogue"? Is it a way of being-in-relationship to another, a specific form of communication, a quality of communication, a certain kind of interpersonal relationship, an experience, or something else?
- How does dialogue happen? Is it an innate ability that all or only some of us possess? Is it the result of skillful practice? Is it something that just happens in a mystical way, for which we should be grateful but which we cannot expect to produce at will? Is it something that happens—or is more probable—in certain kinds of situations?
- Can we increase the probability that dialogue will occur? Is the ability to engage in dialogue learnable? Is it teachable? It is contagious?
- How can we make dialogue the standard operating procedure in our world, nation, organizations, families, schools, and interpersonal relationships? Can we:
  - Command it to happen?
  - Coach people to do it better and more often?
  - Facilitate it?
  - Train/educate people to be more skillful?
  - Regulate our patterns of discourse to make it more likely?
  - Create contexts that contain the preconditions for it?
  - Infect others with a preference for dialogue?
- Is dialogue in public possible, or is it so fragile that it can occur only in sheltered, private places? Is it possible to engage the public in dialogue, or does it require participants who are "ready"? Can the full range of persons and groups in the public arena participate in a public form of communication that has the characteristics of dialogue?

The meaning of dialogue cannot be taken for granted. The term is used loosely, for example, in so-called dialogue boxes on computer screens that prompt (not quite "ask") the user to click on "OK" or

"Cancel." Even though it serves useful purposes, the popular contrast between dialogue and monologue blissfully disregards its etymology. Those of us who carefully parse words for a living also have several different conceptualizations of dialogue. For example, a considerable tradition of practice centered in the Massachusetts Institute of Technology Dialogue Project is grounded in the work of David Bohm (Bohm, 1996; Ellinor & Gerard, 1998; Isaacs, 1999). In this tradition, "dialogue" names particular episodes of communication in which interpersonal dynamics are deliberately set aside and personal assumptions are suspended so that groups can think together. Another tradition of thought and criticism is grounded in the work of Mikhail Bakhtin (Sampson, 1993; Shotter, 2000). The key insight for these scholars is that persons, utterances, and actions do not occur as singletons but are always inherently in relation to all other persons, utterances, and actions. They respond to what other people have said and done, and elicit responses from them. Remembering that persons and all human things are dialogic confers a sensibility (Shotter, 2000) or dialogic wisdom (Barge & Little, in press) that prevents us from acting in a way that is inconsistent with the reality in which we live. My own work uses the adverb "dialogically" more than the noun "dialogue." This usage signals a conceptualization of dialogue as a quality with which we perform the whole gamut of speech acts that comprise social life. This stands in contrast to concepts of dialogue as a specific communication episode (Isaacs), an inherent characteristic of social being (Bakhtin), or a certain kind of experience (Cissna and Anderson's understanding of Buber and Rogers).

Cissna and Anderson develop a distinctive concept of dialogue as moments of meeting. They locate this concept in Martin Buber's philosophy of dialogue and in Carl Rogers's praxis of dialogue. While it would be hard to ignore Buber in any discussion of dialogue, Rogers is not so obvious a choice. For Buber, dialogue is a special kind of meeting in which people allow the other to happen to them (Stewart & Zediker, 2000). The term "dialogue" did not loom large for Rogers, but his person-centered approach to therapy and other forms of practice focused on being congruent, striving for empathic understanding, and extending unconditional positive regard.

In my own learning history, I read Rogers before I read Buber and, to an extent I had not realized, read Buber through the lens of Rogers. While I think this is a particularly good way of reading Buber, my study of chapters 3 and 4 helped me realize that I had been using Buber's language to name Rogers's practices, and that they are not quite the same things. Among other good consequences of reading this book, I have begun to distinguish Rogers and Buber more, to acknowledge how much of my practice is Rogerian (although I had called it Buberian), and to add Rogers to my personal list of seminal figures in the development of dialogue.

In their rhetorical analysis of the encounter at the University of Michigan in 1957 (see also Anderson & Cissna, 1997), Cissna and Anderson find Buber and Rogers agreeing on a concept of dialogue as moments of meeting. Against the prevailing interpretation of Buber and Rogers as disagreeing about the ability of achieving mutuality in asymmetrical relationships, both agreed—so Cissna and Anderson argue—that dialogue is "essentially momentary and fleeting" (see also Cissna & Anderson, 1998). Among other implications, this means that dialogue is possible even when the persons involved are unequal in role, status, or prestige and that dialogic moments can occur in public conversations.

I find the concept of dialogue as momentary to be very helpful. My work involves extended public dialogue projects, in which some of the events do not look very dialogic. At times, participants do not display exceptional empathic understanding and the quality of their unconditional positive regard for each other might best be described as strained. Taking on board the notion that dialogue occurs in significant moments, and its probability is increased by careful attention to the use of language, structure of events, and modeling, I can think of the dialogue *project* (which the leaders will carefully plan and facilitate) as creating the preconditions for dialogic *moments* (which can be encouraged but not commanded).

But Cissna and Anderson's purpose goes beyond (re)conceptualizing dialogue and reinterpreting the conversation between Buber and Rogers. They want to address the potential for public dialogue. Can dialogue occur in public? If so, can it improve the practice of democracy? Can the public become participants in dialogue? Are dialogic moments in public contexts qualitatively similar to those experienced in the more confined contexts of interpersonal communication? Are they more or less likely to occur? Cissna and Anderson offer three data points: the Buber–Rogers public dialogue; the work of contemporary groups; and the characteristics of rhetorics that facilitate dialogue.

The Buber–Rogers encounter makes a great story. Because he experienced a dialogic moment during the event, Buber moved from a public statement that public dialogue is impossible to one saying that it does occur. How satisfying it must be to the authors to tell a story that turns out so well! And Cissna and Anderson deserve their pleasures: we owe them a great debt for their scholarly attention to getting the right text, seeking accuracy in transcription, and interpreting what was said. In a delightful self-referential paradox, they pose six principles of "antimethod" as a description of their self-styled rhetorical analysis of conversation—this section will become required reading for my students who are doing any form of textual analysis.

And yet we might ask if a dialogue-in-public is the same thing as a public dialogue. The answer depends, of course, on what one means by "dialogue." The conversation between Buber and Rogers did not have many of the textual qualities that I would hope or expect to find when people are communicating dialogically. But, if I understand them, Cissna and Anderson are not concerned so much with the qualities of what was said as with the experience of the participants. For them, dialogue is experiential, facilitated by but not identified with specific features of language or conversation. In this, Cissna and Anderson's approach is more closely aligned with Buber's mysticism than with Wittgenstein's ordinary language analysis. This alignment explains why I had to read the book twice before I understood that moments occur in psychological rather than chronological time, and that—following Cissna and Anderson—one would not equate the experience of dialogue with any particular section in the transcript of a conversation.

Buber's concerns about public dialogue involved the constraining effects of an "outsider"—whether audience or tape recorder—on the participants. He learned that it was possible for him to have a moment of meeting even on stage with a recorder running. However, this does not quite demonstrate that the potential for public dialogue includes extending those experiences to the audience or involving the public in forms of communication that have at least some of the characteristics of dialogue. The following are some of the distinctive features of the public that make it a challenging site for dialogue in comparison to face-to-face communication (Pearce & Pearce, 1999):

- There are multiple interpersonal and intergroup relationships and they differ in intensity, affect, and nature. Some relationships are so weak or hostile that it is difficult to sustain the type of conversation in which dialogue occurs.
- So many voices are saying contradictory things simultaneously that anything one says or does has different meanings to various persons and groups within the public. Attempts to "control" the meaning of one's own statements (I'm thinking here of the work of political campaign consultants) generally reduce the likelihood of dialogue.

- Participants often yield to the temptation to play to the audience rather than to address the person to whom they are allegedly speaking. There is no alternative to functioning both in a first- and third-person position.
- Listening skills are challenged: so many voices are speaking simultaneously that no one can attend carefully to them all; many of these voices come from incommensurate cultural or situational contexts; and many of these voices use tones and forms of expression inimical to dialogue.
- Much of the communication in public is done through media that limit the potential for participants to be responsive to each other.
- Even more than face-to-face communication, mediated communication in public is structured by economics, power, and status. People have uneven access to the media and skills in using the media effectively are unevenly distributed.

A number of groups have developed event-designs and processes more sophisticated than the question-and-answer format of the Buber–Rogers dialogue. Because I spend a good bit of my time in one of these organizations, I naturally think that the development of these groups is the best thing since sliced bread. But this work is seriously underdescribed. Although we are beginning to generate what Wittgenstein would call a family of language games that do good things, there are some fairly basic issues remaining to be confronted, including the conceptualization of what we are trying to achieve. Civic journalism and the National Issues Forums, for example, have a well-developed concept of deliberation which is not quite the same thing as the dialogue that the Public Conversations Project has in mind, and the Public Conversations Project creates private conversations about public issues that differ from the Public Dialogue Consortium's events whose open doors attempt to create public conversations about public issues. It will be interesting to see how the work of these groups will be affected as they think through moments of meeting as a conceptualization of dialogue.

I resonate with Cissna and Anderson's nicely nuanced description of the potential for public dialogue: "Dialogue is not a distant hope, but an immediate—if fleeting—potential in all relations. . . . Dialogue is possible, but it is hard-won in the moment, actually achieved in moments of surprise made possible by open listening and contingent speaking. It does not spark just anywhere, but where the soil of communication has been cleared and cultivated, without guarantees, for it." They offer a list of characteristics of rhetoric (here understood as a type of public discourse) that conduces to the experience of dialogic moments. Following this analysis, the task before us is to find ways to make this rhetoric the standard operating procedure of our society. That seems a worthwhile way of spending one's time—even if, as they remind us, this effort is "without guarantees."

In his novel, *2001: A Space Odyssey*, Arthur C. Clarke (1993) envisioned a world challenged by the discovery of an alien "other." As we reach the actual year 2001, it is clear that we are in constant contact with an even more difficult "other"—those people with whom we share an increasingly small and interdependent planet who are not only not us but also not like us. To a very large extent, the quality of our lives depends on our willingness and ability to communicate dialogically with them. During the height of the Cold War, Herman Kahn (1978) dared us to "think the unthinkable"—in that case, that nation-states might survive a thermonuclear war. While the very idea still makes me shudder, I wonder if we might borrow his courage to confront the task before us. Is it unthinkable to imagine implementing effective social processes that will call all of us to those habits of rhetoric, skills in conversation, and disciplines of heart and mind that make moments of meeting more likely? Communicating dialogically with the "others" is the minimal requirement of life in the postmodern, globalized, interdependent, and mobile world in which we live, but it requires both skill and will (as Yankelovich, 1999, puts it). Its costs include setting aside the comforts of xenophobia and the pleasures of narcissistic closedmindedness; its rewards include the pleasures of becoming richer as persons and safer as a community. To paraphrase Clarke's (1968) fiction, we have seen many obelisks attesting to the "other"; we need no further reminders of the need to adjust our thinking about our world and ourselves. What is needed, and what *Moments of Meeting: Buber, Rogers, and the Potential for Public Dialogue* provides, are guides for moving forward together.

Introduction

A difficult challenge for the new century—indeed, perhaps the most basic cultural challenge—is whether democracies will be able to negotiate intense and often polarized group goals in public. When racial, ethnic, lifestyle, and political cultures justly demand recognition and identities that can make a difference, their claims often test older norms of civility and traditional political processes. The public sphere is also complicated by an increasing citizen mistrust of the new electronic media/information environment, and at times by a cynicism that freezes citizens into inaction.

How can a society encourage public dialogue, making it coherent while maintaining a vigorously pluralistic climate for ideas? Are there clues from the past that might help us respond constructively? We need cultural forms that keep citizens and groups talking while maintaining a spirit of open listening as well.

Such questions led to this book, in which we summarize and synthesize our fifteen-year investigation of the intellectual relationship between two of the twentieth century's foremost experts on dialogue, Martin Buber and Carl Rogers. Buber, the century's foremost philosopher of dialogue and a prominent religious thinker, was also active in international literary and political life. His classic *I and Thou* poetically described the option of humane dialogue in a technologized and often objectified society. Rogers, the psychologist who pioneered new approaches to empathy and client-centered therapy, was one of the century's most renowned practitioners of dialogue. His best known books, especially *On Becoming a Person*, bridged academic scholarship and popular culture. Both men worked tirelessly for intercultural understanding across the world. Although each was aware of the other from the early 1950s, they met only once in person. Fortunately, this meeting was preserved on audiotape.

Dialogue, Buber thought, can be shaped in personalized, private, and largely face-to-face contexts. But is *public* dialogue realistic, when communicators are so often tempted to strategize for audiences rather than listen to each other? Buber suspected it was not; Rogers was more optimistic. Debate and discussion can be public, Buber thought, but dialogue depends on something more delicate—a relational spontaneity in which persons are willing to be surprised and might even change their positions. In their 1957 dialogue at the University of Michigan, the critical centerpiece of this book, dialogue was both content and process. Because this meeting was successful in ways Buber didn't predict, he changed his mind about public dialogue. In fact, the Buber–Rogers conversation articulated an implicit theory of dialogic moments that is clearly applicable to our own volatile mediated culture.

Moments of Meeting analyzes the Buber–Rogers dialogue as a "conversational text," but goes far beyond the event itself to explore the intellectual context for public dialogue generally. Supported by original historical research and a variety of interviews, we hope we can illuminate the careers, theories, and practices of both men while we clarify—as no previous study has attempted—what they shared in common. While fully acknowledging the difficulties of public life, this book ultimately affirms its powerful dialogic potential.

PLAN OF THE BOOK

Our first chapter, "Dialogue in Public Space," defines central terms and situates the case study at the core of our research. It asks and answers the crucial question of what kinds of optimism or pessimism should characterize our response to public dialogue.

Chapter 2, "A Rhetorical Approach to Dialogue," builds the rationale for our approach and further defines the practical implications of dialogue, public or private. We argue for a rhetorical, emergent, and essentially coauthored methodology consistent with the shape of the dialogic texts we want to understand and illuminate.

Chapter 3, "Buber and the Philosophy of Dialogue," establishes Martin Buber's life and work as the touchstone for a cohesive philosophy of dialogue. This philosopher, who started writing mature social commentary in the earliest years of the twentieth century, found himself at the center of two of the century's most disturbing political and cultural conflicts, the Holocaust experience in Europe and the persistent Arab-Jewish controversies in Palestine. He was active intellectually until his death in the mid-1960s, and his work is now engaging contemporary scholars in fresh ways in this new century. Although his contributions were central to what he called a philosophical anthropology—the exploration of what makes humans human—some philosophers have also criticized aspects of his work and even whether Buber consistently lived a life of dialogue. A balanced account of Buber's approach to dialogue is necessary for our study.

Chapter 4, "Rogers and the Praxis of Dialogue," is not only a companion chapter to our treatment of Buber, but in some ways an extension of it. If Buber's contributions were often eloquent philosophical statements, Rogers's contributions were stimulated by the immediate lived experience of responding as a psychotherapist to individuals who came to him with immobilizing problems of personal adjustment. In Buber, Rogers found a kindred spirit for some of his basic insights, but he states quite clearly that he never modeled those ideas after any philosophy or theory, Buber's or anyone else's. In spite of his reluctance to adopt others' systems directly, we trace how Rogers's style of therapy became more and more dialogic because he discovered from his clients that dialogue was the core of human relationship, and that relation itself is inherently therapeutic. Rogers did not use Buber as a source of hypotheses that he could test in his therapy; rather, he achieved a parallel realization from a different, more inductive, direction. Rogers also has been an inviting target for criticism from scholars over the years. We account for the rise and fall (and rebirth) of his reputation in terms of how he contributed to an informed collaborative relation we call a praxis of dialogue.

Chapter 5, "Historical Context and the Buber–Rogers Meeting," explores the intellectual context for the Buber–Rogers dialogue. Almost all previous commentary on the dialogue, and on the Buber–Rogers intellectual relationship, appears to assume that this conversation is useful merely for comparing the ideas of the two men. It was far more. We consider it as a *meeting* in the rich sense that Buber himself recommends; it was influenced by a myriad of historical and personal factors that should be unfolded carefully, because these factors influenced how the dialogue unexpectedly changed Buber and Rogers. This chapter begins by tracing important facets of Buber's world at mid-century—the political and cultural tensions that occupied his attention, the concerns for his own writing and philosophy in "what is common to all," the relationship between Buber's philosophy and the psychological sciences. Buber came to that stage not only with preconceptions and a cohesive philosophical outlook on the necessity for interpersonal dialogue; he came with a wide range of experiences and concerns that most commentary on the dialogue neglects to acknowledge. Rogers, too, imagined the meeting in a broader context than just a chance to meet and interview Buber. His new paradigm for therapeutic communication was controversial in 1957; he was engaged in an test of wills with psychological behaviorists and Freudian psychoanalysists, and framed the Buber dialogue in that immediate context. Undoubtedly he saw Buber as an ally in this intellectual quest to redefine psychotherapy and to advocate a broader and more humane discipline of psychology.

Chapter 6, "Interhuman Meeting," the critical core of our book, presents a close reading of the dialogue, both in its essential content and in its process or stylistic elements. Students of dialogue can perceive in action the concrete meeting of a philosophy of dialogue with a praxis of dialogue. Such meeting is the essential tension of this dialogic text and, correspondingly, these are the two tasks we face as a public: Can we develop a coherent sense of what happens when people experience dialogue, even to describing theoretically how dialogue is a richly productive experience for them? And can we develop a coherent way of putting dialogue into practice in the messy everyday world of interpersonal life? We proceed by highlighting the planned and emergent structure of the dialogue as it developed through six basic questions, and build on that foundation by suggesting that three crucial influences—audience, role, and style—could be identified clearly in the interchange and its outcomes.

Chapter 7, "Theorizing Dialogic Moments," builds on the Buber–Rogers case study to speculate about the processes at the core of genuine human dialogue. Buber and Rogers suggested together and separately that dialogue is neither an ongoing state nor an empty aspiration, but instead a matter of momentary insight that is hard-won and ephemeral but at the same time potentially life-changing. Interestingly, theorists have not foregrounded this momentary character of dialogue despite its prominence in the Buber–Rogers dialogue and despite the fact that Buber's essays provided useful clues to such an approach. Rogers, in fact, had been working specifically on a theory of dialogic moments in therapy while preparing for the Buber dialogue, and subsequently referred to this insight often in his articles and books. Beyond these tasks, we briefly examine the implications of a theory of dialogic moments for postmodern thought, political reconciliation, and cross-cultural understanding.

Chapter 8, "Conversations of Democracy," asks the crucial "so what?" questions about our core conversational text and its theoretical implications. Contemporary culture offers sobering challenges for genuine dialogue, and at the same time tantalizes citizens with its potential. We survey the current media landscape, discuss changes in the basic character of information and its relation to public decision making, and compare and critique recent media attempts to contribute to dialogic democratic action.

Finally, chapter 9, "The Next Voices," acknowledges that there are no final destinations in the dialogue about dialogue. But there are landmarks along the way. One of these, the Buber–Rogers dialogue, is richer than many scholars have assumed. In the process of examining it carefully and in context, we illuminate both Martin Buber and Carl Rogers as theorists of dialogue. Their intellectual relationship, ignored for too long, suggests a fresh potential for public and mediated dialogue in this new century. In that spirit, we summarize major themes and anticipate the next voices in the conversation, voices that undoubtedly will surpass ours.

Although Carl Rogers and Martin Buber addressed the problematic of human dialogue from different directions and often varied in their terminology, the intellectual convergence they represented was extraordinary. As we point out elsewhere in this book, the twentieth century rarely witnessed such a convergence of the philosophical and the practical: a European thinker who was immersed in a philosophy of the between is corroborated by an American practitioner immersed, at least in the beginning, in an empirical and inductive psychology of individual experience. Both found that relationship was key, that listening, tough-minded confirmation, and a healthy respect for difference and otherness were the baseline considerations for freeing relationships. This convergence demands our attention, because in it are crucial clues for improving public dialogue, clues that may not be obtainable from either philosophers or practitioners alone.

WHAT SHELF DO YOU PUT THIS ON?

This kind of study does not fit neatly under traditional labels for methods, literatures, or disciplines. As a case study, our project is subject to all the limitations and reservations about overgeneralization inherent in that approach. While we recognize this, we don't apologize for it. The particular encounter that drew our attention is so unique, and its content so richly theoretical, that it invites widespread application. Buber and Rogers together explored basic notions of dialogue that neither man treated much in his individual writing, and their synergy created a conversational text that not only was about, but *was*, dialogue.

Readers are justified in wondering if we are conversant enough with historical methods to attempt a kind of intellectual history; or if we understand philosophical concepts well enough to produce a study of one of the major philosophers of the twentieth century; or if we have enough background in rhetorical criticism or discourse analysis to illuminate a complex conversational text; or if nonpsychologists can grasp nuances of the therapeutic relationship that Rogers and his critics negotiated over the years; or if anyone but academic political scientists can understand political power well enough to evaluate contemporary attempts at public dialogue. We realistically acknowledge the study's limits. At the same time, we suspect any interdisciplinary project involves similar compromises. Ultimately, others will have to determine how serious our compromises or mistakes have been.

CAVEATS

One of the sobering lessons for us on our long path toward the book was to realize that *no one* probably knows enough—or, perhaps, can know enough—to do justice to such a subject. We couldn't put off writing until we had read all that was relevant to the project, for, in all likelihood, that would surely mean that no words would ever reach paper. At some point, authors must send the manuscript into the world, warts and all, hoping that synthesis counts for something and that mistakes here or oversights there will stimulate other students of dialogue to begin their own investigations in earnest. The book is not a tidy package, but what used to be called a prolegomenon—an opening set of remarks that can lead to better or more systematic studies in the same spirit. But if this is a prolegomenon, it is not designed as an abstract one. It is as grounded and specific as we can make it. If it contributes to the human studies, broadly defined, it may be partly because we have tried to be immersed in the detail that enlivens actual talk, and also have tried to hear the wider harmonies and disharmonies of communication that characterize what Buber termed the realm of the interhuman. Theory, properly explored, has dirt under its fingernails most of the time. We want our theoretical statement to be recognizable to both thinkers and practitioners of dialogue. In this way, we might nudge more scholars toward merging philosophy and praxis.

Another caveat comes to mind. Both of us are committed to writing inclusively, in ways that acknowledge different forms of human experience. Racism, sexism, classism, and other types of discrimination become embedded, quite subtly at times, in language. There they reside, influencing us as we talk and write, listen and read, often outside our conscious awareness. One indispensable function of education, we are convinced, is to unwrap language usage in various ways, to disclose embedded assumptions and point out their often unfair effects. This happens in classes, workshops, tutorials, and seminars all the time, as it should. Indeed, our own writing and teaching has touched consistently on the need for inclusive language. Yet, historical studies present unique problems in this regard. For example, 1957 was a time of different sensitivities and, frankly, it was an era that sanctioned what we would now call unfair language choices, especially in gender relations: groups were typically referred to as "men" or, globally, as "mankind"; unspecified subjects almost always seemed to be a "he." Some contemporary scholars have chosen to call attention to each instance of this by a "[sic]" or by inserting in brackets a more contemporary and presumably less sexist term for the offending one.

However, we believe this strategy is itself problematic. The "[sic]" solution wrongly implies that an author had made a mistake in the original text when in fact he or she had used language entirely consistent with the usage of the time. The insertion solution seems to trade one problem for another; the text is rid of a potential offense, but the change calls attention to itself in such a neon-like way that it intrudes on the reader's experience of an author's style and flow, deflecting sense unnecessarily. We know of no perfect solution (obviously, sexist language can be intrusive and distracting for contemporary readers as well). All things considered, though, it makes more sense for us to leave others' language alone. As we point out in succeeding chapters, Buber's language can sometimes appear to English readers more sexist than it is, largely because of prevailing conventions of English translation in his time (rather than "person," *Mensch* becomes "man," for example), and Rogers later became an early pioneer of inclusive language in scholarship. Even so, contemporary readers should understand that their time and culture(s) often encouraged male-oriented language choices.

AUTHORING

Working together has been a dialogic undertaking that itself merged different strengths of philosophy and praxis. It's hard to imagine either of us even attempting, much less completing, such a study alone. And as you learn from chapter 2, we enacted a consciously dialogic style in researching dialogue even though, for the reader's sake, we ultimately decided to write in a cohesive, seemingly singular voice. Although we live half a continent apart, e-mail, long-distance phone calls, heavy

manila envelopes, working visits to each other's homes, and attendance at many of the same conferences gave us plenty of opportunities
to argue, agree, and actualize each other's fragmentary ideas. Although
we each have pursued other projects simultaneously, we resolved not
to ignore this one and not to let distance become a cop-out. And, as we
wrote in another introduction (Anderson & Cissna, 1997), "Cooperation and coauthorship in our ongoing dialogue investigation has been
so multileveled and thorough that we no longer try to keep track of
who is the 'lead' author of each manuscript. Instead, we have adopted
the common convention of alternating the order of our names from
project to project" (p. xii).

APPRECIATIONS

A couple of names may go on the cover, but no one should doubt that
a book's real authority also flows from dozens of other people, many of
whom may not understand how crucial their contributions have been.
Of course, we accept sole responsibility for all errors or failures of vision we perhaps could have avoided if we'd relied even more on these
sources. Because the Buber–Rogers dialogue has fascinated us for so
many years, the list of our debts to others is strikingly long and our
gratitude strikingly deep. It's hard to know where to begin.

Many contemporary readers first encounter Martin Buber's philosophy through the interpretive lens of Maurice Friedman, the moderator
of the 1957 dialogue and now professor emeritus of philosophy, religious studies, and comparative literature at San Diego State University.
Professor Friedman's three-volume biography, *Martin Buber's Life and
Work*, is truly the definitive work in its area, and he has applied Buber's
dialogic thinking, as well as his own original contributions, to intellectual areas as diverse as literary criticism, psychotherapy, and the critique of social science. It is fair to say that nothing like the present
project could have developed were it not for Professor Friedman's remarkable collegial spirit extended in trust to two obscure scholars he'd
virtually never heard of. Having read our earlier work on Rogers, he invited us to present a paper at his 1991 international conference on
Buber's thought and then, despite disagreeing with our interpretations
on several points, included our essay in the subsequent volume he
edited from conference manuscripts. He has been unfailingly gracious
and supportive of this project through his timely correspondence, his
availability for direct interviews, his clues for obtaining an audiotape of
the dialogue, and his willingness to grant access to personal letters

from the 1950s. Most recently, he read two chapters of this manuscript, and helped us clarify several issues related to Buber's life and thought. Despite the substantial debt we owe him, readers should not assume Professor Friedman sanctions our particular analysis of Buber's role in the dialogue; indeed, we suspect that several of our conclusions have rankled our friend and colleague. Fortunately, he has also published his own recollection and analysis of the dialogue (1994, 1996d), with which readers can compare our account.

We obtained our first copy of the taped dialogue from Professor John Stewart of the University of Washington, who had dubbed his from Friedman. Most of our work analyzing the conversational text was done with this tape as our primary source. Later, Barbara T. Brodley sent us the partial copy from the Chicago Counseling and Psychotherapy Center, and DeWitt C. Baldwin Jr. informed us that he had donated the tape owned by his father (the event's primary organizer) to the University of California at Santa Barbara. David E. Russell, director of that university's Oral History Program and its Humanistic Psychology Archive, then provided us with what appears to be the most audible and most complete tape available. We appreciate the kindness of these scholars very much.

Many others also provided invaluable research assistance. The Graduate Schools at both the University of South Florida and at Saint Louis University and the College of Arts and Sciences at USF provided research grants that helped support our writing and travel expenses. A number of graduate students at Saint Louis University assisted in our research; we are grateful to Kevin O'Leary, Thao Dang, Michael Williams, Les Hostetler, and especially Mary Cox. Another graduate student, Marcia Deering of the Centre for the Study of Communication and Culture and the Department of Communication at SLU, invested tremendous interest and energy in the the project's final stages. We also learned much from the students in our undergraduate and graduate seminars and colloquia, whose responses and questions helped us sharpen points we needed to make but hadn't fully anticipated before being pressed on them. Others also supported the research directly but were not connected with our campuses. We depended on staff personnel of the Martin Buber Archives at the Jewish National & University Library; the Michigan Historical Collection at the Bentley Historical Library and the Harlan Hatcher Graduate Library of the University of Michigan; The Carl R. Rogers Collection at the Library of Congress in Washington, D.C.; and the Carl Rogers Memorial Library at the Center for Studies of the Person in LaJolla, California. Martha Mathis and Dominick Biemann graciously served as our research "agents" (to use Martha's term) when we could not be at the Library of Congress or the Buber Archives, respectively, in person. Later, our friend Mike Killenberg read sections of the manuscript and offered helpful suggestions.

Others shared their memories of the dialogue and its principals through correspondence or interviews, or they helped us locate additional important resources. Thinking back over the years, it astonishes us to realize how responsive and thoughtful busy people will be when your curiosity is sincere and when you genuinely want to learn something new. Aside from the people mentioned earlier, we are also indebted to: Judith Buber Agassi, C. Grey Austin, Dorothy Becker, Russell J. Becker, Seymour Cain, Charlotte Ellinwood, Richard Farson, Eugene Gendlin, Tom Greening, Robert Hauert, Nel Kandel, Howard Kirschenbaum, Robert Lipgar, Betty Lou Mahone, Charles Mahone, William McKeachie, Louis Orlin, Natalie Rogers, Len Scott, John M. Shlien, and Brian Thorne. The photograph of Martin Buber was provided by his granddaughter, Judith Buber Agassi, and is reproduced with her permission. The Carl Rogers photograph was provided by his daughter, Natalie Rogers, and is used with her permission.

Although much of our analysis appears here for the first time, we are grateful for the assistance of editors and reviewers from a variety of academic journals who published earlier versions of some of the essays, and we appreciate the permission of the publishers to adapt our earlier work here:

- For portions of chapter 2: *Human Studies*, Vol. 19, #1, January 1996, pp. 85–118, "Criticism and Conversational Texts: Rhetorical Bases of Role, Audience, and Style in the Buber–Rogers Dialogue," Rob Anderson & Kenneth N. Cissna, copyright (c) by Kluwer Academic Publishers, with kind permission from Kluwer Academic Publishers.
- For portions of chapter 4: Kenneth N. Cissna & Rob Anderson, "The Contributions of Carl Rogers to a Philosophical Praxis of Dialogue," *Western Journal of Speech Communication*, Vol. 54, # 2, pp. 125–147, 1990; permission granted by Western States Communication Association.
- For portions of chapter 6: Kenneth N. Cissna & Rob Anderson, "The 1957 Martin Buber–Carl Rogers Dialogue, as Dialogue," *Journal of Humanistic Psychology*, Vol. 34, # 1, pp. 11–45, copyright (c) 1994 by Sage Publications. Reprinted by permission of Sage Publications.
- For portions of chapter 7: *Communication Theory*, Vol. 8, #1, February 1998, pp. 63–104, Kenneth N. Cissna & Rob

Anderson, "Theorizing About Dialogic Moments: The Buber–Rogers Position and Postmodern Themes"; reproduced by permission of Oxford University Press.

In addition, we quote liberally from our own transcript of the Buber–Rogers dialogue, included in *The Martin Buber–Carl Rogers Dialogue: A New Transcript with Commentary* (1997), published by SUNY Press. Each quotation from the transcript is identified by a turn number referenced to the 1997 book, and italics indicate the vocal emphasis we heard on the best extant tape.

Finally, we appreciate the interest and skill of editors and reviewers at SUNY Press, especially Priscilla Ross who encouraged this book, and its 1997 cohort, all the way.

CHAPTER ONE

Dialogue in Public Space

> Dialogic thought in this century is an amorphous
> phenomenon rather than a shared concern. By and
> large, the prominent dialogic thinkers did not hold
> dialogues with each other. . . . You might say that
> each of them was following his own distinctive line,
> with his own authorities and his own disciples.
> —Robert Grudin, *On Dialogue*

Imagine yourself, for a moment, as a time traveler. It's 1957, and you sit eagerly in a plush auditorium at the University of Michigan, anticipating an unusual event. You've driven to Ann Arbor through difficult weather to attend the spotlight evening program of a conference devoted to the thought of one of the world's most prominent intellectual and cultural figures, Martin Buber of Jerusalem—philosopher, theologian, critic, playwright, educator, advocate for cooperation between Jews and Arabs in Palestine. Buber will be on stage soon, but surprisingly he is not going to lecture this evening.

Buber, on his second lecture tour of the United States, has spoken elsewhere recently on such topics as "Elements of the Interhuman," "Guilt and Guilt Feelings," and "What is Common to All." Instead of a lecture, and consistent with his well known appreciation for dialogue, conference organizers have arranged for the seventy-nine-year-old philosopher to spend an hour or so responding to questions from a noted psychologist about "The Nature of Man as Revealed in Inter-Personal Relationship."

You've also heard of Buber's conversation partner, Carl Rogers, although he is not as famous as Buber in the international community of scholars. A University of Chicago psychotherapist, Rogers is one of

1

those rare college professors who imprint popular culture with a striking and fresh point of view. He has been mentioned recently on national radio and television and was profiled in *Time* magazine for his controversial claim that everyday people possess significant psychological resources they can use to help themselves, rather than having to rely on the answers and techniques of professional psychologists and psychiatrists. Professionals need to listen more and diagnose less, he thought. In his vocabulary, therapy ought to be "client-centered" rather than treatment-centered or therapist-centered, and should help clients discover their own answers. Successful therapy, for Rogers, involves dialogue between person and person. Successful therapy, in fact, is based on dynamics not very different from those of any successful relationship.

A dialogue on dialogue, between prominent dialogic thinkers: a rare and intriguing event. Most people in the audience are unaware that it almost didn't happen.

Just a month before the conference, Buber, lecturing at the Washington School of Psychiatry (he gave the same lecture at this conference, too), essentially dismissed public dialogue as impossible, arguing that attempts at dialogue before an audience were "separated by a chasm from genuine dialogue" (Buber, 1957b, p. 113). When people are tempted to perform for audiences in addition to speaking with each other, he said, a vital element of dialogue—spontaneity—is sacrificed. An interhuman relation, according to Buber's thinking at that time, could not rely on performance, and audiences necessitate performances. The spontaneous directness and honesty of dialogic communication is presumably a nonpublic if not private interchange. Buber, however, expressed no reservation about talking with Rogers on stage. Why? According to his friend and translator Maurice Friedman (personal communication, 22 October 1991)—who also moderated the event—he simply didn't expect anything truly significant to occur, much less a dialogue that scholars in the human sciences would remember and consult for decades.

Earlier, behind the scenes, the man responsible for organizing Buber's U.S. tour tried to get the conversation with Rogers cancelled. Leslie Farber, chair at the Washington School of Psychiatry, had invited Buber to the United States and arranged for the bulk of the funding. Although he did not object to Buber speaking at various universities, Jewish centers, and other venues across the country, he did object to this one event at the Michigan conference, and asked the conference organizer to drop the dialogue from the program. Farber evidently thought that the Buber–Rogers conversation might concern psychiatry, a subject he wanted discussed exclusively at Buber's seminars in Washington, D.C. (Baldwin, 1957b). As a result, the event disappeared briefly from the draft program developed for Michigan's conference. Apparently, however, Buber disagreed, and it was reinstated. One important detail, however, remained unresolved, even as people were on their way to Rackham Auditorium for the Buber–Rogers dialogue.

Sitting in the audience, you notice that audiotape equipment has been set up to record the event. The taping almost doesn't happen either.

Buber, you see, didn't want to be recorded. He'd refused to be filmed or even audiotaped at the Washington lectures, even though Farber had arranged for a special grant to support the filming. Buber also believed that technological "contrivances" interfered with dialogue. He explained his refusal to Farber: "My experience is . . . that being filmed slackens the spontaneity of the dialogue, and this is what I need most: full spontaneity. This was my motive when some days ago I refused Dean Pike to have a dialogue with him televised. I am sure you understand that here the negation of certain modern technical means *in this connection* comes from a vital source" (Buber, 1991a, pp. 605–606).

So Buber had personal and conceptual objections not only to attempting dialogue before an audience but also to being taped. Why had he agreed to be taped this evening? Evidently in the hour before the dialogue, during their first introductions to each other, Rogers reassured Buber that he had taped many therapy sessions successfully without the machines or microphones becoming intrusive. Perhaps, too, Buber's low expectations for the interchange with Rogers led him to conclude that the decision to tape wouldn't matter much anyway.

It did matter—very much. Because of the tape, generations of scholars would have a record of an important and revealing event in the history of the human sciences. What Buber and Rogers said that evening would reverberate through the tangle of subsequent decades, addressing concerns and crises that confront world cultures still, as we begin a new millennium. As never before, the challenges of a public sphere are the challenges of integrating or amplifying unfamiliar voices so that they may not only hear and respond to each other across moral and cultural differences, but that these voices may also be heard by relevant new audiences. Democratic dialogue and deliberation depend on a nonacquiescent and informed public forum. That forum is increasingly mediated in ways that would have worried Buber, yet at the gate to the twenty-first century, computerized online culture, to cite only one example, is not only increasingly mediated and technically intricate but more interactive than mediated communication has ever been. But was Buber somehow right? Or is genuine dialogue, after all, possible in a public setting? What might be its contours? Its effectual space? Its limits? Its invitation for change?

Today, looking back from the experience of contemporary challenges to the public sphere, we realize why the 1957 Buber–Rogers conversation is so intellectually rich and suggestive. Because of it, Buber himself changed his mind about the potential for public dialogue. Because of the success of the dialogue, and despite the large audience and tape equipment, Buber realized that public contexts don't necessarily preclude genuine dialogue. When a 1957 Buber lecture/essay was to be reprinted in his 1965 collection, *The Knowledge of Man*, Buber asked Friedman, his editor and translator, to delete a key passage about how publicity taints dialogue; this request was primarily motivated by the quality of his exchange with Rogers (Buber, 1965b, p. 184). Buber, who could be crusty and blunt, told Friedman afterwards that although he treated Rogers gently ("I was very kind to him. I could have been much sharper" [Friedman, 1983c, p. 227]), he appreciated how the psychologist had truly brought himself to the stage as a person, and he thought that real dialogue had occurred. An example of the personal level Rogers sought for the dialogue can be seen in how he didn't back down about their supposed focus. Not only was their dialogue almost cancelled at Farber's request, but Farber had even asked Buber not to speak with Rogers—the psychotherapist—about psychotherapy. Buber mentioned this when the two first met an hour or so prior to the dialogue. Rogers considered it but concluded that there was no better topic they could explore in front of this audience. A colleague later recounted Rogers's sly decision that although "Buber might not be able to speak to him about psychotherapy, there was nothing to stop him from speaking about psychotherapy to Buber" (Pentony, 1987, p. 420). Conversation, the improvised verbal dance of communication partners, can never be controlled from only one side. Rogers knew that, and Buber did too.

So what Buber once thought couldn't happen—a genuine sense of dialogue in a public setting—turned out to be possible after all; he and Rogers created a conversation that rewards our close attention to its content and process. It provides important clues for how to enable dialogue more readily and with greater impact in contemporary public political and cultural arenas.

We are placing the Buber–Rogers dialogue at the symbolic center of an extended study of the implications of dialogue, a study in which personal and interpersonal decisions must be seen in the context of media decisions. Some things these two men did that evening (their process) and some things they talked about (their content) capsulize important insights for sustaining a public democracy in which citizens can speak with voices that are heard and responded to. This has personal implications for identity and relational satisfaction. It has equally crucial public implications for community development and governmental decision making. The personal inevitably blends with the political where dialogue emerges.

PUBLIC DIALOGUE: ASPIRATION AND SUSPICION

Contemporary public life is characterized by vigorous attempts to elevate dialogue as a goal and equally prominent attempts to denigrate it as an unrealistic ideal. Politicians and other citizens have taken to applying the term "dialogue" whenever they want what they say to have a special sheen. "Talk" isn't good enough, "conversation" sounds pretty folksy, and "communication" is too neutral or stilted for their taste. Calling for "dialogue" makes any venture seem solemn, elevated, even noble. Often, however, use of the term apparently means merely that some group wants more air time for a point of view that it's convinced will defeat competitors if heard by enough listeners. Trading opinions does not show that dialogue is happening any more than extensive class discussion necessarily shows that students are learning something.

This superficial linguistic tactic impoverishes what Buber and others wanted to understand as genuine dialogue, transforming it into a freewheeling form of interpersonal advertising. Nothing could be farther from Buber's vision. As he said in one of the Washington lectures presented just prior to the dialogue with Rogers:

> The chief presupposition for the rise of genuine dialogue is that each should regard his partner as the very one he is. I become aware of him, aware that he is different, essentially different from myself, in the definite, unique way which is peculiar to him, and I accept whom I thus see, so that in full earnestness I can direct what I say to him as the person he is. Perhaps from time to time I must offer strict opposition to his view about the subject of our conversation. But I accept this person, the personal bearer of a conviction, in his definite being out of which his conviction has grown—even though I must try to show, bit by bit, the wrongness of this very conviction. I affirm the person I struggle with: I struggle with him as his partner, I confirm him as creature and as creation, I confirm him who is opposed to me as him who is over against me.

> It is true that it now depends on the other whether genuine dialogue, mutuality in speech arises between us. But if I thus give to the other who confronts me his legitimate standing as a man with whom I am ready to enter into dialogue, then I may trust him and suppose him to be also ready to deal with me as his partner. (Buber, 1965b, pp. 79–80)

In this brief passage, Buber both defines the central concept of this book and grounds dialogue as radical availability to otherness, an otherness of cultural differences, interpersonal styles, new ideas, and unanticipated horizons. Some readers who have not studied Buber may only recall that his name has been associated with a weak or soft expressivism, a "have a nice day" or a "wouldn't the world be a better place if we were nicer to each other?" brand of philosophical platitude. Buber was tougher than that; such a curious misreading is undercut by a simple comparison to his published work, and the most cursory survey of his life. We can create dialogue if we are capable of being surprised by what is not-us, and we can recreate it even as we oppose that otherness. In an earlier essay also delivered as a Washington School of Psychiatry lecture, Buber described genuine conversation as involving "acceptance of otherness" (1965b, p. 69) and stipulated an ethic of persuasion that could guide any citizen in the public sphere:

> The desire to influence the other then does not mean the effort to change the other, to inject one's own "rightness" into him; but it means the effort to let that which is recognized as right, as just, as true (and for that very reason must also be established there, in the substance of the other) through one's influence take seed and grow in the form suited to individuation. Opposed to this effort is the lust to make use of men by which the manipulator of "propaganda" and "suggestion" is possessed, in his relation to men remaining as in a relation to things, to things, moreover, with which he will never enter into relation, which he is indeed eager to rob of their distance and independence. (p. 69)

Dialogue in Buber's sense, therefore, involves an exceptional openness to otherness, but it is not an unreflective or gullible acceptance or tolerance. Partners in genuine dialogue also say no: they oppose, explore, argue, and willingly influence others. But all this occurs under the responsible condition of remaining open to influence. When he described his own intellectual development to Rogers in Ann Arbor, Buber reported that even as a young man, "I felt I have not the right to want to change another if I am not open to be changed by him as far as it is legitimate" (turn #4).[1] Can there be a task in contemporary culture that is as important, or as risky, as encouraging such engagement in dialogue?

Perhaps it is the risks of such a dialogue that lead some critics to dismiss it, or to diminish its practicality in an age of mass media that is said to atomize listeners, rob them of their vitality, and make their personal access to each other more and more difficult. Buber himself, remember, worried about this. Others have become convinced that the very project of dialogue is doomed. According to sociologist and social critic Jacques Ellul (1985), when language "uses a loudspeaker and crushes others with its powerful equipment, when the television set speaks, the word is no longer involved, since no dialogue is possible" (p. 23). The increasing dominance of media technology in contemporary life led another prominent sociologist, Franco Ferrarotti (1988), to bemoan "the end of conversation," in part because media merely provide a "vocation for narcissism" (p. 13). The fear that genuine dialogue is diminished or eliminated because people have become too individualized, too selfish, and too used to being passive message consumers is also developed in the highly influential work of Bellah and his colleagues (1985), in Postman's (1985) critique of television, and in Berger, Berger, and Kellner's (1974) attribution of much of the same problem to an increasingly technologized, mass-mediated world that has made humans "anonymous" and experientially "homeless."

Our analysis also enters a somewhat different contemporary cultural conversation (in some ways a debate) concerning how much the public sphere should rely on citizen dialogue. It has a long history but at best an uncertain or amorphous resolution. In the early years of the twentieth century, two other famous intellectuals disagreed about the potential, and in some ways the shape, of open communication in the polity. Their interchange sets the table, so to speak, for our book.

Walter Lippmann, author of *Public Opinion* (1922) and other influential works, profoundly mistrusted the ability of common citizens to cope with the ever more complex choices necessary to engage the modern technologized world. He was especially concerned about how the media system complicated the choices of the worldwide audience for news. Effective newspapers should relay correct versions of events to common people; public opinion was the state of readers' and listeners' ability to apprehend events with minimal distortions such as the "stereotypes" he wrote about so persuasively. Lippmann believed that only a select group of technical or political experts—a scientific intelligentsia working largely behind the scenes—would be qualified enough, or well enough versed in assessing or measuring the truth, to negotiate the maze of new and daunting options. Only experts could be trusted to make the informed choices that could benefit the social order.

In *The Public and Its Problems* John Dewey (1927) argued, to the contrary, that common people can become powerful democratic decision makers to the extent that they have access not just to technical or arcane information, but to *each other*. For Lippmann, the role of the citizen was to be well informed about the experts' opinions and to see things accurately. Dewey thought the citizen's prime role was communication, and he trusted how everyday people understand the importance of mutual participation for shaping democracy. The conclusion of *The Public and Its Problems* makes it clear that interpersonal learning is the essence of public life. "Systematic and continuous inquiry into all the conditions which affect association and their dissemination in print is a precondition of the creation of a true public," Dewey wrote (p. 218). But these means of inquiry are mere tools. "Their final actuality is accomplished in face-to-face relationships by means of direct give and take. Logic in its fulfillment recurs to the primitive sense of the word: dialogue" (p. 218).

In this way, Dewey framed his reply to Lippmann with an impassioned plea for a conversational public life that engages decision makers representing all stations of class, power, citizenship, or cultural identity. James Carey (1989) has characterized the Dewey position particularly well:

> Dewey's response takes a number of turns. Public opinion is not formed when individuals possess correct representations of the environment, even if correct representations were possible. It is formed only in discussion, when it is made active in community life. Although news suffers from many of the deficiencies Lippmann cites, its major deficiency is not its failure to represent. The line between an adequate image and a stereotype is impossible to draw anyway. The purpose of news is not to represent and inform but to signal, tell a story, and activate inquiry. Inquiry, in turn, is not something other than conversation and discussion but a more systematic version of it. What we lack is the vital means through which this conversation can be carried on: institutions of public life through which a public can be formed and can form an opinion. The press, by seeing its role as that of informing the public, abandons its role as an agency for carrying on the conversation of our culture. We lack not only an effective press but certain vital habits: the ability

to follow an argument, grasp the point of view of another, expand the boundaries of understanding, debate the alternative purposes that might be pursued. (pp. 81–82)

In other words, the problem of a democracy *is* a problem of public opinion, but not in the sense that Lippmann meant by the term, where public opinion is shaped by effective information flow. Dewey, like Buber, recognized the primacy of human speech. He conceived democracy as the political process by which dialogue can create a public in the first place, and the "habits" of which Dewey and Carey speak are largely the habits of Buber's dialogue. There is no public until it forms itself, shapes itself, in fact *hears* itself through its own talk. Any politician who proclaims a faith in "the people" is implicitly saying there should be faith in how the people talk with each other about issues of common—that is, community—concern.

CHARACTERISTICS OF DIALOGUE

In a previous analysis (Cissna & Anderson, 1994a), we synthesized eight characteristics of dialogic communication from the literatures of practitioners and philosophers. How do people speak, listen, and respond when their common concerns, and the quality of their relationships, govern communication quality? As we unfold it in this work, the literature is surprisingly extensive and insightful. Dialogue tends to develop in relationships, groups, and communities characterized by:

- *Immediacy of presence.* Presence implies that dialogue partners speak and listen from a common place or space from which they experience access to each other. Communicators sense that, for each other, they are relating *here* (a shared space) and *now* (an immediate moment in time). In many situations, the first task of communicators or planners is to clear such a space, but the clearing doesn't guarantee dialogue so much as it enables it.
- *Emergent unanticipated consequences.* Dialogue presumes a certain spontaneity and improvisation linking communicators. The reason dialogue often seems to repair manipulation is that, in it, all parties enter without full knowledge of the directions that may be taken within the conversation. They are willing to invite surprise, even at the expense of sacrificing strategy at times.

- *Recognition of strange otherness.* By strange otherness we mean that a dialogue partner assumes not only that the other person is different (that is often obvious, of course), but is different in strange—that is, in essentially and inevitably unfamiliar or unpredicted—ways. Strangeness means the other cannot be reduced to an adjusted version of a "me"; there is always more, and confronting the strange implies imagining an alternate perspective. Such strangeness is not necessarily a threat, but is as often an invitation for learning.

- *Collaborative orientation.* By collaboration, we suggest that dialogue partners stand their own ground while they remain concerned about the current and future ground of others. Dialogic collaboration, however, does not suggest happy two-way backscratching. Indeed, collaboration embraces conflict, because by recognizing accurately the other's perhaps antithetical position in relation to one's own, we *confirm* each other.

- *Vulnerability.* Dialogue finds participants open to being changed. We speak from a ground that is important to us, but we do not defend that ground at all costs. Dialogue makes participants willing to be persuaded; dialogue makes us protean creatures. Personalities, understood from a dialogic perspective, are less things that we "have" than they are patterns of changingness.

- *Mutual implication.* A process of dialogue means that speakers anticipate listeners or respondents and incorporate them into messages. In a dialogic process, speaker and listener interdepend, each constructing self, other, and their talk simultaneously. Dewey and Bentley (1949) similarly used the word *trans-action* to suggest a new sense of human causality. Humans aren't changed by actions traded back and forth from one individual to another, but by the very existence of relationship itself. Communication isn't primarily "caused" by either party, but develops through the relation of both, in concert. Even when one person might seem to be the sole speaker, the voices of listeners are already present, said Russian language theorist Mikhail Bakhtin (1981, 1984, 1986). For the same reason, Buber referred to the term *I-Thou* as a "primary word" (not words, plural); what he called "the between," the relation, was a unified phenomenon.

- *Temporal flow.* Understanding dialogue always involves understanding the past out of which it flows and the future that it unfolds so persistently. As we have written elsewhere, it "emerges from a past, fills the immediate present (and thus is experienced as 'wide,' 'deep,' 'immersing,' or 'enveloping' by participants), and prefigures an open future" (Cissna & Anderson, 1994a, p. 15).
- *Genuineness and authenticity.* Dialogue partners base their relationship on the presumption of authentic or genuine experience. This means not that people always tell the truth, but that no sense of genuine dialogue can be based on a participant's self-consciously untruthful, hidden, deceptive, or blatantly strategic set of interpersonal calculations. Rather, in dialogue, communicators are assumed to speak and act in ways that match their worlds of experience. Where such trust breaks down, dialogic potential dissolves.

We suggest in this book that public dialogue exhibiting such characteristics is not only possible but imperative, even considering the extent of contemporary cynicism about the effects of electronic and online media on the quality of personal relations and public discourse. Our position rejects Buber's early belief that media and publicity intimidate dialogue, but affirms the position he took later, after his illuminating public dialogue with Rogers. Our position rejects the one sketched by Lippmann's efficient bureaucracy of planners in favor of the messier process by which Dewey trusted communities to talk a future into existence by fits and starts. When a space somehow is cleared for dialogue and when sincere communicators expect and invite it, we glimpse futures that could not have been available or even imagined beforehand. Sometimes that space will be relatively private and interpersonal, such as a family dispute or a therapeutic relationship, sometimes quasi-public, such as classroom interaction, a church committee, or a corporate training session, and sometimes as fully publicized as a school board meeting or a legislative hearing covered by local or national journalists. Using the Buber–Rogers relationship as a springboard, we will consider a variety of such forums.

Our research complements a chorus of voices now invigorating the concept of dialogue.[2] Most of them do not connect philosophical and pragmatic ideas to touchstone events in intellectual history in quite the way we are attempting, but they make clear and powerful contributions to contemporary life. We will discuss such voices in more detail later in the book. For now, though, consider a representative spectrum of contemporary activities (of course, these are not mutually exclusive categories):

- *Projects to build nontraditional senses of community.* The so-called new electronic media provide new opportunities for dialogue to flourish, as well as new dangers and challenges. Some have noted how online communities can be formed and sustained in nontraditional "spaces" such as chat rooms (Rheingold, 1993) and listservs (Bird, 1999), giving some participants an experience of dialogue they never would have sought out in face-to-face interaction. Magazines such as the *Utne Reader* and television programs such as "Oprah Winfrey" have tried to establish community salons for conversations probing personal and social concerns, creating opportunities to meld participants within coherent, dialogue-focused small groups.

- *Projects to glimpse new potential for personal and interpersonal growth.* The David Bohm Dialogues group (Bohm, 1996) has sponsored many seminars worldwide on personal creativity based on the work of Bohm, a theoretical physicist who believed that dialogue is an essential and creative process underlying all of nature. One of the pivotal points stressed in the Bohm groups is that people must confront the "blocks" that remove them from dialogue, such as role hierarchy, credit/blame, and partial listening. Another program oriented toward improving interpersonal skills, Shem and Surrey's (1998) gender dialogue workshops have involved over 20,000 participants since 1986; their "connection model" stresses the tangible effects of a relational "we," mirroring Buber's concept of "the between."

- *Projects to bring disparate groups and cultures together.* The contemporary recognition of the values of cultural pluralism has increased efforts to bring together people who, in earlier times, would have been pleased to avoid each other except in the political arenas of power. A number of sponsoring groups (National Endowment for the Humanities' National Conversation, National Issues Forums, Public Conversations Project, Public Dialogue Consortium, and others) have developed innovative structures of dialogue that help deeply committed and even ideological citizens listen beyond their previously developed assumptions to include others with contradictory beliefs.

- *Projects to invigorate complex organizations and corporate life.* A powerful trend in recent organizational theory has been the concept of "the learning organization." This vigorous approach, based on the work of MIT professors in that university's Dialogue Project (see Isaacs, 1999; Senge, 1990), stresses systems thinking, cooperative decision making, synergistic knowing, and interpersonal skills.
- *Projects to expand the processes of political participation and choice making.* In one example, James Fishkin (1991) and his colleagues have designed national and international programs involving dialogic "issues forums." These "deliberative opinion polls," quite different from traditional public opinion polling, do not simply tap into what people think about an issue, but instead what they think after their own opinions have been tested in a crucible of conversation with other citizens who take different positions. In addition, much research in "deliberative democracy" is currently exploring how citizens can have access to, and contribute to, wider arenas of opinion and action.
- *Projects to make the institutions of journalism more accessible for public dialogue.* Many journalism researchers, theorists, and practitioners in the 1990s reconceptualized the roles and functions of the daily newspaper and other news media to emphasize public listening and deliberation in addition to message transmission (Anderson, Dardenne, & Killenberg, 1994; Charity, 1995; Rosen & Merritt, 1994). A paper can report the news, for example, and also serve as a community forum for dialogue. The labels "public journalism" and "civic journalism" have become contested terms within the profession, but they generally refer to a movement to frame journalism more in terms of a conversational public sphere.
- *Projects to define literary and philosophical insight in new ways.* Developments in many disciplines now stress dialogue far more than they did just a few years ago. For example, a dialogic discourse ethic has had widespread impact on many academic traditions, especially among critical theorists (Habermas, 1992). New theories of narrative knowing in rhetoric and the human sciences privilege dialogue (Clark, 1990; McPhail, 1996; Shotter, 1993a). Contemporary

anthropologists stress dialogue as a key to their discipline (Crapanzano, 1990; Tedlock & Mannheim, 1995). New forms of discursive and hermeneutic psychology are gaining adherents (Cushman, 1995; Shotter, 1995; Smith, Harrè, & Van Langenhove, 1995). Therapy and counseling also now rely on fresh (and some rejuvenated) senses of dialogic knowing (Anderson, 1997). Political philosophers increasingly rely on metaphors of conversation and dialogue in establishing the bases for democratic life (Barber, 1989; Chevigny, 1988; Guttman & Thompson, 1996; Young, 1990). Feminist thinkers, especially black feminist theorists Patricia Hill Collins (1990) and bell hooks (1994), strongly emphasize concepts of dialogue. Much of the most challenging work in recent media theory has had clear dialogic implications (Poster, 1990, 1995; Snyder, 1996; Taylor & Saarinen, 1994). Influential philosophers and cultural critics also have been drawn to dialogic principles; not only is there a resurgent interest in Buber and Bakhtin, but dialogue also can be seen as a core concept in widespread and well publicized contemporary treatments of Taoist philosophy, in the cultural studies of Stuart Hall and James Carey, in the hermeneutics of Hans-Georg Gadamer, in the postmodernism of Michel Foucault, in the Afrocentric approach of Molefi Asante, in the ethical philosophies of Charles Taylor and Emmanuel Levinas, and in the neopragmatism of Cornel West and Richard Rorty.

CONCLUSION

We are hardly the only researchers or critics, then, fashioning an account of dialogue. Dialogue, you might say, is hot. But is it a fad that will dissipate with little lasting effect? Hardly. Instead, we are approaching a critical mass from which global culture will not be able to turn.

With the newfound interest in dialogue, however, must come a responsible attempt to place it in historical context, to describe it carefully, and to sketch its realistic contributions to contemporary public life. That is the direction in which we are pointing. Beginning a journey in that direction means we must think seriously about what approaches or methods support such a project.

CHAPTER TWO

A Rhetorical Approach
to Dialogue

> A part of what we must learn in growing up, if we
> want to be perceived as speaking authoritatively about
> factual matters, is how to respond to the others around
> us should they challenge our claims. We must speak
> with an awareness of the possibility of such challenges,
> and be able to reply to them by justifying our claims.
> [This is] a *rhetorical* rather than a referential form of
> language; for more than merely claiming to depict a
> state of affairs, our ways of talking can "move"
> people to action, or change their perceptions.
> —John Shotter, *Conversational Realities*

Scholars have long been interested in analyzing rhetorical texts—
speech, writing, and action intended to influence other people. One approach has been for critics to illuminate authors' strategies, audience
reactions, and persuasive effects in the relatively formal contexts of
important orations and literary documents. In contrast, many recent
studies of spoken interaction have focused on less formal settings, analyzing the dynamic components of everyday talk even when the
speakers seem not to be trying to influence each other or the situation
they share. The former tradition has often been labeled rhetorical or literary criticism, while the study of informal speech events has developed as conversation analysis, discourse analysis, and ethnography.

Each of these has made its own contributions to the human studies, yet they have remained, for the most part, conceptually insulated
from each other. However, a creative blend of these traditions can help

us understand dialogue in fresh ways. People are probably never motiveless, and neither are they, in dialogue, selfless. Communication researchers want to know more about the dynamics of such interaction. Rhetorical researchers of dialogic encounters must be able to note the purposes that guide communicators uniquely and seemingly separate them at times, even while we acknowledge that communicators remain fundamentally interdependent.

We argue that such a rhetorical approach to dialogue should be based on an emergent methodology in which critics, whatever their philosophical preferences, find their primary clues about how to proceed embedded in the texts and contexts they choose to study. That is, the materials to some extent "make the call" for critics; to decide beforehand on a methodology and apply it as a technique may miss many of the central invitations or questions of any text. Critics may be neo-Aristotelian, postmodernist, or Marxist, with a narrative or a Burkean bent, but the specific *how* of a successful study is ultimately a creative encounter—a dialogue—with the text that invites and animates the study in the first place.

Typically, conversation- or discourse-analytic studies, however creative otherwise, rely on a series of predecided methodological moves. Scholars in this genre have tended, with notable exceptions, to use conversational texts primarily to explore and describe. McLaughlin (1984) notes: "a number of issues related to the actual doing of research on conversation . . . pertain regardless of discipline or perspective, to wit, issues of *observational and explanatory adequacy*" (p. 235). "How often?," "When?," and "What happens?" tend to be the kinds of questions answered by such studies, and their authors have been analysts more than critics. Critics attempting to understand or explicate a text, on the other hand, could be expected to have far more interpretive goals, goals more in line with emergent methodologies. But scholars, despite their interest in speeches, plays, and novels, rarely attempt to address in critical ways what we call conversational texts (for exceptions, see Branham & Pearce, 1996; Farrell, 1983; Foss & Foss, 1991; Glaser & Frank, 1982; Sharf, 1979). Among other goals, we want to identify and engage a centerpiece conversational text and show how it is a creative rhetorical accomplishment, much in the same way that a rhetorical, literary, or hermeneutic critic might confront any other text.

To do this, we begin this chapter by claiming that the central concept for a critical approach to conversation is dialogue, and that the current resurgence of interest in dialogue as a quality of discourse is an encouraging trend indeed. We also suggest (see also Goodall, 1991) that a scholarly sensitivity to dialogue depends on methods that are fundamentally emergent, and on a subjective reliance on coauthorship at several important levels. Finally, we close the chapter by justifying a series of critical (anti)methods that guided our research choices at various moments along the way, and which we would suggest for other researchers contemplating similar work.

THE QUALITY OF DIALOGUE
AS RHETORICAL ACCOMPLISHMENT

The term "dialogue" can commonly suggest a wide variety of meanings in everyday life. Scriptwriters produce dialogue that actors interpret; that is, dialogue in one sense often refers simply to what is said on stage, and, by extension, in everyday conversations. A second sense flows from the first; dialogue is sometimes considered to be any communicative event in which the partners engage in relatively equal back-and-forth interchange. Some politicians are likely to say of a given meeting with a diplomat, for example, that he or she was "open to dialogue"—by which they mean that the other person didn't monopolize or monologize the occasion. Finally, and also linked to the interchange sense of dialogue, some social scientists use the term simply to refer to the conversation's essential characteristic of alternating turns (Riegel, 1979).

However, thanks to Buber and others, the human sciences have recovered a philosophical sense of dialogue as a particular quality of human relating, one that sparks in those moments when communicators most fully realize their relationships. We will look more closely at Buber's dialogue in the next chapter, as he is one of the key players in our exploration. But, in brief, Buber claimed that human living is not contained within private human psyches, but emerges from "the between," the relational arena in which humans meet and confront each other as separate persons. Buber distrusted the modern tendency to psychologize existence, and discounted the feelings and cognitions of an individual mind as basic criteria by which to judge communication. Rather, he stressed, it is not in minds but in meeting that a particularly human existence develops, and such meeting becomes dialogical as each person truly comes up against the otherness or differentness offered by the other. Stereotypes, assumptions, objectifications, and abstractions won't do; Buber's dialogue depends neither on agreement nor on soft, accepting responsiveness. Even opponents can build dialogue, confirming each other and the quality of their talk by their willingness to encounter how different their positions really might be. Although

Buber's philosophy was once claimed to be the clearest statement of the perspective of a "new rhetoric" (Smith & Douglas, 1973), scholars in the last half of the twentieth century were more likely to cite Buber's influence on interpersonal theory than on rhetorical studies (e.g., Arnett, 1986; Stewart, 1985; for an exception, see Czubaroff, 2000).

Hermeneutical scholars, approaching dialogue from a slightly different direction, emphasize processes of interpretation—the myriad ways by which persons understand texts from unique perspectives through addressing, questioning, and discovering phenomena. The philosopher currently most helpful in exploring the communicative implications of hermeneutic thought is Hans-Georg Gadamer (1976, 1982; Palmer, 1969; Warnke, 1987).

Language to Gadamer cannot be a tool or instrument for conveying prior meaning to a receiver, because language is the living ground of all uniquely human existence. Implications are clear for a rhetorical understanding of texts: rhetoric cannot belong to authors. We do not *have* ideas and then decide to *say* them; the ideas and their saying are inextricable. Humans don't *use* language as much as they *live within* it, subject to its conditions. Because persons are born into an experience of language, all understanding—even critical commentary—becomes analogous to dialogic conversation in which the partners find themselves playfully going past what they already know or already believe, even as they are constrained by this same tradition.

A hermeneutic rhetoric, therefore, would go beyond merely attempting to discover effects of messages on audiences as though communication was a one-way process of delivering influence. Gadamer and others want to illuminate how rhetors co-influence each other to create a text of mutuality that would not have been possible monologically. Listening is as intimately a part of rhetoric as is speaking, and just as linguistically embedded. The rhetorical contributions of listening style become especially crucial in the Buber–Rogers dialogue, as we will see in chapter 6.

Gadamer (1989) implies a justification for a textual perspective on conversation when he asks, "What is communication between speakers? And why is it that something like texts can be given to us in common? What does it mean that in this process of communication with each other something emerges that, like texts, is one and the same thing for us?" (pp. 27–28). At the same time, Gadamer recognizes the difficulties of such textualization when he refers to "antitexts," spontaneous speech forms such as jokes and irony that "resist textualization" because they are so highly interactive, and depend so much on the event's context and supportive prior understanding of speakers (p. 37).

From a different tributary, the long neglected Russian literary theorist Mikhail Bakhtin has impressed contemporary scholars with his dialogic insight into novelizing experience, the phenomenon of inner speech, and the nature of existence itself (Bakhtin, 1981, 1984, 1986, 1993; Clark & Holquist, 1984; Holquist, 1990; Morson & Emerson, 1990; Todorov, 1984). Bakhtin, for example, reasoned that each person's sense of self is constructed through a dialogic process of coauthorship, describing how authorial or creative responsibility does not develop through the psychological directions of a creative individual, but within the creativity necessarily found in human otherness, the meeting with the not-me, and therefore in human language.

Language reverberates with its own history. The "already-spoken" nature of any word, the voices present *before*, retain their presence in any utterance. Bakhtin stressed the vitality of the presence of many different historically active speech styles of any language (he called this *heteroglossia*), and also the vitality within any utterance of the many alternative voices that the utterance implies (he reserved the better-known term "polyphony" for this phenomenon). Thus, any discourse provides multiple invitations and works at many levels for speaker-listeners, and for critics.

WHAT KIND OF RHETORIC IS DIALOGUE?

Because rhetoric was understood by Aristotle as the study of the available means of persuasion, and because dialogic scholars typically do not focus on contexts in which one party attempts to manipulate others to fit predetermined goals, it is probably clear by now that we believe conceptions of rhetoric need not be confined to obvious occasions of speaker-to-listener, goal-derived, goal-directed behavior. Indeed, the movement away from an exclusively intentional, unidirectional, formulaic, and agonistic influence model is, with some exceptions, the vector of twentieth-century rhetorical thought (see Czubaroff, 2000; Foss & Griffin, 1995; Ong, 1982, pp. 110–112; Schrag, 1986; Simons, 1990). Increasingly, we must examine contexts of practical discourse in which communicators seek simply to understand a common problem. Many human contexts challenge us to synthesize, not to analyze; to facilitate or catalyze, not to win; to understand, not to oversee. The scope of theory has expanded to include rhetoric's status as a constitutive force, a phenomenon of identification and relationship.

The hermeneutic reach of rhetoric as described by Buber, Gadamer, Bakhtin, and others is at least broad enough to include conversational dialogue—talk that can be considered coauthored intentional texts responding to human needs and the symbolic means by which persons address those needs. Such texts transcend the control of individual rhetors, but for that very reason define a valid communicational emphasis within rhetoric. Kenneth Burke's (1969) work, expanded by Brown (1987, pp. 84–96) and others into a "society as text" metaphor, provides a nonlinear, symbolic, processual, constitutive, and transactional approach to rhetorical life. Indeed, the textual metaphor is itself in many ways limiting and objectifying, turning the dynamic and ephemeral into a staticized representation, unless we understand Bakhtin's position that even seemingly static texts can constitute dialogic situations. *Text*, in the sense we intend, refers collectively to those subtle traces of discourse—written, spoken, recorded, or remembered—with which respondents, by replying, build interpretations. Society is dialogic conversation in the ways suggested by Buber, Gadamer, and Bakhtin, and reinforced by the symbolic interactionist tradition (Blumer, 1969; Denzin, 1992; Dewey, 1927; Mead, 1934). It is toward conversational texts, then, that we turn in order to glimpse the protean potential of rhetoric.

Considering dialogue rhetorically reminds us that language forms the ground of human being and that successful critics ideally account for two parallel phenomena, *tradition* and *surprise*, that, despite surface differences, are far from contradictory. Dialogic theorists must stress the necessity of both: language has a forward sweep that is dependent on its own history; it is the environment for our meetings, not simply a tool kit for talk. Language is the expected. As Ong (1982) said, "To speak, I have to be somehow already in communication with the mind I am to address before I start speaking" (p. 176) and "To formulate anything I must have another person or other persons already 'in mind.' This is the paradox of human communication" (p. 177).

At the same time, language also remains the province of the unexpected. It cannot avoid being a medium for surprise, for serendipity, for the unexpected meaning jumping at us from around the corner. As Gadamer suggests, when we approach discourse from the position of genuine questioning, when we truly do not know what to expect, even when we're aware that we must somehow be prejudiced, we are most free to learn. Certainty and entrenchment justify monologue, not dialogue, as Buber himself knew when he encouraged his students and friends to question him persistently. Ong (1967) shows why a questioning dialogue is the ground of rhetorical change:

> Dialogue constitutes the basic use of the spoken word, and in
> its normal stage dialogue is entirely unrehearsed. It moves

from determined points of departure toward an undetermined goal, for in dialogue the utterance of each individual is decided not merely by the individual himself but by the preceding remark of the interlocutor to whom his remark is a reply. (pp. 300–301)

Traditional rhetoric that privileges persuasion analyzes how speakers' messages move from "determined points of departure" toward predetermined goals; dialogic rhetoric presumes a wider and less content-inscribed playing field for talk. A dialogic rhetoric cannot ultimately grant individual speakers possession of their "own" utterances, but finds conversational texts to be profoundly, even mysteriously, coauthored. Individual utterances, heard in this context, no longer seem so individualized. Talk is not for persuasion but for inviting more talk, and more consideration.

Ong (1995) later elaborated on this theme. He shows how "the most radically unambiguous words in any language are the words for 'I' and 'you,' as spoken in direct dialogue" (p. 22). This is because these words demand no interpretation or hermeneutic; they refer, as linguistic 'floater' terms, only and always to the *persons* of speaker and listener in the moment of dialogue—and possess no deeper meaning-layers to be interpreted. Thus:

> Discourse founded in the direct relationship of "I" and "you" (singular sense, formerly expressed by "Thou") represents a different level of discourse from that where only nouns (representing not persons directly, but things, and persons only indirectly) are in control, as Martin Buber decades ago made clear. . . .
>
> Since each "I" must sense the "you" whom the "I" addresses before speech begins, dialogue demands, paradoxically enough, that the persons addressing one another be somehow aware of the interior of each other before they can begin to communicate verbally. Although we have no way of retrieving the point in human history at which the first words [sic] or words were spoken, we can be quite sure of certain underlying features that speech possesses from the beginning. In verbal communication, the hearer must be aware that the speaker intends the utterance to be a word or words and not just noise; the speaker must know that the hearer knows this, and the hearer must know that the speaker knows that he or she (the hearer) knows it. The hermeneutic circle again. We

are somehow inside one another's consciousness beefore we
begin to speak to another or others.

Otherwise, there is no way to *say* anything. (Ong, 1995,
p. 22)

What kind of rhetoric, then, is dialogue? Essentially, it is coexpe-
riential and collaborative rhetoric, open rhetoric, expansive rhetoric,
constitutive rhetoric, and paradoxically perhaps, radically traditional
rhetoric. What can *radically traditional* imply? Dialogue is radical in
that it not only assumes but mandates an openness to change; it is traditional, as Ong implies, in its necessary links to an historical context
for forming and understanding any utterance. Dialogic rhetoric becomes the field for the growth of fruitful and open conflict and confrontation. It is the experiential field in which the knowns and the
maybes, what's settled and what's surprising, can be held in profound
tension with each other. Where humans cannot converse, they probably cannot negotiate or deliberate, either.

EMERGENT DIALOGIC SENSITIVITY:
BEYOND TEMPLATE METHODS

To make your own holiday cards, you might want to decide on a design, say a dove in flight with a stylized tree in the background. You
could paint each separately, and friends would love you for it. Or, because you have so many to do, you could cut along the outline of your
best dove and tree and make your cards by dabbing paint within your
stencil. Although still individualized, the similarity of the cards is also
a decision you've made artistically. A *template*, of which a stencil is
one example, assists a craftsperson in creating a new work, in effect, by
borrowing liberally from previous efforts. Crafts are, of course, composed of histories of action; they are a kind of carefulness in motion
over time. The template, when overlaid on unrefined material, connects the current task to the tradition and becomes a shortcut to shaping and designing the new piece. A pattern for sewing clothing is
another obvious example of a template, along with teachers' scoresheet
overlays for exams, cookie molds, and a variety of other everyday tools.

Templates can be useful and necessary, but not because they lead
to surprising and creative discoveries. Rather, the value of templates is
that they preserve the ongoing tradition of a work and facilitate the
production of similar and relatively predictable works. In fact, schema
somewhat like mental templates develop in many artists, allowing

them to produce many superficially similar works (dolls, songs, essays, culinary dishes, brooms, totems, etc.) that subsequently can be individualized creatively. In the same way, critical essays that seek novel insights should transcend the application of a template method provided by a critical approach, and move to a level of creative response.

The best critics, of course, always have done so, but it's tempting—even seductive—for them to formalize their own orthodoxies, or for followers to prove they can "make the team" by parroting fashionable template-style language. When Roderick Hart (1986, p. 290) lamented that, too often, "critical systems are super-imposed willy-nilly on some innocent rhetorical event until, for example, the remarks of some Georgia peanut-farmer are rendered in the critical patois of some continental existentialist," he was essentially critiquing this template mentality. If we avoid using their systems as templates, theorists can guide us well in understanding dialogic texts. For example, writing from a Bakhtinian perspective in dialogic cultural criticism, Giles Gunn (1987) suggests that "the most appropriate model for human experience is discourse or conversation, but the aim of this conversation or discourse is anything but unanimity or truth; its aim is rather the enlargement of consciousness through dialogic engagement with alterity" (p. 145). Further, because dialogic criticism "ultimately boils down to a question of the polyphony of our interpretations, our discourses, our critical practices" (pp. 145–146), criticism becomes much more grounded in listening for different voices than in the application of method. This, of course, was Gadamer's (1982) central critique of method itself in his most famous book, *Truth and Method*. Truth or understanding will not be the outcome of applying correct methods, because the method-based inquiry will always miss the point of alterity or difference itself.

In a similar vein, philosopher Abraham Kaplan (1964) once wrote perceptively of "the law of the instrument," by which he meant that a tool or method can be applied so much and so thoroughly that an inquirer will only be able to see the world in terms of that tool. "Give a small boy a hammer," he claimed, "and he will find that everything he encounters needs pounding" (p. 28). Effective cultural or rhetorical critics hoping to make conceptual contributions do not carry methods around searching for target texts to which to apply these methods. Instead they discover texts that somehow choose their attention, so that criticism then "celebrates the real-ization of human events in public dialog" (Rosenfield, 1974, pp. 494–495). In other words, critics enter the process as full dialogical partners—ready to be changed and surprised, respectful of the "otherness" of a text, not enrolled in a prescribed critical school, listening to messages for implications not yet disclosed, divulged, or even developed, and ready to weave their tentative meanings into the emerging public dialogue.

Therefore, the critical process assumes many of the characteristics of conversation itself: emergence, co-construction of meaning, surprise-within-tradition, temporal flow, a degree of spontaneity, an absence of strategic manipulation, and the experiential immersion of participants. Conversational criticism does not suggest that methods, as such, are unimportant or harmful. It implies only that methods cannot become templates, and critics must accept Halling and Leifer's (1991) invitation to do what they call "dialogal" research, where "with increased competence there is decreased reliance on abstract rules or procedures and more attention to specific cases" (p. 2). Halling and Leifer show how dialogic and collaborative research "is more process than procedurally oriented, and yet is responsive to the same methodological concerns that other phenomenological approaches attempt to address through theory and the development of procedures" (pp. 2–3).

The notion that critics must be capable of being surprised by what they discover is consistent with naturalistic and social approaches to discourse. We have grounded this study in assumptions similar to those explored in a stimulating forum on social aproaches to communication theory (see especially Jorgensen, 1992; Lannamann, 1992; Leeds-Hurwitz, 1992, 1995). Our work is also consonant with more broadly defined social constructionist tendencies in the human sciences as exemplified by Gergen (1994, 1995), Shotter (1993a, 1993b), Pearce (1989, 1993), and others. In such a perspective, reality is socially constructed, and inquiry into interpersonal process is best characterized by recognizing the benefits of research reflexivity, the necessity for persistent questioning, the centrality of cultural context to any analysis, and the ascendance of dialogic assumptions over "individually owned personalities" merely trading actions (Lannamann, 1992, p. 142). Approaches like ours, in fact, presuppose that "research requires a dialogic model of understanding" (Lannamann, 1992, p. 146). This fundamental research dialogue asks scholars to go beyond merely recognizing the mutuality of communication as and when they discern it. Rather, part of the research dynamic itself becomes fundamentally dialogic and mutually defined.

Dialogical anthropologists have adopted a similar stance that avoids philosophical or methodological prescription (Crapanzano, 1992; Maranhao, 1990; Tedlock, 1983; Tyler, 1987). Dialogical anthropology is concerned directly with communicative praxis, and by implication with how rhetorical critics must confront their tasks as well. The first similarity is the necessity of investigator presence. Much criticism appears to proceed almost anonymously and invisibly, as if the critic were absent but for the pronouncements. The tone is elevated explication, a type of objectification far from the immersive tone advocated by dialogic scholars. If a cultural field researcher cannot be "not there" as a story is told, the only alternative is to presume inevitable participation in the shape of the story that emerges. Meaning and personhood emerge, as Buber reminds us, from betweenness, not from speakers' intent. A second reminder of dialogical anthropology is that who the critics are and the critics' relation to texts and contexts are at least as important to the quality of understanding as the tools the critics possess. Third, like dialogical anthropologists, rhetorical critics of conversation must maintain a healthy respect for differentness; the other is not simply a demonstration of something, a conduit for a disembodied message, a representative of a group, or a pale reflection of one's self. Rather, others are persons whose lives in process maintain and presume their own distinctive logics that demand and deserve respect.

RESEARCH (ANTI)METHODS

If critics expect to encounter conversational rhetoric meaningfully, we believe some unconventional moves are often justified. At the same time, we should report the decisions we made as co-researchers in this Buber–Rogers project, and even tentatively suggest how useful they might be for other researchers interested in related studies. Of course, it would be ironic indeed if what we think of as "(anti)methods" would be read as prescriptions.

In general, we suggest that rhetorical critics of conversation:

- Study what they enjoy;
- Avoid critical templates;
- Stand on their humility;
- Avoid lionizing what scholars invoke as "the literature";
- Live with the text, experiencing it in different modalities; and
- Emphasize coauthorship.

Suggesting these things is a bit like suggesting that someone should make new friends, watch a wider range of television programs, or lose weight. At one level, these are specific directions that could be helpful. At another level, they provide few clues as to how these goals might be accomplished. This prescriptive distance is probably appropriate. However, to recomend (anti)methods seems to invite us to personalize our own involvement with studying one particular conversation.

Study the Enjoyable

For many years, we were intrigued with the Buber–Rogers dialogue, consulting it often in order to crosscheck other ideas of these two significant twentieth-century intellectuals. We found in this public dialogue the expression and clarification of ideas that neither man had elaborated elsewhere. A recent volume of Rogers's intellectual dialogues (Kirschenbaum & Henderson, 1989b) provided an additional resource, as its transcript of the Buber–Rogers meeting was somewhat different than the most commonly cited transcript (Buber, 1965b; see also Friedman, 1964, pp. 485–497; "Dialogue Between," 1960). Maurice Friedman, perhaps the world's foremost Buber scholar, not only moderated the dialogue in 1957 but has maintained his interest in this event as a fundamental clue to Buber's thought, especially to Buber's concern with the limits of mutuality. Friedman cites the dialogue often in his work, and other scholars, especially in recent years, have found that it illuminates concepts in education, psychotherapy, and interpersonal theory (Anderson, 1982; Anderson & Cissna, 1996, 1997; Arnett, 1981, 1989; Brace, 1992; Brink, 1987; Burstow, 1987; Cissna & Anderson, 1990, 1994b, 1996; Friedman, 1994, 1996d; Peterson, 1976; Roffey, 1980; Seckinger, 1976; Thorne, 1992; Van Balen, 1990; Yoshida, 1994). Beyond the intellectual invitation of the dialogue, we came to appreciate the interchange as itself a lively conversation that still engages relevant ideas decades later.

Avoid Critical Templates

As we have seen, critics tend to develop specialized vocabularies that characterize their conceptual systems. These vocabularies are designed to illuminate texts, but are not themselves such illumination. However helpful they are theoretically, they are diminished—dialogically speaking—by the very nature of being essentially prior to and displaced from the immediate involvement with a text that engages and questions a critic's experience. The character of surprise may be sacrificed for the comfort of tradition. Fresh insight is most likely to be stimulated by a critic's careful participative questioning and "reading" of a first-level communicative event, based on the ground from which he or she moves to encounter relevant rhetoric. Criticism, then, is second-level dialogic participation in the multiple voices, actual and potential, of language—participation that leads to fresh appreciation from a third-level audience. Morson and Emerson (1990), in their synthesis of theoretical implications of Bakhtin's prosaics, point out that from a dialogic perspective, truth must always be *conversation* rather than *proposition*. A critic should not look for "what something means," as if meaning could be monadically determined, but to the most elastic extent possible should free the multiple voices inherent in linguistic experience. As they argue:

> When two . . . voice-ideas come to interact, they may produce a dialogue changing both of them and giving rise to new insights and new dialogues. The "unity" of truth becomes the unified "feel" of a conversation, not the unity of a single proposition, however complex, that may result from it. When monologic thinkers encounter such conversations, they usually try to extract just such a finalizing proposition, but in doing so they are false to the dialogic process itself. (p. 237)

For Bakhtin (1981), the key to understanding Dostoevsky, for instance, and to a successful criticism of his poetic, is to know that reading for the "origins and consequences" of ideas is unprofitable because this strategy presumes monologic, cause-effect propositions. Even worse would be a critic who brings unassailable propositions to the rhetoric. Rather, Morson and Emerson (1990) suggest, the best strategy is virtually no strategy at all: "One must read not for the plot, but for the dialogues, and to read for the dialogues is to participate in them" (p. 249).

The key to understanding conversation rhetorically is to regard text not as a product or an object-of-study but as a moment of dialogic invitation within which critics must participate. Conversations are environments in which critics move—essentially atheoretically—as conversants or interlocutors themselves. They may be especially well-formed (or ill-informed) interlocutors, grounded in their own distinct times and places, and biased from their own cultural and experiential perspectives. But all communicative understanding is based on such differences and such limits.

Stand on Humility

Criticism can be a prideful activity. Critics sometimes appear to float above the fray as omniscient or objective commentators whose judgments are asserted as if they count more than those of ordinary people. In critical essays, what is claimed as "understood" is typically spotlighted, while what remains mysterious or ineffable is omitted or downplayed. In contrast, we argue that conversational criticism is necessarily an exercise in humility. What dialogic critics do not know, or are not sure of, or are led to misunderstand, is so vast that making any assertion should feel a bit arrogant. For example, critics are limited simultaneously by the intentional, predictable factors of dialogue, and also by the surprises inherent in any dialogic encounter.

Dialogic rhetoric, thus, is an interweaving of two dialectical tendencies—extensions of tradition and surprise—that might be called *ploy* and *play*. Ploy refers to the tendency of communicators to experience tangible connections to their past behaviors, attitudes, cultures, and intentions, and their impulse to make communication more manageable, predictable, and understandable. A concern with ploy creates a continuity between past and future; we plan at times to have effects on situations and on other persons, whether those effects are actualized or not. Yet the ploy factor by itself is insufficient for dialogue and needs the complement of interactional play. Play is the tendency of communicators to anticipate open futures, to be surprised, to invite the unfamiliar, and to be affected in serendipitous ways by others. Yet if interaction is persistently overconcerned with play, dialogue is diminished because persons can lose the ground on which they can stand experientially in encountering a world. Critics of dialogic rhetoric are limited in the understanding of ploy by an obvious inability to read minds or to know fully another's experience, and limited in the understanding of play by the constant flux of a process world.

Because conversation is a transitory functional expression of the immediate moment, its essence cannot be captured or possessed, nor can its context be recovered. Essence is lost with the moment, receding. Although textual artifacts such as transcripts might resuggest the arc of a conversation, they fail to convey the force of either context or discovery that infused the original dialogue, and critics should not assume that the verbal code provides the cleanest clues to actors' meanings. Once a printed page or an audiotape makes the conversation analytically manipulable, the talk as preserved loses the very characteristics that created emergent conversation in the first place. Conversational critics, to be honest, might admit that something like the physicist Werner Heisenberg's (1930) venerable uncertainty principle affects their work: any apparatus of observation alters the conditions of the observed. We might observe and comment, but observation is its own kind of participation, and observers will inevitably experience the event plus (or minus) whatever subtle or elaborate, but often invisible, changes they introduce.

Avoid Lionizing the Literature

H. L. Goodall Jr. (1991) once warned communication researchers against investing too much in the shape of established scholarship. The corpus of studies and extant knowledge in a field, known collectively as "the literature," is potentially a source of guidance and support. Any scholar needs to understand how current lines of inquiry complement or contradict others, and significant gaps in the literature define useful opportunities for investigation.

However, Goodall observes, many researchers act as if the literature is a sacred text whose legitimacy should not be questioned (p. 33). When it is tested at all, it is usually in the form of dramatic politicized battles over which interpretive positions are proper—hardly a dialogic approach. If we are not careful, the literature functions as monologic judge, settling open questions primarily by the weight of precedent or the dominance of fashionable templates. Scholars choosing unconventional ways to shape their research might abandon them before they are even attempted, because they remain (as yet) unsanctioned by the literature. Scholars intrigued by preliminary results could mistrust them because they diverge from the literature. Researchers might not persist in unpopular or unusual lines of inquiry long enough for their value to be recognized more widely. Or, as Goodall suggests, scholars might compare their methods and results against the literature in a search for a mythical proper interpretation, leading to what Buber called a "technical dialogue" (1965b, p. 19) in which different voices are heard, but heard monologically, not in genuine conversation.

Live with the Text, Experiencing It in Different Modalities

Textual specification and verification are problematic for any critic. Which "Close Encounters of the Third Kind" does a film critic evaluate —the "original" cut as first released, or one of the later expanded versions? (The first theatrical release was hardly the original to the director, Stephen Spielberg, as he had been shaping and reshaping the film all along.) Which "I Have a Dream" speech engages a rhetorical critic—the one first reprinted, or the one as spoken by Reverend King to his Washington, D.C. audience? In conversational criticism, the problem is even more complex. Although some interviews are reprinted in magazines, newspapers, and books, they are almost invariably edited extensively to delete repetitions, speech errors, unconsidered generalizations, and reconsidered opinions. Occasionally, too, published interviews are a hybrid form, mixing the original oral language with subsequent written emendations.

Genuine and unscripted face-to-face conversations are only rarely preserved in writing, although modern technologies of film, audiotape, and videotape are capable of recording salient features of such events for later transcription. Some people, including Buber, think recording devices and procedures create uncomfortable intrusions on otherwise spontaneous conversations. The recorder could make the audience-context more artificial, a problem to which we return later. Whatever the limitations, how the transcription is done becomes crucial.

Unless the transcriber's intent is strict conversation analysis, transcription is unlikely to be systematic, and relatively few communicative cues will be preserved. Simple mistakes of hearing and listening naturally creep into the transcriptions, and these happen quite often, even with experienced transcribers (Stubbs, 1983, pp. 227–230). Beyond aural mistakes, though, most readers would presume that transcribers would retain the conversants' original word choices (they often don't) and not omit utterances of significance (they often do). Presumably also, transcribers will note problems or features of context such as intermissions or disturbances from an audience. Informal transcriptions, when compared with taped conversations, often display the transcriber's implicit judgments of what should have been said, rather than what was actually said. Ease of reading, rather than verisimilitude with the original dialogue, becomes the typical criterion for transcription. Interestingly, given the importance of transcribers' decisions, many transcriptions appear to be created anonymously, or at least are uncredited in publication. Mishler (1986, p. 50), writing of the theoretical implications of transcription decisions, recalls the experience of one researcher whose typist had simply "filtered" relevant information from the transcript, presumably because it seemed repetitious. To Mishler, each transcriptual representation is necessarily also, to some extent, a transformation (p. 48).

Because even tape recordings are only extracts and partial representations of full communicative dialogue, a critic should experience as many different voices and modalities within a conversational text as possible. Repeated visits to our text, we found, far from torturing the richness of the conversation, enhanced it. In addition, although the essence of interpersonal understanding cannot be quantified, we decided not to renounce counting and measuring phenomena if that seemed appropriate and helpful.

Our informal investigatory design emphasized interpretive and performative ways of experiencing the dialogue and testing our ideas about it, including:

- Individual readings of the transcribed dialogue in which each coauthor highlighted textual inconsistencies with the tape;
- Collaborative sessions discussing the flow of the dialogue;
- Several occasions of "role-play replays" in which the coauthors each took the part of Rogers or Buber, playing with possible inflections, intentions, and nuances in order to explore the polysemic possibilities of language choices;
- Several collaborative and several separate listening sessions during which two somewhat variant transcriptions (Buber, 1965b; Kirschenbaum & Henderson, 1989a) were compared word by word with the audiotaped dialogue;
- Several sessions in which the coauthors tested each other's interpretations of the underlying dynamic of the dialogue;
- Interviews with audience members, subject matter experts, colleagues of the principals, and, in one case, a participant in the dialogue (moderator Maurice Friedman);
- Primary documentary research in the Library of Congress and other relevant repositories; and, finally,
- Development of a refined and corrected transcript of what Buber and Rogers said that evening in 1957, complete with annotations, which resulted in the publication of *The Martin Buber–Carl Rogers Dialogue: A New Transcript With Commentary* (Anderson & Cissna, 1997).

Clearly, the shape of this research project could not have been foretold or prescribed. Allowing it to emerge developmentally was not merely a philosophical commitment or goal but also a consequence of the cooperation of two researchers trying to make sense together. We are convinced that neither of us working alone would have explored most of the dialogic nuances invited, often subtly, by the original coauthored conversational text. To the same degree that all conversational meaning is ultimately coauthored, research is its own brand of coauthored conversation. This leads us to our final suggestion for critics of conversation.

Emphasize Coauthorship

Published criticism in literary and communication scholarship is usually the work of single authors, perhaps because criticism has been most often perceived and defined as a solitary activity of judging products against artistic or effectual standards. In conversational criticism from a dialogic perspective, we necessarily sacrifice criterial precision in order to retain and disclose as much of the life of the interchange as possible. When the success of dialogue depends in part on spontaneity and playing off the contributions of the other, success in dialogic criticism should grow from similar roots.

For Bakhtin (1981, 1986), human existence, and even the human self, is never simply authored but is always coauthored. The dynamic relation of person with person creates human meaning. This does not mean the individual person is confined to monologue. Because language subsumes and carries the dynamic relation, dialogue can flourish even within inner speech. The person-with-person dimension adds another level of richness to the dialogic mix. Goodall (1991) suggests that to "capture multiple selves within contexts," scholars might consider "multiple authorship" of studies in which subjects literally assume roles as authors or respondents (p. 25)—a good suggestion that is unfortunately impractical or impossible in many rhetorical studies of conversation. Yet, such a goal might be approached by ensuring that multiple voices are considered. This is much more easily facilitated by co-investigators in a study than by single authorship. Conversational criticism is, by definition, meta-dialogical. Thus, it makes sense to emphasize the relationship of scholars, as well as a reminder of the constant presence of Buber's "between" as the site of meaning. Simply put, it is not *within* us that we "get" or "have" ideas, but *between* us.

As coauthors, we compared, considered, coalesced, and sometimes contrasted our differing interpretations, and engaged the only living participant from the dialogue, philosopher Maurice Friedman, through correspondence and direct interview. Although Professor Friedman disagrees with some of our interpretations (see Friedman, 1994, 1996d), our case study would have suffered significantly without his direct and indirect contributions to the informal authorial mix.

CONCLUSION

A rhetorical approach to dialogue can sharpen our critical senses and make us alert to the large consequences that flow from relatively transitory interpersonal events. More than one person has asked us a version of this question: "You're writing a whole book about a 1957 event that only took an hour or two?" Well, yes and no. We begin with that evening: an event, a dialogue about dialogue, that is the departure point for a series of other dialogues it stimulated. This conversation's rhetoric reverberated far and wide, not only by changing its participants in ways that surprised them both but by influencing countless other intellectuals by becoming a touchstone text in twentieth-century intellectual history. It launched a new dialogue about the nature of conversational possibility in us. And that is why this book is ultimately "about" far more than the Buber–Rogers dialogue.

Our own journey through these ideas of mutuality, confirmation, acceptance, and otherness led us to rethink the potential for public dialogue itself. Subsequent chapters will elaborate what these two men said, but far beyond that, the book will explore implications of Buber's and Rogers's ideas—and what we call the "Buber–Rogers position" that emerged during their conversation—for a mediated world that neither of them fully anticipated, a world in which the questions of dialogue frequently become the questions of social and cultural crisis.

In this chapter, we have refined our initial discussion of what dialogue entails and introduced the possibility of treating conversations as coauthored rhetorical texts worthy of critical response and subsequent theorizing. That response, however, cannot be based in template thinking, nor can it be specified in advance. Research into dialogue must itself be dialogic, we suggest, and ultimately participative even when it is focused on historical texts. We trust that keeping the conversation alive as we examine it will be justified in the richness of the results. This chapter describes our interpretive and performative attempts to enliven a conversational text; beyond that, though, it recommends (anti)methods for accomplishing dialogic rhetorical research within different historical contexts. To let history live, we not only preserve and critique its speech; we must somehow speak it too, and respond. To do so is to hear its voices in fresh ways. To do so is also to hear our own voices more clearly, in our own time.

The next two chapters will amplify the voices most prominent that spring evening so many years ago, Martin Buber and Carl Rogers. Despite their obvious contributions to their respective fields, each man also had vocal critics. To provide context for our study, we need to clarify their basic concepts and, as friendly critics ourselves, evaluate how these ideas can continue to shape dialogic theory.

CHAPTER THREE

Buber and the Philosophy of Dialogue

Because word and deed were as one to [Buber], he was able to concentrate with an intensity he brought to bear on everything he did. This power of concentration, focused like the rays of the sun through a burning glass, was one of the many enduring things I learned from him. He taught me to live in what he called the given moment—the moment in time through which we were passing. We could allow it to float by emptily, or we could fill it with meaning. But we could do this only if we lived intensely in the moment through which we were passing and did not use it for halfhearted actions or speech.

—Aubrey Hodes, *Martin Buber*

Buber . . . has shown with the greatest possible cogency that only what he calls a philosophy *des Zwischen*—I would say, for my part, a philosophy of intersubjectivity—can rescue us from either the impasse of an individualism which considers man solely in reference to himself or the other impasse of a collectivism which has eyes only for society. . . . It is true that the human personality first attempts to escape its isolation by adding itself to the mass. Yet therein lies an illusion that reflection suffices to dispel. In the midst of a collectivity, man is not *with* man or *alongside* man. The isolation is not surmounted, it is smothered as a sound may be drowned out by noise. . . . It is only when the

> individual recognises the other in his very otherness,
> as a human being other than himself, and when on
> this basis he effects a penetration to the other, that he
> can break the circle of his solitude in a specific,
> transforming encounter.
> —Gabriel Marcel, "I and Thou"

No one has contributed more to a philosophy of dialogue than has Martin Buber. Born late in the nineteenth century, he lived eighty-seven years, dying 13 June 1965, after a career of groundbreaking interdisciplinary scholarship and cross-cultural social and literary awareness. His numerous essays and books influenced thought and practice across a myriad of fields, including philosophy, sociology, theater, biblical studies, theology, Jewish studies, education, and psychology.[1] Buber translated the Hebrew Bible into German, prepared the Hasidic tales of an earlier century for a modern audience, and even authored a few novels and poems. The most complete bibliography of his work (Cohn & Buber, 1980) includes more than 1,400 items in 19 languages.[2] He produced such an astonishing body of work not just because he was a prolific writer, but because he was such a hungry and skillful reader. Buber had accumulated a personal library of 20,000 volumes by the 1930s and, according to Shmuel Eisenstadt, graduate student and later a colleague at Hebrew University, was able to read 300 to 400 pages an hour, accomplishing "in an afternoon what it would take an ordinary person a week to read" (Friedman, 1983b, p. 286).

THE LIFE OF MARTIN BUBER

Contemporary readers may find it hard to imagine how different Buber's world was from our own, as he grew up in nineteenth-century Europe, reached adulthood at the dawn of the twentieth century, and experienced firsthand the horror of two World Wars.[3] Born in Vienna, Austria, on 8 February 1878, Buber spent most of his formative years in the home of his paternal grandparents. His mother left home mysteriously when he was three, apparently without explaining anything about this to young Martin,[4] and Buber did not see her again for twenty years. Buber's father took him to his own parents' home, near Lemberg, 450 miles away, in what was then part of Austria. This area became part of Poland between the World Wars, was annexed into the Soviet Union after World War II, and most recently became Ukraine following the breakup of the Soviet Union in 1991. There Buber lived until he was fourteen, when he rejoined his newly remarried father.

Buber received his early education at home primarily from his grandmother, who stressed language learning—Hebrew, Latin, Greek, and French, as well as his native German. As an adult, he would be fluent in nine languages—adding English, Polish, Yiddish, and Italian. At nineteen, he left home to study philosophy at the University of Vienna, and also attended lectures on art, economics, and philology. As he tells Rogers in their dialogue many years later, he also studied psychology and psychiatry for three terms in Leipzig and Zurich, where he first learned about "man in the *so-called* pathological state." Even then, he said, he wanted to meet and to establish a real relation between himself and people who were called pathological. And this, as he put it to Rogers, he learned in some measure "as far as . . . a boy of . . . twenty or so can learn such things" (turn #4).

Buber received his Ph.D. from the University of Vienna in 1904 and lived in Germany for most of his early adult life, active in such intellectual and political circles as the Zionist movement of the late nineteenth and early twentieth centuries. He worked as a writer and editor. His most famous book, *I and Thou*, begun shortly after the First World War, was published in December 1922. The next year he took his first university post as a professor at the University of Frankfurt. Shortly after Hitler came to power in Germany in 1933, Buber resigned his professorship without waiting for the official dismissal that all Jewish professors eventually received. Although others, including his friend and houseguest, Albert Einstein, left Germany shortly thereafter, Buber stayed, organizing adult education programs for his fellow German Jews. Only in 1938, on the eve of his sixtieth birthday, and only after much preparation and negotiation, did Buber leave. He emigrated to Palestine and took a position in social philosophy at the recently formed Hebrew University, which he had helped to found. He retired from the university in 1951 so he could travel more extensively, eventually making three lecture/seminar tours of the United States in 1951, 1957, and 1958.

Buber was thus a mainstay of the global intellectual landscape for sixty years. His early work as an editor brought him into contact with many literary figures, and his involvement in Zionism introduced him to many others who held a variety of positions about the future Jewish state. Buber served early notice of his writing talents in 1906 and 1908 when he published his first two Hasidic books, *The Tales of Rabbi Nachman* (1956) and *The Legend of the Baal-Shem* (1955). His wife, Paula (Winkler) Buber, was herself a novelist, publishing under the pseudonym Georg Munk; her interests expanded Buber's literary network even farther. Buber's fame following the publication of *I and Thou* and his influence on a dozen fields introduced him to even more intellectuals worldwide. Celebrated intellectuals who knew Buber and with whom he corresponded included, among many others, Bertrand Russell, Hermann Hesse, Francois Mauriac, and S. Y. Agnon (all recipients of the Nobel Prize for Literature), as well as novelist Franz Kafka; poets Ludwig Strauss, T. S. Eliot, and Else Lasker-Schuler; physicists Niels Bohr and Albert Einstein; philosophers and writers Eugen Rosenstock-Huessy, Reinhold Niebuhr, Franz Rosenzweig, Ernst Simon, Paul Tillich, Samuel Hugo Bergman, Rabindranath Tagore, and Albert Camus; politicians Chaim Weizmann, Levi Eshkol, David Ben-Gurion, and Dag Hammarskjöld; educator Robert Maynard Hutchins; and humanitarian leaders such as Eleanor Roosevelt, and Albert Schweitzer.[5] Surely this was a man whose influence uniquely positioned him at the crossroads of twentieth-century cultural, literary, and political life.

Buber received many honors, including most prominently the Erasmus Prize, the Hanseatic Goethe Prize, and the Peace Prize of the German Book Trade. A volume in the prestigious Library of Living Philosophers series was devoted to his thought. Buber was the first Israeli citizen elected to honorary membership in the American Academy of Arts and Sciences and the first president of the Israel Academy of Sciences and Humanities. Several times he was nominated for the Nobel Prize for Literature and once for the Nobel Peace Prize, although he received neither.

One of the honors most gratifying to Buber occurred on the evening of his eighty-fifth birthday, an event celebrated not only in Israel but throughout the world. Five hundred students from Hebrew University paraded from the campus to Buber's home, where they serenaded him and made him an honorary member of the Jerusalem Students Association (Hodes, 1971, pp. 209–212). Buber was deeply moved, remarking, "I have a drawer full of honorary degrees, in everything from theology to medicine, but this is the first time I've been made an honorary student. This is a great honor for me" (Friedman, 1991, p. 442). No doubt he would have been touched, too, by an unprecedented event two years later at his funeral in Jerusalem, a high state function. A delegation from the Arab Students' Organization placed a wreath on his grave, in recognition and respect for a self-described arch-Jew who strove so mightily for peace between the two peoples of Palestine. Buber has been regarded variously as philosopher, theologian, mystic, teacher, biblical scholar, and political Zionist, labels he denied in one form or another, or others denied him. Labels fail to capture careers like Buber's. Although many commentators justifiably note that his preparation and contributions made him a philosopher (see Schilpp & Friedman, 1967), Buber typically just wanted to be known as a person and a writer.

INFLUENCES ON BUBER'S THOUGHT

Buber was influenced by many intellectual forces, as he enjoyed a first-rate philosophical education as a young man. He was well-read in classical philosophy from the pre-Socratics on, particularly Immanuel Kant and René Descartes, whose *Discours de la Méthode* was the only philosophy he read in the two years before he produced the final version of *I and Thou*. Buber was especially well versed in German literature, but few literary traditions escaped his curiosity. He read carefully such nineteenth-century intellectual predecessors as Ludwig Feuerbach, Friedrich Nietzsche, and Søren Kierkegaard, and studied the social theories of Georg Simmel and Wilhelm Dilthey. Buber was an especially careful biblical scholar, translating the Hebrew Bible (for Christians, the Old Testament) from the Hebrew into German, a commitment he undertook in the 1920s with his friend Franz Rosenzweig and finished (after a lengthy interruption following Rosenzweig's death) thirty years later. Of course, he was also deeply influenced by Jewish thought and tradition, especially the eighteenth-century Hasidic movement, for which Buber became a twentieth-century voice with his retelling of the Hasidic tales.

An additional source of influence is harder to assess. Before the First World War, Buber published a translation and commentary on the Taoist classic, *Chuang Tzu*, which was followed shortly thereafter by a translation of a series of Chinese folktales.[6] In 1924, immediately after the publication of *I and Thou*, Buber gave a series of seminars in the Netherlands on the other central text of Taoism, Lao Tzu's *Tao Te Ching*. The mysticism of the *Chuang Tzu* was congenial with Buber's own mysticism at the time. Although he later said (1957c, p. xv) he could not stand by "The Teaching of the Tao," the essay that introduced his version of *Chuang Tzu*, he included it in the collection *Pointing the Way* because it was too important to the development of his thought, he said, to be withheld from readers.

Whether the Taoist philosophy had an abiding and deep influence on Buber, or whether he simply found it a temporary resonance, something like the Taoist teaching of *wu-wei*, or noninterfering action of the whole being, "remained central in Buber's mature thought" (Friedman, 1991, p. 135). Specifically, the not holding back oneself, not interfering with the development of the other, and not preaching at but being in harmony with others are all themes that, according to Friedman (1981), Buber imported from the Taoist *wu-wei* "into the heart of the second part of *I and Thou*" (p. 212).[7] One traditional translation of the Tao, for example, articulates a sense of noninterference that Buber's dialogic philosophy would also later reflect in its mistrust of technique and the entrenched position-taking of ordinary debate:

> True words are not fine-sounding;
> Fine-sounding words are not true.
> The good man does not prove by argument;
> And he who proves by argument is not good.
> True wisdom is different from much learning;
> Much learning means little wisdom.
> The Sage has no need to hoard;
> When his own last scrap has been used up on behalf of others,
> Lo, his stock is even greater than before!
> For Heaven's way is to sharpen without cutting,
> And the Sage's way is to act without striving.
>
> (Waley, 1958, p. 243)

Despite obvious influences, Martin Buber did not simply import his philosophy of dialogue from anyone else, nor did he merely deduce it from his reading of other philosophers. Rather, his philosophy of dialogue was synthesized, as Friedman (1955) wrote, from a "life of dialogue." Buber wrote no book-length autobiography, evidently believing that ideas should stand for examination and interpretation without being reduced by biographical or psychological analysis. He did, however, author a series of "autobiographical fragments," collected initially in *The Philosophy of Martin Buber* (Schilpp & Friedman, 1967) and later published as a small book, *Meetings* (Buber, 1973). Here he identified the episodes that "had a decisive influence on the nature and direction of my thinking" (p. 17). In the earliest fragment, "My Mother," Buber recalls standing with an older girl, the daughter of a neighbor, on a balcony of his grandparents' home a year after his mother left. He was still expecting that he would see his mother again soon but never mentioned that to anyone. Although he doesn't recall what led up to this, the older girl told him that "she will never come back." Buber wrote that from then on he never doubted the truth of her words. The episode was significant for two reasons.

Buber recognized the failure to establish a relationship with his mother, and he later coined a term *Vergegnung,* or "mismeeting," to indicate "the failure of a real meeting" between people. This episode was not merely a negative learning, however, for Buber closed these few paragraphs by saying, "all that I have learned about genuine meeting in the course of my life had its first origin in that hour on the balcony" (pp. 18–19). He seems to imply both that his motivation to inquire into human meeting was founded in that moment of realization of the absent relation with his mother and that his relationship with the older girl in that moment evidenced many of the characteristics of genuine meeting that came to represent much of the work of his adult life.

Another particularly memorable episode was "The Horse." Buber's grandparents lived on a farm where they kept horses. He recalled that when he was eleven, he would often go out to the stable to stroke the neck of his favorite, a dapple gray. The astonishingly wild and powerful vitality beneath his touch was experienced as palpably Other to young Martin, and yet it allowed him to approach it as Thou to Thou. On one occasion, though, he became conscious of his hand and of what fun this was to stroke such a majestic horse, and thereafter something changed. Although he continued to feed and stroke the horse, it wasn't the same after this moment of analytical consciousness. "A few years later," Buber wrote, "when I thought back to the incident, I no longer supposed that the animal had noticed my defection. But at the time I considered myself judged" (pp. 26–27). The direct relationship between I and Thou, Buber would later write, involves going out to the other, rather than "reflexion"—the bending back on one's self. Analysis in the moment is not possible; every I-Thou moment must inevitably return us to the realm of I-It.

In another episode, "The Conversion," Buber tells of a young man who came to talk with him one afternoon during the First World War, as many younger people did throughout his life. Buber had spent the morning deep in religious enthusiasm. Without in the slightest being unfriendly or unresponsive to his guest—"I conversed attentively and openly with him"—Buber did not "guess the questions which he had not put." Somewhat later Buber learned that the young man had come to him not "for a chat but for a decision" and that he had died in the war of a "despair that did not oppose his own death." Buber learned from this the importance of being fully present to the other, with the whole of his being, rather than, as Friedman put it, bringing only "the intellectual and social fragments left over from his preoccupation with his morning of mystic ecstasy" (1973, pp. 10, 45–46).

In addition to these autobiographical fragments, we have another unique source of information about the origins of Buber's philosophy of dialogue. In their dialogue, Rogers asked Buber how he came to learn so deeply about people and relationships. Buber's answer was extraordinary, for he responded immediately and fully to Rogers's invitation to make himself personally available in their conversation. After mentioning his early training in psychology and psychiatry, Buber said that two things "mainly constituted" what Rogers was asking about. First, he told Rogers that early in his life he had a profound inclination to meet people with the twin desires of changing something in the other and letting himself be changed by the other. He said that he felt that he did not have "the right to want to change another if I am not open to be changed by him as far as it is legitimate" (turn #4). The two-sided mutuality Buber is describing here was fundamental to his conception of dialogue, and it guided him all his life.

Buber also told Rogers of his response to the First World War. The war had a profound impact on Buber. Although he was too old to serve in the armed forces of his country, Buber said that, nonetheless, he felt compelled to live the war in his imagination—not just in his feelings, but with his body. This phenomenon, Buber told Rogers, could be called "imagining the real," a concept that became critical to Buber's dialogue. The influence of the war on him, he told Rogers, culminated in May 1919, when he learned the details of the brutal and barbaric killing of his friend, Gustav Landauer. Buber's biographer, Maurice Friedman, reports that this was the one autobiographical fragment that Buber declined to write. Two years before his own death, and despite Friedman's urging and Buber's awareness of its significance, Buber said he was still "too close" and "too preoccupied" by this forty-year-old event ever to write about it (Friedman, 1973). Nevertheless, he talked briefly to Rogers about it, and it is a testament to their dialogue that this was evidently the only time that Buber ever wrote or spoke publicly about the impact Landauer's death had on him (Friedman, 1981, pp. 257–258).

Friedman called Landauer's death (along with the "conversion" episode and the departure of his mother) one of the three most important events of Buber's life. He learned from the four years of imagining concretely the horror of the war, culminated by imagining the particular blows struck upon his friend and felt by his friend upon his body, that from then on he had to go beyond just meeting people and exchanging thoughts and feelings: "I had to give," Buber told Rogers, "the fruit of an experience" (turn #11).

BUBER'S PATH TO *I AND THOU*

Some observers have marked Buber's long life with three phases or periods; others have delineated two phases. The events we have already noted happened relatively early in Buber's life, from his childhood in the 1880s through the First World War (Buber was nearly forty when it ended). These events shaped his thinking about what mattered in human life and how human life and human relationships can and should be thought about. Our focus on Buber's philosophy of dialogue, however, leads us to examine most throughly his writing during the second half of his life, following the First World War and beginning with the publication of *I and Thou*.

In 1916, at the height of the First World War, Buber first conceived this work, which would become his most famous. In this book, described by the first English translator (Smith, 1958) as an expression of "revolutionary simplicity" (p. v) with a unique argument in the form of a spiral that "mounts, and gathers within itself the aphoristic and pregnant utterances of the earlier part" (p. xi). If there are passages in an author's early work that can be said to capsulize and even preview later interests, surely this is one of Buber's:

> The primary word *I-Thou* can be spoken only with the whole being. Concentration and fusion into the whole being can never take place through my agency, nor can it ever take place without me. I become through my relation to the *Thou*; as I become *I*, I say *Thou*.
>   All real living is meeting. (Buber, 1958, p. 11)

But however poetic and elliptical *I and Thou* was, it did not come to Buber in a rush of complete inspiration, as has sometimes been assumed. Buber said his 1918–19 draft was set aside for a year or two in favor of further work on Hasidism. In 1921–22, he revised the work extensively and continuously, so much so that even the term "I-Thou" was added in the summer of 1922 and the title *I and Thou* was a product of his discussions with the book's eventual publisher.[8] *I and Thou* was written during a period of active dialogic correspondence and conversations with Franz Rosenzweig, with whom Buber discussed every facet of the book. The process of producing *I and Thou* was itself transformative for Buber. Although he had always been concerned—and always would be—with what he called man's relation to God, *I and Thou* turned out to deal much more with relationships between human beings. From the time of *I and Thou*, Buber was as concerned with our relationships with human "thous" as he was with our relationship with the Eternal Thou. *I and Thou* was Buber's seminal book, and he said that much of the remainder of his work, especially the essays collected in *Between Man and Man* (1965a) and *The Knowledge of Man* (1965b), was essentially a working out and clarifying of the themes and issues first raised in *I and Thou*.

CRITICISMS OF MARTIN BUBER

Before we consider Buber's philosophy of dialogue in more detail, and the implications of what he called the "primary words" I-Thou and I-It that he introduced in *I and Thou*, we should acknowledge that Buber's work and personality have drawn a wide range of criticism. Despite his fame, or perhaps partly because of it, he has had his share of intellectual opponents.

Some critics object to the central distinction of *I and Thou*, for example. Buber discussed his book, before it even had its final title, with his dear friend Franz Rosenzweig, and he sent the page proofs to Rosenzweig for his comments. Although we cannot know what they said to each other in private, Rosenzweig's letters to Buber regarding the book (see Glatzer & Mendes-Flohr, 1991, letters 274, 278, and 279) make him the first to question the distinction between the I-Thou relationship and the I-It. Rosenzweig's complaint is that Buber's I-It is a "cripple" (letter #274, p. 278): Buber attempted to compress too much, "all authentic life," Rosenzweig thought, into the I-Thou.

Walter Kaufmann, translator of a second English edition of *I and Thou*, advances a similar criticism. In Kaufmann's view, there are many modes of what he preferred to translate as the "I-You" relationship:[9] "The total encounter in which You is spoken with one's whole being is but one mode of I-You" (Kaufmann, 1970, p. 17). Kaufmann calls Buber's distinction between the two primary words, I-Thou and I-It, a "misleading dichotomy" (1980, p. 278). Although he credits Buber with "opening the issue up for discussion," Kaufmann asserts that "it is not true . . . that a genuine relationship to another human being can be achieved only in brief encounters from which we must always relapse into states in which the other human being becomes for us merely an object of experience and use" (1980, pp. 257–258). Kaufmann's position seems to be the antithesis of Buber's and of what we call the "Buber–Rogers position" about dialogic moments that emerged during their dialogue (see chapter 7).

Kaufmann claimed that Buber's errors could be attributed to personal difficulties in his youth, including the absence of his mother. Kaufmann thought something was "lacking in [Buber's] life, and . . . his relationships to other human beings had fallen short of . . . a sustained I-You relationship." Buber assumed "falsely," Kaufmann wrote, that the limitations of his life and relationships were "part of the human condition" (p. 260). Kaufmann described Buber as a "lonely heart" who had "come to grief in every human relationship" (p. 266).

Other scholars (e.g., Edwards, 1970) have also suggested that Buber thought and wrote in artificially dualistic terms that were not nuanced enough for the complexity of human experience. Maurice Friedman (1996c), however, explains that Buber's emphasis on the dialectical tension with which we must hold such terms as I-Thou and I-It should not be confused with dualistic or polarized thinking:

> [Buber] opposed with all his force the polarization as well as the politicization of reality that is so common in our day. . . . He seemed to think in dyads, not only I-Thou and I-It but also person and individual, *gnosis* vs. *devotio*, *emunah* vs. *pistis*, being vs. seeming. Yet to turn that into a kind of Manichean dualism, as Walter Kaufmann said in 1978, is to miss entirely what he was doing, namely holding the tension. . . . Buber really meant these dyads as ideal types; he did not mean for us to choose one or the other. That is why it has always been a complete misunderstanding of the I-Thou relationship to imagine that Buber thought it was possible or desirable to have only the I-Thou, or that he saw the I-It as evil in any way. (pp. 4–5)

Perhaps because Buber's work was popular in the 1960s among humanistic theorists of a variety of persuasions, some observers assume that Buber advocated a soft personalism, a mystical trust in the ability of interpersonal intimacy to dissolve misunderstandings, or an unthoughtful acceptance of an authentic core self to which a person must remain true. As an example, consider the impressions of the political theorist and critic Michael Walzer (1988). Walzer generalized that Buber's philosophy was "obscure and portentous" (p. 64). As Walzer describes Buber's approach,

> The life of dialogue is too heavily weighted with significance ever to have been lived by mere mortals; angels, intimate by nature, might manage it. But perhaps we should think of Buberian dialogue as an early version of what contemporary

critical theorists call ideal communication: in Buber's case not
so much face-to-face as soul-to-soul, a "pure" exchange from
which all traces of vanity and self-interest have been eliminated. His emphasis is on personal intensity, absolute openness, the gift of the self to the other. (p. 64)

Later, Walzer critiques Buber by implying that Buber advocates a form
of emotional mindreading in which one can "possess . . . the soul of the
stranger" (p. 68). "Our imaginations don't," he argues, "in fact, reach to
true or certain knowledge of the other person's reactions. We don't
enter into his head when we step into his shoes. To think that we do is
a characteristic mistake of philosophers who believe that heads have
no histories" (p. 68). It's hard to imagine a reading of Buber more at
odds with what he actually wrote. Buber thought that dialogue involves entering someone else's experience? Absolute openness? Buber
thought that "heads have no histories"? As we will see, Buber was
quite clear in renouncing the concept of empathy precisely because he
thought it involved the abandonment of personal ground in an attempt
at mystical identification with the other.

It is natural perhaps, even if unfair at times, to wonder how well
philosophers of communication communicate in their everyday relationships. On the one hand, many have remarked that Buber was a
master of establishing real dialogue in his private life. Friedman (1955)
was deeply impressed by Buber: "Everywhere he has spoken, the ar-
resting man with the white beard and the penetrating, yet gentle, eyes
has shown those present what it means to ask 'real questions' and to
give real answers" (p. 8). And a great many others described Buber's impact on them similarly (e.g., Hodes, 1971).

On the other hand, some colleagues and acquaintances questioned
whether Buber really lived the dialogue about which he wrote so eloquently. They experienced Buber quite differently than Friedman did
(see Friedman, 1983b, p. 286). One critic, for example, remarked on
Buber's "tendency to resolve difficulties by verbal fiats" (Edwards,
1970, p. 36), hardly a dialogic posture. Haim Gordon's (1988) approach
to this question was interesting. Over a decade after Buber's death, he
arranged to interview thirty-two family members, students, and other
associates, asking them to recall Buber the man and his relationship
with each of them. Only rarely did an interviewee report feeling comfortable or relaxed in Buber's company. Some thought Buber was not dialogic in his personal life because he did not seem open to being
influenced. Jochanan Bloch put it this way in his interview: "But I
must add a point that is well known. Buber was not a dialogical person.

He seemed to know the answers and was not open to learning from other persons. His ideas were crytallized and systematized, and he did not budge an inch from these ideas" (in Gordon, 1988, p. 72). Some found Buber very hard to talk to, and his students, especially, were disappointed at times that Buber did not establish more personal relationships with them.

The psychotherapist Stephen Schoen (1994), after surveying the literature on Buber's life and work, reached a conclusion that balanced his subject's insight with the suspicion that Buber's "grand view" was more grandiose and self-congratulatory than it needed to be:

> All that life gives us of loss, of pain, of irony, he takes into his grand view, accommodating them, greatly illuminating them. And yet, in part, they stay in shadow; the grandeur suffers from a certain loss of pathos. That may come from an arrogance in the man. For instance, after the conversation with Carl Rogers, he remarked to Maurice Friedman, "I was very kind to him. I could have been much sharper." When Buber is right, he is totally, unshakably right. This grants him majesty. But it crimps his sense of humor and, perhaps too, his awareness of God's humor, the wryness of life given to us, with which our own wry candor can reckon. (p. 117)

Despite his reservations about Buber the person, Schoen found Buber's vision invites "fullness of response, and gives us, in all aspects of life, a new way to ask after this fullness. For psychotherapists in particular, it provides a clear goal: the reclaiming of the client's freedom to feel himself, or herself, a *Thou*, and be able to say *Thou* to another" (p. 118).

Even friendly accounts give the impression of a man who was not given to, or perhaps not good at, casual conversation: "He tolerated no commonplace conversations; he forced people to conduct a real dialogue," recalled Grete Schaeder (1991, p. 61). Another friend, Aubrey Hodes (1971), reported that "All my conversations with Buber began in the same way. He would greet me at the door and lead me into his study. Neither of us spent much time on the usual social preliminaries. Our minds were already on the coming talk. After we sat down there was always a silence—not a tense silence, uneasy as between two people who were not sure of each other, but a silence of expectation" (p. 14). As Gordon (1988) summarized it: "Meeting him was an engagement, a task, a commitment, a responsibility" (p. xi). Of course, intensity is not itself a problem, unless it is perceived as intimidating by potential dialogue partners.

One interesting story about Buber as a communicator was described for us by Eugene Gendlin[10] (personal communication, 18 April 1996). Gendlin was invited to a small gathering at the Hillel Foundation following a talk Buber gave at Rockefeller Chapel at the University of Chicago, during Buber's first trip to the United States in 1951. He remembered sitting next to a rabbi, who asked Buber: "Could you tell me anything to take back to my congregation for their spiritual quest?" Gendlin reported that in response Buber stood, waving his arms passionately, and replied: "If I had such a thing, I would be a criminal if I hadn't told it long ago!" Now, such words could be framed as a joke, a light moment of self-deprecation, even. But Gendlin's impression was that Buber didn't consider the question deserving of an answer, and perhaps didn't care much for the questioner.

This event was so powerful for Gendlin, he said, that its effect is still with him. Whenever he is asked questions now in public gatherings —even ones that seem pointless at first—he always tries to think of something to say, some way to answer without dismissing the question or the questioner. Buber was known for not appreciating general questions, preferring to be asked specific questions grounded in particulars of the questioner's life or of his thought. Taken literally, the rabbi's question might have been interpreted as a request to reveal a general secret of spiritual life, which surely Buber did not possess. As Maurice Friedman explained when told of Gendlin's story, Buber might have been saying that he could offer no answer to such a query that could be divorced from the situation and relationship, no solid answer that the rabbi could take back to his congregation (personal communication, 18 March 2000). That's fair. But what feelings or problems might have lurked behind the question's surface? We don't know, but presumably neither did Buber. Buber did not learn what might have motivated his questioner and whether there was a "real question" he might have had. In this instance, Buber apparently did not attempt to meet this unique questioner who had addressed him.

Listeners rarely doubted, however, that Buber frequently strove to establish dialogic relationships. Even in his letters—he often wrote twenty or thirty a day—weeks would go by, he told Franz Rosenzweig, with him only "taking care" of his correspondence and without writing a "real letter"—that is, "without an attempt at summoning to mind the real presence of the addressee, but also none with a real giving of the self" (Buber, 1991b, p. 288). Whether in letter or in person, Buber valued dialogue and almost certainly succeeded more often, probably far more often, than most of us. But not even a Martin Buber (nor a Carl Rogers, as we will show) can establish dialogic relationships with each person enountered in everyday life. This is necessary and inherent in the nature of dialogue and of human beings. If there is a failure, it is not so much a failure of Martin Buber, much less evidence of hypocrisy on his part or a weakness in his philosophy of dialogue, but a failure of those relationships. Apparently some people, at some times, sought a quality of meeting with Buber that was not achieved. This, of course, is inevitable. Buber, like all of us, had moments when he wasn't particularly open or inviting as a listener, moments where he might have been tendentious, moments where immodesty or pride might have assumed more prominence than he would have liked. And no one, no matter how much they might wish it or how hard they might try, can make dialogue happen with others.

Buber has been criticized for a number of other failings—or at least they were failings in someone's eyes. Biographers such as Friedman recount, and answer, a variety of other criticisms of religious and political importance. Buber supposedly appropriated the Hasidic traditions to his own use without faithfully reproducing their wisdom for a contemporary audience. He supposedly feigned devotion to Judaism while ignoring its laws and traditions himself. Although assuming a prominent position in Zionism, he was criticized for moving to Palestine very late and doing so not because of his belief in a future Jewish state there, but only because his remaining in Nazi Germany became untenable. He was accused of meddling in politics, advocating simplistic, unrealistic, and idealistic solutions to complex political issues, in Palestine and elsewhere. Some have said he adopted a pose that was not genuine but designed to produce a certain strategic effect in audiences. We could go on.

Buber lived a long and full and active life. He worked in more fields than virtually any contemporary scholar would dare attempt. Our intention is only to summarize, not to investigate or answer in detail, the various objections to Buber's thought or personal demeanor. He was a man fully engaged, not only in his scholarship, but with other people and with the issues of his time. Of course, he drew criticism, and some of it was probably deserved.[11]

BUBER'S PHILOSOPHY OF DIALOGUE

The essential insight of Martin Buber, and the foundation of his philosophy of dialogue, is simply this: "The fundamental fact of human existence is man with man" (Buber, 1965a, p. 203). Thus, for Buber, what is most basic, most fundamental in human existence, is not the solitary individual who then comes into relation with others, nor is it to be found in the realm of the social or society. Buber directs our attention not to the individual or the collective, nor can his thinking be associated with either individualism or collectivism. Instead, Buber focuses on the possibility of each person's *relationship with* another, which he called "the sphere of between." "In the beginning," Buber wrote in *I and Thou*, "is relation" (1958, p. 18).

The opening sentence of *I and Thou*, "To man the world is twofold, in accordance with his twotold attitude" (1958, p. 3), makes clear what a radical turn Buber has taken from the philosophy that preceded him.[12] From at least the time of Descartes in the seventeenth century, philosophers have attributed to human beings a single orientation toward the world, an orientation of subject and object. Buber breaks with this tradition. Although acknowledging the orientation of subject and object, which he calls the "I-It" relation, Buber suggests that another orientation is not only possible but more fundamental. I-It relations are ones we can have toward things, nature, and even people, when we are experiencing them as objects of use. Relations of I-It are not only inevitable, they are essential to our lives: "Without *It*, man cannot live. But," Buber continued, "he who lives with *It* alone is not a man" (p. 34). So, Buber was announcing that another mode of relation is available, one that is essential to our becoming fully human. Although not easily described, a direct encounter of person with world is possible, which Buber called the "I-Thou" relation.

In his philosophical anthropology, Buber distinguished between two realms of human life: one he called the social, the other the interhuman. The *social* happens whenever human beings interact with one another. In this realm, no real personal relation, no existential relation, is created (Buber, 1965b, pp. 72–75). Friedman explains that "the 'social' includes the I-It relation as well as the I-Thou: many interpersonal relations are really characterized by one person's treating the other as an object to be known and used" (1983a, p. 6).

By contrast, Friedman continues, consider "the unfolding of the sphere of the between Buber calls the 'dialogical'" (1986, p. 6). In this *interhuman* relationship, each person happens to the other as the unique and particular person that he or she is:

> As the sphere of the interhuman I do not designate the relationship of the human person to his fellowman in general, but the actualization of this relationship. The interhuman is something that takes place from time to time between two men; but in order that it may take place again and again, in

order that genuine meetings may occur and ever again occur, the Thou in relation to his fellowman must be inherent in man. (Buber, 1967, p. 711).

The interhuman relation, therefore, is not one of subject to object, but of partner to partner.

Meaning in such a relationship is not found in one person or the other, or even in the two together. For in the realm of the interhuman, meaning relies on both parties together and cannot be reduced to either or to both of them separately. Meaning dwells in the "between" of their relationship, in the dialogue in which they participate together. Buber was highly critical of the tendency in the modern world toward what he called "psychologism" or "psychologizing of the world" (1967, p. 152), which refers to the tendency to think of what is real as that which is within the person. "Psychologism is a habit of mind. It is the tendency to divide the reality that is given to us into two parts—one is an outer world into which we fit ourselves, and the other is an inner psyche into which we fit the world" (Friedman, 1992, p. 18). This elaboration of the problem of psychologism is not an attack on psychology or psychotherapy; it is an attack on the tendency to locate meaning strictly within the individual person. For Buber, the relationship is primary.

Buber tends not to define and categorize dialogue precisely, preferring to offer examples. One of his examples concerned a meeting in 1914 of representatives of various European countries to discuss establishing a supranational European authority. Their conversations were unreserved and, Buber said, had a "substance and fruitfulness I have scarcely ever experienced so strongly" (1965a, p. 5). When they turned to how a public initiative on these questions could begin, one man, of "passionate concentration and judicial power of love," was concerned that so many Jews had been nominated and that several countries would be represented disproportionately by their Jews. Buber continued:

Obstinate Jew that I am, I protested against the protest. I no longer know how from that I came to speak of Jesus and to say that we Jews knew him from within, in the impulses and stirrings of his Jewish being, in a way that remains inaccessible to the peoples submissive to him. "In a way that remains inaccessible to you"—so I directly addressed the former clergyman. He stood up, I too stood, we looked into the heart of one another's eyes. "It is gone," he said, and before everyone we gave one another the kiss of brotherhood.

The discussion of the situation between Jews and Christians had been transformed into a bond between the Christian and the Jew. In this transformation dialogue was fulfilled. (pp. 5–6)

Buber distinguished between *genuine dialogue* and two counterfeits, *technical dialogue* and *monologue disguised as dialogue* (1965a, pp. 19–20). Technical dialogue is motivated solely by the need for objective understanding. Hence, a conversation with a co-worker may be pleasant enough, yet not genuine dialogue, although, as Buber said, real dialogue hides in odd corners and breaks through the surface sometimes in surprising and even inopportune occasions. Monologue disguised as dialogue includes debates in which the speakers make their points so they "strike home in the sharpest way" (p. 19), conversation in which one attempts to make a predecided kind of impression on the other, or even a friendly chat or the talk of lovers, when the focus is more on the self than on the reality of the other. In genuine dialogue, by contrast, "each of the participants really has in mind the other or others in their present and particular being and turns to them with the intention of establishing a living mutual relation between himself and them" (p. 19).

Buber described the life of genuine dialogue with a vivid metaphor of embodiment: dialogue involves most basically a *turning toward* the other. This happens all the time, of course, at its simplest level, when one person turns to face another to talk and gives the other attention while listening to what he or she has to say. More fully, though, one turns to the other with openness and responsiveness—openness in the sense of being willing to say what is on one's mind and openness to hearing the response of the other. In so doing, one establishes a dialogic partnership with the other. Here the key communication skill would appear to be listening. Listening both opens a person's world and simultaneously advertises her or his willingness to confirm and take seriously the other.

Three things impede the growth of the life of dialogue. The first of these Buber called the "invasion of seeming" (1965b, p. 82). He regarded this as so important that he called the duality of *being* and *seeming* the "essential problem of the sphere of the interhuman" (p. 75). There are two distinct modes of human existence, one of which "proceeds from what one really is, the other from what one wishes to seem" (p. 76). None of us lives entirely in one mode or the other, nor can we always reliably or precisely categorize specific people in particular settings. However, Buber believed we can distinguish between people in which one or the other of these predominates. The person characterized by being engages the other without regard to the image of himself or herself that is formed by the other. This person is usually spontaneous and acts without reserve. The person characterized by seeming, on the other hand, is primarily concerned with how he or she looks to the other and with the impression the other forms. In a powerful and well-known paragraph, Buber gives an engaging illustration of the impact of being and seeming on relationships between people:

> Let us now imagine two men, whose life is dominated by appearance, sitting and talking together. Call them Peter and Paul. Let us list the different configurations which are involved. First, there is Peter as he wishes to appear to Paul, and Paul as he wishes to appear to Peter. Then there is Peter as he really appears to Paul, that is, Paul's image of Peter, which in general does not in the least coincide with what Peter wishes Paul to see; and similarly there is the reverse situation. Further, there is Peter as he appears to himself, and Paul as he appears to himself. Lastly, there are the bodily Peter and the bodily Paul. Two living beings and six ghostly appearances, which mingle in many ways in the conversation between the two. Where is there room for any genuine interhuman life? (p. 77)

In the realm of interhuman relationships, Buber's dialogue suggests that people must communicate themselves to others as they really are. This authenticity does not require saying everything that comes to mind, but only that we let "no seeming creep in between" us.

Buber noted the inadequacy of interpersonal perception as the second difficulty with achieving a life of dialogue. In dialogue, we become aware of the other, aware of how the other is not like me and aware of the other as the unique being that he or she is, and we accept the other in this way also. This involves being aware of the wholeness or unity of the other, the "dynamic centre which stamps his every utterance, action, and attitude with the recognizable sign of uniqueness" (1965b, p. 80). Buber used a number of different terms to refer this process of interpersonal perception, including experiencing the other side and inclusion, which are virtually synonymous terms. By *experiencing the other side* Buber referred to feeling an event from one's own position as well as from the position of the other. Buber distinguished this, though, from what he called "empathy," which, as he saw it, involved one so going over to the other's side as to lose track of one's own position, indeed to lose one's own self, an issue to which we will return in the following chapter. When Buber used the term "inclusion," he was noting that, without forfeiting anything of one's own experience or one's own side of an event, one also at the same time "lives through the common event from the standpoint of the other" (Buber, 1965a, p. 97). Buber also called this special kind of awareness *making present*—making the other, as a whole and distinctive being, present to one's self. At the other extreme, the analytical and reductive perception, which is probably more typical in human relationships, is contrary to realizing a life of dialogue. Related to making the other present is what Buber called *imagining the real*, which he referred to in the dialogue with Rogers. Imagining the real involves "a bold swinging . . . into the life of the other" (p. 81). By imagining just how real something is to the other, I make the other present to me as a whole, a unity, and a uniqueness.

Finally, Buber distinguished between *imposing* and *unfolding*, two ways of attempting to affect the life and attitudes of others (1965b, pp. 82ff.). The desire to impose on the other is the method of the propagandist. The propagandist is not concerned with the person that he or she attempts to influence. The qualities or characteristics of the other are important only when they allow the propagandist to design more effective persuasive messages. The goal of the propagandist is wholly strategic: to impose one's own thoughts, beliefs, and values on the other. The second basic way of affecting others Buber called unfolding, by which one shows and invites, helping to open the potentiality of the other. Although Buber calls this mode of influence the work of the educator, influence occurs not through telling or one-way instruction but more simply through meeting.

One especially crucial consequence of dialogue, yet still a fully relational element of the interhuman or the between, is *confirmation*. Confirmation involves "acceptance of otherness" (Buber, 1965b, p. 69). We become selves together in and through mutual confirmation. Buber is referring to confirmation when he says, in his poetical metaphor, that "it is from one man to another that the heavenly bread of self-being is passed" (1965a, p. 71). In dialogue we confirm and are confirmed. To be confirmed as a person is a fundamental need of our species, and, in Buber's words, "a society may be termed human in the measure to which its members confirm one another" (Buber, 1965b, p. 67). "That this capacity lies so immeasurably fallow constitutes the real weakness and questionableness of the human race: actual humanity exists only where this capacity unfolds" (p. 68). Confirmation does not mean mere agreement or approval—one may confirm by struggling with the other, by disagreeing, and by calling forth potentialities in the other that, until then, had remained entirely latent.

In *The Confirmation of Otherness: In Family, Community, and Society*, an excellent book on dialogue in everyday relations, Maurice Friedman (1983a) illustrates how Buber's confirmation is at the core of how we define a self. Confirmation, he writes, "is central to human existence, but human existence is itself problematic, and the heart of its problematic is that of confirmation" (p. 37). How can this be so? Simply because the genesis of a self, our experienced identity, comes from mutual connection that cannot be willed but instead is a gift of "the between," built with another person who notices and cares without thinking it over, neither party relying on a ledger of pros and cons or profits and losses. At the same time, Friedman and Buber do not urge confirmation as a feel-good state of unreflective good will; it is a relation of noticing and being noticed realistically. According to Friedman (1983a),

> Because confirmation is a reality of the between, no one can offer a blanket of unconditional confirmation, regardless of what the other says, does, or is. We can only give what we have, and what we have, first of all, is not a technique of confirmation but our personal selves—selves which can make another present and "imagine the real" but selves which also respond from where we are. Further, because confirmation means a confirmation of our uniqueness, a blanket confirmation would be valueless. We need to be confirmed in our uniqueness as what we are, what we *can* become, and what we are called to become, and this can only be known in the give and take of living dialogue. (pp. 40–41)

This issue will arise, as we will see, in the Buber–Rogers dialogue, and in this context Friedman is apparently writing with Carl Rogers in mind—believing that it was a "blanket of unconditional confirmation" that Rogers wanted to use to cover his clients. Rogers, though, as we also will see, denied that this "anything is all right with me" attitude was his intent. In fact, both Buber and Rogers appear to suggest (although their language varied) that confirmation helps to create a relational space for dialogue, but does not guarantee acceptance of, or agreement with, all the other person(s) might say or do.

Confirmation, as Buber conceived it, also could involve conflict. Being in relation, Friedman interprets, is a matter of not leaving behind your own ground, your own positions and uniqueness, as you attempt to hear and understand the other. You may need to confirm by saying "no" in order to see and hear the real person you are with. As Friedman (1974) puts it:

> We are inclined to think that we have to choose between being ourselves and shutting him out, on the one hand, and being "unselfish" and going over to his side, on the other. Actually, we cannot know *his* side of the relationship without standing our ground because we can only know him *as a person* in a relationship in which his uniqueness becomes manifest in coming up against our uniqueness. Otherwise, what we see is a distortion of him—the way he is when he has no real person to come up against. . . .
>
> One reason people do not have the courage to show themselves to others as they are is that they wish to avoid conflict. They propitiate and conciliate the other, not wishing the wrathful parent to make his appearance in the form of the friend, the beloved, or the teacher. The truth is the exact opposite. (p. 314)

If we want to avoid unnecessary conflict, Friedman and Buber argue, we should ensure through an honest approach to confirmation that each of us is a full person for the other to "come up against." How else can we know what kind of dialogue is required and how we—individually and together—must contribute to it?

Throughout Buber's philosophy we find similar instances where apparently simple ideas take on interesting and challenging nuances in everyday practice. Confirmation is intimately related, it turns out, to a kind of personal congruence and honesty in which each person must remain true to his or her own style of uniqueness. No pseudofriendly acceptance will do.

CONCLUSION

When Martin Buber died in 1965, the *New York Times* eulogy was appropriate to his stature as a worldwide emissary of peace and humane learning. The *Times* captured the sweep of Buber's influence and the depth of his gift:

> Martin Buber was the foremost Jewish religious thinker of our time and one of the world's most influential philosophers. He

was a theological bridge-builder long before ecumenism achieved its present popularity. He served as a kind of patron saint for such towering Christian intellectuals as Paul Tillich, Reinhold Niebuhr, Jacques Maritain, and Gabriel Marcel. For many in the Jewish community, the bearded old man in Jerusalem was the quintessential scholar, the teacher and exponent of a tradition that reaches back to the biblical ages.

If today the ancient cold war between the faiths is being replaced by dialogue and friendly personal confrontation, much of the credit must be given to Martin Buber. It was he, with his doctrine of "I-Thou" personalism, who showed the way. For Buber, the God of Abraham was no icy abstraction or loveless Prime Mover but a Person, infinitely lovable and loving.

Love, he said again and again, is the key to the mystery of existence and points the way to divinity. "Every particular Thou is a glimpse through to the eternal Thou." Men find God by discovering each other. There is no other way. (in Theroux, 1997, pp. 108–109)

Scholars of dialogue might identify two hallmarks of Buber's conceptualization. First, he stressed an awareness of the other as a unique and whole person, which encourages turning toward the other, imagining the reality of the other, receiving the other as a partner, and hence confirming the other as a person. This sphere of the between, as he called it, was not just a site for communication, but the basic ground of humanness; we become persons through our connections with others. Dialogue was neither a technique nor a means to an end, but an ontological perspective.

Second, Buber's philosophy encouraged a genuineness or authenticity that, although not requiring full and complete disclosure, nevertheless involves dialogic partners not pretending with one another, not being concerned with how one appears to the other, and not holding back what needs to be said. This open spirit was manifest not just in Buber's work but in how he lived his life—with intensity, enthusiasm, and commitment. In an authentic relationship, one might struggle hard to affect the other, but never to the exclusion of being open to self-change in the process. Dialogue is no calculus for manipulation, although persuasion often happens within its sphere. It depends on respect and a willingness to allow a mutual reality and possibility to unfold, rather than the imposition of opinions and attitudes on the other.

CHAPTER FOUR

Rogers and the Praxis
of Dialogue

I first read Carl Rogers' books in the 1950s when, as a
graduate student, I was immersed in the complex and
fascinating world of academic psychology and the
poetic vision of psychoanalysis. I found little to interest
me. . . . I thought he was mostly of historical interest.
 Many years later, preparing a course, I set about
rereading Rogers. I was utterly astonished. The
simplicity of his view of the clinical relationship,
which previously had seemed so naive to me, now
seemed to have profound beauty and importance.
 —Michael Kahn, *Between Therapist and Client*

Over the years I watched [Rogers] take positions that
were in striking contrast to the mainstream thinking
of the day, defend them successfully, and eventually
see them incorporated so thoroughly into the
mainstream that most people now don't even
know where the ideas came from.
 —Richard Farson, *Management of the Absurd*

When he died in February 1987, Carl R. Rogers was famous throughout
the world as a therapist, scholar, teacher, researcher, theorist, best-selling
author, group leader, and intercultural emissary. Perhaps best known as
a spokesman for a humane redefinition of psychology, his professional
contributions were both wider and more seminal than many scholars
now acknowledge.

59

Born of well-to-do parents in a Chicago suburb, Rogers developed his interest in growth-oriented psychologies from a mix of Protestant family experiences and an abiding curiosity about science and agriculture. He was at first drawn toward the ministry, and attended New York's liberal Union Theological Seminary after graduating from the University of Wisconsin. While at Union, Rogers took courses at the nearby Teachers College of Columbia University, where he was influenced by William Heard Kilpatrick, an intellectual ally of pragmatist philosopher John Dewey. When Rogers's interests developed even more in the secular directions of psychological science, he transferred officially to Teachers College to complete the doctorate. A personality assessment instrument for children he developed for his dissertation was published several years later and remained in print for fifty years. After graduate school, a Rochester, New York clinic gave him his first job, where he worked with significant success, primarily with troubled children. His decade at Rochester convinced him of the practical importance of relationship development in therapy, an insight that resulted in his first book, *The Clinical Treatment of the Problem Child* (1939). Shortly after moving to Ohio State University (it enticed him by offering this clinician-practitioner a fast-track appointment as a full professor!) came *Counseling and Psychotherapy* (1942), an early statement of the approach of "nondirectiveness" that would receive fuller development in the coedited *Psychotherapy and Personality Change* (Rogers & Dymond, 1954) and his more famous books, *Client-Centered Therapy* (1951) and the 1961 academic best-seller *On Becoming a Person*.

Rogers's most productive theoretical work was done during his years at the University of Chicago (1945–57) at a time of exceptional intellectual ferment on campus. He founded a new Counseling Center to coordinate a variety of clinical and scholarly projects and provide the structure necessary for many colleagues to share research data. Rogers led a project that developed one of the world's most thorough research bases for therapeutic communication to that time. His reputation spread even farther as he became known for facilitating others' work effectively. Not surprisingly, he was recruited by other campuses. In 1957, Rogers was attracted to his alma mater, Wisconsin, by dual appointments in psychology and psychiatry, and the opportunity to conduct intensive research into the most challenging forms of in-patient schizophrenia. After a six-year stay in Madison that Rogers himself characterized as a bad mistake (primarily due to an unpleasant interpersonal climate, including what biographers describe as a turbulent relationship with a seemingly unethical colleague), he took up another calling. Leaving academe in 1963 to move to LaJolla, California, he affiliated with the Western Behavioral Sciences Institute and later helped form the offshoot Center for Studies of the Person, which is still active. Rogers continued to write and facilitate growth groups from his California base, and by the mid-1960s he was recognized worldwide as one of the two or three leading spokespersons for the humanistic psychology movement. Rogers continued to write, speak, conduct workshops, and consult, although his contact with individual clients and his involvement in conducting original research declined during these years.

Rogers was elected president of the American Psychological Association, the American Academy of Psychotherapists, and the American Association of Applied Psychology. His many awards included the Distinguished Scientific Contribution Award and the Distinguished Professional Contribution Award of the American Psychological Association; for each, Rogers was recognized in the initial year the award was given. He was elected a Fellow of the American Academy of Arts and Sciences, and a documentary film of one of his growth groups won an Academy Award. Sadly, Rogers died just before he would have received word of his nomination for the Nobel Peace Prize, an honor largely based on his persistent efforts to foster intercultural trust through workshops in the Soviet Union, Northern Ireland, South Africa, Asia, and the Americas.

However, some observers of intellectual life have found Rogers's ideas outmoded—of quaint historical value perhaps, but of little practical concern for contemporary scholars. Many academic and cultural critics actively oppose his ideas. They characterize Rogers as a dangerous proponent of selfishness, as an enemy of community morality and fundamental religious values, and as a dinosaur-like icon of a troubled 1960s era of excess and social irresponsibility. He is also invoked as a condensation symbol and target in the so-called culture wars declared by vocal conservatives against a twentieth-century individualist liberalism they argue has been a profound failure. In this chapter, we reconsider Rogers as a contributor to a broader intellectual landscape, and as a teacher whose lessons for contemporary society are far from exhausted. Specifically, we claim:

- Despite criticism, some of it deserved, Rogers was a vital link between vastly different cultural psychologies, and therefore helped to change our view of what communication can mean in a pluralistic society.
- Despite his often-announced suspicion of theorists, Rogers's focus on *praxis*—theorizing-in-action that is constantly inflected by practical implications—significantly

enhanced a concept of dialogic potential appropriate for the contemporary public sphere.

• Despite his reputation as an advocate of an autonomous core self, Rogers contributed significantly to a humane conception of dialogue by stressing listening styles and relationship as much as speaking and self-disclosure.

TWO FACES OF ROGERS

For reasons we will explore, Rogers's legacy polarizes scholars who believe he was a potent intellectual force at mid-century. Indeed, reading about him away from the backdrop of his own work, it's almost possible to imagine radically different personae, a Good Rogers and a Bad Rogers. These two faces have been constructed by acolytes and opponents over the years as he—or, more precisely, his reputation—has achieved iconic status through their eyes. He has been interpreted like an inkblot by different observers who perceive him through lenses tinted by their own agendas. The image of Rogers offers two faces, not because he was personally "two-faced" or disingenuous, but because his strong critics and strong advocates seemingly never can agree on what he, or his approach, was about. But contemporary observers, whichever face they see, can agree on the extent of his influence if they simply put it in intellectual context.

Clearly, significant aspects of Rogers's basic approach informed the eclectic mix of late-twentieth-century psychotherapies. One vital indicator of any theorist's success, in fact, is the heuristic criterion, the extent to which the thinker's insights work—perhaps subtly or even invisibly at times—to guide others' research and practice. Few matters in the intellectual world can be reduced to simple binary distinctions, and few if any thinkers are solely responsible for revolutionary change. There are too many contextual and interwoven factors for simplistic this-versus-that comparisons to be trusted without qualification. That said, there are few thinkers in the human studies who understood the tone of an era well enough, or tuned in to his or her own experience in relationships well enough, to symbolize a kind of intellectual watershed. To some extent, Rogers appeared to be such a pivotal person—or at least he was fortunate to have lived during a pivotal time during which these changes were infused into the intellectual climate of psychology at mid-century. According to many observers (e.g., Gendlin, 1974; Yalom, 1995), Rogers was so successful that many contributions profoundly shaped—if not virtually invented—by him are now part of the basic intellectual repertoire of psychotherapy. He was one of a very few famous symbols of psychology's movement toward a more open and dialogic conception of itself.

If Rogers symbolized change, what did he help change? Consider how Rogers's historical role helped to reshape the rhetoric of psychotherapy. Important analysts note how he helped psychotherapy and psychology itself move to a more dialogic system of premises. Although not all observers agree, as we will see, and although such historical generalizations are always risky, Rogers's research and professional presence contributed in crucial ways to the following transitions:

- *From a medical model of helping to a relational model.* Before Rogers, psychotherapy was typically based on psychoanalytic Freudian assumptions that were clearly quasi-medical and in some cases "pseudomedical" (Gendlin, 1974, p. 213). Freudian psychoanalysts and other therapists diagnosed personal problems and applied techniques, presuming that those techniques were the treatments that made people well. After Rogers, therapists increasingly presented themselves, even in role, as *persons* who could meet others in more genuine and less formulaic interaction, and this relationship was itself presumed to be have therapeutic value beyond the application of any technique. Another way to say this is that Rogers helped to revolutionize how the therapeutic sites of trust are conceptualized professionally; Rogers's theory and research efforts were crucial in nudging the field away from a primary faith in expertly applied technique and toward trusting the inner resources of each person for dealing constructively with his or her problems, if only those resources could be mobilized through genuine relationship with another.
- *From "patients" to "clients."* Before Rogers, psychotherapy had its "patients," labeling a particular medical-model role that suggests sickness or deficiency in the person seeking help. After Rogers, "patients" customarily became "clients" for much of the field, as it freely adopted Rogers's conceptualization. This subtle linguistic change radically altered the implied power relationship, and granted potent agency to those who seek help.
- *From closed doors to openly shared research data.* Before Rogers, psychotherapy was touted with claims of success and cautioned by tales of occasional failure, but researchers reviewing the literature had to rely on inferences filtered

through the therapists' own presumably somewhat biased accounts. Rogers was the first in the field to tape record and analyze actual therapy sessions for critical moments of success and failure and then to share these conversational texts with colleagues and students. After Rogers, such pooling of research texts became far more common. Because of Rogers and others, we now have a vast empirical body of data that can be analyzed and interpreted in relatively more objective ways (e.g., see Farber, Brink, & Raskin, 1996). For Rogers, the possible embarrassment of his mistakes, misstatements, and perceptual failures becoming public was secondary to the scientific advantage of reviewing his work more objectively and receiving others' feedback on it. In a research sense, he often said, "the facts are friendly."

- *From impressionistic research to a more scientifically controlled research program.* Before Rogers, psychotherapeutic approaches and methods were rarely if ever tested by scientific investigations with stringent controls. But Rogers was not content to tell stories about his own successes as a therapist; he wanted to know if his hunches, experiences, and perceptions worked for others in similar ways. Rogers wanted more facts about therapy and its effects. Without denying the phenomenological implications of therapy, he wanted to bring something like the scientific method to an otherwise mysterious field. After Rogers, experimental and empirical testing of therapeutic variables and outcomes became common. One psychologist (Thorne, 1992) observed that Rogers brought to his brand of psychotherapy "more research studies than had ever been undertaken previously" (p. 36).

- *From clique ethics to an ethic of relational and clinical confidentiality.* Before Rogers, "'professional ethics' [among therapists] mostly meant a doctor's duty to protect other doctors" (Gendlin, 1988, p. 127). After Rogers, therapists developed a new sense of ethical obligation to clients. As Gendlin further states, "[Rogers] proclaimed new ethics: Recording requires the client's permission. Confidentiality was emphasized, and the answer to all inquiries was only 'The person was in therapy here.' In spirit, his ethics is now accepted, but at the time it was new" (p. 127). Rogers's expression of concern for the client elevated the therapeutic dialogue to a matter of ethical importance;

he was considered a professional helper, but his primary professional responsibility was to clients as persons rather than to colleagues, to techniques, or to an abstraction called a "profession."

- *From the past to the present.* Before Rogers, most therapists exhibited a "total focus on the past" when trying to help persons work through their problems (Gendlin, 1974, p. 213). After Rogers, therapists focused much more on the present, especially on the importance of the immediate lived relation of client and therapist. Supposedly expert analysis of long-past causes gave way to more attempts to understand—and acknowledge—the impact of one-to-one presence. If "here and now" seems like a tired cliche in the contemporary world of ideas, it may be because Rogers was part and parcel of a 1950s and 1960s philosophical revolution of the present, as were sociologists of knowledge such as Peter Berger and Thomas Luckmann (1967, pp. 28ff.) and Alfred Schutz (1967, pp. 163ff.).

- *From the couch to a dialogue of mutual face-to-face recognition and presence.* Before Rogers, the prototypical physical context of therapeutic communication, at least in the popular mind, was a psychoanalyst sitting apart from a patient who would recline on a low couch looking away. After Rogers, therapeutic interaction is usually conducted face-to-face if possible, permitting maximum potential for confirmation and other forms of dialogue to develop.

- *From the therapist-as-expert/diagnostician to the therapist-as-listener/learner.* Before Rogers, therapists typically interpreted and analyzed patients in essentially private ways, primarily using the sessions themselves to elicit data in the forms of memories, associations, and interpretations. After Rogers, therapists developed a more personalized voice and learning style; they checked out their inferences and associations aloud, enlisting clients as a co-discoverers of meaning. In effect, Rogers elevated the status of listening for the profession, especially in counseling settings, and consequently elevated the status of clients by inviting them to become the experts and teachers when considering their own experience. The influential recent collaborative, narrative, and "postmodern" approach of Harlene Anderson (1997), for example, relies heavily on this Rogerian insight without directly attributing it to him:

A client brings expertise in the area of content: a client is the expert on his or her life experiences and what has brought that client into the therapy relationship. When clients are narrators of their stories, they are able to experience and recognize their own voices, power, and authority. A therapist brings expertise in the area of process: a therapist is the expert in engaging and participating with a client in a dialogical process of first-person storytelling. It is as if the roles of therapist and client were reversed: *The client becomes the teacher.* (p. 95)

- *From monocultural to multicultural therapy.* Before Rogers, therapy was largely a province for a middle- or upper-class and largely white population, except for the very disturbed who were desperately in need and were referred for treatment because of serious social disruptions. After Rogers, therapists and counselors more consciously attempted to treat persons from a broad range of cultural and socioeconomic groups in everyday interaction. Eugene Gendlin (1988), referring to Rogers's facility at the University of Chicago, observes that in the emerging concern for multicultural opportunity, he was "ahead of the country":

    In 1945, Blacks, women, gay people, and others felt helped at the Counseling Center, because these therapists knew that every client had to teach them a new world. A Black client might spend months teaching a therapist about Black experience. Yet, another Black client might say, with relief, after one hour, "With you I can forget about race." These therapists never forced a policy on a client. They would not coerce a woman to stay in a marriage, as the psychoanalysts then did. Nor would they decide what another person's sexuality should be. To therapists trained by Rogers, it was obvious that every person is at the directing center of a life. (p. 128)

The irony of Rogers's success is the extent to which he has become *dispensable* to present-day professional psychologists, as Farson (1996, pp. 15–16) suggests in a quotation introducing this chapter. Rogers's innovations have become absorbed so thoroughly that many in the culture of psychotherapy simply aren't conscious anymore of their roots. Ironically, many of his ideas have become so influential and so seductively simple that they are simply part of an immersive conventional wisdom, the thorough incorporation into the mainstream that Richard Farson noted. Irving Yalom (1995), a pioneer of group therapy, observes that "today, a half century later, Rogers's therapeutic approach seems so right, so self-evident, and so buttressed by decades of psychotherapy research that it is difficult to appreciate the intensity of these battles or even to comprehend what they were all about" (p. ix). Contemporary commentators, he is saying, too easily ignore how radical Rogers's ideas about therapist-client communication were in their own historical context.

Philip Cushman's popular "cultural history of psychotherapy," *Constructing the Self, Constructing America* (1995), ignores Rogers completely except for a single mention in a long list of humanistic psychologists Cushman wants to criticize collectively (p. 242). This omission is especially surprising, given the author's stance that psychotherapy is one of only a "few dialogic opportunities available" in contemporary society and even though Cushman is quite comfortable exploring dialogic notions of Gadamer and other continental philosophers. Although the noted therapist and best-selling author Peter Kramer could claim in 1995 that "certainly Rogers's ideas prevail within the mental health professions" (p. x), newer trends in self psychology give Rogers "nary a word of credit" (p. x). On the other hand, this may tell us more about preferences of North American psychologists than about Rogers, as he is better appreciated in other countries. Gendlin (1988) estimated not long ago that "half the therapists of Europe and Japan are client-centered" (p. 128). In fact, international interest in Rogers's "person-centered approach" is flourishing, with international conferences and publications appearing regularly (see Barrett-Lennard, 1998; Hutterer, Pawlowsky, Schmid, & Stipsits, 1996; Thorne, 1992).

In a fascinating countertrend, scholarly interest in Rogers's work has increased since his death. To mention just a few contributions: In 1989, two volumes edited by Kirschenbaum and Henderson were published and widely reviewed: *Carl Rogers: Dialogues* and *The Carl Rogers Reader.* New editions of two classics, *On Becoming a Person* and *A Way of Being,* appeared in the 1990s with fresh and appreciative forewords by two of today's most famous psychologists, Peter Kramer and Irving Yalom. Two recent intellectual biographies (Barrett-Lennard, 1998; Thorne, 1992), several new texts on client-centered and person-centered communication (Barrett-Lennard, 1998; Mearns

& Thorne, 1988; Teich, 1992b; Thorne, 1991), and significant new anthologies considering Rogers and his implications for human studies (Brazier, 1993a; Hutterer, Pawlowsky, Schmid, & Stipsits, 1996; Lietaer, Rombauts, & Van Balen, 1990; Suhd, 1995) are also available. Greenberg, Rice, and Elliott's (1993) *Facilitating Emotional Change* is a recent conceptual extension of Rogers's principles into newer forms of therapy.

In 1995, a special issue of the *Journal of Humanistic Psychology* celebrated "Carl Rogers—The Man and His Ideas" with seven long articles and a substantial commentary by the editor, Tom Greening. Our own 1997 book, *The Martin Buber–Carl Rogers Dialogue: A New Transcript With Commentary*, is one of many works from many authors—mostly scholarly articles—that recently have explored the connection between Rogers's and Buber's philosophies. In 1996, Farber, Brink, and Raskin published *The Psychotherapy of Carl Rogers: Cases and Commentary*, a work that revisits some of Rogers's classic sessions to examine them with fresh perspectives. A journal with a Rogerian orientation, the *Person-Centered Journal*, was inaugurated in the 1990s by the Association for the Development of the Person-Centered Approach. In addition, the recent American Psychological Association-sponsored anthology on empathy and its psychological and behavioral implications (Bohart & Greenberg, 1997) prominently analyzes and credits Rogers's work as well as summarizing recent research into one of the basic Rogerian concepts.

Rogers, though, was always more of a lightning rod for controversy than an intellectual guru. Many critics have responded to Rogers with a negativity, and at times a venom, rarely heard in the academic world. They evidently consider Rogers not only wrong or ineffective, but downright dangerous, too. One examination of various "growth psychologies" claimed that his client-centered and person-centered philosophy lacked "a sense of responsibility to others" and "clear-cut goals and purposes," and that Rogers "appears to invite the individual to exist in a state of total selfishness and self-indulgence." The author of this survey argued that Rogers's concern "is solely with one's own existence, not with fostering the growth and development of another" (Schultz, 1977, pp. 36–37). Another critic charged that Rogers presented "the erroneous if not incoherent assumption that the true self is an immaterial, unchanging thing-like substance" that "cannot be shaped or formed through interaction with others. It remains outside of and invulnerable to experience" (Geller, 1982, p. 59).

This alleged atomism of the self is further highlighted in an obvious reference to Rogers in the highly influential social critique by Robert Bellah and his colleagues, *Habits of the Heart*: "the ultimate purpose of the therapist's acceptance, the 'unconditional positive regard' of post-Freudian therapy, is to teach the therapeutic client to be independent of anyone else's standards" (Bellah, Madsen, Sullivan, Swidler, & Tipton, 1985, p. 99). "Unconditional positive regard," of course, was Rogers's own specific and almost proprietary term. When critiquing the "therapeutic attitude," the authors claimed that it "denies all forms of obligation and commitment in relationships, replacing them only with the ideal of full, open, honest communication among self-actualized individuals. Like the classic obligation of client to therapist, the only requirement for the therapeutically liberated lover is to share his feelings fully with his partner" (p. 101). Further, this attitude supposedly "liberates individuals by helping them get in touch with their own wants and interests, freed from the artificial constraints of social roles" (p. 101).

Former psychoanalyst Jeffrey Masson (1989) used large sections of his book *Against Therapy* to attack Rogers. He painted Rogers as a manipulator whose overt egalitarianism papered over an essentially false empathy. No matter how much a therapist asserts that his or her listening style won't distort a client's experience, Masson claimed, all therapists are power brokers, and self-proclaimed benevolent ones like Rogers, who deny or downplay the ultimate power of their positions, are simply more dishonest than most. To Paul Vitz (1994), writing from a Christian tradition within psychology, Rogers's work is even more dangerous; it undermines the fabric of Western religious spirituality with a secularism that makes a *selfish* psychology equivalent to its own religion. It presents an "implicit antireligious model" that has "rendered Christianity and other traditional religions permanently out of date" (p. 107). In Rogers's relationship with clients, "the encouragement to narcissism, solipsism, and self-indulgence is obvious" (p. 43). Wallach and Wallach (1983) assert that Rogers's brand of selfishness "see[s] all external determination as a source of evil and what comes genuinely from within as leading to good" (p. 157), and that in families it is obvious that Rogers would recommend that "our own fulfillment, actualization, or development always should be the paramount consideration" when compared with one's responsibilities for others' welfare (p. 159).

One of Rogers's most persistent and vocal critics since his death has been William Coulson, a former student and later his colleague at the Western Behavioral Sciences Institute and the Center for Studies of the Person. Coulson, whose primary forums during this time period evidently have been broadcast media interviews and legislative testimony, has claimed that he was one of the troika of theorists who originally launched humanistic psychology in the 1960s, along with Rogers and Abraham Maslow. According to Coulson, Rogers's basic ideas ruined school systems, religious groups, and other organizations that attempted to apply them—and Coulson evidently feels obliged to repent and apologize for these actions. Further, they have had ruinous effects on the American family, the American school system, and Catholic life; in Coulson's indictment, Rogers urged people to worship themselves, treating inner impulses, in Coulson's words, as "sacred and irrefutable." He further argued that Rogers "got honorary doctorates from Santa Clara and Gonzaga, both Jesuit universities, for, in effect, destroying Catholic discipline" (quoted in Neumayr, 1995, p. 2; for further summaries, quotations, and examples of Coulson's charges, see Kirschenbaum, 1991; Neumayr, 1995). Coulson, the repentant sinner, now warns: "In a way, we are raising up the next generation of [moral delinquents] when we continue to allow Rogerian psychology to determine the shape of . . . religious education, because Rogerian psychology doesn't believe in the Bible" (Neumayr, 1995, p. 2).

Because Rogers thought interpersonal relationships were crucial in human life, it is not surprising that early academic specialists in interpersonal communication found particular relevance in his work. Rogers's influence was often greater outside academic psychology in allied fields such as counseling, education, nursing, social work, English, and communication. Yet his reception has hardly been unqualified there either. For example, despite the common application of his concepts in early interpersonal communication texts in the discipline of communication studies, consider how some in communication have characterized his basic ideas.

Rogers, according to an early edition of an influential communication theory text (Littlejohn, 1983), thought that people should "stick to their personal ideals without variation and without adapting to or adjusting to others" (p. 199). Although this reference was later changed, it probably represented a prevailing attitude at the time. In another theory textbook (Trenholm, 1986), students were told that Rogers argued how "self-acceptance, total honesty, and willingness to self-disclose lay at the heart of rewarding interaction"; the author contended further that such humanists as Rogers "preached" not only "total honesty" but "complete consistency" as well (pp. 112, 114).

In other cases, criticisms, even when not blatant put-downs, seem based on historically suspect conclusions. Another introductory theory text (Griffin, 1994) claimed without qualification that Rogers propounded a theory that was not testable (p. 36), and stated that "Carl Rogers' client-centered principles have generated many devotees, but it has received virtually no testing by empirical researchers" (pp. 36–37). Critics justifiably might question the equivocality, ambiguity, or validity of research into Rogers's "facilitative conditions" of congruence, positive regard, and empathy, for example, but these conditions have been researched in a variety of empirical studies by hundreds of scholars over six decades, as we show later in this chapter. Indeed, the chief frustration of some client-centered therapists with the research literature is not that Rogers's concepts are untestable, but that the studies so seldom reflect the crucial (to Rogers's theory) criterion of ensuring the facilitative conditions are *perceived from the client's perspective*, not just according to externally validated scales imposed artificially within the research design. We also should remember that therapists before Rogers rarely even attempted to research their approaches objectively, other than to record their own clients' successes and failures.

Prominent critics from communication studies have sought to identify Rogers's thought with "expressivism," "doing one's own thing," an unrealistic ignorance of the impact of social roles, a reified self, and a "psychologized" rather than a relational conception of meaning (Arnett, 1981; Arnett & Nakagawa, 1983; Hart & Burks, 1972; Phillips, 1976; Stewart, 1983). In a widely cited analysis, Arnett (1981) claimed that "Rogers' emphasis on the psyche" and on other inner variables "is incompatible with the fundamental dialogical notion of the 'between'" (p. 204); in fact, according to Arnett, Rogers "theoretically advocates obliterating roles" but it's not clear where this advocacy appears in Rogers's writing. Arnett (1982, 1989), to his credit, later moderated his position about Rogers's listening emphasis being psychologistic, undialogic, and focused only on internal meanings—and now (Arnett & Arneson, 1999) clearly appreciates Rogers as a dialogical theorist.

To some critics, then, Rogers is at best a naïve and romantic commentator on an idealized human condition, and at worst an irresponsible advocate of selfishness. Evidently wanting to position Rogers as an easy target, they often characterize his work with absolutes. To highlight only a few from our account in this section: the selfishness he supposedly advocates is "total"; Rogers is concerned "solely" with an isolated self; a genuine self to Rogers is said to be "unchanging," "without variation" or adaptation, and "cannot" be shaped also by interaction; honesty in Rogers's system must be "total" and consistency must be "complete"; the Rogerian conceptual system is so thinly constructed and impressionistically grounded that it has generated "virtually no" empirical testing by researchers; in Rogers's theorizing, social roles are not just de-emphasized as behavioral criteria, but "obliterated." Whatever else Rogers is to his intellectual critics, he is not subtle.

But *did* Rogers stand for total reliance on selfishness? Did he advocate that people should pay no attention to others' needs, and feel
no responsibility to them? Did he teach that a core self can be objectified simplistically and assumed to be either authentic or inauthentic?
Did he advocate sole reliance on an irresponsible technique in which
listeners merely parrot back what they've just heard? If such characterizations are accurate, then Rogers certainly could add little to a nuanced understanding of human dialogue or effective communication.
To the contrary, however, such critiques too often seem to depend on
a patchwork of interpretations of Rogers that are, to be generous,
based more on stereotypical reactions and ideologically motivated
readings than on a careful consideration of what he actually wrote or
said. Rogers can be criticized on a number of issues, but absolutistic
interpretations do not survive a thorough documentary analysis of
client-centered therapy or the person-centered approach. It would be
ironic indeed if a person who devoted his professional career to facilitating human understanding was not himself understood about matters so central to his life and his thought.[1] As Rogers once remarked,
"When people try to describe my theories, I find I don't even recognize
them" (Evans, 1975, p. 91).

Anyone's writing invites various interpretations, of course; we
should not quibble with critics without direct evidence, preferably evidence also available to those same critics. In the remainder of this chapter we thread such evidence into a description of how Rogers's work
reflects a coherent dialogic vision, one that emphasizes both the theory
and practice of everyday relationships. We argue that Rogers was neither
naïvely idealistic nor obsessed with an individualized objectified self;
contrary to how he is often characterized, his concepts of therapy and
human relationships were firmly grounded in the practical consequences of mutual existence and meeting. Rogers believed that his theory of communication was inadequately considered and understood,
calling his most precise statement of it (Rogers, 1959b) "the most thoroughly ignored" of his writings (1980, p. 60). His work, considered in
this context, offers a responsible and specific approach to dialogue, and,
more important, demonstrates and operationalizes its practicality.

PRAXIS

Rogers's work embodies a relationship among the practical, the theoretical, and the philosophical that we term a *praxis of dialogue*.

Praxis seeks to explore systematically the practical implications of everyday human experience. Stephen Toulmin (1988) noted "the recovery of practical philosophy" in intellectual life, and Rogers could be identified within this tradition as well. Practical philosophy, writes Toulmin, had its origins in the work of Aristotle, and was developed in the twentieth century especially by John Dewey. Practical philosophy addresses oral, particular, local, and timely issues, and is anchored in contemporary experience. Practical philosophy and theory, in other words, listens to people and how they enact and characterize their experience.

Praxis, a concept that links systems of ideas and systems of concrete practices, is central to contemporary discussions of philosophy and the social sciences. Raymond Williams (1985) skillfully applies what he terms "historical semantics" to explain important cross-disciplinary terms in the social sciences, such as theory and practice. Theory in one sense is "a scheme of ideas which explains practice" (p. 316), and in this way is "always in active relation to *practice*: an interaction between things done, things observed and (systematic) explanation of these. This allows a necessary distinction between *theory* and *practice*, but does not require their opposition" (p. 317).

For the purposes of this study, the term "praxis" unifies practice, theory, and philosophy. Williams's account is especially useful in considering the work of such a thinker-practitioner as Rogers:

> *Praxis* is *practice* informed by *theory* and also, though less emphatically, *theory* informed by *practice*, as distinct both from *practice* uninformed by or unconcerned with *theory* and from *theory* which remains *theory* and is not put to the test of *practice*. In effect it is a word intended to unite *theory* . . . with the strongest sense of *practical* (but not conventional or customary) activity: *practice* as action. *Praxis* is then also used, derivatively, to describe a whole mode of activity in which, by analysis but only by analysis, *theoretical* and *practical* elements can be distinguished, but which is always a whole activity, to be judged as such. The distinction or opposition between *theory* and *practice* can then be surpassed. (p. 318)

In these terms, Carl Rogers was a philosopher of praxis. He consistently attempted to ground and test his experience of dialogue in particularized face-to-face encounters, philosophical assumptions underlying dialogue, and theoretical (i.e., explanatory and predictive) propositions for communicative action. The philosopher of praxis attempts above all to unify—valuing "what works," but forever seeking the reasons and the contexts; valuing the "premises" and "propositions" but never denying their rootedness in the practical consequences of humans creating relational meaning. Kurt Lewin (1951) is widely acknowledged for this recognition of the practical value of good theory—"There is nothing so practical as a good theory" (p. 169). Rogers demonstrated the theoretical value of good practice.

THE EMERGING PRAXIS OF DIALOGUE

Because Rogers was far more influenced by his professional experience than by any systematic philosophical positions, we achieve only partial insight into the development of his praxis of dialogue by tracing intellectual roots. Rogers thought the pragmatic philosophy of John Dewey was an important early influence (Evans, 1975, pp. 110–111), and also acknowledged influences from Christian existentialist Søren Kierkegaard, from his friend, the post-positivist philosopher of science Michael Polanyi (Rogers, 1980, p. 63), and from Martin Buber, whose writings Rogers assigned in his classes as early as 1952 after Chicago theology students recommended them to him (see Rogers, 1952).

John Dewey's writings reinforced Rogers's faith in individual experience, and Dewey's educational philosophy provided a theoretical context in which Rogers would develop his ideas about experience, change, and learning (Zappan, 1980). Kierkegaard's writings helped Rogers explore existential issues, and they also "loosened me up and made me more willing to trust and express my own experience" (Kirschenbaum, 1979, p. 231). Kierkegaard's implicit theory of communication (Anderson, 1963; Galati, 1969) probably further sensitized Rogers to the nature of a reflective self in its social context. Michael Polanyi's enlarged conception of science, his identification of tacit sources of valid knowledge, and his recognition of the role of personal commitment in scientific inquiry resonated deeply with the experience Rogers had gained from the realm of psychotherapy (Rogers, 1980; Kirschenbaum, 1979). The influence of Buber is perhaps more pervasive, however. Beginning in the early 1950s, Rogers's writing often pointed directly or indirectly to Buber's dialogical philosophy, especially to the I-Thou concept and the fundamental respect for otherness it entailed. Maurice Friedman, Buber's most prominent biographer and interpreter, has frequently

noted (see especially 1985, pp. 48–55) the influences and parallels that
Rogers attributed to Buber.

A final philosophical influence is less tangible but still important.
In 1922, Rogers was one of a handful of young Americans chosen to attend an international youth conference in Beijing, China. This opportunity, which expanded into a six-month journey through the Far East,
was an immensely educational and liberalizing experience for this
rather fundamentalist Christian youth. Perhaps it was then that Rogers
was first exposed to Taoism, the Chinese philosphical system he peri-
odically quoted in his later life. Although it is difficult to discover precisely how influential the philosophical tenets of Taoism have been in
the development of his thought, the parallels at least are clear. Just as
Martin Buber had found Taoist thought to be a fertile ground for his dialogic philosophy (even though he decided later it was too "mystical"
for him), Rogers came to appreciate its essential attitude of noninterference, a not-forcing, and an acceptance of the natural order of things.
Noninterference in Taoism is often expressed as *wu-wei* or "effortless
effort." It is an approach to responsible behavior that accomplishes
without manipulating accomplishment.[2] Rogers used the word "nondirective" to describe his counseling relationships, not to suggest that
passivity or lack of direction were desirable states; rather, like the
Taoist, he refused to impose directions, diagnoses, prejudgments, prescriptions, or easy advice on the therapeutic relationship, preferring to
let the directions emerge from the dialogue between counselor or therapist and client.

The Taoist concept of *mutual arising* was reflected in Rogers's emphasis on the relationship and the contributions persons inherently
make to each other's growth. This transactional (Dewey & Bentley,
1949) view of nature sees "every thing-event . . . in relation to all others" and recognizes that "individuality is inseparable from community"
(Watts, 1975, p. 43). Similarly, "self" for Rogers cannot be analyzed apart
from the personal relationships that form the ground of its arising.
Those who believe that Rogers advocated a "thing-like," static, or
"true" self invulnerable to social influences should find it difficult to
explain his clear position, expressed as early as 1951 and reiterated in
variant forms throughout his published work thereafter:

> As a result of interaction with the environment, and particu-
> larly as a result of evaluational interaction with others, the
> structure of self is formed—an organized, fluid, but consis-
> tent conceptual pattern of perceptions of characteristics and

relationships of the "I" or the "me," together with values attached to these concepts. (Rogers, 1951, p. 498)

Consistent with the Tao, self for Rogers became a dynamic perspective of mutuality and a relational phenomenon. Persons constantly affect each other's senses of self. As we interpret Rogers, self is a concept useful for discussing individual uniqueness, but as this quotation indicates, it is not *within* a self that a primarily subjectivist meaning for a relationship is contained. Self is a perceived *pattern of relationship*, and therefore is simultaneously both individualized and socially constructed.

Yet Rogers's approach to human communication did not develop out of an allegiance to prior philosophical positions, nor did he conceive of himself primarily as a philosopher. In a rather unusual and self-deprecating admission, Rogers suggested that he was not a scholar and that his reading of the ideas of others served largely to "buttress" his own experientially developed views (1980, p. 63).[3] Of three broad sources of his learning (1980, pp. 61–64), Rogers gave by far the greatest weight to his therapy and counseling (see also Evans, 1975, pp. 109–111). His conception of dialogue was drawn from this crucible of experience. His is a philosophy of dialogue, to be sure, but is first and foremost a praxis of dialogue. Of all currently influential thinkers in dialogic theory, Rogers was perhaps the most immersed—professionally—in day-to-day applications and testings.

Rogers's label for his theory of dialogue evolved from "nondirective therapy" to "client-centered therapy," and finally broadened beyond therapeutic realms to the "person-centered approach." This theory is empirically grounded in many thousands of hours of direct contact with clients and therapy groups, experiential learning groups, and intercultural encounters. Especially in his descriptions of therapy and in others' descriptions of his behavior with clients and groups (De Ryck, 1982; Kirschenbaum, 1979; Slack, 1985), it is clear how a theory of dialogue may be based not only on abstraction, but on an immediacy of experience often in very trying human circumstances. As a psychotherapist, Rogers responded constantly to people who felt lost, isolated, and confused, unaware of their place in a complex world; among his extraordinary contributions was the confirmation of very disturbed and disoriented persons. The importance of his example, this concrete "living-through," should not be underestimated. The writings of most philosophers of dialogue are eloquent and often inspiring. Rogers demonstrated in *practice* the viability of dialogue.

In 1938 Rogers became the first therapist to record his therapy sessions and make them available to others (Farson, 1975, p. xxxiv;

Kirschenbaum, 1979, p. 205; Kirschenbaum & Henderson, 1989b, p. 202; Rogers, 1942a, pp. 17, 261; Rogers, 1942b). Before his breakthrough, therapists could provide only post hoc and often somewhat self-serving descriptions of the processes of their therapy. Rogers provided oral recordings and written transcripts, accessible to all (see Rogers, 1942a, pp. 258–437, for a transcript of a complete psychotherapy case). He studied the recordings and transcripts carefully, analyzing them to understand when he said or did something helpful, and when he perhaps hindered client growth. He did not begin with an a priori conception of what the therapeutic relationship "should" be; indeed, his initial development of the "client-centered" approach in the 1940s was a significant departure from his earlier training and practice (Kirschenbaum, 1979; Rogers, 1980, pp. 27–45). His theory of therapy was simply an attempt to systematize the conditions, processes, and outcomes (Rogers, 1959b, p. 193) that he noted in his therapy sessions.

Rogers's perspective on dialogue was apparent in his exchange with Polanyi in a televised discussion on the possibility of a human science of knowledge. Polanyi seemed more interested in the global and theoretical implications of new approaches to knowledge, while Rogers sought to personalize the focus:

> I'm particularly impressed with the distinction you draw between knowledge, as the larger field, and science. It perhaps bears on one item that has been a very real puzzle to me. As you know, I'm a therapist, a counselor, and the majority of my life has been given over to working with individuals who are in some sort of personal or psychological distress. I certainly feel I have been able to be of some help to some of them, and if I ask myself what has been the real element which has been helpful, it would seem to be the intimate, close, mutual subjective relationship—something similar to what Buber describes as "I-Thou" relationship. It's that personal experience of relationship that seems to be the element that brings about change, and yet, when trying to do research in psychotherapy, you can study the way in which the verbal behavior changes, you can study the changes in the person's way of perceiving himself, you can study the way his friends perceive him, the changes in such perceptions—you can study all kinds of external cues, and yet, so far as I can see, you can never get to the really essential experience which brought about change. Now, I relate that to what you're saying by thinking that, perhaps, it must remain a part of our

knowledge but cannot be a part of our science. I don't know. (Polanyi & Rogers, 1968, pp. 196–197)

This statement yields important clues for how to interpret Rogers's praxis. First, he focuses directly on the process of communication, rather than on behavioral or even psychological data. Although in other writings he emphasizes self and personality and his faith in what he terms the "actualizing tendency" of the organism (1959b, 1961, 1971b), for Rogers these are not the primary determinants of human growth. The "real element which has been helpful" is the relationship of mutuality. "I've learned through my experience," Rogers said in his 1957 dialogue with Martin Buber, "that when we *can* meet, then help does occur, but that's a by-product" (turn #81). Growth occurs *from* mutuality, and *toward* it. When people are "helped," it is so they can form more satisfying relationships in their lives.

Second, Rogers's learning style was not only experiential, but also fundamentally and rigorously inductive. He built generalizations in order to explain an accumulation of specific events. Perhaps the best example is his notion of self, which we introduced earlier. Self is crucial because it has been thoroughly misunderstood in the literature on Rogers. He stressed what he called a "self" not because he developed an original model of the way humans "really" are, and not because he believed persons somehow possessed a self. This construct assumed importance only because he listened so carefully to his clients over the years. Originally somewhat suspicious of the term "self" by his own admission, he "was slow in recognizing that when clients were given the opportunity to express their problems and attitudes in their own terms without any guidance or interpretation, they tended to talk in terms of the self" (1959b, pp. 200–201). Rogers didn't ordain or even surmise but instead—in the best tradition of descriptive and exploratory scientific research—*discovered* that "the self was an important element in the experience of the client, and that in some odd sense his goal was to become his 'real self'" (1959b, p. 201). And, as we have seen, the experience of self that Rogers discovered was essentially relational and socially based.

Although some followers of Rogers may approach his teachings with a simplistic "wouldn't the world be nicer if " mind-set, it is clear from his career of work, and from the introspective accounts of his own growth from mistakes and failure (1980, pp. 13, 227–252), that was not his own motivation. Consistent with Buber's advice in their dialogue, Rogers allowed himself to be surprised in his meetings with others, building theories from events without imposing theories on them. At the moment of meeting, no matter what the cumulative status of a therapist's learning or theorizing, Rogers realized that therapeutic presence must be as atheoretical as possible:

> [I]t is the existential encounter which is important, and . . . in the immediate moment of the therapeutic relationship, consciousness of theory has no helpful place. Another way of stating this is that to the extent that we are thinking theoretically in the relationship, we become spectators, not players—and it is as players that we are effective. (1971b, pp. 189–190)

Of course this does not mean that communicators can forget or renounce at will their previous insights or theoretical biases. Rather, respondents cannot work to build a uniquely present relationship while imposing previous analysis and theories on it. Rogers is very close to Buber in this belief, as Friedman (1960, p. 192) first observed. Recall how Rogers qualified and concluded his response to Polanyi: "so far as I can see," "perhaps," "I don't know." Here is the openness to experience he also noted in his successful clients, and which he has discussed in himself as well (Rogers, 1959b, pp. 188–191)—an attitude essential to dialogue. A singular person's perspective is necessarily provisional and limited; one must invite others' words; certainty is at best elusive; and theory is always changing.

ROGERS'S THEORY OF COMMUNICATION

Central to Rogers's concept of dialogue is the theory of communication he derived from his therapy relationships (1959b). Ordinary human relationships, Rogers believed, had much in common with the therapeutic relationship: "I have long had the strong conviction—some might say it was an obsession—that the therapeutic relationship is only a special instance of interpersonal relationships in general, and that the same lawfulness governs all such relationships" (1961, p. 39). The growth-promoting potential of all relationships results from the quality of the relationship established between persons. What Rogers felt, said, and did with clients, when successful, became what Rogers called the "characteristics of a helping relationship."

But is "helping" the prime objective and theme of Rogerian thought? Not really; he was convinced that his abiding commitment to

communication was primary: "[P]eering back . . . I can see what is perhaps one overriding theme in my professional life. It is my caring about
communication" (Rogers, 1980, p. 64). His concepts were among the
most influential support for speech and communication faculty who
were establishing new courses in interpersonal communication at mid-
century. His brief article describing the "necessary and sufficient conditions of therapeutic personality change" (Rogers, 1957b) and his
lengthy essay for Koch's multivolume review of psychology (Rogers,
1959b) essentially presented a communication-based theory of personal
growth and relationship development.

The expression of his theory of communication changed only
slightly after the mid-1950s. Rogers came to apply the theory more
broadly, as evidenced in the terms "person-centered approach" and "a
way of being" rather than "client-centered therapy." Late in his life,
Rogers (1986a) also broadened his view to recognize the value of intuition. But neither his own experience nor the research literature led
Rogers to make fundamental revisions in his description of the basic
conditions of effective human relationships.

Although others have summarized Rogers's intellectual contributions quite thoroughly (Thorne, 1992; Kirschenbaum, 1979), they have
focused on psychological implications. Only a few scholars have summarized his work with a specific eye toward illuminating directly either
its implications for communication relationships broadly or for the quality of dialogue more specifically. In fact, before our work (Cissna & Anderson, 1990), few dialogic communication scholars sympathetic to his
approach have examined his theoretical propositions at all, and then only
briefly (Anderson, 1982; Gaw, 1978; Johannesen, 1996; Sillars, 1974;
Thomlison, 1982; also see Friedman, 1985, pp. 48–55; Van Belle, 1980).

Rogers described four conditions necessary for a growth-promoting
relationship to develop. The first is a degree of "contact" or psychological involvement between people. Late in his life, Rogers (1987) used
the allied concept of *presence* to discuss what brings people together, a
concept also important to Buber and other dialogic theorists. The other
three conditions are qualities of interpersonal communication. Rogers
frequently called these "attitudes" in order to distinguish them from
narrowly construed behaviors or techniques, but he also consistently
said they must be perceived or understood by the other person. Rogers
named these conditions somewhat differently over the years. In much
of his work he gave the greatest attention to *congruence*, or what he
sometimes called genuineness, realness, or transparency. A second condition is created by *acceptance*, a feeling of warmth, caring, or concern
for the other; he sometimes called this "unconditional positive regard."

Finally, he stressed *empathy*, a kind of tentative and inferred sense of the unique feelings and interpretations of the other.

Rogers did not prescribe these conditions from any sense of "oughtness"; that is, he did not start out to claim that people ought to behave this way in order to be ethical or moral, or even to assure effectiveness. These were not *prescriptions* based on a presumed ideal of humanistic psychology (or any other perspective) but *outcomes* as firmly rooted in praxis as Rogers knew how to make them. He found these things through empirical observation of how clients and therapists established relationships in the recordings and films he made of his therapy sessions. When effective therapy *tends* to develop, he discovered, the therapeutic relationship *tends* to be based on the facilitative conditions. Rogers clarified and qualified his theoretical constructs with meaningful caveats that have been overlooked often by both true believers and ideological opponents. He and his colleagues then developed hypotheses that sharpened their subsequent empirical research. Yet the true believers and the ideological opponents often stuck to their stereotypes.

We should address more directly Rogers's willingness to subject his theory to rigorous research, and whether it is true, as some assert, that a Rogerian system can never stimulate systematic and effective empirical inquiry. While at the University of Chicago in the 1940s and 1950s, Rogers and colleagues tested client-centered hypotheses with dogmatism, Minnesota Multiphasic Personality Inventory, Rorschach, Thematic Apperception, and other instruments, including measures of self-perception, anxiety, galvanic skin response, heart rate, and instruments designed to measure the various qualities of the therapeutic relationship. Further, grants from the Rockefeller and Ford foundations, among others, supported psychotherapy research "with larger populations and more elaborate controls than ever employed before" in such studies (Kirschenbaum, 1995, p. 33). Rogers adapted William Stephenson's (1953) Q-methodology to the client-centered framework in an attempt to model and portray subjective perceptions systematically, and as best they could, Rogers and his co-researchers designed effects studies that easily surpassed the scientific controls of contemporaneous psychotherapy research.

After a 1949 issue of the *Journal of Consulting Psychology* presented a symposium of client-centered research, the *Encyclopedia Britannica* would report in its next yearbook that "These first efforts of Rogers to subject his methods of non-directive therapy to scientific test constituted a landmark for clinical psychology" (quoted in Kirschenbaum, 1995, p. 33). Rogers and Dymond's 1954 book, *Psychotherapy*

and Personality Change, was selected as the year's outstanding research work by the American Personnel and Guidance Association.
One review called it "the first thoroughly objective study of outcomes
of psychotherapy in which adequate controls have been utilized"
(p. 33). It was not surprising, therefore, that two years later Rogers was
presented the American Psychological Association's first Distinguished Scientific Contribution award, with the following citation of
appreciation:

> . . . for developing an original method to objectify the descrip-
> tion and analysis of the psychotherapeutic process, for formu-
> lating a testable theory of psychotherapy and its effects on
> personality and behavior, and *for extensive systematic re-
> search to exhibit the value of the method and explore and test
> the implications of the theory.* His imagination, persistence,
> and flexible adaptation of scientific method in his attack on
> the formidable problems involved in the understanding and
> modification of the individual person have moved this area of
> psychological interest within the boundaries of scientific psy-
> chology. (American Psychological Association, 1957; empha-
> sis added)

Rogers's research into "the therapeutic relationship and its impact" continued after his move to Wisconsin (Rogers, Gendlin,
Kiesler, & Truax, 1967). Colleagues, students, and other researchers
struggled to create research designs that take into account relational
dialogue while also tapping the subjective worlds of clients and others in light of possible behavioral and attitudinal outcomes. Some
were more successful than others, and a specific problem Rogers always worried about was the (inevitably) small number of partici-
pants/"subjects" in some studies. But few could doubt that a base of
empirical research was being constructed, on which further research
would be built. Grummon (1979) suggested that by the late 1970s the
empirical research supporting Rogers's ideas was larger than for any
other helping theory except perhaps for behavior modification (an
ironic comparison for Rogers, to be sure). Patterson (1985), summarizing the literature in his book *The Therapeutic Relationship*, wrote
that "considering the obstacles to research on the relationship between therapist variables and therapy outcomes, the magnitude of
the evidence is nothing short of amazing. It might be ventured that
there are few things in the field of psychology for which the evidence
is so strong. The evidence for the necessity, if not the sufficiency, of

the therapist conditions of accurate empathy, respect or warmth, and therapeutic genuineness is incontrovertible" (p. 244).

Although observers such as Watson (1984) rightly interrogate the quality of some of the research and remind us that the whole package of Rogerian theory still awaits definitive empirical support (which theoretical systems *have* achieved unarguable support?), clearly research in this area is neither nonexistent nor largely impressionistic. Rogers was the pioneer in scientifically researching psychotherapy relationships, and consequently used methods that some contemporary social scientists would critique. But not long before Rogers's death, Watson (1984) acknowledged that "over the past 25 years there has been a substantial amount of research on the theory of the mechanism of effective therapy from a client-centered perspective" (p. 17). Gurman (1977) found that "there exists substantial, if not overwhelming, evidence in support of the hypothesized relationship between patient-perceived therapeutic conditions and outcome in individual psychotherapy and counseling" (p. 523).

More recently, Bozarth (1993) surveyed a wide range of psychological research into Rogers's facilitative conditions that were thought to be both necessary and sufficient. Although Rogers's ideas may be undercut in some areas, Bozarth found that when the studies were placed in the context of what Rogers actually suggested, "examination of recent reviews of research, relevant literature, and the theoretical underpinnings of the person-centered approach leads to the conclusion that there is no substantial evidence to refute Rogers' position" (p. 102). Therefore, the concepts Rogers thought were so crucial—first the availability of contact and then of the three facilitative conditions of congruence, acceptance, and empathy—formed the foundation for a psychologically inflected theory of communication that was as well researched for its time as reasonably could be expected, and as well supported as any theory of its kind.

Contact

Contact is a necessary precondition of a therapeutic relationship, and also emerges out of that relationship as it develops. But Rogers did not mean by this word merely being physically present to one another or even talking to or with the other. Rather, *contact* in his system involves a psychological availability, a willingness to enter into a relationship with the other person. It occurs "when each [person] makes a perceived or subceived difference in the experiential field of the other" (Rogers,

1959b, p. 207). Rogers first called this phenomenon "relationship" but switched terminology to emphasize it does not refer to "the depth and quality of a good relationship" but only to the "least or minimum experience" that occurs in human relationships (p. 207). In the absence of this contact—a mutual attending to and involvement with the other—the growthful possibilities of human relationships will not occur.

Congruence

Congruence is the term Rogers used most frequently to refer to the first of the communicated conditions of growthful relationships. In everyday language he has described it as being real, not pretending, not assuming a facade. In more precise and technical terms, congruence refers to how a person correlates experience, feelings or awareness, and overt communication. "Experience," used here as a noun, includes "all that is going on within the envelope of the organism at any given moment which is potentially available to awareness" (1959b, p. 197), including both conscious and unconscious phenomena. Awareness refers to the symbolization of some aspect of experience; it may be sharp and vivid, or dim and vague. Rogers was especially concerned with awareness of feelings, emotionally tinged experiences, and their personal meanings. Overt communication refers to the things a person explicitly says or does that serve as messages to others. Congruence is therefore a "close matching . . . between what is being experienced at the gut level, what is present in awareness, and what is experessed" (1980, p. 116). The closer the similarity between the person's experience and his or her awareness of that experience, and between the person's awareness and the communication of that awareness, the more congruent the person is being.

Some scholars interpret congruence in ways that would have surprised Rogers.[4] In one reading, Rogers supposedly is suggesting that people should not assume or enact socially derived roles (Arnett, 1981). A second characterization of this aspect of his work suggests that he advocated full and constant disclosure (see Hart & Burks, 1972; Phillips, 1976). Rogers did not urge that we obliterate or avoid roles, and indeed much of his professional writing and career was devoted to describing how to function most helpfully in the therapist role. His books also examined the roles of teacher (1969, 1983), group facilitator (1970), marriage partner (1972a), and social change agent (1977a). Rogers would not wish to abolish roles; rather, he was well aware of the significance of social expectations on personal behavior (recall that he defined self as a transaction of diverse social influences) and suggested that persons should select roles carefully and enact them genuinely and congruently whenever possible (Anderson, 1982, p. 353). He did suggest that many people rely on roles unnecessarily to invoke power or to depend on outmoded ways of thinking, but this is a far cry from a blanket condemnation of the concept of social role. To be congruent does not mean a sort of cavalier "do-your-thing" attitude without regard for other people. To the extent that we can, Rogers would suggest that we approach our tasks in as integrated a way as possible.[5]

The issue of self-disclosure presents another interesting misunderstanding. Rogers did not suggest that people should tell all their feelings to anyone who would listen. His emphasis was always on relationship, and not on the individual or unrestrained expressivism that many of his critics allege. There are many paths to congruence or genuineness in a relationship, as there are many levels of experience and feeling. Further, not all feelings should be shared. Rogers typically discussed sharing *significant* and *persistent* feelings that are *relevant* to the relationship:

- Should [the therapist] also express or communicate to the client the accurate symbolization of his own experience? . . . [S]uch feelings should be expressed, if the therapist finds himself persistently focused on his own feelings rather than those of the client, thus greatly reducing or eliminating any experience of empathic understanding, or if he finds himself persistently experiencing some feeling other than unconditional positive regard. (1959b, p. 214)
- I am not saying that it is helpful to blurt out impulsively every passing feeling and accusation under the comfortable impression that one is being genuine. (1971a, p. 88)
- I have learned that in any significant or continuing relationship, persistent feelings had best be expressed. (1980, p. 44)

Rogers also recognized degrees of congruence (see 1961, p. 51), and made clear that congruence is a relative rather than an absolute condition when he wrote that "no one fully achieves this condition" (1971a, p. 87). He even discussed his own deliberations about whether to describe a feeling or thought to a client (e.g., 1959b, p. 214; 1971a, pp. 87–89). Rogers did seem to believe that most people, most of the time, could form closer relationships if they disclosed in ways that were more "real" for them, and he often provided examples of how risky it was to ignore or deny one's inner states, to the extent they were relevant to the relationship. Still, the decision not to disclose could also be viable and appropriate, depending on the situation and relationship, and well within the guidelines of congruence Rogers discussed. Persons who are "rhetorically sensitive" (Hart & Burks, 1972), adapting their messages to the listening styles, vocabularies, or attitudes of their hearers, would not be identified ipso facto by Rogers as incongruent, even though some accounts in the communication literature present the rhetorical sensitivity construct and congruence as incompatible (e.g., Littlejohn, 1983, p. 199; Trenholm, 1986, pp. 112, 114).

Positive Regard

Rogers often called his second facilitative condition acceptance or unconditional positive regard, and also discussed it in terms of respect, caring, warmth, prizing, and confirmation. To Rogers, positive regard means to understand that the other is uniquely valuable and important, and to communicate a baseline acceptance of him or her. The person expressing positive regard is able to let the other be, as he or she is, without external judgments designed to fix the person, or to impose externally derived conditions of change. Regardless of the appropriateness or desirability (or social correctness) of a feeling or perception, the other is given permission to experience it without fearing that he or she will be considered less worthy as a person in the relationship. Regard, even when it is unconditional and positive, does not necessarily require in Rogers's system that one "likes" the other, nor does it involve endorsing all the person says or does. And surely regard does not refer, as one scholar interpreted it, to "total acceptance of whatever a client has done as appropriate and normal for this person in this circumstance" (DeVito, 1986, p. 329). The concept of regard refers to a fundamental respect for otherness, in all its uniqueness, even when the observer cannot fully understand the relationship and even in conditions of intense conflict. In Rogers's (1959b) classic formulation, it means "to value the person, irrespective of the differential values which one might place on his specific behaviors" (p. 208).

This attitudinal move is far more than mere sunny optimism about human nature, and it is far more practical, too. The therapeutic or growth-promoting importance of this attitude is relatively simple, and amply supported by research in the helping professions. Clients who feel judged, especially unfairly judged, by externally imposed standards will often become defensive and will unduly clamp their openness to dialogue. In addition, from the other side, helpers who rely on such judgments are likely to lock in conclusions too rapidly, becoming fragmented listeners at best. Rogers, among many others, found it much more practical to hold judgmental conclusions in abeyance while the dialogue emerged. This was Rogers's way of reminding himself that he had to be willing to be surprised by the next comments or feelings or disclosures of the client—and the next.

Greenberg (1996) has analyzed a number of Rogers's representative psychotherapy transcripts with a particular client ("Jim Brown"; see Rogers et al., 1967) to examine how this valuing acceptance influences the relationship in particular moments of creative insight. These moments, he suggests, create a relationship similar to Buber's I-Thou, and one that frees the client to be different:

> The most striking initial feature of Rogers' sessions with Jim is that the relationship is . . . a true encounter between two human beings attempting to make contact in a helping context. The relationship is much more a real, caring relationship between two people than it is an analysis of the client by a therapist that focuses on the client's past experiences projected into the present. The relationship manifests qualities of presence, immediacy, inclusion, confirmation, and nonexploitativeness that characterize the I-thou relationship (Buber, 1958). Rogers' caring presence, in fact, appears to be central in breaking through Jim's defensive shell. The primary conditions of the client-centered relationship can be seen . . . in all their power. The prizing of one human being by another and the experience of acceptance and nonmanipulative caring for another's inner pain, without any direct attempt to change it, has a tremendously nourishing effect. . . . We see how the acceptance of "what is" leads to the acknowledgement of the avoided or obscured inner self-organization. . . . This allowing and accepting of pain in the often hidden and vulnerable self-organization is a crucial therapeutic movement—a real moment of change. (Greenberg, 1996, p. 252)

Greenberg believes that although the core conditions, including prizing or regard, are important, they may be less important at times than the respondent's simple flexible presence in the moment, a presence that is explicitly *for* the other. This presence did not need to be tinged with positive feelings in order to be powerful: "It seems to me that Rogers himself did different things at different times, and that his actions—especially at certain key moments in therapy—were not always intended purely as the provision of understanding and relational acceptance, as important as these conditions are" (Greenberg, 1996, pp. 252–253). In chapters 6 and 7, we will elaborate on a consistent Buber–Rogers theoretical position demonstrating how relational dialogue emerges not as an ongoing state but only in such key moments of insight, growth, surprise, and change that are facilitated by nonjudgmental presence.

Some critics have argued that Rogers's concept of acceptance/positive regard has contributed to an unhealthy trend toward moral relativism (any behavior is okay), a selfish individualism ("I'm in this for myself"), and an abdication of personal responsibility toward a larger community. It is at best difficult to imagine how this can be so after a careful reading of Rogers's work or that of his commentators. Rogers's therapy often involved persons who were by their own descriptions too reliant on the definitions of others; they let others define them, and they essentially existed for and through those others. Rogers's goals and approaches affirmed neither this problem ("I am nobody without others telling me what I should do") nor its opposite ("I should be invulnerable to what others say to me"). Clearly, both of these extremes would preclude dialogue in many ways, and the lives of persons consumed by one or the other would be impoverished. Dialogue partners who have no personal ground from which to speak cannot contribute meaningfully, but neither can partners who believe theirs is the only justifiable ground from which to speak. Instead, when a listener displays some form of positive regard that is not fundamentally conditional, the client can feel able to establish a balance. That balance is interdependence, and Rogers's work explicitly forecloses unrestrained selfishness as an outcome. It does not diminish the importance of community or relation in any noticeable way, and is "relativistic," philosophically speaking, only in two obvious and literal senses: that Rogers does not want to impose _his_ reality and goals on people who need not share them, and that he has faith that all humans—despite obvious shared commonalities—will have constructed aspects of reality at least somewhat uniquely.

Again, the similarity of Rogers's and Buber's approaches seems clear. Rogers associated his concept of regard or acceptance with Buber's notion of confirmation, and frequently cited Buber when he discussed a listener's accepting or prizing the other without wishing to impose change (e.g., 1961, p. 55; 1969, p. 232; 1980, pp. 19, 41–42, 155). In their dialogue, as we will see in a later chapter, Buber clearly wished to preserve a distinction between accepting and confirming, but the distinction seemed to rest on Buber's concept of accepting rather than on the meaning Rogers intended for the term. To Buber, acceptance is tied to who the other is, and can be a starting point for confirmation, while confirmation involves recognizing and calling forth the the potentialities of the other. Rogers, however, encompassed recognition of the person as he or she is and can become within the one term of acceptance. To Rogers, regard, prizing, confirmation, and acceptance all point to a fundamental respect for the integrity of the other as a person, both in being and in becoming.

A poignant example further clarifies how Rogers confirmed by "struggling with" another. His biographer Howard Kirschenbaum (1979, pp. 416–417) provides an account of Rogers's communication with Helen, his wife of over fifty years, who in 1976 was bedridden and apparently dying. She was becoming increasingly dependent on him and difficult to care for. At one point she said to him that she really had nothing to live for except to live for him. Rogers responded, "Then I can understand why you want to die." This is not a response of a "blank slate" or "mirror," as Maurice Friedman (e.g., 1994, p. 63) often characterized Rogers's views (nor of merely "reproductive" or "reflective" listening), but represents an authentic call to the other. Perhaps in part realizing that "living her life for her husband was not a sufficient reason for living," she greatly improved and survived for three more years. It is revealing that in his most intimate and long-term relationship, where some would say that the risks are the greatest, and at perhaps one of the most significant moments in that relationship (and in his wife's life), Rogers made the communicative choice to confirm by "struggling-with."

Empathy

Empathic understanding provides a key link for Rogers in his theory of communication. *Empathy* involves perceiving the "internal frame of reference" of the other as accurately as possible, and understanding the other's emotions and personal meanings as if one were experiencing the world from the other's vantage point (without, Rogers usually stipulated, losing the "as if" quality). Keeping in mind the essential "as if" means simply that Rogers recognized the danger of losing oneself in the other. He thus emphasized that empathy is not an abandonment of personal ground but demands an active and relational imagining of how real another's ground might be (Anderson, 1984). Empathy for Rogers (1959b) is a form of knowing that is neither objective nor subjective, but which provides the basis for genuine interpersonal understanding. It requires that one be tuned closely to the "flow of experiencings" of the other (1980, p. 142). It involves "being sensitive, moment by moment, to the changing felt meanings which flow in this other person," "sensing the meanings of which he or she is scarcely aware," and "communicating your sensings of the person's world" while "frequently checking with the person as to the accuracy of your sensings" (1980, p. 142). Empathy is not a static or steady condition (although Rogers once used the term "state" in explaining it), but is closer to being an ongoing and dynamic process; Rogers described it as "a complex, demanding, and strong—yet also a subtle and gentle—way of being" (1980, p. 143).

Martin Buber, whose work Rogers assigned to graduate students years before he met Buber at Ann Arbor, also addressed the importance of acknowledging the reality of another person's sense of the world. In his famous essay on "Education" (1965a), Buber writes of the importance of the "elemental experience" of "experiencing the other side" (p. 96). This, he cautions, cannot be expected at all times in every meeting, but this "inclusion," as he says, is at the base of what he called dialogue: "A relation between persons that is characterized in more or less degree by the element of inclusion may be termed a dialogical relation" (p. 97). Further, "all conversation derives its genuineness only from the consciousness of the element of inclusion—even if this appears only abstractly as an 'acknowledgement' of the actual being of the partner in the conversation; but this acknowledgement can be real and effective only when it springs from an experience of inclusion, of the other side" (p. 97). This seems to be a fundamental if somewhat more abstract support for Rogers's empathy, and a rationale for its crucial contributions to dialogic potential.

Buber (1965a) disliked the notion of "empathy" because of its historical connotations, largely from nineteenth- and twentieth-century psychoanalytic sources. He cautions that "it would be wrong" to identify his ideas with empathy, because to him that means "to glide with one's own feeling into the dynamic structure of an object, a pillar or a crystal or the branch of a tree, or even of an animal or a man, and as it were to trace it from within, understanding the formation and motoriality of the object with the perceptions of one's own muscles. It means to 'transpose' oneself over there and in there" (p. 97). Rogers has occasionally been criticized, therefore, for superficiality because he stressed empathy in lieu of Buber's supposedly more nuanced and sophisticated formulations of "experiencing the other side," "inclusion," or "imagining the real" and "making present" (1965b, pp. 70, 81). Yet it's not difficult to see how this problem is more semantic than conceptual. Rogers's basic definition shows he was never interested in "transposing [himself] over there" to "glide with his own feeling" into a client's world, taking it over and analyzing it. Instead, read in tandem, these two descriptions seem different only in their different praxic emphases; both stress mutuality and concern for the moments of dialogue with an acknowledged other whose differences are valued. Both stress the importance of retaining one's own ground while perceiving those differences. In other words, Rogers and Buber basically agree despite using the term "empathy" very differently. Other theorists of the therapeutic relationship evidently have reached this same conclusion, that a Rogers-like approach to empathy is quite consistent with Buber's work (e.g., Havens, 1986; Katz, 1963). As Katz (1963) pointed out:

> Effective empathy . . . calls for moving into the situation of the client rather than attempting to simulate within oneself one or more of what is presumed are the intrapsychic states or zones of feeling. You do not simply listen to the pulse of feeling with an empathic stethoscope, moving the instrument from one spot to another to pick up the range and intensity of the heart beat. You are not even conscious of the rhythm of feeling as something in itself, because as a participant you are lost in the situation itself. You become an active agent in your imaginative role-play. You experience a situation, participate in a drama, and respond to live cues. The effective empathizer does not try to recapture a "feeling" as if it were an object located within the body of the client. As he feels himself into his client, he, like the client, becomes *connected* with the people and objects in the client's experience. (pp. 180–181)

None of this, however, shielded Rogers from criticism—first for advocating a supposedly empty technique, second for advocating that a Rogerian-style empathizer must leave self behind in order to enter the other's perception, and third for championing a simplistic and individualistic style of listening that only attempts to reproduce another's inner meaning. Rogers advocated none of this.

Thomas Bruneau (1989), after reviewing the literature in empathy and listening, noted that the most frequent misunderstanding of empathy equates it with mere technique or skill: "reflecting" back the words of the other, sometimes called "active listening." However useful the concepts and skills of active or reflective listening may be, they do not adequately capture the concept of empathy as Rogers has presented it.[6] In fact, although Rogers and Richard Farson published a short booklet called *Active Listening* (Rogers & Farson, 1957), the fundamental nature of his conception of empathy was so badly misapplied that for many years Rogers virtually quit writing and talking about it (1980, pp. 138–140). For Rogers, empathy is a relational and not a linear concept; it is a dialogical, not strictly a psychological, one. It is not an avenue to knowing with certainty the meanings of another, but a way of checking on, and affirming, otherness. Empathy is a way of being in relationship, something created with another person, and certainly not something done to another. It cannot be reduced to a list of tips for active listening.[7] This "reflection of feelings" has been taught as a "wooden technique," Rogers lamented in one of his last publications. "I am not trying to 'reflect feelings,'" he wrote; "I am trying to determine whether my understanding of the client's inner world is correct—whether I am seeing it as he or she is experiencing it at this moment" (1986b, p. 376).

Friedman (1986) and Stewart and Thomas (1986) justifiably criticize Rogers for a passage (1980, pp. 142–143) in which he writes that an empathic communicator "lays aside" self in order to enter "the perceptual world of the other." This passage appears inconsistent with dialogical thinking, because it suggests abandoning one's own ground in a relationship, and because it implies that an empathic communicator can reproduce accurately the other's feelings, thoughts, and intentions. But this passage is atypical, as Friedman noted (1986, p. 428); Rogers persistently warned against the therapist losing touch with his or her ground or personal uniqueness in empathy, as we have seen. How, then, can his "laying aside self" comment be explained? First, the passage appears in a book in which Rogers attempted to write personally and informally, often through reminiscence, for a wide lay audience. This was hardly a theoretical essay. Second, the passage appears not as a primary definition but as an informal elaboration of a prior definition; it appears in the same essay as, and soon after, his "highly rigorous" and "formal" 1959 definition that clearly states the "as if" qualification cited above. Third, the passage in question is highly metaphorical, imprecise, and qualified ("In some sense it means that you lay aside yourself . . ."), no doubt to appeal to his large nonscholarly audience. In context, Rogers is only reminding us that our own values and views are necessarily different from the other's, and to expect this uniqueness. Finally, he admits in his next section that the popularized statement to which his critics object is "hardly an operational definition" (1980, p. 143). Rogers here is not being self-contradictory as much as he is being rhetorically sensitive to the expectations of an audience not inclined to theoretical and philosophical nuances.

Another criticism equates Rogers's empathy with psychologizing—psychological, internal, purely reproduce-the-other's-intent listening—in contrast to seemingly more rich forms of interpretive, hermeneutic, or productive listening. Most listening theorists stress that listening is both reproductive (attempting to understand another's meaning as he or she does) and productive (stimulating a freer play of meaning involving insights that likely transcend another's intentions). As far as we are aware, Rogers talked about listening per se largely in practical terms to lay audiences. Otherwise, he did not isolate this part of his communicative praxis. Empathy for Rogers was a way of being, not merely a way of listening, and can be isolated from congruence and regard only for purposes of discussion. When empathy, congruence, and regard are seen as closely integrated, Rogers seems in step with Stewart (1983) and Gadamer (1982), and surely far from the hypothetical conversational caricatures that have sometimes appeared (e.g., Arnett & Nakagawa, 1983, p. 373; Stewart & Thomas, 1986, p. 182).

Carl Rogers, of course, was an American psychologist whose clinical work was primarily with individuals. It should surprise no one that such a practitioner could be said to approach his work with some form of relatively individualized praxis. He understood from his background and education that the person is inherently important and that the pursuit of that which enhances the individual's freedom is a predominant value. As a psychologist, he was trained not only in a scientific method founded on prediction and control and on operationalism, but also in the belief that the real stuff of human life and of therapy is psychological. *Against that training*, Rogers struggled throughout his career to find a vocabulary in which he could express the reality of human relationship as he experienced it. Although he was a psychologist, his focus was beyond the psyche and on dialogue. Rogers urged empathy in order to recognize and, to borrow Sampson's (1993) term, "celebrate otherness," not to mind-read or to size up or diagnose clients as if they were objects of analysis. He did not have a background in European phenomenological thought, but surely Gadamer's (1982) description of being open to otherness would resonate for Rogers as well:

> In human relations the important thing is . . . to experience the "Thou" truly as a "Thou," ie [sic] not to overlook his claim and to listen to what he has to say to us. To this end, openness is necessary. But this openness exists ultimately not only for the person to whom one listens, but rather anyone who listens is fundamentally open. Without this kind of openness to one another there is no genuine human relationship. . . . When two people understand each other, this does not mean that one person "understands" the other, in the sense of surveying him. (p. 324)

Yet this quotation is applied by Stewart (1983, pp. 383–384) to show the difference between the reproductive empathic listening paradigm and the more effective productive interpretive listening paradigm. Clearly Rogers often discussed empathy in terms that Stewart (1983; Stewart & Thomas, 1986) has labeled "reproductive" listening. In his work as a therapist it was essential to be open to and to understand the feelings and meanings of the other — to "reproduce" them, as accurately as he could, in himself so the client (for instance) would feel understood. But Rogers also recognized, even if he discussed it less often, the process in which self and other share in participating in and "producing" meaning together. Rogers extended his notion of empathy far beyond the so-called reproductive or reflective listening (Bowen, 1986; Rogers, 1986a). Of course, Rogers attempted to understand the other's inner directions and intentions, but a therapist or any other respondent must also use intuition and other interpretive capacities to let new meanings emerge. Bowen (1986) used excerpts from Rogers's interviews to illustrate a Rogerian form of empathic response she terms "integrative impressions." These integrative impressions do not simply support or reflect the other's meanings, but also can identify underlying issues, create new and striking metaphors in an interpretive way similar to that advocated by Stewart and Thomas (1986), and suggest the use of behavioral and imaginative experiments in order to integrate emergent meanings (Bowen, 1986, pp. 303–306). David Cain (1996) uses the term "inferential empathy" to refer to a similar process.

Unlike Buber, Gadamer, and other philosophers, Rogers was not schooled in a tradition of European phenomenology or existential thought. Moreover, Rogers worked professionally as a therapist, not as a philosopher. His work demonstrates neither the systematic consistency nor the careful explication of all the implications of ideas that would be expected of a professional philosopher. Rogers was attempting to articulate the relationally oriented conception of human life that he experienced (including the role of empathy) with inadequate preparation and in an inhospitable environment. He also tried, in very practical ways, to give people ideas that could help them and, as we said earlier, attempted to do so in terms they could understand readily.

FACILITATING DIALOGUE

In addition to identifying three basic elements of growth-promoting communication, Rogers also discussed the priorities among them and described their functional interrelationships within dyads or small groups. At different times Rogers emphasized one of these core conditions over the others. Often he described congruence as the beginning and fundamental point of effective communication in and out of therapy. Later, Rogers focused more on empathy. Our own reading of the research evidence on this issue parallels his: "Over the years, . . . the research evidence has kept piling up, and it points strongly to the conclusion that a high degree of empathy in a relationship is possibly *the* most potent factor in bringing about change and learning" (Rogers, 1980, p. 139). Nevertheless, research also shows that empathy, genuineness, and respect are often, but not always or necessarily, significantly and positively correlated (Cissna & Keating, 1979, p. 53; Truax & Carkhuff, 1967, pp. 132–133).

Rogers also speculated that each of these three elements might assume priority in different situations. In ordinary relationships between spouses, friends, colleagues, teachers and students, and parents and children, congruence "is probably the most important element." In nonverbally based relationships such as parent and infant, therapist and mute psychotic, or physician and very ill patient, prizing, caring, or regard "may turn out to be the most significant element." Finally, in helping situations, when dealing with a hurt, troubled, anxious, or alienated person—one "doubtful of self-worth, uncertain as to identity"—then "the empathic way of being has the highest priority" (1980, p. 160).

In an interpersonal relationship, congruence on the part of one person most often is experienced by the other as clear communication. This encourages greater congruence in the other as well. Sensitive empathy helps the other to feel understood and to experience positive regard to some degree. Positive regard or prizing of another allows him or her to feel more caring about self, although it never can guarantee that result. As the second person's feelings of being prized and understood lead to greater caring for the self and more accurate listening to internal messages of the self, the enhanced self-caring and self-listening help him or her to be more congruent. An interplay exists between two partners in dialogue such that when one partner is able to listen more sensitively, to respond with greater caring and respect, or to be more careful in identifying and expressing feelings and needs, both parties and the relationship tend to benefit (Noel & De Chenne, 1974).

For Buber, genuine dialogue occurs "where each of the participants really has in mind the other or others in their present and particular being and turns to them with the intention of establishing a living mutual relation between himself and them" (1965a, p. 19). "The basic movement of the life of dialogue," he reminds us, "is the turning towards the other" (p. 22), and this is precisely the goal of Rogers's therapy. Rogers's thought can also be integrated into other definitions of dialogue. Poulakos (1974) describes dialogue as "a mode of existence manifested in the intersubjective activity between two partners, who, in their quest for meaning in life, stand before each other prepared to meet the uniqueness of their situation and follow it wherever it may lead" (p. 199). Arnett (1989) paraphrases Friedman (1960) in describing dialogue as involving "'meeting' the other as a person, not as an object, being sensitive to the relational nature of communication, responding to the unique, concrete other, and recognizing that one must start with oneself, but 'real' living begins in the partnership of dialogue" (p. 47).[8] For such reasons, the philosopher Abraham Kaplan (1969) prefers to identify dialogue with "communion" (p. 98).

Dialogue, therefore, identifies a quality of human relationships that is experienced on a moment-to-moment basis and which, as Rogers discovered, can be characterized productively by several core relationship and communication conditions. When these conditions are present to a significant degree, dialogue is probably occurring. Rogers refuses to provide a set of techniques, despite the popular misconception that client-centered therapy is based on such techniques as "reflecting feelings"; no formulas can guarantee dialogue (see Farson, 1978). Fundamentally, the core conditions are facilitative relational attitudes that find expression in behavior. They are invitations that open the space for dialogue. For Rogers dialogue is a potential of human life that no person or relationship will actualize all the time. Although one may be able to enhance its likelihood through attention to the core conditions, Rogers, Buber, and Friedman all emphasize that dialogue is not something one person can will. Further, any "therapeutic gains" one may achieve in empathy, regard, and congruence in one moment must be reclaimed in every new relationship, every new encounter.

CONCLUSION

Across the span of a half-century career as therapist, researcher, teacher, group facilitator, intercultural representative, and popular author, Carl Rogers developed a sophisticated praxis of dialogue that others have built on and advanced. This is a contribution of philosophical praxis for which he is insufficiently credited. He was not an advocate of a simplistic and slavish devotion to a static "true self"; he did not encourage total or indiscriminate disclosure; he did not want to abolish social roles; and he did not present empathy as if it meant giving up one's own ground in the relationship or as if it were a mere technique for "reflecting feelings." Some of the misunderstanding of his thought may have stemmed from his perhaps unrealistic attempts to reach both professional and lay audiences simultaneously. Certainly, some of his popular writing on empathy, for example, must be read by academics in the context of his scholarly theoretical writing and experience. The other side of this coin is brighter, though, in that he brought an essentially dialogic message to a wider range of professionals and lay audiences because of his breadth of application even when the conceptual distinctions were less precise than some scholars would have liked.

Rogers clearly did not try to mimic philosophers, but broke his own pragmatic ground. This was reasonable, for "the 'dialectic of humanness' cannot be captured by any one approach, but must emerge at times in conflict between approaches" (Arnett, 1986, p. 67). Despite the intellectual debts Rogers often cited, the most persistent source for his view of dialogue was his experience with clients and group members all over the world. The wisdom of the dialogical perspective he shared came less from ethical "shoulds" or prior philosophical commitments than from the always-changing practice in which he saw trust emerge under extraordinarily trying circumstances. In this way, Rogers may have contributed as much to our collective hope for dialogue as anyone else in this century.

John K. Wood, a former colleague at the Center for Studies of the Person, understood Rogers's reliance on communication and praxis:

> Rogers practiced therapy through a method that does not work for some, but worked superbly for him. His practice was purity itself. He practiced with an intense and devoted desire to listen and to understand, and with genuineness and acceptance he adapted to the situation and his client. Rogers was also curious, good humored, humble, believed he could help, and that it was the most important thing in the world he could do at that moment. He also exerted a steel will to make this belief a reality. (1988, p. 388)

It is difficult, and more than a little dispiriting, to see how such a life and praxis has stimulated so much derision among critics. Criticism is natural, and every strongly stated position will have, and should have, opponents. Yet many dismissals of Rogers from some quarters have become so automatic, and often so virulent, that we must ask ourselves whether they match well with the actual work he did.

Rogers demonstrated one way of opening ourselves to dialogue. He exemplified the importance of listening and caring in growthful human relationships. He showed how confirming otherness by listening carefully can occur both in and out of therapy, and his work grounded dialogue as a more accessible human possibility in everyday life. His was a unifying philosophical praxis of dialogue, complex yet enactable.

CHAPTER FIVE

Historical Context and the Buber–Rogers Meeting

> Conversing with the other . . . necessitates both the
> construction of sameness and familiarity and the
> recognition of otherness and strangeness. The true
> understanding of dialogue may be reached only when
> disparate selves are acknowledged within the larger
> common framework of meaning.
> —Z. D. Gurevitch, "The Other Side of Dialogue"

> Everyday talk, as well as formal dialogues, does not
> take place in isolation. Each turn or move of the
> ongoing discourse as well as the whole verbal exchange
> is an integral part of a situation and inextricably
> connected with a relevant selection of social objects,
> namely, the context. . . . [T]his context is not objective
> but is an intersubjectively interpreted or constructed
> setting.
> —T. A. van Dijk, "Dialogue as
> Discourse and Interaction"

It might be tempting to assume that Martin Buber and Carl Rogers approached their meeting fully aware of its importance for future students of dialogue. In that case, the two would have realized their dialogue had important conceptual implications—even "momentous" ones, in Friedman's (1994, p. 47) estimation—that would eclipse contemporary expectations for the event. They might even have prepared differently for it if they had known that a single unrehearsed conversation would span eras for scholars. Had they anticipated its future importance, organizers might have kept detailed records of the planning and logistics of the occasion, and we would have a more reliable historical record than the one we've been forced to piece together from widely dispersed notes, programs, letters, recollections, and news accounts. Someone might have thought even to take a photograph of Buber and Rogers together. Unfortunately, as far as we've been able to determine, no systematic records were kept, and no joint photo of the two men—or any photograph of this event—exists.

No one, famous or not, can predict fully how later generations will attribute meaning to public talk. Certainly neither Buber nor Rogers had many clues that their moment on stage, while interesting in the temporary context of this three-day conference on Buber, might seem pivotal to future intellectual historians.

They took the event seriously, and brought off the occasion successfully for each other and for the audience. Yet Buber himself evidently had relatively low expectations for the dialogue and, as chapter 1 described, it was once considered marginal enough to be dropped for a time from the tentative program. Both Buber and Rogers undoubtedly framed the dialogue in terms of what they perceived as somewhat larger issues in their lives—issues that affected both what they said to each other and how they subsequently explored the ideas raised in the conversation. We examine those personal commitments in this chapter, as well as the role of intellectual context in shaping talk. Despite some similarities in their thought, quite different background influences affected Buber and Rogers even as they prepared for their conversation. With the exception of some of Maurice Friedman's biographical work on Buber, the context for the dialogue is essentially unexamined in the literature.

Rogers evidently experienced the dialogue as a valuable opportunity to meet an admired kindred spirit face to face, but also, at least in part, as an opportunity to receive support from Buber for his position vis-à-vis both psychoanalysts and behaviorists in the psychological community. Buber, as a more senior scholar who was retired from his teaching post, probably experienced the dialogue in quite different contexts—he was to some extent thinking about his legacy in the intellectual world and attempting to synthesize key ideas in readily available collected volumes. He was refining a series of lectures and essays in his second U.S. tour, and encountered Rogers at a time when psychology in Buber's estimation was generally in "crisis" (Friedman, 1983c, p. 207). We must remember, too, that for this prominent Jewish philosopher,

World War II and the specter of the Holocaust were barely a decade past, and Buber, among others, was seeking to account for the existence of antihuman forces within a secular and increasingly technologized world in which God was in "eclipse" (Buber, 1952). After examining the intellectual milieus of Buber and Rogers more fully, we describe how such matters of intellectual and cultural context influence our perceptions of the potential for public dialogue itself.

Although the content of the dialogue has been explicated relatively often, and although Buber's participation has been considered in the context of his 1957 U.S. lecture tour, scholars have tended to neglect the complexity of Rogers's participation and contributions, and his role has never been considered in the context of his own career and immediate intellectual involvements of 1957.

BUBER'S WORLD IN 1957

As Grete Schaeder (1991) noted, "The years 1957 and 1958 were high points in Buber's creative vigor and world renown" (p. 56). His influence across disciplines and traditions of thought, long recognized in Europe and especially among German-speaking intellectuals, had by this time become well known in the English-speaking world also. The classic *I and Thou*, first published in 1922, waited fifteen years to be translated into English (by Ronald Gregor Smith), but after World War II, Buber's fame as a commentator on the human condition spread rapidly. Almost inexplicably, however, *I and Thou* would not be published in the United States until the year following the Buber–Rogers dialogue.

Buber's Career at Mid-Century

Buber toured Europe in early 1947, presenting over sixty lectures in six countries (Schaeder, 1991, p. 54). Shortly thereafter, an impressive series of his works began to be published in many countries, appealing to a broad and growing intellectual audience for his style of spiritual and humane engagement. He first visited the United States in 1951–52, speaking not only about his philosophical anthropology but also finding himself a designated spokesperson for worldwide themes of Jewish identity and thought. Buber not only lectured during his visits to campuses, but also taught various courses in theology and philosophy.

One of his stops was at the University of Chicago's Rockefeller Chapel. Carl Rogers could have heard Buber speak on his campus.

According to Maurice Friedman (1983c, p. 147), about two thousand people crowded into the chapel, reflecting the intellectual significance of the lecture for a wide array of disciplines. Surely Rogers would have tried to attend if possible; around that time he was planning a seminar in which Buber's dialogue would be explored in terms of both counseling theory and democratic communication principles (see his syllabus: Rogers, 1952). However, indirect evidence suggests he probably was not in the audience. Not only does Rogers's correspondence at the time not mention Buber's lecture, but no one we talked to could recall him describing it. In addition, Rogers's opening remarks in their dialogue do not mention hearing Buber lecture a few years earlier, but easily could have ("it was only an hour or two ago that I met Dr. Buber, even though I have met him a long time ago in his writings" [turn #3]).

Lecture tours allowed Buber to explore ideas in front of audiences and also provided, as with many writers, occasions to finish essays in process. In a 1956 tour of Europe, he explored issues of commonality by which human beings could be united meaningfully even in their diversity. "What is Common to All," an important essay for Buber's later philosophy, originated in a lecture refined in these 1956 speaking engagements. It was in this essay that Buber contrasted his philosophy of otherness and difference with other philosophical systems stressing the essence of unity:

> When taken seriously in the factual, waking continuity of intercourse with one another, the ancient Hindu "That art thou" becomes the postulate of an annihilation of the human person, one's own person as well as the other; for the person is through and through nothing other than uniqueness and thus essentially other than all that is over against it. And even if that supposed universal Self should remain in the ground of the I, it could no longer have intercourse with anyone. But we see in human existence, in the intercourse of men with one another that grows out of it, the chance for meeting between existing being and existing being. In this meeting each of the two certainly does not say to himself, "He over there is you," but perhaps each says to the other, "I accept you as you are." Here first is uncurtailed existence. (1965b, p. 96)

For Buber, whatever philosophical or ethical systems might *say* about a unified human self, actual people in concrete everyday situations respond to, and define their existence in terms of, difference. When he employs the unusual phrase "all that is over against" uniqueness, Buber was not suggesting interpersonal conflict or dissension by the word "against," but simply that we constantly define our lives in terms of comparisons. We forever live at or near borders of difference. It is not useful to assimilate others to yourself in an artificial, tidy, or polite unity; rather, dialogue and "uncurtailed existence" mean that what is common to humanity is the experience of otherness that can be fully accepted: "I accept you as you are" (Rogers's use of "acceptance" in therapy is strikingly similar). Stated this way, otherness does not separate persons irretrievably, but is the very thing that creates the possibility of a world: "Man has always had his experiences as I, his experiences with others, and with himself; but it is as We, ever again as We, that he has constructed and developed a world out of his experiences" (1965b, p. 107).

What humankind has in common must have weighed heavily on Buber's mind as the Jewish scholar struggled to reconcile the unfathomable horror of the Holocaust with an abiding faith in the human capacity for dialogue. The ordeal of World War II was hardly a decade past, a nightmare in which over 6 million Jews and other minorities were murdered and countless others openly persecuted. When Buber was awarded the Peace Prize of the German Book Trade four years before his dialogue with Rogers, he commented on this curious choice from the German literary establishment and how he, a prominent Jew, felt at receiving an award in a country that had in many ways countenanced the evil of the Nazis: "I, who am one of those who remained alive, have only in a formal sense a common humanity with those who took part in this action" (1957c, p. 232). Buber's acceptance speech developed a theme that would also arise in his conversation with Rogers: how good and evil affect the experience of everyday citizens. As he said in concluding his speech, "The name Satan means in Hebrew the hinderer. That is the correct designation for the anti-human in individuals and in the human race" (p. 239). Evil is what keeps us from saying yes to dialogue. Buber's belief that refusing the possibility of meaningful relation constituted evil was reflected in his comment to Rogers in 1957 that human nature is not to be described in terms of good or bad but is instead "polar" in the sense of yes and no (turns #100ff.). Obviously, the atrocities of the war years would have maintained their intense hold on Buber these few years later.

For readers many decades later to understand how close Buber was in the mid-1950s to his experience of Hitler's regime, they must recall some sort of emotional landmark, perhaps a parent's memory of the birth of a child, and realize that the time between World War II and Buber's conversation with Rogers was barely longer than the time between the child's birth and when he or she might be allowed to ride a bicycle to school alone in a safe neighborhood. Or, taken another way, it is only several years longer than the administration of a reelected U.S. president. In other words, World War II's emotional wounds were still experienced as immediate and concrete, and Buber, among many others, was still struggling to understand the widespread acceptance of Hitler's inhuman rhetoric and the devastation it created.

By his second visit to America in 1957, Buber's fame had grown so much that entire conferences were devoted to his thought; they drew important figures from the academic and intellectual community, as well as newspaper reporters from local papers. At the time, the initial stimulus—and the acknowledged high point—for this tour was Buber's William Alanson White Lectures at the Washington School of Psychiatry in Washington, D.C. There, Buber discussed "Elements of the Interhuman," "Distance and Relation," and "Guilt and Guilt Feelings" (originally titled "Guilt and Modern Psychology"), which were published in the journal *Psychiatry* and subsequently revised for one of Buber's most accessible books, *The Knowledge of Man*, published in 1965. The 1957 tour, which included lectures at Princeton University, Northwestern University, and the University of Chicago, as well as the conference at Michigan to which Rogers was invited, was so successful that he returned to the United States the next year to deliver more lectures and participate in a seminar on "Key Religious Concepts of the Great Civilizations." It would hardly be an exaggeration to call Buber at mid-century one of the world's most influential intellectuals.

Buber's Intellectual Commitments at Mid-Century

In chapter 3, we examined Buber's commitment to adult education in Israel, an interest that extended the commitment to Jewish adult education he began in Germany in the 1930s. In addition, he was an advocate for Jewish-Arab dialogue, much to the chagrin of Prime Minister David Ben-Gurion and other Israeli political figures. In both of these efforts Buber extended the principle of dialogic relation based on recognizing otherness in concrete situations, even when conflict and frustration were inevitable.

Perhaps most important for his meeting with Rogers, Buber recently had been evaluating the contributions of psychology to the modern world. As he would mention to Rogers at their dialogue, he studied psychology and psychiatry when he was a student, and had some background in its issues and intellectual status. When Leslie Farber, the chair of the faculty at the Washington School of Psychiatry, invited Buber, he specifically mentioned his awareness that Buber had been working on a critique of Freud (Farber, 1991, pp. 595–596). This piece, which was never completed in its projected form, was originally intended by Buber to be one of the Washington lectures. In addition, Buber's critique of Jung, regarded by Buber as the leading psychologist of the era, was well known at the time (Friedman, 1983c, pp. 170ff.).

When Buber replied to Farber's invitation, he specifically referred to a revision of psychological concepts that he could suggest: "The ultimate question should be: What can anthropology, as I understand it, give psychology?" (Buber, 1991a, p. 597). Buber had written to Maurice Friedman in early 1956 about his "conviction that all the main concepts of psychology are 'in crisis'" (Friedman, 1983c, p. 207). Buber, however, was no opponent of psychology. He believed psychologists were important in the modern world. However, for years he had critiqued what he termed "psychologism"—the tendency for people to believe that the most valid and elemental experience is internal, individual, and psychological rather than based on interhuman meeting. Presumably the thrust of this criticism was directed at Freudian and Jungian psychologies.

Interestingly, Rogers, in later years, would speculate that what he considered Buber's misinterpretation of some of what he said in their meeting might have been based on Buber's connecting such issues as schizophrenia to the earlier psychologies he studied as a young student at the turn of the twentieth century rather than with Rogers's own client-centered therapy (which he presented as a radical break with psychological and psychoanalytic tradition). Late in his life Rogers told oral historian David Russell (Rogers & Russell, 1991) that Buber denied the possibility of therapy with a schizophrenic, but, referring to their dialogue together noted that "I said, 'I just had such an interview with a schizophrenic before leaving,' and he didn't understand that at all" (p. 201). In fact, Rogers misremembered what he said—he did not specifically mention a particular interview. But he did recall that "the next morning at breakfast we talked again and I found that his courses in psychiatry had been around the year 1900 when dementia praecox [schizophrenia] was [considered to be] a real damage to the brain, and so on. So he was thinking that I couldn't possibly have an equalitarian relationship with someone who was so damaged" (p. 201).

However, Buber's understanding of psychology was evidently often on the mark. His powerful critique was influential with the Washington school and also with later generations of dialogical psychotherapists (e.g., Hycner, 1991). Psychology, Buber believed, must consider the limits of human existence with more care. Although therapists can help those who come to them, they should recognize more fully the normative limits that characterize the therapeutic relationship. This issue would be raised in the April Buber–Rogers dialogue, but Buber was well prepared to respond when Rogers brought it up. Just prior to the Michigan conference, Buber had heard a similar question from therapist Margaret Rioch, who wanted to know Buber's thoughts on the therapist-patient and teacher-student roles (Friedman, 1983c, p. 223). During the Washington seminars, Buber was also moved to talk about a personal experience with a friend who had been treated for schizophrenia, and that tragic condition was probably also on his mind as he participated in the Michigan conference. His friend, who had been helped by therapy to make some behavioral adjustments, was nevertheless not healed, in Buber's estimation, of his "atrophied personal center" (Friedman, 1983c, pp. 221–222). His friend's experience might have bolstered Buber's belief, later to be expressed during the dialogue with Rogers, that schizophrenics are "shut" in some ways and unavailable for relatively mutualized relations with therapists. The limitations of the therapeutic context meant that the therapist had sufficient resources for acknowledging his or her own experience and the experience of the "patient," while the one seeking help did not and could not have the same resources for imagining how real another person's experience would be for them. Thus, although dialogue can be encouraged in such a context, its quality will be transitory, and it could never develop into a fully equal relationship.

Buber's concern with limits within the roles of therapy did not mean that he sanctioned the tendency of many psychoanalysts to rely on authority and even, some would say, authoritarian tactics in diagnosing patients' difficulties. Buber thought that meeting others in relationship was itself a healing process, and wished for a psychology generally—and a psychotherapy more specifically—that encouraged dialogue. He was much impressed with Leslie Farber's essay relating his own work to psychiatry, and wrote to Farber that "We need now in psychology, as elsewhere, a phase of real freedom" (Friedman, 1983c, p. 206). In addition, his "Healing Through Meeting" essay, written in 1951 and reprinted in *Pointing the Way* (1957), suggested that, at the time, academic and professional psychology was dominated either by Freudian and Jungian psychoanalysts or by the emerging empiricism of behaviorists, all of whom employed modes of therapy based on systems of expert knowledge and methods normal people could not hope to possess. Among American psychologists there were few who agreed with Buber more than the man he was about to meet in Ann Arbor, and few who shared more thoroughly his double-edged critique of psychoanalysis and behaviorism.

In 1956 and 1957, Buber was considering a new edition of *I and Thou*, to be published also in the United States, and asked Friedman to prepare a list of questions people had about this work (Friedman, 1983c, p. 252). Although the book was well known in the global intellectual community, it was also notorious for its ambiguous passages and densely poetic syntax. Although he was reluctant later to revise it to improve readability, he still wanted his most famous work to be relevant for the intellectual community. As it turns out, some of the facets of *I and Thou* that he clarified in his postscript to the 1958 edition involved psychological and psychotherapeutic implications. At least one passage reads as if it was a direct reply to Rogers (pp. 131–134).

Some months after the Rogers dialogue, Buber used the forum of a *New York Post* interview article to propose a "grand dialogue" (Friedman, 1983c, p. 310) on a global scale. This meeting, to be held in secret, would bring together philosophers and other intellectual leaders to discuss what citizens of the world hold in common; they would then return to their respective countries to convince political leaders and other opinion leaders of the benefits of peace. Buber was the kind of philosopher who was visionary in two senses: he not only generated compelling visions, but he did what he thought he could to enact them concretely. Friedman (1983c) described this venture as an end run around political interests:

> Again Buber proposed a grand dialogue between the disinterested, independent spirits of East and West, bypassing the politicians, diplomats, hucksters, and journalists for "philosophers," persons who think independently about the roots of things, and about the ends as well as the means. An occasional politician of sufficient intellectual independence might be welcomed to such an experimental dialogue, which Buber said should be secret so that the members could talk unreservedly to one another, and only after the conferees had come to some meeting of minds—*if* they did—should they try to influence the politicians of their respective countries. The presidents of the high courts of justice of various lands might be one type of representative, although the best would be the real spiritual representatives of each people, if these could be determined (they would not, Buber opined, be identical with the heads of the various churches). As long as peace can be maintained, Buber saw hope for all despite the world crisis. (p. 310)

Earlier in the decade, Buber had told his American friend Robert Maynard Hutchins that such a dialogue among spiritual leaders should not involve the press and the public, contrary to what Hutchins advocated in suggesting a worldwide intellectual dialogue in the United States: "I had opposed rather strongly the introducing of an atmosphere of publicity into such talks," he said, "one drop of publicity being sufficient to poison the whole undertaking" (Friedman, 1983c, p. 188).

We can speculate that when Buber and Rogers met they were exploring different tributaries of the concept of public dialogue. Their positions—as we have suggested and will explore in more detail in chapter 8—revisited, although inexactly, the John Dewey–Walter Lippmann interchange from the first decades of the century about what constitutes an educated democratic public. Whereas Rogers's position was closer to philosopher John Dewey's faith in the everyday person's resources of strength, understanding, and response, Buber's perspective—while far from elitist and quite different from Lippmann's in many ways—resonated to a more European tone. His mistrust of public dialogue was similar to that of Dewey's intellectual sparring partner. Lippmann argued that only select members of a democracy have the perspective, the resources, and the breadth of knowledge about social issues to deliberate in depth and make effective decisions about the public good, although a vigorous journalism can certainly widen effective political participation. Lippmann was suspicious of Dewey's (1916) optimism when Dewey assured readers that "democracy" is a form of extended public mutuality:

> More than a form of government, it is a mode of associated living, of conjoint communicated experience. The extension in space of the number of individuals who participate in an interest so that each has to refer his own action to that of others to give point and direction to his own, is equivalent to the breaking down of those barriers of class, race and national territory which kept men from perceiving the full import of their activity. (p. 101)

Such concerns still chart the dialectic of our faith in a public, indeed in a conversational, democracy.

Buber, as a European Jewish professor steeped in the history of tensions among cultural, religious, and ethnic elites, was concerned for good reason with the fragility of dialogue, even as he recommended it and believed in its necessity. Dewey's American model of a widening dialogue that is constantly starting over, constantly inviting the freedom to make mistakes, and make them publicly, estranged many European cultural critics and philosophers. To Buber, for example, media technologies did not present inviting opportunities for including wider audiences in the rhetoric of the interhuman realm. Rather, they were agencies of dehumanization, and they imposed artificial impediments between conversants that could stifle the genuineness and presence of dialogue.

Buber believed audiences presented nearly insurmountable obstacles for dialogue partners who strove for candor in discussing issues and relationships. As we have seen, he had recently claimed that public attempts at dialogue were "separated by a chasm from genuine dialogue" (Buber, 1957b, p. 113). Because the contemporary age was motivated by propaganda motives more than dialogical ones, it created more anonymous audiences. Public interaction encouraged what he called "seeming" (conforming to roles and image expectations of others, for example) rather than "being" (spontaneous and flexible behavior responsive to a situation). In contrast, Rogers, who was also interested in problems of seeming versus being, as his emphasis on genuineness in therapy demonstrates, was developing a more fluid and optimistic philosophy of the dynamics of public meeting, and—influenced early in his career by many of Dewey's ideas—was seemingly more tolerant of its fits and starts, its failures and dysfluencies. Just as clients can energize therapists, audiences, even large and public ones, can energize dialogue. If clients can teach themselves and their therapists about their own life tragedies without even being expert in their diagnoses, perhaps everyday people in public groups can create real conditions of dialogue—if we accept the inefficiencies, the occasional posing and politicized playing to an audience, and the possibility of being surprised by the talk of nonexperts. It is no accident that Rogers's work after his dialogue with Buber became not only more self-referentially dialogic, but also became far more public, and increasingly less focused on narrowly professional applications. Rogers's vision, like Dewey's, was to intellectualize less and publicize the theories and hypotheses from his psychotherapy work to broader and more prosaic everyday situations. Almost all of his subsequent books, starting with *On Becoming a Person* (1961), appealed to both professional and lay readers.

Despite his suspicions, Buber was not opposed to all forms of public talk that could develop dialogic characteristics. He often encouraged public educational settings in which the surprises and tensions of dialogue were present. The difference was that Buber often expected that a primary interchange was between a single communicator—usually an expert commentator whose credibility could be established—and

the genuine issues, concerns, criticisms, and questions raised spontaneously by audiences who listen attentively and are willing to risk
themselves in response.

The ideal form for this educational public dialogue, Buber appeared
to believe, was when listeners questioned him about his ideas. According to a variety of sources, he enjoyed the process of audiences seeking
clarifications of his thought, or asking him about its implications.
Through this give-and-take, he often articulated nuances and extensions of ideas he'd not explored before. Buber believed that in a very
real and tangible sense, he learned more about what he believed when
others elicited those beliefs by good questioning. On such occasions, he
was clearly the expert and the focus for the talk, yet he was an expert
who admitted he didn't have all the answers. He was committed to
open-minded thinking on his feet. Seminars and question-answer sessions for Buber, therefore, were not intellectually stale recitations of
what he already believed, but occasions for fresh thinking. He did not
appreciate questions that simply set up or requested reiterations of
older ideas nor did he encourage questions that suggested the questioner was quibbling rather than really inquiring. For example, Friedman (1983c) observed that during Buber's first U.S. tour, "In the most
public settings he would only answer 'real questions,' questions in
which the questioner staked herself or himself. 'This is really pilpul,'
Buber said of [one] question that night" ("pilpul" referring to when
Talmudic study became silly and hair-splitting) (p. 148).

In Rogers, Buber would encounter a questioner who generated real
questions, one who would keep the focus on the visiting scholar, one
who would listen intently to the responses, one who could elicit fresh
disclosures from Buber, and one who, as Buber would remark later to
Friedman, really brought himself honestly as a person. Rogers, of
course, had a stake in the questions because of his own personal and
professional milieu in 1957.

ROGERS'S WORLD IN 1957

Martin Buber's conversation partner was a man whom his contemporaries saw as a rising—if controversial—star in the academic firmament.
Rogers prospered while living and teaching in the rich interdisciplinary
environment of the University of Chicago, the institution of Buber's
friend Hutchins and a school whose tradition symbolized the intellectual turn to community service as a goal of higher education (Rudolph,
1962, p. 356). After World War II, psychologist John Shlien (1997) wrote,

the Chicago campus was a "neighborhood" (p. 67) of ideas, many of which supported "empathy" as a way of knowing and understanding human relationships. At various times, the university had been the academic community of John Dewey, Robert Park, George Herbert Mead, Herbert Blumer, and others whose versions of symbolic interactionist philosophy and social psychology would revolutionize interpretive approaches to social science. The Division of Social Sciences was "full of intellectual and interdisciplinary ferment" (p. 68), with Bruno Bettelheim and Heinz Kohut achieving prominence. Rogers, "already a major figure" (p. 68) at Chicago, had begun to elaborate how the concepts and research reported in his 1951 book, *Client-Centered Therapy*, could be applied as a philosophy of therapy designed to assist everyday citizens in a wide range of direct and concrete ways. Rogers and his counseling center exemplified the university's commitment to community service as it radically repositioned therapeutic role expectations toward a learning/listening model in which the client explicitly functioned as the expert regarding his or her own life.

Rogers's Career at Mid-Century

As we suggested in previous chapters, Rogers hypothesized that people he worked with were not resourceless and in need of expert intervention, as a medical model would suggest, but instead could summon impressive resources of their own if they were listened to as persons rather than as objects. Consequently, his therapy treated patients as "clients," and redefined in many ways the psychotherapist's role as a helping, facilitative one. These were more than semantic changes; they effected a radically different interpersonal politics that won Rogers a measure of notoriety, some friends, and much derision within his own field.

On 2 September 1956, during the fall semester before meeting Buber in April, Rogers was one of only three scholars honored with a "Distinguished Scientific Contribution" award sponsored by the American Psychological Association, the organization he served as president ten years earlier. Rogers's honor, given in the first year of the award, was for work representing a "lifetime or a significant portion thereof . . . [of] distinguished contributions to the development of the science of psychology" ("The American Psychological Association," 1957, p. 125). Although Rogers was justifiably proud of this professional recognition, portions of the citation supporting it might have rankled or at least surprised him. In addition to formulating a "testable theory of psychotherapy and its effects on personality and behavior" and the "extensive systematic research" to test the theory, he was honored for "developing an original method to *objectify* the description and analysis of the psychotherapeutic process," and for his understanding of the problems of "understanding and *modification* of the *individual* person" (p. 128; emphasis added). Even in honoring Rogers, his professional colleagues managed to translate his ideas into a language of objectification and control. Still, this honor, bestowed only months before the dialogue with Buber, to some extent symbolized Rogers's faith in testing inferences and theories by applying the solid facts of everyday direct experience. He was curious about philosophies such as Buber's, even intrigued by them, but, as we stress in chapter 4, it was the concern with praxis that distinguished his work and won adherents. He brought to the conversation with Buber a humanist's values, a scientist's concern for data and evidence, and an engineer's interest in what works.

By 1957, the year of the dialogue, the waves Rogers was making within psychotherapy began to break on wider and more distant shores. *Time* magazine profiled him and the counseling center at Chicago ("Person-to-Person," 1957), writing that Rogers was a "maverick" whose ideas about therapy were distinctly non-Freudian but seemingly effective. The article quotes one opponent, however, who "snort[ed]" that "Rogers' method is unsystematic, undisciplined and humanistic. Rogers doesn't analyze and doesn't diagnose. We have no common ground" (p. 34). Rogers, if not as famous worldwide as Buber, also had become controversial and newsworthy in ways few professors could expect.

The *Time* article was not his first brush with a more public fame. The previous year, Rogers had been mentioned in April and again in September on national television newscasts by American Broadcasting Company commentator Edward P. Morgan, one of the most popular celebrity broadcasters of the day. Rogers and his work was discussed in the context of whether modern life dehumanized and manipulated persons. In September, Morgan described for his viewers the 1956 American Psychological Association (APA) meeting where Rogers first debated freedom and determinism with his most famous antagonist (and friend), the Harvard behavioral psychologist B. F. Skinner (see letters from Morgan to Rogers with attached transcripts of broadcasts [Morgan, 1956a; 1956b]).

Rogers's concern with the deterministic implications of the underlying philosophy of behaviorism, which was best articulated at this time by Skinner, consumed much of his attention during the 1950s. This interest crystallized at that late 1956 APA meeting just prior to the dialogue with Buber. Beginning with an invitation from "Fred" Skinner dated 27 December 1955, they began to plan a joint appearance and later a publication that would move their divergent interpretations into a public forum. The Skinner–Rogers correspondence in 1956 detailed in fascinating ways how the two intellectual antagonists in effect became teammates for advocating public dialogue on a divisive issue. Rogers's no-nonsense but friendly tone and his conception of the program is represented well in a May 14 letter:

> I believe that your paper should come first. As I see it, you are a little bit more of a proponent of a new point of view than am I in this connection. I am not wedded to this and if you feel strongly that I should come first I will do so but I would prefer it the other way. If you are in agreement that you should probably speak first then I believe that it would hlep [sic] a great deal if I could have at least an outline or a rough draft of your paper before I put mine into shape. The more closely our papers are related to each other the more the meeting will have a significant flow of thought and the less we will be battling straw men or heading off toward unrelated goals. . . .
>
> I have always liked your idea of each of us making some additional comments, certainly not more than seven or eight minutes in length on the other's paper. If we follow the conventional formula for debates—which I insist is only a partially true description of this meeting—then I think you should have the privilege of making a last comment. I think it would be too complex to try to exchange these comments in advance and besides I feel it would be profitable if the meeting contains some newness for us as well as the audience.
>
> Please let me have your reactions to these suggestions and let's at least try to set up a tentative time table. It seems to me it should be good fun and that it will have the value of getting the profession thinking about an issue which in my experience [illegible] psychologists are reluctant to think about. (Rogers, 1956a)

Skinner replied with some reactions to the logistical issues, and affirmed: "I believe we are in agreement as to the importance of this topic for American psychology, and I share your concern that our presentation should be more concerned with putting the issues in the clearest light than in trying to establish any personal position" (Skinner, 1956a). Rogers responded immediately with a letter that began, "We may differ somewhat in ideas but we seem to have no difficulty in working together. I like the possibilities you suggest," and ended, "I am really looking forward to the opportunity to think through myself and think through with you the important questions which are involved" (Rogers, 1956b). In a later letter, Rogers brings up the interest that the ABC broadcaster Morgan and *Time* magazine have shown in his work, and how these media might be interested in publicizing the APA symposium with Skinner too:

> I don't know how you feel about this, but I favor such steps. Part of my purpose in the symposium is to get psychologists and the public thinking about these issues. I believe this is your purpose too. So I would propose that as soon as our papers are in final shape, and in any event several days prior to the APA, that we submit copies to the *Time* man and to Morgan, informing Mike [name illegible] (APA office) of this, and perhaps getting other suggestions from him. I don't crave publicity, but I think it would be good to get the public thinking, and I believe it would be good for our profession in that it presents psychologists as a definitely significant group. (Rogers, 1956c)

Both men warm to the task, and their informal dialogue in preparation for their presentation begins to clarify issues. In August, Skinner wrote on a postcard that "I think I am beginning to see light—a real area of agreement between us. So far—a very creative experience for me. Cordially Fred" (Skinner, 1956b).

Therefore, at the time of his conversation with Buber, Rogers had been thinking seriously about the relationship between privately developed intellectual ideas and their dissemination and discussion in the common ground of public dialogue. Rogers saw dialogue as a testing of ideas, but not fully a "debate," even when the ideas seemed philosophically contradictory (as Skinner's initially appeared to him). Rogers, the proponent of active listening, valued full opportunities to be heard. He wanted participants to enter the forum with a comprehensive knowledge of the issues they were facing, as well as the issues they were advocating. He welcomed the wider audiences that national broadcast and print media could deliver, although he was suspicious of "crav[ing] publicity." And, perhaps most important for a theory of dialogue, he wanted to ensure the possibility of something surprising happening in the interchange, not just for the audience but for participants as well.

Rogers framed his conversation with Buber in terms of the Skinner dialogue and the challenges of a behaviorist worldview. In notes from this period, he observed that "Reading Buber after Skinner is like stepping into another world" (Rogers, nd-c). In a document Rogers prepared evidently for use at his late 1956 appearance with Skinner at APA, he invoked Buber:

> I think that man's "freedom" and his "determined behavior" are both there, just as the contradictory theories of light as waves and light as corpuscular units are both true. We simply lack the over-arching intelligence to see how these are reconciled. Like Buber [written insert: "& Geo Kelly" (the constructivist psychologist)] I believe that the freest man freely chooses the behavior which is also determined, and thus at least in the ideal case the contradiction is reconciled. (Rogers, nd-a, p. 4)

On page 6 of the same document, Rogers wrote that in his kind of approach, "man will never need to sacrifice the 'I,' will never need permanently to become an 'It.' He will be freely available for the most profound and meaningful subjective 'I-Thou' encounters with other men, and with the universe."[1]

It should be no surprise, then, that when Rogers prepared to meet Buber, the foil of the behaviorist agenda was probably his preeminent intellectual concern. He took several pages of his paper, "Some Issues Concerning the Control of Human Behavior" (Rogers, nd-e; published as Rogers, 1972b), drafted for the APA encounter with Skinner, to Ann Arbor with him for the Buber dialogue ("Early Draft p. 11–16 removed for Buber mt."). He subsequently revised this section for what he labeled the "Next to final draft." Perhaps more important, Rogers's written notes on "Questions not used" for the Buber dialogue includes a two-page typescript, resembling a class handout, titled "BUBER'S CONCEPT OF INCLUSION," drawn "from a paper on 'Education,' written in 1925." This excerpt contains Buber's distinction between inclusion and empathy, the latter being to Buber the "exclusion of one's own concreteness" (Rogers, nd-d). Thus, we know that even before their dialogue Rogers was aware of Buber's narrower and negatively tinged meaning for one of Rogers's basic terms. He understood that there could be terminological problems in discussing interpersonal behavior with Buber. In addition, one of his several planned questions that he didn't get to ask (see chapter 6) concerned the issues of the Rogers–Skinner dialogue generally, and more particularly, involved whether Buber thought current social and scientific trends expanded the objectifications of the world of "It." In all likelihood, Rogers's anticipated meeting with Buber seemed secondary if not marginal when compared with his recent interchange with Skinner about human freedom and control and his ongoing disagreements with Freudian and neo-Freudian psychoanalysts on their view of the essentially negative and destructive nature of the human condition.

Clearly, two professional and conceptual issues weighed most heavily on Rogers's mind in 1957: (1) his renunciation of the diminution of human subjectivity and human potential that Skinnerian behaviorism represented to him, and (2) his objections to entrenched psychoanalytic and psychiatric models of treatment that foregrounded diagnosis and expert analysis. He saw both issues in the specific context of psychological practice, but he also framed both as wider challenges for psychology as a discipline and, indeed, for society as a whole. Yet this is not to say that the philosophical commentator Buber was trivial for the pragmatic Rogers; far from it. In developing his rhetorical stances on these fronts, he relied on essentially dialogic thinking, and undoubtedly he thought Buber was a conceptual ally in response to both Skinnerian behaviorism and Freudianism.

Maurice Friedman certainly did his part to suggest that Buber's approach buttressed the relational emphases of client-centeredness and, conversely, that Rogers's therapy was one valid expression of Buber's dialogic philosophy. Buber had been corresponding with Friedman in the early 1950s about the contents of Friedman's book, *Martin Buber: The Life of Dialogue*, which was published in 1955, only two years before the dialogue. In that book, Friedman's description of Rogers's work might also have reflected how Buber understood Rogers at this time, because Friedman had sent Buber a number of Rogers's unpublished papers.[2] Friedman wrote that Rogers's approach was "a striking parallel" to Buber's, and "a significant confirmation of Buber's attitude toward psychotherapy" (p. 191). Previewing a topic of their dialogue (regarding the relationship between acceptance and confirmation), Friedman observed that "For Rogers as for Buber it is important in the process of the person's becoming that he know himself to be understood and accepted, or in Buber's terms made present and confirmed by the therapist" (p. 191). Further, therapy "implies for both a laying aside of the preoccupation with professional analysis, diagnosis, and evaluation in favour of an acceptance and understanding of the client based on true attitudes of respect which are deeply and genuinely felt by the therapist" (p. 192). Friedman goes on to quote a passage from Rogers that he argues is "remarkably close to Buber's spirit":

> To enter deeply with this man into his confused struggle for selfhood is perhaps the best implementation we now know for indicating the meaning of our basic hypothesis that the indi-

vidual represents a process which is deeply worthy of respect, both as he is and with regard to his potentialities. (Rogers, 1951, p. 45; quoted by Friedman, 1960, p. 192)

Readers—including, presumably, both Buber and Rogers—thus learn that to Buber's most famous student, Rogers's concept of acceptance was another way of referring to Buber's confirmation (p. 191). Friedman acknowledged that, for Carl Rogers, respecting and accepting clients as persons extended not only to their immediate presence but also to their "potentialities."

Although Friedman later came to perceive some of the subtle differences between Buber and Rogers in new ways, he did not revise his assessment of the basic similarity when the book went into its second and third editions in 1960 and 1976.[3] If we can assume that Rogers read Friedman's 1955 chapter on Buber and psychotherapy before the dialogue (which seems safe because Rogers's papers contained an excerpt from the book, although from a different chapter, and because Rogers was following Buber's thought and career carefully), we also might assume that Rogers anticipated an encounter with a congenial intellectual spirit. From Rogers's perspective, Buber's wide-ranging philosophical anthropology and theological insights on healing through dialogue seemed to converge at premises similar to those derived from Rogers's own clinical experience. For example, in an essay written shortly after the dialogue, Rogers (1960) summarized the trends in client-centered therapy from the 1950s, claiming that therapists like himself were becoming more "dialogical" in many of the ways philosophers like Buber were recommending.

Rogers's Intellectual Commitments at Mid-Century

Van Balen (1990) identifies 1957 as a major watershed in Rogers's professional life, in part because the dialogue with Buber helped him emphasize with renewed vigor how the therapist-client relationship is vitally important in determining the quality of help and growth experienced by the client. Thorne (1992) in a slightly different way assumes the same thing about Buber's influence on Rogers. Perhaps, too, we could note other factors in Rogers's life that catalyzed the influence of this dialogue, and that—just as important—could clarify why Rogers said what he did.

Rogers had several research projects in the forefront of his mind in the first months of 1957. First, he had for some time been contemplating a move to the University of Wisconsin, and in fact was teaching in

Madison that spring as a visiting professor. In addition to the recognition and prestige that came with a rare dual appointment in both psychiatry and psychology, one of Rogers's main attractions to a permanent Wisconsin appointment was the opportunity to do research and engage in therapy with institutionalized schizophrenics—an important test, he thought, of the tenets of his developing theory and a broadening of his clinical experience. He had dealt with schizophrenia before in his own clients, but had not specialized in treatment of the deeply troubled chronic schizophrenics he would encounter in Madison. Critics had suggested that client-centered therapy may work with less disturbed middle-class clients at the Chicago center, but that more chronic problems would expose the weaknesses of Rogers's approach. Significantly, Rogers's therapy with schizophrenics became an issue in the dialogue when Buber suggested that such conditions and relationships produced severe normative limits on the extent to which mutuality could develop in therapy. Rogers, while agreeing on one level, disagreed to the extent that moments of mutuality can still be sparked in such relationships.

Second, in late 1956 and early 1957 Rogers was working on a paper in which he elaborated on the theoretical importance of dialogic moments. He described the core conditions of therapy as having their greatest impact not globally or holistically, but *particularly* within what he called "moments of meeting," "moments of meaning," and "molecules" of change (see our more thorough discussion in chapter 7). Clearly, then, when Rogers framed his comments to Buber about equality and mutuality in therapy relationships, they emerged from his scholarly preoccupation at that time with describing how clients and their therapists experienced each other as equals primarily in momentary, transitory incidents of growth—precisely how he would phrase his questions to Buber on this point. In the drafts of his "moments" papers and in the questions for Buber he developed from them, Rogers was wrestling with how to express this subtle conceptual appreciation for how limited and transitory dialogue could be. This fact is particularly ironic, considering how often the dialogue has been invoked to illustrate how Rogers naively assumed that he and his clients were fully equal in a completely dialogical relationship.

Third, the year of the dialogue was when the famous Rogers and Farson (1957) piece on *Active Listening* was first published, as we have seen. The extended essay, printed as a booklet by the University of Chicago Industrial Relations Center, was an early attempt to extend client-centered thinking to a wider audience with more practical and everyday problems of interaction; it became a landmark text in applied communication. When Rogers was invited to meet with Buber on stage, it undoubtedly was partly on the strength of his intellectual reputation. But equally influential for conference organizers must have been Rogers's reputation as a skillful listener with an ability to draw out his interlocutor. Richard Farson (personal communication, 11 August 1993) told us that he drafted most of the *Active Listening* document while Rogers was involved in other projects, but Rogers's ideas were at its core. No doubt the concepts of active listening were part of the context of Rogers's thinking in April 1957, and the habits of active listening are readily apparent in his conversational invitations to, and clarifications of, Buber's insights. Indeed, although he presented several of his own ideas in the dialogue, he more often downplayed his own thought in the interest of facilitating Buber's contributions. He seemingly defined his role as an interviewer who was especially concerned with active listening.

Fourth, 1957 also saw the publication of the article Rogers (1977b) would later call "the most significant paper I have ever written, and the most far-reaching in its effects," as well as the one "spark[ing] more research investigations than any other"—the famous "Necessary and Sufficient Conditions of Therapeutic Personality Change." He had been working on the general theory that stimulated this research for two years and had first presented this analysis to a conference, ironically enough, at the University of Michigan. There, he discovered how unpopular some of his ideas could be among colleagues whose roles of power, expertise, and authority he seemed to be questioning. Although his impact was growing to some extent within psychology, many in his field denigrated his work and found it especially hard to believe that these conditions of genuineness, unconditional caring, and sensitive empathy were more influential in therapy than therapist expertise. Rogers recalls that his Michigan audience was composed of psychoanalytically oriented academics: "They were expectant and critical. I was at that time a controversial figure. . . . I believe I was regarded as presumptuous for having set forth what I regarded as sufficient conditions to account for effective psychotherapy. I know that I shocked many by stating that 'special intellectual professional knowledge' is not essential in psychotherapy. Another controversial statement was that a psychological diagnosis is only helpful in making the therapist feel secure" (Rogers, 1977b).

Surely, Rogers probably assumed, the seasoned philosopher of dialogue would understand these issues of human communication better than academic behaviorists or psychoanalysts. Buber's writing explained why persons in therapy change in the context of relationships that stress listening. And we can see why Rogers might have assumed, in discussing therapist "genuineness," that Buber would agree with him that there are certain role differences limiting what is said in therapy, but that on certain occasions therapists might find it necessary to disclose something of a personal nature. Buber, of course, *did* agree that role differences in therapy precluded a full mutuality. Rogers would presumably be surprised, however, that some commentators, as we suggest in chapter 6, could interpret the dialogue as evidence that he failed to fathom or acknowledge the role differences, and he'd be surprised too that commentators could so completely overlook his stipulation that equality was found in the *transitory moments* of therapeutic insight, not throughout the client-therapist relationship.

In his 1957 "Necessary and Sufficient Conditions" article, Rogers attempted to operationalize his fundamental concepts around the time of the dialogue. He thought of that article as a component in a larger project: a conceptual specification that would turn out to be the piece Rogers was proudest of, the essay he believed best captured the essence of his approach, and—almost inexplicably—one that was largely and unfairly neglected in discussions of client-centered therapy and the person-centered approach, much to his disappointment. In 1956 and 1957 Rogers was writing his extensive "A Theory of Therapy, Personality, and Interpersonal Relationships, as Developed in the Client-Centered Framework," published in Sigmund Koch's important *Psychology: A Study of a Science* series in 1959. In other words, while Rogers was preparing to meet Buber and during the months immediately following that meeting, Rogers was engaged in a systematic exploration and synthesis of the theoretical implications of his life's work to that point. The national organization of professional psychologists had just honored him for a "lifetime" of contribution to a science of psychology; now he wanted to synthesize those contributions into an organized theory. If Buber in 1957 was synthesizing much of his own work through preparing seminal lectures that would later appear in *The Knowledge of Man* and elsewhere, Rogers prepared to converse with Buber when he too was tracing the threads that connected his many projects. At this historical juncture, each was emphasizing coherence in his own lifework, and attempting to create metastatements reflecting their careers.

Early 1957 was clearly a time of particular confluence in Rogers's professional life. It was not when he first "met" Buber, except in a literal and physical sense; he'd discovered Buber through his writings some years earlier. He had been conceptualizing a wider frame for client-centered theory for some years, although most of that work had been practical, with less focus on wider relational issues of dialogue. However, in 1956 and 1957 Rogers's work started to become more theoretical, more public, more concerned with philosophical context, and more relational. The evidence reinforces Van Balen's (1990) conclusion that the Buber conversation was pivotal for Rogers and his career, although surely not in an "aha" sense of illuminating exactly what he needed to do next. He was undoubtedly invited to be Buber's interlocutor because he was skilled at interviewing. But he also brought a developing praxis and experience with dialogue in concrete troubled circumstances that certainly complemented Buber's philosophy and, he probably expected, would be heard as confirmation of Buber's eloquent observations about dialogue.

An otherwise minor event from Rogers's busy year of 1956 seems more relevant now than it must have appeared to anyone at the time, and it presages an issue to which we return in the next chapter. In our analysis of the dialogue itself, we will discuss Buber's "rhetoric of cannot"; Buber's speech style, while dialogic in many ways, also at times dismissed others' positions with what Edwards (1970) called "verbal fiats." And although many of Buber's friends and colleagues over the years testified to his conversational openness, others noted this tendency to dismiss disagreement by moving to a higher plane of pronouncement. Undoubtedly a man of dialogue, we have seen that Buber could be an abrupt conversation partner at times (Gordon, 1988). Thus, it seems in retrospect like a faint warning signal for their meeting when Rogers published in 1956 a widely read review of theologian Reinhold Niebuhr's book *The Self and the Dramas of History*. In it, the psychologist takes the theologian to task for his style of pronouncing truth:

> As I lay the book down, I find that I am impressed most of all by the awesome certainty with which Dr. Niebuhr *knows*. He knows, with incredible assurance, what is wrong with the thinking of St. Thomas Aquinas, Augustine, Hegel, Freud, Marx, Dewey and many, many others. He also knows what are the errors of communism, existentialism, psychology, and all the social sciences. . . . I find myself offended by Dr. Niebuhr's dogmatic statements and feel ready to turn back with fresh respect to the writings of science, in which at least the *endeavor* is made to keep an open mind. (Rogers, 1956f, p. 13)

Obviously, Buber is not Niebuhr, although Friedman observed that Niebuhr's book was "based on Buber's philosophy of dialogue" (Friedman, 1991, p. 352). Yet we believe Rogers's evaluation of Niebuhr's linguistic style may clarify and contextualize his reaction to Buber's interpersonal style during their subsequent dialogue. Consistent with his radical democratizing of the therapy relationship, Rogers discounted seemingly dogmatic pronouncement as a way of teaching or as an avenue to truth, especially if unaccompanied by practical evidence or by invitational open-mindedness; he wanted at least a spirit of active listening to accompany strong expressions of opinion. Of course, Rogers could be seen as somewhat inconsistent in this matter. He later criticized much of the research conducted under the rubric of social science himself, but here rides to its defense against Niebuhr's attack that he regarded as too dismissive. Rogers plays the role of the practical scientist who trusts the concrete data of direct experience. In Ann Arbor early the next year, he would admire Buber's ideas but also would seem puzzled by some of Buber's demeanor and pronouncements, wondering once out loud whether on a certain point he might be more Buber-like than Buber himself.

SUMMARY

Taking a wide view of Buber's and Rogers's careers, we can see how the early- to mid-1950s constituted a turning point for each man, and that 1957 particularly focused their work for later generations. Buber subsequently drew together many of his ideas about dialogue in role-based contexts like therapy and education, focusing increasingly on the interhuman aspects of his philosophical anthropology, and he appeared to revise his negative evaluation of public dialogue and its possibilities. Rogers more overtly emphasized relational descriptions of his concepts, liberally adopting Buber's language and philosophy. In this brief chapter we have extended our discussions of each man's work, for the purpose of glimpsing intellectual context—what Buber and Rogers were working on, and what they were worried about, at the time of their dialogue. Within this context, the dynamics of their conversation will be more meaningful.

CHAPTER SIX

Interhuman Meeting

Now Martin Buber and Carl Rogers are dead, but . . .
the issues raised in their dialogue still seem to me
momentous.
　　　　　—Maurice Friedman, "Reflections on
　　　　　　　　　the Buber–Rogers Dialogue"

Almost all scholarship on dialogue has focused on individual philosophers or theorists, applying their ideas to particular contexts such as epistemology, education, ethics, or political deliberation. Few, if any, extended studies have attempted to study dialogue itself through a close, critical examination of the efforts of particular persons to engage in dialogue.

Yet one prominent review of the interpersonal communication literature (Ayres, 1984) highlighted both the scarcity and the importance of this type of research in the dialogic tradition:

> Additional attention might also be devoted to the identification of dialogic communication characteristics—of particular interest would be analyzing the styles of talk associated with dialogue. . . . The goal of this work should be to search for the existence of genuine dialogue and describe those characteristics that are associated with it. (p. 411)

A more recent review of emerging methodologies in interpersonal communication research (Poole & McPhee, 1994) also recommended that scholars undertake more "historical-critical" studies of "interpersonal interaction patterns"; this perspective assumes that "patterns of interpersonal communication are constituted and influenced by larger social, economic, and cultural contexts" (p. 88). These recommendations encourage researchers and critics to place historically important occasions of dialogue into comprehensive sociocultural and intellectual context. Around 1985, we began to plan an extended research program that could meet this goal. We have come to believe that our analysis also has implications for democratic theory and public policy.

The Buber–Rogers meeting provided a nearly ideal text for this kind of study. It was a public conversation bringing together two of the twentieth-century's foremost proponents of dialogue in a cross-disciplinary dialogue of their own—Buber the globally influential philosopher talking with Rogers, one of the most famous of American psychologists and psychotherapists. Much of their talk was about dialogue, but as we suggest in chapter 2, we were as interested in the process of their interaction as in the content of their talk. Buber and Rogers were both distinguished interpersonal communicators. What can we learn from how they, with moderator Maurice Friedman, coauthored this dialogue? What does this particular conversation tell us about successful dialogue in general? The answers will come only from a careful reconsideration of their talk in the same hermeneutic spirit that Buber himself recommended. He wrote that no textual interpretation "coincides with the original meaning" (presumably the intent of authors), and that an interpreter's "own being" always influences the interpretation. However, he stressed, "if I attend as faithfully as I can to what it contains of word and texture, of sound and rhythmic structure, of open and hidden connections, my interpretation will not have been made in vain—I find something. . . . And if I show what I have found, I guide him who lets himself be guided to the reality of the text" (Buber, 1957b, pp. 100–101).

The principals of the Buber–Rogers dialogue definitely considered the event an occasion of dialogue. Maurice Friedman (1983a, 1986, 1991, 1994, 1996d), the moderator, called it a dialogue—at its conclusion and subsequently several times in print. In an interview immediately after the event, Buber called it a "genuine dialogue" (Friedman, 1983a, 1986, 1991, 1994, 1996d). Clearly, Buber thought it was a dialogic event, and Rogers, too, said he thought the dialogue "went very well" (Pentony, 1987, p. 420).

Friedman has been the foremost interpreter of the dialogue (see especially Friedman, 1986, 1994, 1996d), although he has primarily explicated its content, comparing the merits of what Buber and Rogers said. Perhaps because of our focus on the interaction process itself (in the context, of course, of the content), we reach conclusions that differ in some respects from Friedman's. Further, because Friedman focused on the participants' ideas, even when he quotes extensively from the dialogue, the quotes are often not in the sequence in which they were spoken. Friedman's goal was neither to illuminate the structure and flow of the conversation nor to learn about dialogue from examining that structure or flow. We will comment on the ideas, but we also hope to clarify the coherence of the dialogue as a conversational accomplishment by analyzing influences of audience, role, and style on the process. Finally, previous commentaries have tended to focus only on particular issues, such as the relevance of the dialogue for educators, or for a theory of confirmation or mutuality. We show in this and subsequent chapters that a close reading offers more comprehensive insight about dialogue generally and public dialogue particularly.

BACKGROUND

Buber's 1957 U.S. tour gave Rev. DeWitt C. Baldwin, coordinator of religious affairs at the University of Michigan, the opportunity to invite the internationally known scholar to Ann Arbor for a special three-day event, the "Mid-West Conference with Dr. Martin Buber," which became a highlight of the tour. It attracted many luminaries in the American intellectual circuit to participate in panels, discussions, and presentations on Buber's philosophy, including economist Kenneth Boulding, anthropologist Dorothy Lee, theologians Perry LeFevre and Ross Snyder of the Divinity School at the University of Chicago, the literary critic R. W. B. Lewis then at Rutgers, the famous University of Michigan educator William McKeachie, and Maurice Friedman, a thirty-five-year-old Sarah Lawrence College philosophy professor who was already recognized as the foremost American authority on Buber's thought ("Attendence" [sic], nd; Friedman, 1983c, p. 225; 1991, p. 368; "Program," 1957).

The "most notable event" of the conference (Friedman, 1991, p. 368), though, was to be an evening in which Buber would engage in dialogue with Carl Rogers. There is some evidence (Rogers & Russell, 1991, p. 201; see also Friedman, 1957) that Chicago's Ross Snyder played a liaison role in planning the Buber–Rogers conversation as part of the conference, and may even have suggested it initially. Baldwin's correspondence with Buber and Rogers (Baldwin, 1957a, 1957b, 1957c, 1957d) led to an agreement about arrangements and the topic (suggested by Rogers [Baldwin, 1957c, 1957d]) that would be their starting point: "The nature of man as revealed in inter-personal relationship." The meeting was scheduled for a Thursday evening, the second day of the conference, in the most beautiful meeting hall on campus, Rackham Auditorium.

About four hundred people attended, including Buber's wife Paula and his granddaughter Judith Buber Agassi, now a noted sociologist. Although Rogers's presence attracted faculty and students in counseling and psychology to the sessions, surely most of the audience was primarily interested in hearing Buber.

Rogers was detained by bad weather and arrived late; he and Buber were able to meet for only an hour or so before the dialogue began. Rogers later reported that Buber then disclosed that his sponsors who brought him to the United States had, as we mentioned earlier, "told him not to speak with Rogers about psychotherapy." According to one report, Rogers did not know what else they could meaningfully discuss and decided that although Buber "might not be able to speak to him about psychotherapy, there was nothing to stop him speaking about psychotherapy to Buber" (Pentony, 1987, p. 420). Thus, Rogers's opening question to Buber (along with others that followed) seems somewhat less whimsical and much more assertive in this context. And Buber's willingness to ignore the advice of his sponsors (not only in responding to the first and second questions, but throughout the dialogue) indicates his willingness to engage Rogers.

Their conversation immediately before the event was apparently intense and also decisive in creating a record of the event. One of the conference organizers, Grey Austin, believes it was then that Rogers successfully encouraged Buber to let the conference proceed with taping their dialogue on stage, although Buber had not wanted to be taped or filmed at other tour appearances. Rogers, however, had recorded many client sessions over the years with good results, and Austin believes that Rogers successfully assured Buber that this event could be handled in an equally sensitive way. An accurate transcript would be valuable, and Rogers's office could produce such a document easily (Austin, personal communication, 1 January 1996; 12 February 1996). According to Friedman, Buber probably agreed to this because he had low expectations for the dialogue (Friedman, personal communication, 22 October 1991).

DeWitt Baldwin opened the program with a few words of welcome and introduced the moderator, Friedman, who then clearly described the participants, their roles, and the ground rules for the event. The principals would explore similarities in their thought, and see what issues would emerge. His "role as moderator is only . . . , if occasion should arise, to sharpen these issues or interpret one way or another."[1] The relationship of Buber to Rogers is even clearer: "And the form of this dialogue will be that Dr. Rogers will himself raise questions with Dr. Buber and Dr. Buber will respond, and perhaps with a question, per-

haps with a statement" (turn #2). Rogers from the beginning understood that his role was to be more like an interviewer than an equal
conversation partner; he prepared and brought to the dialogue a series
of nine questions, most of which were not asked. Later we return to the
interesting consequences of this interviewing presumption, including
how it influenced their discourse. For now, though, note that their dialogue was never intended to be either freeform or totally spontaneous,
but was built on a mutually assumed framework built from content
and role assumptions.

Later we also speculate about the implications of such a framework for clearing a discourse-space necessary to invite dialogic spontaneity. Dialogue is not likely to happen if it is left to chance or
serendipity, but neither is it likely to happen if its participants force,
script, or manage it. Instead, the optimum dialogic move could be said
to be *the clearing*: the establishment of an open space in which moments of genuine meeting might, but only might, occur.

We were not present for the dialogue, and no analysis can pretend
to be the final word on such a rich historical event. Still, we think intriguing portrayals—of Buber, of Rogers, and of dialogic process itself—
emerge from a close examination of the dialogue as a conversational
text. In effect, we confront a problematic text as an invitation for
rhetorical criticism. We interpret, but through a somewhat different
lens than used by Friedman or by other commentators to date.

PROBLEMS OF PREVIOUS COMMENTARIES

Speech events are often considered to be of scant historical importance
if they aren't oratorical or political, and conversations seem especially
dismissable. Yet the richness of the Buber–Rogers dialogue, together
with its ready availability to scholars over the years, has ensured its
status as an object of persistent study. Although the first publication of
the dialogue was in a small Japanese psychology journal ("Dialogue between," 1960), it appeared in excerpted form in a widely circulated anthology a few years later (Friedman, 1964), and the following year was
reprinted virtually in its entirety (but with considerable editing and numerous errors) in perhaps the most influential collection of Buber's essays (Buber, 1965b). It received significant attention there in part
because it explored topics Buber had never written about in much detail. The transcript also was reprinted more recently in Kirschenbaum
and Henderson's (1989a) collection of Rogers's dialogues with important intellectuals of his time. With this long tradition of reference,

however, comes a quite uneven record of accuracy. A brief review of the major commentators will set the stage for our own discussion:

- Maurice Friedman, in biographies of Buber (1983c, 1991) and in analytical papers and articles (1986, 1994, 1996d), has made the dialogue an exemplar of differences and distinctions between Buber's nuanced philosophical anthropology and Rogers's (and similar thinkers') supposedly more naïve psychologistic individualism on the other. He does not claim these gaps are huge; for him, the differences are subtle but crucial. Friedman rightly has inspired many to consider Buber, Rogers, and their conversation, and his contributions have been impressive. At the same time, we must note that some of his accounts—perhaps overrelying on memory at times—relay somewhat inaccurate quotations from the dialogue, and some characterizations have been hard to reconcile with the words actually preserved on the tape (see our analysis in this chapter).
- Grete Schaeder (1973a) devoted a lengthy section of her intellectual biography of Buber to the dialogue. She uses Rogers as a useful foil for understanding Buber's "more realistic" thinking about limits on mutuality and equality, and about the process of confirmation of persons. She writes, however, that in the dialogue Rogers "always returned" to his presumably less realistic view of acceptance, and "in this he proceeded from the premise that it is the task of the doctor to probe to the deepest layer of the patient's being, where he will surely find that in him which is positive and constructive" (p. 208). However, Rogers never stated or implied in this dialogue that it was his task to "probe to the deepest layer of a patient's being," and such probing is not even a close approximation of client-centered theory.
- Donald Seckinger (1976) applied the dialogue's lessons to the problems of education, attempting a neutral summary with a number of longer quotations. Seckinger is not convinced that Rogers advocated full equality between therapist and client; instead, he interprets Rogers's responses on this point as "at least a tacit acceptance by Rogers of the therapeutic relation as being 'one-sided' while it is taking place" (p. 147). Seckinger does not note Rogers's persistent emphases, qualifications, and reservations about dialogic

moments. What is less clear about Seckinger's analysis, however, is why he believes the dialogue "should be useful both in distinguishing the concept teaching from the concept therapy as a general case and specifically in differentiating existential psychotherapy from Buber's theory of instruction" (p. 144). Actually, the content of the conversation does not distinguish teaching from therapy at all; if anything, it implies correspondences between them in that in both, role definitions between helper and helpee are essentially unequal.

• R. D. Laing ("Still R. D. Laing," 1991) demonstrates the vagaries of memory, or transcription, or of moving one degree of separation away from an event. His account of what Rogers told him about the Buber meeting most closely resembles the last message from the children's game of "gossip" in which facts are more or less recognizable but become laughably skewed or rearranged. Laing said:

> [Rogers] told me about a meeting with Martin Buber in the late '40s in which he told Buber that schizophrenics were the most evil people. Buber was very much in agreement with that and told Rogers that schizophrenics are incapable of an I-Thou relationship.
>
> Some time later, Rogers did expose himself to a therapeutic relationship with a schizophrenic lady that drove him over the edge. He went completely crazy himself but had the social prudence to get out. One day he got in his car and disappeared from his family and his practice and drove up to Canada. It was three months before he found his balance again. When he came back, he decided to never, ever listen to a schizophrenic again. (p. 29)

It's hard to know where to begin in sorting out this tangle of errata. Rogers's only meeting with Buber was in the late 1950s, not the late 1940s. Rogers didn't tell Buber that schizophrenics were evil, nor would Buber agree with that point, but they did discuss the limitations of mutuality by referring to schizophrenics. Rogers did have an episode with a woman client (whose behavior might today be described as close to "stalking") from which he needed to extricate himself, but this was between 1949 and 1951 according to his biographer (Kirschenbaum, 1979, pp. 191–194), *long before*, not "some time later" than the dialogue with Buber. He didn't go completely crazy himself, but felt himself on the verge of a breakdown. He didn't disappear from his family, but left with his wife Helen. Staying away for two or three months, he returned to become a client himself. Did he decide "never, ever [to] listen to a schizophrenic again"? No; immediately following the dialogue with Buber, he moved to the University of Wisconsin because they offered him outstanding research support to study just such schizophrenic clients and to assess the impact of his client-centered therapy with them.

- Bonnie Burstow (1987) uses the Buber–Rogers dialogue as her centerpiece example for an analysis of claims of equality in humanistic psychotherapy, presenting a quoted interchange out of context. In the dialogue, Rogers frames his comments not in terms of claiming a fully equal relation but in the context of a relationship that allows only *moments* of equality (with which Buber agrees) and in terms of a basic agreement with Buber that this relationship will look, and in some ways will be, unequal. None of this was noted by Burstow as she attempted to show that Buber had demonstrated that Rogers and therapists like him "are mistaken, that therapy is not an equal relationship" (p. 11). She follows with some fairly bold mindreading of Rogers: He "becomes quite uncomfortable"; he "is angry"; he "understandably . . . is disappointed"; he "may even feel betrayed. My suspicion is that he is also threatened" (p. 11). Later she also reads Buber's mind, deciding that when he says a schizophrenic client cannot "see" Rogers or "look on [Rogers's] experience" meaningfully, he really doesn't mean that, but instead has exaggerated to make a point. Burstow's account contains other misleading information as well; for example, the postscript Buber wrote for *I and Thou* is said to be "earlier" than the 1957 dialogue although it was actually written after the dialogue, and was probably influenced by the conversation with Rogers.

- Debora Brink (1987) comments on the dialogue briefly to reply to Burstow (1987), and to point out that Rogers's then-recent involvement in therapy with a hospitalized schizophrenic had affected how he conceptualized equality when talking with Buber. In this complex and challenging relationship, Brink reports (partly based on personal communication with Rogers) that therapist and client (known as "Jim Brown") did experience together moments of equality (for instance, after Rogers shares with Jim that he himself had experienced similar feelings) (p. 28). Rogers never claims the relation is fully equal, or that the roles make it fully mutualized. Rather, in this concrete context, he had an actual example in mind of a time when "without denying the actual, objective inequality of the helper/ helpee relationship, therapist and client together for a moment nevertheless step seemingly into a different dimension where, for the moment, all inqualities drop away and the two meet on an equal plane, as persons. It is a moment of *felt* equality in which the usual barriers are transcended and they *live* their common equal humanity in an I-Thou relatedness of essential mutuality" (Brink, 1987, p. 30).

- Richard Van Balen (1990) offers an interesting account of the dialogue because he recognized that Rogers and Buber were not talking about full relationship equality between therapist and client but rather about "a relationship-moment within the relationship" (p. 73). When the two disagree, or at least talk past each other, about the impact of role on experienced equality, Van Balen observes that "For the time being, the viewpoints of Rogers and Buber seem irreconcilable. In my opinion it appears as a—temporary—misunderstanding" (p. 75) that later, as we will see, becomes somewhat resolved. The outcome of the dialogue for Rogers, Van Balen suggests, is that "Rightly, and probably more than is often realized, Rogers thus recognizes Buber's decisive influence on his own evolution towards increased 'realness'" (p. 77).

- Brian Thorne (1992) treats the Buber dialogue as a significant event in his brief biography of Rogers and his ideas. Thorne thinks the event had the tone of "debate" (p. 69); this, we suggest, is somewhat misleading because the conversation as a whole was less a comparison of distinctly different positions (as in a debate) than it was an exploration of subtleties between two similar approaches. Still, Thorne is correct in noticing that there were a few moments in

which disagreements and apparent disagreements were discussed explicitly. As he put it, the dialogue

> ended with Buber clearly unconvinced about the
> nature of the relationship which Rogers experi-
> enced with his clients. . . . Indeed, in the closing
> minutes . . . Buber implies that the therapeutic re-
> lationship resulting from client-centred therapy
> may produce individuals rather than persons, and
> he roundly declares himself to be against individ-
> uals and for persons." (p. 69)

This is "because he [Buber] is unconvinced about the reciprocity of the therapeutic relationship" (p. 69). Although we
strongly recommend Thorne's book for its other contributions, this particular conclusion is not well supported by the
dialogue transcript. As we show later, Buber's final point
about individuals versus persons is not tied to the earlier
discussion of reciprocity or equality, and in fact not only
doesn't contradict, but actually *echoes* an essay Rogers had
written earlier. In addition, we note how Buber's position actually began to resemble Rogers's as they talked about the
issue of moments of mutuality, although neither man acknowledged that movement during the conversation.

- Atsuhiko Yoshida (1994) applies the Buber–Rogers dialogue
  to the issue of "compulsion or freedom?" in education, and
  similarly wants to believe that Rogers said the therapist
  and client "are equal to each other" (p. 91). Rogers's interpretation is portrayed as "rather simple" and "very naive"
  (p. 95). Buber reminds Rogers, according to Yoshida, that
  "there is an essential difference between the therapist and
  the person being helped" (p. 92). Rogers is chastised for "not
  understand[ing] Buber's objection," and the author wonders
  derisively, "Why did Buber have to point out to Rogers that
  the helper and the helped are not equal, an almost self-evident fact implied in the definition of helping relationships?" (p. 92). The only problem with all this is that
  Rogers never says that the two roles are objectively equal to
  each other; in fact, he acknowledges, as we show, that essential differences between therapist and client make them
  unequal in power, prestige, insight, preparation to address
  mental turmoil, and so forth. Rogers, in fact, said to Buber
  that the therapeutic relationship when seen from the out-

side could be perceived as quite unequal. Rogers becomes a target of opportunity in Yoshida's essay, which also conveniently chooses not to acknowledge Rogers's context of asking about *moments* of equality. The piece further relays errors that should disturb scholars: (1) in at least one place a quotation attributed to Buber is nowhere to be found in any of the transcripts ("you must play a role different from the client's" [p. 92]); (2) Rogers's concept of acceptance is characterized as "unconditional approval of all the attributes which characterize the other person at a certain point in time" [p. 95]), a position that—as we saw in chapter 4— Rogers never took; (3) Rogers is said to have advocated "complete confidence in the innate instincts of human beings" (p. 99), although this is a striking mischaracterization of his "actualizing tendency" concept (see chapter 4); (4) Buber's "confirmation" concept supposedly "extends absolute affirmation and acceptance of the other person's fundamental existence," a description Buber would surely hesitate to endorse.

- Carl Rogers himself (Rogers & Russell, 1991) recalled the dialogue with Buber in an interview with oral historian David Russell not long before his death. In addition to reporting other interesting details, Rogers said:

> we had a very good dialogue, but really differed on one point. I said that I thought that the best of the therapeutic relationship was very much an I-Thou relationship of the sort he'd described. Well, he didn't think so—that couldn't be because the therapist was the expert, the upper level. And finally, to clinch it, he said, "Well, that's certainly not in dealing with a schizophrenic—that wouldn't be an I-Thou relationship." I said, "I just had such an interview with a schizophrenic before leaving," and he didn't understand that at all.
>
> The next morning at breakfast we talked again and I found that his courses in psychiatry had been around the year 1900 when dementia praecox was [considered to be] a real damage to the brain, and so on. So he was thinking that I couldn't possibly have an equalitarian relationship with someone who was so damaged. (1991, p. 201)

Rogers's memory has captured a basic theme of the dialogue accurately, but he seems to recall Buber's points
selectively and to dismiss his concepts too readily. He re-
members accurately that he claimed in the dialogue that
therapeutic relations could be "I-Thou" quality—but only
when the relationship was considered in terms of "the
best" moments. Even as he recalls the event in the year before his death, Rogers does not claim a fully equal or totally mutual relation. However, he did not tell Buber
specifically that he'd *just* had such an interview with a
schizophrenic, which to him validated that the I-Thou experience was really possible even with the normative limits of role Buber stressed. Perhaps this is what he later
wished he had said. He may have been thinking of "Jim
Brown," as he later told Debora Brink (1987, p. 28). Overall, Rogers's memory of Buber's objections credits his partner with little nuance and appears to dismiss the role
issues far too readily.

CONVERSING ON STAGE

The dialogue explored six questions, the first four asked of Buber by
Rogers, and the last two asked of both Buber and Rogers by Friedman.
We consider the interaction as it developed, using the six major ques-
tions to organize the account.

Previous scholarship on the dialogue, unfortunately, has treated
the text of the dialogue as a given. But the transcripts on which these
commentators relied, unfortunately, have always been more than problematic, as we have pointed out:

If errors in existing transcripts were trivial or sporadic, it
would not be necessary or reasonable to publish a new version. On the contrary, quotation errors and other changes introduced in previous transcripts are surprisingly frequent and
often thematically significant, even when Buber's and
Rogers's basic positions seem clear enough. Stylistic editing,
occasionally introduced with the expressed purpose of enhancing readability, has removed readers even further from
what Buber and Rogers actually said, even when their speech
on the tape made perfect sense. Both connotation and denota-
tion have been affected, and some changes warped the con-

texts within which accurately transcribed utterances could be interpreted. (Anderson & Cissna, 1997, p. 111)

Hundreds of errors, major and minor, dot the most cited transcripts (Buber, 1965b, pp. 166-184; "Dialogue Between," 1960; Friedman, 1964, pp. 485–497; Kirschenbaum & Henderson, 1989a, pp. 41–63), most of them probably attributable to a flawed typescript originally circulated by Rogers after a secretarial assistant or assistants produced it (see Anderson & Cissna, 1997 pp. 6–7, 102). Readers interested in our systematic methods for verifying and retranscribing the text should consult our companion book, but we should warn readers who are already familiar with the dialogue: some quotations may sound faintly unfamiliar, and at least a couple are likely to be downright jarring in their new, accurate incarnation. In addition, the earlier book gave us the opportunity to discuss the meaning of the errors and changes more fully than would be appropriate here.

Question 1: Invitation and Stories

Following Friedman's introduction, Rogers took an interesting opening tack, asking a question that Buber labeled as biographical and that Friedman (1991) subsequently called amusing (p. 368). Even Rogers said it "may sound a trifle impertinent" but added that when he explains the question it won't seem so. He asked: "I have wondered: How have you lived so deeply in interpersonal relationships and gained such an understanding of the human individual, without being a psychotherapist?" (turn #3). Buber laughed. Rogers then explained that many people, himself included, had reached similar insights as Buber through their work as psychotherapists. He concluded his question by inquiring: "And so, . . . if it is not too personal, . . . I would be interested in knowing what were the channels of knowing that enabled you to, to really learn so deeply of . . . people and of relationships?" (turn #3).

This question was critical to the dialogue, in that it established a personal context and informal mood for the talk—the question was playful in a way and indicated that Rogers was open to having some fun while they did their serious intellectual and dialogic work that evening. It was a signal, too, and almost a private joke, because we now know that the two men had conversed earlier about how tour organizers had not wanted Buber to talk about psychotherapy with Rogers. The question puts Rogers's cards on the table with immediacy, humor, and irony. The question also compliments Buber, in recognizing that the older scholar's ideas about being and relationship were established, as were Rogers's, through a lived reality of immersion in human engagement. Rogers disclosed just a bit in the question itself and invited Buber to respond with something from his life and experience also. Yet the question was also sensitive to the limits Buber might wish to establish for the evening.

Buber accepted the invitation and perhaps responded in even greater detail than Rogers had expected. In fact, his long and detailed reply indicates how seriously Buber took the seemingly lighthearted question. Buber began by mentioning his years as a student where he "studied three terms . . . psychiatry," not to become a psychotherapist but because he wanted to meet and establish a "real relation" with "man in the *so-called* pathological state" (turn #4). He mentioned his "inclination" to meet people and "to change something in the other, but also to let me be changed by him" (turn #4). He concluded his answer by discussing the impact of the First World War in developing his concept of "imagining the real" (turn #8). Two other characteristics of his response are especially noteworthy. First, midway through his answer, Buber paused in midsentence for 5.7 seconds, an exceptionally long silence in ordinary conversation. Few listeners have the patience and confidence in the other not to fill in such a pause. But Buber was thinking, and Rogers waited silently to allow Buber to continue. Second, a little later in this response, Buber told the story—which we introduced in chapter 3—about how he was influenced by the murder of his friend the revolutionary Gustav Landauer (although he did not name Landauer). He spoke quite personally, if somewhat elliptically, with Rogers about this event. Yet it was an experience that Buber felt "too close" to write about extensively (Buber, 1973, p. 8), despite urging from Friedman (1991, pp. 114–115) to do so. That this "impertinent" and "amusing" question allowed Buber to talk about such a moving experience and one he hadn't addressed well in his autobiographical writing is further indication that Buber and Rogers were already deeply involved with one another.

In addition, during Buber's response, Rogers can be heard several times vocalizing indicators of his focused listening (e.g., "Uh huh"). Further, at one point Buber misstated a date, saying 1819 when he meant 1918 (Buber: "The first phase went til the year eighteen, eighteen nineteen, . . . meaning til . . . I was . . . about forty" (turn #4). Rogers: "Hm-hmm. Till you're about forty?" Buber: "Just so. . . . And . . . then I, in eighteen nineteen, I felt something" [turn #6]). Rogers quickly checked his understanding of Buber's chronology, but without correcting Buber. One sentence later, after Buber repeated the mistaken date, Rogers checked again, asking: "In . . . nineteen eighteen?" (turn #7). Buber responded: "M-hmmm. . . . It ended then, and . . ." (turn #8) and he proceeded to talk about his experience of the murder. At the conclusion of Buber's response, Rogers checks his understanding and reorganizes Buber's response into a "threefold answer" (turn #11), to which Buber says "Just so" (turn #12) and then elaborates even further, showing a close connection between the participants even at this very early stage of the dialogue. Buber not only accepted Rogers's invitation to discuss the genesis of his learning, but both men mentioned friends, an interesting symmetry in the form of their talk. Rogers referred to a "psychiatrist friend" (turn #3) and Buber to a "friend of mine, a great friend, a great man" (turn #8). The reciprocity of disclosure and the invoking of their networks of friends are further indications that these two near-strangers have made considerable progress toward mutuality even in these early minutes.

Rogers then pauses in the discussion to suggest adjusting the table at which they are sitting. He explains that "I can't face the mike and face you at the same time" and asks if Buber would "mind if I turned the table just a little?" (turn #15). Although this interrupted them, it also verified for Buber and the audience how seriously Rogers approached the conversation. He cared enough about the quality of their conversation to interrupt it in this way so he could be even more involved—so his loyalties to the audiences (the people present in the auditorium and those who might someday hear the tape or read the transcript) would not have to be tested against his commitment to listen to Buber.

Friedman then told a story about a naïve theological student who had read Buber's work, a story that might be interpreted as a comment on Rogers's first question, whether this was Friedman's intention or not. The punchline was the student's parting question to Friedman: "Professor Buber is so good. How is it he's not a Christian?" (turn #22). What are we to make of such a joke? It might be more than just a story to fill time. Rogers had begun by asking a question that even he recognized could be heard as impertinent; and although we interpret Buber's laughter as a marker of shared understanding of the context for the question, we can appreciate that others, perhaps Friedman, might view the question differently. Interpreted literally, Rogers's question might be seen not only as impertinent but even insulting, for it implies that in normal circumstances only therapists (like Rogers) could learn what Rogers knew.

These are subtle but common conversational issues, and are the stuff from which communication choices are made. Some analysts (e.g., Goffman, 1981; Grice, 1975), have called this shared recognition of unspoken subtleties "conversational implicature." It's probably safe to assume Rogers did not intend to insult Buber, but the question does call attention to their different professions and experiences, and seems, even if just a little, to privilege the experience of the psychotherapist as the more effective route—or at least the more common one—to learning about human relationships. Similarly, then, Friedman's story might be interpreted in context as commenting on Rogers's opening question by implying that it was somewhat disrespectful or naïve, even patronizing—a kind of psychotherapeutic parochialism. Although listeners should also not assume Friedman intended his story to insult Rogers or to put him in his place, it is possible that a Buber devotee might respond in this context by sharing the humor of Rogers's question, yet turning it in a way that emphasizes its impertinence more than its amusement.

Buber then tags Friedman's story with one of his own ("a true . . . story, too, . . . not just an anecdote" [turn #23]) that has essentially the same theme, this time the naïve ignorance of Jews by Christians. This story might have been intended to surpass Friedman, with a story that is "true" and not an anecdote (implying that Friedman's was not true—does he mean his is *also* a true story?). But it could also be heard as a continuation of an implicit analogy that Rogers, as a therapist, is somehow like the story's ignorant and parochial Christians. Another interpretation is that Buber, recognizing the implication and perhaps even inferring a rhetorical intent to Friedman's story, wished to deflect attention away from it by telling another similar one. Buber may have thought that if he told such a story there would be less occasion for any offense to be taken. Buber enjoyed stories, and much of his teaching was done through them. We see no evidence that Buber was offended by Rogers's question or that his story had any particular competitive intention. He has simply found an appropriate moment for a brief and entertaining narrative.

Rogers, however, sounds flummoxed, and perhaps a bit puzzled about how to continue after the round of stories. Perhaps he was pondering their significance. Another possibility is raised by Friedman (1987, pp. 392–393), who felt after the dialogue that Rogers was somewhat "annoyed" and "irritated" with him (the accuracy of which was later confirmed through a mutual friend). Friedman inferred that Rogers was annoyed because, as Friedman put it, a moderator was "getting in the middle of his [Rogers's] dialogue with Buber." If so, this might have been one of those spots where Rogers thought Friedman was intruding. Rogers might simply have felt that telling a joke after the table had been moved and when Rogers was prepared to continue was an unnecessary distraction, or perhaps he thought one or both stories were somehow critiques of his question. In any event, Rogers does not respond to the content or possible implications of the stories, and follows Buber's joke with an abrupt "Well, I'd like to . . . shift to a question that I have often wondered about" (turn #27).

Question 2: Mutuality and Therapy

The discussion of the second question focused on conceptual ground the two men shared, and as such it occupied fully half of the dialogue. Rogers was a psychotherapist who thought of his relationship with clients as a specialized form of dialogue. Buber was a philosopher who had written about dialogue in terms of an "I-Thou" relationship that to Rogers caught the tenor of therapy at its best moments. For most of his adult life, too, Buber had been sought out especially by younger people to establish informal helping relationships. Although Buber was not a professional therapist, he knew he frequently engaged in conversations that had some degree of therapeutic intent.

Rogers phrased his basic question to focus precisely on the convergence of these two perspectives, Buber's I-Thou where it confronted Rogers's emphasis on dialogic moments: "I have wondered whether [3.1] your concept—or your experience—of what you have termed the I-Thou relationship is . . . similar to what I see as the effective moment in a therapeutic relationship."[2] He continued: "And I wonder . . . —if you would permit me—I might take a moment or two to say what I see [Buber: Yes, yes] as essential in that, and then perhaps you could comment on it from your point of view" (turn #27). He then developed at some length his views on entering the relationship as a "subjective person" rather than a "scrutinizer," on being "whole" or "transparent" in the relationship, on accepting or being willing for the other "to be the person he is," on viewing the other's experience "the way [it] seems to him," and on having the other "sense something of those attitudes." As a consequence, Rogers said, there may occur "a real, . . . experiential meeting of persons, in which . . . each of us is changed" (turn #27). The question privileged neither view and simply asked Buber to compare Rogers's description with his own experience. Rogers concluded with the sort of provisional statement, inviting exploration, that characterized his approach over the years: "Now . . . I see that as having some resemblance to the sort of thing you have talked about in the I-Thou relationship. Yet, I suspect there are differences" (turn #27).

Rogers's clearly stated focus on the *effective moments* in therapy, not on the whole relationship or any ongoing dialogic state, is a key for evaluating subsequent scholarly commentaries on the dialogue that we

believe have misstated Rogers's position. He described what he and
clients experienced during those crucial but fleeting moments and
asked Buber if that was similar to the I-Thou concept. During Rogers's
statement of the question, Buber can be heard several times responding
vocally in ways that indicate close attention. (Such nonverbal vocaliza-
tions by both principals happened frequently throughout the dialogue.)

Buber responds by beginning to set limits or boundaries for using
the term "dialogue." The therapeutic relationship, he begins, is "a very
good example for a certain mode of . . . dialogic existence" (turn #28).[3]
Buber continues with a fairly lengthy two-part response about the "essential difference" (turn #34) between therapist and client roles. The
tone is rather like a lecture, which Rogers interrupts twice. First,
Rogers asks permission to interrupt, and Buber replies, "Yeah, please
do" (turn #30). Rogers then takes issue with Buber's use of the term
"sick" to designate a client. He says that if he thought of the client as
truly sick, he was "not going to be of as much help as I might be" (turn
#31). Buber interrupts to say, "I don't mean this. I . . . let me . . . leave
out this . . . word 'sick.' . . . A man coming to you for help" (turn #34).
Buber then continues the analysis he had begun. Rogers interrupts a
second time to check his understanding of Buber's first point:

> BUBER: . . . And now this is the first point, as far as I see it. And
> the second is—now, please, you—
>
> ROGERS: Uh, yes, I'm not . . . entirely sure—
>
> BUBER: You may . . . interrupt me any moment.
>
> ROGERS: Oh, all right. I . . . really wanted to . . . understand that.
> . . . The fact that I am able to see him with less distortion than he
> sees me [3.1], and that I do have the role of helping him and that
> he's not . . . trying to know me . . . in that same sense—that's what
> you mean by this "detached presence"? . . .
>
> BUBER: Yes, h-mmm hmm.
>
> ROGERS: I just wanted to make sure I—
>
> BUBER: H-hmm. Hmmm.
>
> ROGERS: OK.
>
> BUBER: Yes . . . only this.

Buber continues with his second point, that the therapist can "see it, feel
it, experience it from the two sides" (which Buber often called *inclusion*),

whereas the client "cannot do it at all." In other words, "You are not equals and cannot be" (turn #44).

Rogers responds that what Buber has said "stirs up lots of reactions," and he begins "on a point that I think we would agree on," that "if this client comes to the point where he can experience what he is expressing, but also can experience my understanding of it and reaction to it, and so on, then really therapy is just about over" (turn #45). Buber seems to agree: "Yes. This is just what I mean" (turn #46).[4]

Rogers then begins to address the issue that divides them for the rest of their exploration of this question and even beyond. Rogers explains his experience of psychotherapy to Buber:

> I've sometimes wondered whether this is simply a personal idiosyncracy of mine, but it seems to me that . . . when another person is . . . really expressing himself and his experience and so on, . . . I don't feel, in the way that you've described, different from him. That is—I don't know quite how to put this—but I feel as though [3.8] in that moment his way of looking at his experience, distorted though it might be, . . . is something I can look upon as . . . having equal authority, equal validity with the way I see life and experience. And it seems to me that that really is the basis of helping, in a sense. (turn #47)

To this, Buber responds with a simple "yes" (turn #48). Rogers provides a succinct statement of his position: "And I do feel that's a real sense of equality between us" (turn #49). In discussing this issue with Buber, Rogers relies on the validity of his own experience, in the same way that he says he assumes the validity of his clients' experience to them. We note Rogers's emphasis on a *sense of equality* rather than denying some tangibly "real" *in*equality (see Rogers, 1987). Buber's response is pointed: "No doubt of it. But . . . I am not speaking now about your feeling but about a real situation" (turn #50). Rogers is grounded in his own experience; Buber seems to want to make a wider and more abstract point about the human condition. Buber accepts the validity of Rogers's experience for Rogers himself, but he denies its applicability to the question of the "real situation," concluding, "You cannot change it" (turn #50).

With some disagreement or misunderstanding having emerged, Rogers attempts a joke, apparently to indicate his agreement with Buber's last comment: "Well now, now I'm wondering . . . who is Martin Buber, you or me, because what I feel—" (turn #51), whereupon

Buber and the audience laugh. But Buber objects, stating that he is not "Martin Buber" (turn #54) in the sense of a "quoted man that . . . thinks so and so and so on" (turn #54). Perhaps Buber was anticipating (correctly, as it turned out) that Rogers was not merely agreeing with what Buber had said, but that Rogers was in some sense going to bring "Buber the Author" into the conversation, and Buber was reminding him that it is Buber the person, not Buber the author, who is engaged with Rogers on stage. Buber attempts to restore the focus with a summary of what they had been talking about, when Rogers interjects, "Now, let's forget that facetious remark. What . . . I wanted to say is this . . ." (turn #59). Rogers agrees that an objective situation of inequality exists but insists that "it has been my experience that that is reality when it is viewed from the outside, and that that really has *nothing* to do with the relationship that produces therapy. . . . That is something . . . immediate, equal, a meeting of two persons on an equal basis—even though . . . in the world of . . . I-It [a reference to a concept of Buber the author!] that could be seen as a very unequal relationship" (turn #59). Buber responds, "Hmm. Now, Dr. Rogers, this is the first point where we must say to one another, 'We disagree'" (turn #60), to which Rogers responds "Okay" (turn #61), followed by audience laughter.

But they don't simply agree to disagree. Buber continues to press his point and then asks Rogers, first, if he has dealt with schizophrenic and, second, with paranoid clients. Rogers says "some" to both questions (turns #63, 65, 67).[5] Buber then asks Rogers whether he can form "the same kind of relationship in the one case and in the other? . . . Can you . . . meet the paranoiac just in the same kind?" Rogers qualifies his answer by saying he has never worked in a psychiatric hospital, so may not have seen the worst cases, but then responds not from a theory but from his experience of attempting to establish dialogue with these persons:

> And . . . one of the things that I say very tentatively, because I realize this is opposed by a great weight of psychiatric and psychological opinion, . . . but I would say that there is *no* difference in the relationship that I form . . . with a normal person, a schizophrenic, a paranoid . . . —I don't really feel any difference. (turn #71)

Rogers then again emphasizes the qualifying theme of moments of equality: "It seems to me that . . . the moments where . . . persons are most likely to change, or I even think of it as moments in which people *do* change, . . . are the moments in which perhaps the relationship is experienced the same on *both* sides" (turn #73). Clearly he is not asserting by the word "same" that both persons have mystically fused or identical perceptions; rather, he evidently means that for a unique moment the unequal roles fall away and each experiences the other's presence apart from the role.

Friedman interrupts to pose a question, but Buber says, "No. Would you . . . wait a moment?" (turn #76). He then explains in impersonal and certain terms the differences in the limits set for dialogue by paranoid and schizophrenic persons. When Rogers attempts to respond (Rogers: "Yes, I think I see that as . . ." [turn #77]), Buber interrupts him to allow Friedman to speak (Buber: "Yes, now, Dr. Friedman may want to come—" [turn #78]). This is not one of the dialogic highlights of the evening.

Friedman indicates that he is acting in his moderator role, and wishes to ask Rogers to explore the reciprocity issue "one step further." He summarizes what he heard from Buber and Rogers and concludes, "And I wondered if this might not be . . . perhaps just a difference, if not of . . . words, of viewpoint, where you [Rogers] were thinking of how you feel *toward* him [a client], that is, that he is an equal person and you respect him" (turn #79). A brief pause is followed by laughter from the audience. Perhaps Buber or Rogers engaged in some nonvocal behavior that elicited the reaction. At any rate, although the query was directed to Rogers, Buber responds: "There remains a *decisive* difference" (turn #80), and he reiterates his point in particularly dramatic terms: "This is— . . . I used to say, totality of different . . . by the whole heaven, but I would rather prefer to say by the whole *hell*, a difference from your [Rogers's?] attitude. . . . This is a man in hell. . . . A man in hell cannot think, cannot imagine . . . helping another. How *could* he? (turn #80)" Rogers continues by explaining that in the "most real moments of therapy" he isn't motivated by a desire to help either. It is "a desire to meet a person" rather than a motive of "now I want to . . . help" that is primary to his work as a therapist. He concludes: "I've learned through my experience that when we *can* meet, then help does occur, but that's a by-product" (turn #81).

Friedman pursues the point further by asking Rogers whether he would agree "this is not fully reciprocal" (turn #82) because his client does not have the attitude of wanting to understand him. Rogers agrees with Friedman, excepting only that "perhaps in the moments where real change takes place, then I wonder if it isn't reciprocal in the sense that . . . I am able to see this individual as he is in that moment . . . and he really senses my understanding and acceptance of him. And that I think is what *is* reciprocal and is perhaps what produces change" (turn #83). Buber then agrees regarding Rogers's experience, but when he looks "on the whole situation"—the therapist's and the client's—he sees that Rogers gives the client something to make him equal, and that equality "may not last but one moment." "It is not the situation, as far as I see, not the situation of an hour; it is a situation of minutes. And these *minutes* are made possible by you. Not at all by him" (turn #84). Rogers says that although he agrees with the last part, he does "sense some . . . real disagreement." What he gives a client, Rogers states, is "permission to be. . . . Which is a little different somehow from bestowing something on him" (turn #85). Buber's response is gracious: "I think no human being can give more than this. [3.1] Making . . . life possible for the other, if only for a moment. [3.3] Permission" (turn #86). Rogers then observes wryly that "if we don't look out, we'll agree" (turn #87), which stimulated laughter. Buber then takes the initiative, suggesting, "Now let's go on" (turn #88).

This interchange has extraordinary implications for how persons with unequal status might imagine or fashion a mutual experience of dialogue. Such knotty problems occur often in human affairs as we struggle with cultural differences, bureaucratic power, political decision making, and even personal or family roles.

Rogers had asked a general question of Buber—to compare Rogers's concept of the effective moments in a therapeutic relationship with Buber's view of the I-Thou relationship. In his question, Rogers premised that the *effective moments* might be the crucial factor. Of the many relevant issues to which Buber might have responded, he selected what Friedman (1985, 1991) has called the "problematic of mutuality." In chapter 7, we revisit this problematic to stress how the notion of the dialogic moment was essentially agreed on by Buber and Rogers, and how much it contributes to a theory of dialogue.

Perhaps the larger issue on which they disagree in this segment of the dialogue is an epistemological question, one largely unacknowledged in previous scholarly commentary. Although Rogers usually wants to be quite tentative in drawing conclusions from what people say about themselves, he is typically also insistent on respecting the validity of first-person reports of experience. In the dialogue, Rogers repeatedly described his subjective experience; Buber accepted Rogers's description of his personal feeling (Rogers had the habit of using "feeling" as a near-synonym for perception or belief) but analyzed the therapeutic relationship as an "objective situation" almost from the perspective of an outside observer. Rogers's commitment to personal experience as a more or less phenomenological way of knowing clearly contrasted with Buber's rhetorical commitment to an objective definition of limits placed on knowing, limits imposed by interpersonal roles, for example (cf. Brink, 1987). In other words, Rogers communicated as though he thought it should make a difference to Buber that he (Rogers) had experienced something to be true in his therapy. By and large, it didn't. Buber communicated as though he thought he could convince Rogers that he (Buber) had a privileged insight into the objective limits placed on mutuality and dialogue in any therapy. By and large, he couldn't.

Buber's discourse did become somewhat more provisional as the dialogue developed, but the cumulative impression is one of Buber describing concepts that seem real and independent of anyone's conception of them, and asserting a reality that is not dependent on individual experience. Here, as elsewhere, Rogers reflects on what he thinks, believes, or has experienced; then Buber replies with what is "really" true.

Question 3: Inner Meeting and Problems of Terminology

After Buber suggests "Now let's go on," Rogers moves to another topic: a "type of meeting which has a lot of significance to me in my work that, as far as I know, . . . you haven't talked about." Consistent with the provisional style he advocated, Rogers allows, "Now I may be mistaken on that, I don't know" (turn #89). He puts it this way:

> it seems to me one of the most important types of meeting or relationships . . . is the person's relationship to himself. . . . In . . . therapy, again, which I have to draw on because that's my background . . . of experience— . . . there are some very vivid moments in which the individual is meeting . . . some aspect of himself, a feeling he has never recognized before, . . . something of a meaning in himself that he has never known before. (turns #89, 91)

Rogers appears to be speaking metaphorically of the surprise element of dialogue, that persons who think they know what they have to say can, within certain moments of a good conversation, surprise themselves by saying something fresh, new, interesting, and maybe even strange. Rogers suggests this personal surprise may be similar to the surprise of encountering someone or something new, and this is phrased metaphorically in Buber's terms as a sort of "meeting." Buber's response is clear and direct, but evidently surprises his questioner.

Buber says that with this question they "approach . . . a problem of language," and that "you call something . . . dialogue . . . that I cannot call so" (#92)—although Rogers did not use the term "dialogue" anywhere in his question. Buber wants another term for this, and asserts that "for what I call dialogue, . . . there is essentially necessary the moment of surprise [Rogers: Moment of surprise?]" (turns #92, 93). Buber explains further that although "a man can surprise himself," it is "in a very different manner . . . from how a person can surprise another person" (turn #94). He also adds that in true meeting or dialogue the differences between partners are "prized." (The "prized," which sounds more like Rogers's language than Buber's, is from a paraphrase describing the brief time while the tape was being changed; the paraphrase appeared in the original typescript circulated by Rogers and has appeared with each republication of the dialogue transcript.) The tape resumes with Rogers saying that he would like sometime to play recordings of interviews for Buber to show how "the *surprise* element really can be there," but he also accommodates Buber's view by allowing that typically the otherness within is "not something to be prized" (turn #95).

Buber then decides to discuss—as a lecturer might—the importance of "appreciat[ing] terms," which "modern psychology," Buber says (turn #96), generally does not. Although Buber uses the examples of *consciousness* and *the unconscious* to illustrate this problem (not particularly apt terms for Rogers's approach or for the topics of this dialogue), by implication Rogers, clearly a psychologist, and not overtly excepted by Buber from his complaint, is also guilty of this error. Consider the context: Buber had just been talking with a psychologist about a terminological disagreement in which he thought the psychologist missed the point, and then immediately generalizes about psychologists' problems in defining terms; it would not have been much of a stretch for his partner to interpret this as a rebuke based on an overgeneralization (Buber's examples appear to represent a psychoanalytic literature that Rogers himself had critiqued). Rogers chooses to ignore this issue and abruptly caps it by moving on somewhat tersely to a fourth question area by saying "I agree with you very much on that"—that different experiences "deserve . . . different term[s]" (turn #97).

Buber has clearly explained his objections to using the term "dialogue" to refer to the phenomenon of self-meeting, illustrating his insistence on rather precise use of terminology. Rogers was willing to accept that calling self-meeting "dialogue" was pushing the analogy too far and was not appropriate or useful (although Rogers did explain that the element of suprise is often present, and we should note that he did not assert that inner meeting was dialogue as Buber used that concept). But, unfortunately, we did not learn from this exchange much of what Buber thought of the phenomenon of intrapersonal self-meeting, or a "person's relationship to himself" (turn #89)—whatever it might be called. We did not even learn what, if anything, Buber would call it.

Question 4: Human Nature as Positive or Polar

Rogers wanted to bring up another question, he said, but "I don't know quite how to put it." He began:

> As I see . . . people coming together *in* relationship in therapy, . . . [2.5] I think that one of the things I have come to believe and feel and experience is that . . . what I think of as . . . human nature or basic human nature—that's poor, a poor term, you may have a better way of putting it—is something that is really to be trusted. . . . [I]t seems to me in some of your writings I catch that, something of that same feeling. . . . Now, I don't know. Again, I just . . . hope that perhaps . . . that would stir some comments from you. (turn #97)

Buber responded obliquely, perhaps wanting more time to think, perhaps not understanding fully, or perhaps even wanting a literally focused question: "I don't yet see the exact question in this" (turn #98). Although the basic issue about which Rogers invited "some comments" seems clear enough, Rogers initially takes Buber literally: "The only question that I'm raising is: 'Do you agree?' I suppose. . . . Or, if I'm not clear, please ask me other questions. I'll try to put it . . . another way." Rogers then rephrased the question, with a new context of "orthodox psychoanalysis," which according to him believes the person "consists mostly of instincts and attitudes and so on . . . which must be controlled." That belief, Rogers said, "runs *diametrically* contrary to my own experience" (turn #99). Perhaps this rephrasing was partly a response to Buber's earlier chastisement of psychology; Rogers may be attempting to identify with Buber by distancing himself from psychoanalytically oriented psychology and its major terms or to remind Buber (and the audience) of the difference between himself and the psychoanalysts.

Buber now responds by explaining what he calls the *"polar* reality" (turn #100) of the person: the so-called good and the bad, what can most and least be trusted, the best and the worst, are all "dependent on one another, attached to one another" (turn #102). This observation, of course, is not only consistent with the Taoist thought that engaged Buber (and Rogers) for a time, but is squarely in the tradition of dialectical theory in interpersonal relations that has developed a research tradition with even more sophistication in recent years (see Baxter & Montgomery, 1996). In helping another, "we can strengthen, we can help *him* strengthen, the one positive . . . pole. . . . And even, perhaps, we can strengthen the force of direction in him because this polarity is very . . . often directionless" (turn #102). Rogers attempts to articulate his understanding: "And if I get the last portion of that particularly, you're saying that perhaps we can help the individual to strengthen the 'yes,' that is to affirm life rather than refuse it" (turn #103). Buber basically agrees when he says that "I differ only in this word, I would not say 'life.' I would not put an object to it. [Rogers: Uh huh.] I would say simply 'yes'" (turns #104, 105, 106). Rogers then vocalized "uh huh" four times, followed by a significant pause of four seconds, after which he calls on Friedman: "You're . . . looking as though you want to say something" (turn #108). Friedman, again initiating his contribution by referring to his "function as a moderator," pursues an additional topic (turn #111).

This discussion, brief as it was, became perhaps the sharpest conceptual difference that emerged during the dialogue. Rogers had consistently stressed the *actualizing tendency* to describe how persons grow in positive directions as long as they are not thwarted by other influences. Buber recognizes that his view is "near to what you [Rogers] say, but somewhat different" (turn #100). He frames the human person in a twofold or polar way, in which the poles are not good and evil, but acceptance and refusal, direction and a chaotic state. Rogers seems to reflect the optimism that came to characterize much of humanistic psychology; in Buber, we see reflections of Jewish theology and of existential philosophy (Friedman, 1976, pp. 27–33; 1986). Both understand the self as socially constructed and as responding to internal direction. A similar difference is found in the exchange of published letters between Rogers and Rollo May (see Kirschenbaum & Henderson, 1989a; and for comment, Friedman, 1982, 1991). The two positions may not be as different as they initially appear. At one point, Rogers seems to agree with Buber on this matter, and we discuss elsewhere (Anderson & Cissna, 1997, p. 83) that Buber had said in his lecture the previous evening that he had never met a young person who seemed hopelessly bad. Rogers did not believe that all humans are inevitably good, but that they will *tend* ("actualizing *tendency*") to make constructive decisions for growth when they see the opportunity to do so. The basic direction is toward actualization, or meeting one's potential. While stressing the polar reality of human existence in ways Rogers did not, Buber also optimistically affirms—as did Rogers—the potential for direction and growth if humans can create a socially appropriate kind of directedness.

Question 5: Acceptance and Confirmation

Friedman posed the final two questions of the dialogue. In the first, he introduced Rogers's use of the term "acceptance" and quoted two sentences from Rogers's then unpublished essay "Some Hypotheses Concerning the Facilitation of Personal Growth," which would later appear as a chapter in *On Becoming a Person*. He then asks "whether Professor Buber would look on confirmation as similar to that, or would he see confirmation as including, . . . perhaps, not being accepted, including some demand on the other that might mean in a sense a nonacceptance of his feelings at the moment in order to confirm him later" (turn #111). Friedman seems to have asked what is sometimes called a leading question, one that presumes or implies the answer the questioner expects to hear.

Buber replies that "every [2.9] true . . . existential relationship between two persons . . . begins with acceptance," by which he means "being able to . . . tell, or to, rather not to tell, but only to make it felt to the other person, . . . that I accept him just as he is." But "confirming means [4.5] first of all, . . . accepting the whole potentiality of the other . . . and making even a decisive difference in his potentiality. . . . I can . . . recognize in him, know in him, more or less, the person he has been . . . *created* to become" (turn #112). Buber's response is not provisional: his definition of confirming is not just what the term means *to him*, as he uses it, but evidently what confirming inherently means. This wording might, of course, be an artifact of Buber speaking a nonnative language. But such assuredness and certainty does not clear much space for disagreement, nor does it allow for his partner's definition that may differ from his own. Buber concludes with a question: "This is what you mean?" (turn #114).

Rogers still says "yes," and then explains his somewhat broader use of acceptance: "I think that sounds very much like the quality that . . . is in the experience that I think of as acceptance, though I have tended to put it differently. I . . . think that we do accept the individual *and* his potentiality" (turn #115). This sort of acceptance, Rogers continues, is "the strongest factor making for change that I know" (turn #115). Rogers evidently believes that Friedman has asked about a mere semantic difference—the two men use different terms for the same concept. For Rogers, acceptance includes recognizing and responding to the potential of the other, whereas Buber wants to "distinguish between 'accepting' and 'confirming'" (turn #116) because for him the former does not include the recognition of human potentiality.

In the most frequently cited transcript from the decades following the dialogue, the appendix to Buber's (1965b) *The Knowledge of Man*, it appears that Friedman then interjects another question that might have kept Rogers from responding. In fact, Rogers did have such an opportunity but didn't take it. In his version, Friedman (as editor) was generous to Rogers. Perhaps out of sensitivity to the time constraints established by conference organizers, and cognizant of his role as questioner, Rogers seems to be seeking to end the conversation. Yet he does so somewhat awkwardly and at a time that could appear self-serving if the audience thought Rogers was trying to avoid replying to Buber's strong reassertion of his own position (i.e., helping others even in the struggle against themselves can happen "only" if one distinguishes between acceptance and confirmation as Buber does). Buber, it is clear, is willing to continue and rejects the implication that he is tiring (see the interchange itself, which we quote in the opening of the next section of this chapter). So Friedman raises what becomes the final major question of the evening.

The issue of acceptance and confirmation is complex and difficult, and the parties themselves do not discuss it sufficiently for us to know precisely what they think of each other's positions. Buber spoke twice; Rogers once. At the end of Buber's first comment, he asked if what he'd said is what Rogers means, to which Rogers replied in the affirmative, while suggesting they are just using the terms differently. Although Friedman (1986, 1994, 1996) sees a significant difference in the views they express about confirmation/acceptance, the dialogue itself does not disclose whether the difference is solidly conceptual or merely semantic. Scholars might wonder how crucial the distinction was to Buber when, in an essay revised subsequent to the dialogue, he used the two terms basically synonymously, without asserting the distinction he did with Rogers. In genuine dialogue, Buber (1965b) wrote, "The true turning of his person to the other includes this confirmation, this acceptance" (p. 85). Friedman (1976), too, has used Rogers's term "acceptance" as essentially interchangeable with Buber's "confirmation" (pp. 191–192). In a famous essay written a year after the dialogue, "Characteristics of the Helping Relationship," Rogers (1961) cited their dialogue and referred approvingly to Buber's phrase "confirming the other" (p. 55). In this essay and thereafter, Rogers used the terms "acceptance" and "confirmation" synonymously.

Friedman has cited the dialogue on this issue to separate Buber from Rogers conceptually, but without crediting Rogers's stipulation much. Contrary to Friedman's (1986, 1992, 1994, 1996) implication, Buber's confirmation and Rogers's acceptance both appear to be dynamic, not static, concepts; and Rogers's notion of congruence should not be conflated with acceptance and confirmation. Friedman (1991) summarized his position regarding Buber and Rogers on this issue in this way:

> People do not just naturally develop so that all I have to do is accept them—in this I agree with Buber. They are in a struggle themselves about their own direction. While I cannot impose on you what your direction should be, I can listen and respond to you and, thus walking that stretch of the way with you, I can help you in your struggle. (1996, p. 368)

Although Friedman intends to support Buber *in contrast* to Rogers's position, it is difficult in the context of Rogers's writings or the dialogue's interchange to imagine Rogers disagreeing. Acceptance is *not* enough; surely no client-centered therapist who worked with Rogers—if indeed any therapist—could believe that "all I have to do is accept" clients and then they will "just naturally develop" without an inner struggle of some sort. Rogers's therapy was attuned to such internal struggle, and he wrote about how acceptance, however powerful, was only one of three facilitative conditions (see chapter 4). Yet Friedman wants to distance Rogers's view even further from Buber's: "I don't confirm you by being a blank slate or blank check. I can confirm you only by being the person I am. You'll never be confirmed by me simply by my putting myself aside and being nothing but a mirror reflecting you" (1986, p. 426; also see 1992, p. 49; 1994, p. 63; 1996, p. 368).[6] These metaphors do not accurately reflect Rogers's position, and surely Rogers would have agreed that these conditions would not constitute confirmation or acceptance. "Being the person I am" and not "putting myself aside," in fact, are good indicators of congruence, another of Rogers's facilitative conditions. Perhaps Friedman has overstated his case for emphasis, but Rogers does not describe acceptance, in the dialogue or elsewhere, as anything like a "blank slate," a "blank check," or "nothing but a mirror reflecting you."

Perhaps the most supportable position is that Buber and Friedman made more of the struggle to confirm (to "wrestle with" the other—see Friedman, 1994, 1996), whereas Rogers (perhaps because of his unique professional praxis) gave greater emphasis to the need, especially at the

outset of a therapeutic relationship, to accept the other uncondition-
ally even while remaining open to struggling with the client to achieve
the change that is the client's potential (Cissna & Anderson, 1990).

Question 6: Within and Between

Friedman asked, "May I be so unmerciful as to just ask one last question?" (turn #122), which turned out to be about the locus of value. He
said that he understands Rogers as locating value "as being inside one,"
whereas Buber locates value "more in 'the between.'" "I wonder," he
asked, "is this a real issue between the two of you?" (turn #124). The
answer is that listeners don't really find out. Rogers spoke first after a
silence of almost six seconds: "I might . . . give one type of expression
to my view on that that . . . puts it in quite different terms than what
you've used, and yet I think . . . really relates to the same thing."
Rogers then explained the goal of therapy being "'becoming,' or . . .
being knowingly and acceptingly that which one most deeply *is*." He
continued, "In other words, that too expresses a real trust in the . . .
process which we *are* that . . . perhaps may not entirely be shared between us" (turn #125). In a previous study (Anderson & Cissna, 1997,
pp. 101–102), we speculated why previous transcripts had added
"tonight" at the end of this sentence, as though Rogers was referring to
his present relationship with Buber. It seems more likely, considering
the syntax and tone of Rogers's statement, that he meant to refer to the
therapist-client relationship generally. Buber responded in different
terms entirely. He thought "perhaps it would be of a certain aid if I add
. . . a problem that . . . I found when reading just this article . . . of yours,
. . . or a problem that approached *me*." "You speak about persons, and
the concept 'person' is . . . seemingly . . . very near . . . to the concept
'individual.' I would . . . think that it's advisable to distinguish between
them." Buber explained the difference in how he uses the terms (one
can become more uniquely individualized without becoming more of a
"person"), and concluded, "I'm *against* individuals and *for* persons"
(turn #126). Rogers responds simply, "Correct" (turn #127).

   This is a curious point to press with Rogers. Buber first substitutes
"individual" for what he knew was Rogers's term ("person") and then
analyzes his problem with the word "individual." He does so as if he
was responding to Rogers, but Rogers's construct of "person" is entirely
consistent with Buber's point. Essentially Buber has agreed with
Rogers's central argument in the cited article, which was published subsequently as chapter 6 of *On Becoming a Person*—that to become a per-

son is a social and interpersonal accomplishment, and that to become a person is, among other characteristics, to open oneself to experience and be more able to meet the world in, as Buber says, *"real contact, in real reciprocity* of the world in all the points in which the world can meet man" (turn #126). At any rate, Buber's response was not closely aligned to Friedman's question, nor to Rogers's prior response to that question. This was the weakest interchange of the evening. Despite their willingness to continue some minutes earlier, both men were probably tiring, and perhaps they were signaling that the session should end.

The event concludes with Friedman thanking Rogers and Buber for a dialogue that was "certainly unique in *my* experience: . . . it is a *real* dialogue, taking place in front of an audience" (turn #128). Friedman's comment points to the connection between the dialogue's content and its process—the what and the how of their talk. Let us now turn to a more complete look at how process issues of audience effects, role enactment, and conversational style influenced the interaction of Buber and Rogers on stage.

THE RHETORIC OF AUDIENCE, ROLE,
AND STYLE IN PUBLIC DIALOGUE

Influences of Audience in Public Dialogue

From the dialogue (turns #117–121):

ROGERS: I just feel that one um difficulty with a dialogue is that there could easily be no end, but I think that uh both in mercy to Dr. Buber and to the audience, this is—so I will not—[Buber overlaps] [Laughter]

BUBER: This—what do you say?

ROGERS: I say that out of, out of consideration for you and consideration to—

BUBER: Not for me. Heh heh.

ROGERS: Oh, all right—[Laughter] just just consideration for the audience—

People usually assume that speakers say what they have to say and then audiences hear their speech, or fail to. The speaker is presumed active; the audience passive. However, as Buber and Rogers both knew, every auditor actively coauthors the developing meanings of discourse. Speakers can hardly make speech decisions independent of some sort of estimate of who will listen: "Who is with me?" "What do they need or expect to hear?" "What assumptions guide what's okay to say?" "What will they think of me?" "How can I continue to ask for their attention?" These questions do not exhaust the possibilities, of course, and they aren't usually asked and answered explicitly by speakers. Rather, questions of audience are enfolded within an utterance at deep cultural levels. Audience-sense is an active element of basic humanity—so audiences are active elements of speaking, not simply receivers of speech.

Unfortunately, researchers have largely neglected how an audience that overhears a conversation affects how communication develops. Limited research on the broadcast news interview (Heritage, 1985, pp. 99–112), a speech genre similar in some respects to the Buber–Rogers meeting, suggests that audience presence does influence such psychological and linguistic factors as *footing* (how participants frame their own and others' status in conversation) and *formulations* (overt characterizations of the talk of others). Given the paucity of such research, however, we have found it useful to speculate on other rhetorical effects of the presence of audiences on public conversation.

At one level, Buber and Rogers were speaking to each other as a primary audience. Beyond that, each expected Friedman, the designated moderator, and DeWitt Baldwin, who coordinated and introduced the event, to be auditors as well. This much is obvious. Less obvious to readers of the transcript are the 400 additional audience members who "silently participated" (turn #128), as Friedman said, in the discourse. Whether any of the participants could have imagined the many thousands of interested readers of their dialogue over the next half century and beyond is impossible to know.

In his essay, "Elements of the Interhuman," where Buber claimed that dialogue in public was impossible (1957b; see also 1965b, pp. 72–88, 184), he explained something of his reasoning. We infer that Buber was worried about the tendency of speakers to address themselves not to each other, but to court audience favor by becoming conversational "duelists," and that he considered dialogue to be compromised when an occasion defined certain persons in nonspeaking roles. Both of Buber's reasons thus reinforce our concern for the potential effects of audience on dialogic interaction.

At the time of their meeting, however, he even told Rogers, "I would . . . recommend to do it without an audience" (turn #76). And because no question-and-answer period was scheduled, the audience members were literally spectators, albeit occasionally vocal ones. Consistent with Buber's reservations, we should consider how observers might affect participants engaged in dialogue. We cannot know with certainty what influence the presence of two audiences—the live one observing that evening and a more distant potential audience represented by the tape recorder—had on Buber, Rogers, and their conversation. Nevertheless, we found indications in the discourse of seven potential influences of audience:

1. *A sense of competition.* Buber warned that although speakers in front of audiences might appear to be speaking to each other, they might merely be representing themselves and the other in persuasive packages for the consideration of the audience. Under such conditions of public commitment, a speaker could suffer a loss of face by changing his or her mind, or could lose face by appearing to be the loser in a competitive exchange. This doesn't mean that changing minds in public is impossible but that it is improbable, or perhaps less likely to be acknowledged publicly. However, openness to change and willingness to be surprised are basic dialogic criteria to Buber and other dialogic theorists. Although it is impossible to be certain, some evidence suggests that Buber, at least, considered the interchange partly in terms of a comparison between the force of his assertions and those of Rogers. After the dialogue, Buber remarked, "I was very kind to him. I could have been much sharper" (Friedman, 1983c, p. 227), and Friedman (1987), probably recalling the same comment, has also reported that Buber said "I could have been much harder on him" (p. 393). It sounds as if Buber was reacting in terms of the interpersonal dynamics of public competition—for example, the issues of Rogers's face and footing relative to his own—even while being complimentary about Rogers bringing himself "as a person" to the dialogue (Friedman, 1983c, p. 227).

2. *A desire of speakers to speak for those in the audience who do not have a voice.* Rather than to speak always for self, a speaker sensitive to an audience might be more likely to say, as Rogers did, such things as, "since I see time is going by" (#97) or "out of . . . consideration for the audience" (turns #119, 121). Such statements sound appropriate because the audience is, in Erving Goffman's words, a "ratified participant" in the dialogue (Goffman, 1981, p. 234). Just as Goffman and Fr. Walter Ong (1977, pp. 84–85) show in their analyses of broadcast talk—that the announcer-interviewer usually will be more responsible to, and mindful of, the audience than the interviewee—we might expect that Rogers, given the designated roles of this event, would be more sensitive to this function in his conversation with Buber.

3. *A preoccupation with the permanence of the current remarks.* Few public conversations these days are conducted without videotaping

or audiotaping, even if they aren't taped for broadcast. Compared with less formal personal dialogue, awareness of this kind of permanence could tend to make many speakers extra-cautious in making claims, and reluctant to risk creative spontaneity. Public and publicized conversations, therefore, are more likely to sound "canned" or managed, even if they are not intended to be so. Buber once advised against taping conversations because it artificially deflects talk away from a present audience and toward an absent hypothetical audience represented by the device:

> If two people are trying to talk with one another directly, honestly, and this electrical device is placed between them, to record what they say, they will no longer be talking to one another but to the machine. And the vital human response will be lost. They will not say the same things to one another that they would have said if the machine had not been taking it all down. So the machine not only sets up a wall between them, it also distorts what they actually say. (Hodes, 1971, p. 12)

No one can be certain how much, if any, spontaneity was sacrificed in this way in the Buber–Rogers meeting. In this dialogue, however, Rogers demonstrated he was particularly concerned with how the table and microphone were configured, and in adjusting them, referred to the audience's requirements for hearing and seeing, as well as to his own. Perhaps the satisfaction of both men with the dialogue indicates that they believed they met this challenge successfully.

4. *More accommodation to the dramatic requirements of a public occasion.* Goffman (1974) demonstrated that "often what talkers undertake to do is not to provide information to a recipient but to present dramas to an audience. Indeed, it seems that we spend most of our time not engaged in giving information but in giving shows" (p. 508). As media theorist Neil Postman (1985) has suggested, a high-intensity media culture has further reduced audience tolerance for shows that are merely "interesting" or "informative." Public events are expected to be entertaining dramatic performances. Television, a chief agency of this trend, influenced American society in 1957, although it was not nearly as entrenched in our psyches or our households as it has become since then. The desire to entertain might partially explain some moves in public dialogue toward light humor, cleverness, and storytelling. Rogers, who opened with a funny twist on a question, performed this role often in the dialogue. Both Friedman and Buber joked about the naïvete of Christians regarding Jews and Jewish religion, even though these jokes might have implied a not-altogether-friendly interpretation of Rogers's opening question; and all three principals attempted to

manage their talk to suggest that serious matters could be confronted in an atmosphere of good will.

5. *An exaggerated sense of agreement mixed with exaggerated distinctions between the speakers' positions.* Speakers might want to seem to agree in order to appear to their partner(s) to be cooperative, and to be seen as cooperative by the observing audience. At the same time, the presence of an audience might encourage speakers to highlight differences so the audience can "tell who the players are" and to increase interestingness. Cooperative public conversants, therefore, may assert or imply an agreement they might not actually experience—or, for reasons of identity, exaggerate a distinction. Both tendencies appear to contradict the dialogic advice of Buber and others, and yet, as we show later in the section on interpersonal styles, both tendencies can be found in this text.

6. *A tendency for speakers to take longer conversational turns.* Speakers may presume that a voiceless audience (in this case, persons who could not be assumed to be thoroughly familiar with the thought of either Buber or Rogers) would need more context for their remarks, or more amplification. Indeed, Robert Nofsinger (1991) reports that in broadcast interviews, both interviewer and interviewee "tend to get more extended turns than in everyday conversation" (p. 106). In this conversation, Rogers never asked a short question, and Buber rarely gave brief answers. Although discourse analysts often disagree over what qualifies an utterance technically as a "word," the tendencies are clear if we simply cite ballpark figures. For example, Rogers's first question took about 300 words, and Buber's reply was more than 750 words, equivalent to over three double-spaced pages of typing or printing with normal font and margins. Later, when Friedman became more involved, this pattern continued. His first question involved about 270 words, Buber's first reply was over 425 words, Rogers responded in about 180 words, and Buber completed this topic in another 245 words or so.

7. *A need to satisfy the time requirements of the event.* Whereas in daily life, conversations often last as long as their momentum sustains the participants, public dialogues (like television programs, then or now) are expected to last thirty minutes, an hour, or two hours. Audience members may have driven a long way or invested high expectations for their attendance, and regardless of whether they paid for admission, they usually expect their "money's worth." This investment introduces an element of planning not normally characteristic of genuine dialogue. As we wrote earlier, Rogers's own notes in preparation for the dialogue (Rogers, 1957a), for example, show that he drafted nine questions for Buber, presumably to raise interesting topics and to facilitate smooth transitions (see Anderson & Cissna, 1997, p. 18). He chose to ask only four of them, probably due to time constraints.

Rogers first remarked that "time is going by" (turn #97) in prefacing his fourth and (as it turned out) final question. In concluding that question he apparently began to terminate the evening's program. However, Friedman then began to ask his first question concerning acceptance and confirmation. After Buber's second response to this question, rather than further elaborate on his own views, Rogers again attempted to end the program, at which time Friedman seeks to ask "one last question" (turn #122). When Rogers first attempted to close, they had already gone well past the hour that the audience had been promised—and we suspect that Rogers had noticed, as we did when listening to the tape, that Buber's speech had slowed, he was using more and longer pauses, and he was making more speech mistakes and subsequent "repairs." Surely listeners would have been the poorer if we had not had Friedman's first question and the two responses; and we even wish Rogers had seen fit to extend his ideas one last time in response to Buber's second statement. On the other hand, the responses to Friedman's second question seemed the weakest of the evening and surely few would have minded had the conversation terminated prior to this point.

A taped dialogue before a public audience presents many rhetorical challenges to speakers, and critics of conversational texts should acknowledge and account for them. On the one hand, conversants (especially considering the reputations of these two men) are expected to be spontaneous and open not only to each other's ideas, but to possible changes in their own positions. Yet the dynamic of the public conversation in which they find themselves places certain decisive cross-pressures on them. Their speech is not just "for" this dialogue, but for immediate as well as temporally removed audiences that cannot be fully anticipated by the speakers. We should not be surprised that conversants, in this case Buber and Rogers, adapt to this contingency by adjusting what they have to say to the requirements of their roles.

Influences of Role in Public Dialogue

From the dialogue (turn #3):

ROGERS: One thing I think I would say to the audience before starting to talk with Dr. Buber is that this is most certainly an unrehearsed dialogue. Uh, the weather made it necessary for me to spend all day arriving here, uh, and so it was only an hour or two ago that I met Dr. Buber, even though I have met him a long time ago in his writings.

I think that the, uh, first question I would like to ask you, Dr. Buber, um, may sound a trifle impertinent, but I would like to explain it and then perhaps it won't seem impertinent. I have wondered: How have you lived so deeply in interpersonal relationships and gained such an understanding of the human individual, without being a psychotherapist? [Rogers adds I is explanation for the question]

BUBER: Hmmm. Er, It's rather a biographical question. Eh, eh, I think I must give instead of one answer, two [Rogers: Uhm huh]. One, eh, eh, [unclear: "aber" (German for "but") or perhaps "rather"]—this is only just a particular—is that I'm not eh entirely a stranger in, eh, let me say, psychiatry [Rogers: Uhm huh], because when I was a student—it's long ago—I hmm studied three terms uh psychiatry, and uh what eh they call in Germany "Psychiatrische-Klinique." [Buber further describes his studies and his inclination to "meet people"]

The 1957 meeting was advertised as a "dialogue," and both principals and most subsequent analysts have used the same term. We agree that dialogic communication developed. Yet, because of the presence of an audience and because of some relatively specific delineations of role, this conversation also resembled other public forms of communication. We have suggested that it seemed somewhat like a broadcast interview complete with "turn-type preallocations" (Greatbatch, 1988; see also Nofsinger, 1991, pp. 105–106). In other ways, it was like a classroom lesson in which an experienced teacher replies to an inquiring and less-experienced student. In yet others, its sharp responses and several lapses of listening suggested, although faintly, a debate tone, complete with a couple of near-put-downs. We analyze these issues because they influenced what Buber and Rogers said, and how they listened and reacted to each other. This was not a freeform and spontaneous conversation in which each conversant was equally free to engage ideas, but rather a demonstration of how a kind of dialogic interchange can develop even in a politically inflected public context.

Roles are patterns of behavior that become identified with social positions. The role distinctions in the Buber–Rogers dialogue are illuminating, if only because role distinctions are so seldom built into the structure of conversation. This does not mean, of course, that roles are inconsequential in conversation. If a district manager is having a conversation with a new trainee, both will probably be aware of how their different roles affect what they say and how they say it. Roles influence conversation, but the roles typically are preexisting ones: a mother speaks as a parent (role) to a high school principal (role) about discipline procedures at home and school, for example. These could be called "social roles." Roles that emerge informally and naturally from the flow of talk could be called "emergent roles": for example, one partner in a relationship finds that he or she more often breaks the ice, or jokes, or challenges the other. But rarely are conversational roles explicitly manufactured to guide talk, especially when genuine and spontaneous dialogue is desired (it would seem nonsensical to suggest, for example, "Let's have a spontaneous dialogue and see what develops; my job is to suggest topics and questions and your job is to reply to my topics"). This assumption, that communication in dialogue needs to be managed, creates what we call *enfolded roles*, which are real but not always obvious aspects of the dialogue that exist in the folds of the conversation's process rather than on the surface of its content.

An interchange involving enfolded roles suggests something more akin to an interview than to either a conversation as it is normally understood, or a dialogue as usually defined. Certainly interviews can, and often should, be "conversational," but that does not mean that everyday conversations would be better if structured as interviews.

Participants and organizers clearly specified the relevant roles. When Friedman said that Rogers was to "raise questions" to which Buber would respond, this made sense in the context of the Michigan conference. The theme of the conference concerned Buber's work, not Rogers's, and the audience surely was more interested in Buber's views. In journalistic terms, Buber's visit to the United States and his appearance on the University of Michigan campus were newsworthy (in fact, covered by campus and local newspapers), and it was normal for him to be placed in the role of expert. Because Rogers was an American who had acknowledged an intellectual debt to Buber, perhaps it was equally natural for him to assume a role that was, by comparison with Buber's, secondary and functional. Rogers's reputation as a facilitator and interviewer probably influenced the role decision as well. But what interactional price was paid for this choice?

However reasonable it was to rely on these roles, they clearly shaped the interpersonal politics of the ensuing conversation. Neither Buber nor Rogers disparaged roles, yet it is fair to ask how enfolded roles influence the quality of dialogue itself. Buber (1965b) suggests that dialogue partners must each be willing "to say what is really in his mind about the subject of the conversation," and to say it "without reduction and without shifting his ground" (p. 85). Further, "each must be determined not to withdraw when the course of the conversation makes it proper for him to say what he has to say" (1965b, p. 87) And: "No one . . . can know in advance what it is that he has to say; genuine dialogue cannot be arranged beforehand" (1965b, p. 87). Interviewers might have some difficulty with such suggestions, to say the least, because their role is dual. *Interviewers must contribute to the conversational content, because they are present, and at times they must not, because their role is also overtly facilitative.*

This dilemma means that often they enable the other's talk, sometimes at the expense of their own, because they bestow a particular gift of attention. To help another person talk before an audience (Rogers's assigned role in this dialogue), a conversant might occasionally deflect self-interest. Although an interviewee might be expected to be responsive, as Buber certainly was, a "questioner" is *expected to have questions or probes* should the conversation lag (as Rogers had). Thus, one role is spontaneously responsive; the other by definition requires planning what might later be said, or asked. The planning role reduces spontaneity as it asks the person to assume responsibility for *process* or, as social scientists sometimes say, the "maintenance functions" of communication. In Goffman's (1981) terms, Buber's and Rogers's different footing could not help but influence the potential for dialogic surprise. The enfolded roles, in the context of our *ploy-play* distinction developed in an earlier chapter, placed more responsibility for the ploy dimension of interaction management on Rogers, and gave Buber more freedom for ideational play.

Differences of enfolded role help explain why this dialogue developed as it did. Communication specialists customarily point out that all messages are dual messages in that they provide commentary on the topic addressed in the conversation and at the same time also comment on the relationship that connects the conversants. Bateson (1951, pp. 179–181) first referred to these functions as *report* and *command*; Watzlawick, Beavin, and Jackson (1967) called them the *content* and *relationship* levels of meaning. The point is that every message performs both functions; report and command, content and relationship, are inextricably interwoven. For example, one person asks a question of another. The question is literally about a topic, suggesting a content involvement; but at the same time, the question signals an assessment of relation with the partner (e.g., "I know less than you do here," or "I am confused by your earlier statments," or "I want to test you," or "I'm taking the responsibility to help order our talk by asking questions," etc.).

When we suggest that the choice to have Rogers ask questions was a political one, we are considering this relational dimension. Occasionally, questions are moves within a conversation that can suggest, for example, the questioner's superiority, as when a prosecutor interrogates an accused criminal in court, or when a teacher tests students. Jay Haley (1963) called these *maneuvers*. More often, the questioner occupies an inferior position; daily, students ask teachers questions to clarify what they haven't understood, travelers ask for directions when they are lost, and young children constantly must ask parents "why?" Yet all of these can also be maneuvers, too: students may want to impress the teacher with their strong motivation, travelers may want to point out to the locals how poorly signed their area is, and children at times seek not only to learn but to test their parents' vulnerabilities, consistencies, and values.

Students of the politics of conversation should not be surprised to find that dialogue partners who define themselves as questioners would tend to speak less than their interlocutors, to develop their ideas with less depth, defer and yield the floor more often, facilitate the other's talk more with assists and encouragements, check more often on the other's meanings, introduce more topic transitions, and be less overtly concerned with maintaining face. All of these artifacts of role were present in the interpersonal styles of Buber and Rogers in their encounter.

Influences of Interpersonal Style in Public Dialogue

From the dialogue (turns #47–50):

ROGERS: Okay. But the, the other, one other thing that I feel is this. I've, I've sometimes wondered whether this is simply a personal idiosyncrasy of mine, but it seems to me that uh when another person is, is really expressing himself and his experience and so on, um, I don't feel, in the way that you've described, different from him. That is—I don't know quite how to put this—but I feel as though [3.8] in that moment his way of looking at his experience, distorted though it might be, um, is something I can look upon as as having equal authority, equal validity with the way I see life and experience. And it seems to me that that really is is the basis of helping, in a sense.

BUBER: Yes.

ROGERS: And I do feel that's a real sense of equality between us.

BUBER: No doubt of it. But eh I am not speaking now about your feeling but about a real situation. I mean, you two look, as you just said [Rogers: Uhm huh], on *his* experience. Neither you nor he look on *your* experience. The subject is *exclusively* he and his ex-

perience. . . . So, eh, I, I see and feel very well your feeling, your attitude, your taking part. But you cannot change the given situation. There is something objectively real that confronts you. Not
only he confronts you, the person, but just the situation. You cannot change it.

Although Buber and Rogers developed similar theories of communication, their styles of expressing these ideas on this occasion were
quite dissimilar. This conversation illustrated how differences of floor,
focus, and terminology could influence dialogue.

The floor for talk. Buber (1965b, p. 87; and in the Rogers dialogue)
consistently stressed that silence can contribute to dialogue, and
Rogers's relationships with clients underscore the same conclusion.
Dialogue, as a quality of communication, cannot be measured in words
or minutes. Still, the clear differences in expansiveness between Buber
and Rogers are instructive. Measured in lines of type, Buber talked
53 percent more than Rogers. Because Buber spoke quite slowly and deliberately, measuring actual speaking time produces even more dramatic differences. Overall, of the approximately 93 minutes on the best
tape available to us, Buber spoke for 64 percent of the time, Rogers for
30 percent, and Friedman for 6 percent. Clearly, the spotlight was on
Buber's thought, and both principals adjusted their expectations for
conversational dominance accordingly.

An additional factor in the dialogue's ratio of contribution was
the moderator role of Maurice Friedman. Friedman spoke much more
in the later portion of the dialogue (4.3 percent of the conversation
before the tape was changed, 15.3 percent after that—measured in
lines, and excluding his introductory and concluding comments),
when he assumed the responsibility of becoming a secondary questioner. Strikingly, after Rogers asked his fourth question and the advertised "hour" had elapsed, Friedman talks almost as much (13%) as
Rogers (14%).

Focus of talk. Rogers developed his ideas primarily in order to
structure questions for Buber. This development was rarely more than
sufficient to carry the question; he did not refer specifically to his research, nor did he make much effort to explain his reasoning after the
turns when Buber disagreed with his concepts or applications. Often,
Rogers deferred to Buber's meanings and distinctions. Consistent with
the "active listening" style he advocated, Rogers inserted many
"checks of perception" in which he attempted to discover how Buber
framed the issues from his side. Buber did not attempt to verify through
perception checks that he understood Rogers's ideas in roughly the
same manner as Rogers meant them. In fact, Buber asked very few

questions of any type. Although at one point Buber said he was about to ask Rogers a question, he did not do so. Later, Buber asked Rogers about his experience in talking with schizophrenic and paranoid clients, but his curiosity seemed more related to making his own point than it was to discovering Rogers's experience. Another time, Buber said he saw and felt what Rogers meant, but he did not attempt to verify or check his interpretation against Rogers's own experience. Buber was clearly interested in Rogers's ideas, but he seemed to want them phrased as reactions to his own distinctions. Rogers, for his part, was willing to accommodate.

Rogers kept his conversational focus primarily on three tasks: invitation, clarifications of his own understanding, and sharing or testing his own experience in relationships. As we have already considered the first two in some depth, we now focus on Rogers's emphasis on limiting claims to concrete experience. Rogers frequently qualified his conclusions by such phrases as "it seems to me," "in my experience," and "although I might be wrong." He believed such reservations were consistent with contemporary scientific evidence on the limitations of perception and individual knowing, and with his philosophy of taking responsibility for one's own perceptions and beliefs (Rogers 1980, pp. 96–108). For Rogers, absolute knowledge was not within a person's realm. Consistently, in fact, he called into question his own concepts, inviting research that could disprove them (1959b; 1961, p. 15).

Predictably, when talking with Buber, Rogers kept his own statements and claims provisional and open, and grounded in his own experience in therapeutic relationships. (This dialogue occurred before Rogers's popular work in encounter groups, intercultural workshops, teacher-student interaction, interpersonal politics, forms of relation in marriage, and community-building in large-group settings.) Note the pattern—which we have emphasized in italics—in the following representative comments excerpted from various sections of the dialogue:

> "it *seems to me*" (turn #3)
> "I have *wondered whether [3.1] your concept . . . is uh similar to what I see* as the effective moment in a therapeutic relationship" (turn #27)
> "I might take a moment or two to say *what I see . . . as essential* in that, and then *perhaps you could comment on it from your point of view*" (turn #27)
> "I, I feel that um, if, if *from my point of view*" (turn #31)
> "it *seems to me . . .* I don't feel, in the way that you've described, different from him" (turn #47)

"But um *it has been my experience* that . . ." (turn #59)

"*I would say that there is no difference* in the relationships *that I form* . . . with a normal person, a schizophrenic, a paranoid . . . —*I don't really feel any difference*" (turn #71)

"In in, uh, therapy, again, *which I have to draw on because that's my background* [Buber: Sure] *of experience*—[Buber: Of course]—um, there are some very vivid moments in which the individual is meeting uh some aspect of himself" (turns #89, 90, 91)

"*I hope that perhaps sometime I could play some recordings of interviews for you to indicate* how the surprise element can be there" (turn #95)

"That *runs diametrically contrary to my own experience*" (turn #99)

With this tentative speech style, Rogers offered his experience as data, in a scientific sense, not as conclusions. In a sense, Rogers provided the perspective of someone who can speak only for himself, but nevertheless wanted to invoke decades of thoughtful practical experience in attempting to facilitate dialogue under difficult circumstances.

Buber's style, also predictable in some ways, was different, even though the dialogue produced an unusually high quality of communication for a public forum. If Rogers's talk was based on invitation, Buber's emphasized replies, corrections of Rogers, and a reliance on precise terminological distinctions. If Rogers's rhetorical style could be characterized as provisional, Buber's was certain. Consider some representative examples, again drawn from different phases of the dialogue, and again presented with our emphasis added:

"The difference—the, the *essential difference*—between your role in this situation and his *is obvious*" (turn #34)

"He *cannot, by far, cannot see you*" (turn #34)

"He *cannot be but where he is*" (turn #44)

"Your inner necessity may be as they are. I accept that. I have no objection at all. But *the situation has an objection*" (turn #44)

"But eh I am not speaking now about your feeling *but about a real situation*" (turn #50)

"So, eh, I, I see and feel very well your feeling, your attitude, your taking part. But you *cannot* change the given situation. There is *something objectively real* that confronts you. . . . *You cannot change it*" (turn #50)

"This is . . . different, eh *by the whole heaven, but I would rather prefer to say by the whole hell*, difference from your eh attitude. . . . A man in hell *cannot* think, *cannot* imagine eh helping another" (turn #80)

"You see, I, eh, of course, am entirely with you as far as your experience goes. *I cannot be with you as far as I have to look on the whole situation*" (turn #84)

"*We we cannot say* this is psychic and this is psychic" (turn #96)

"*you cannot say*, 'Oh, I detect in him just what can be trusted'" (turn #102)

"Because *accepting, this is just eh accepting* how the other is in this moment, in this eh actuality of his. *Confirming means [4.5] first of all, eh, accepting the whole potentiality of the the other*" (turn #112)

"perhaps it would be of a certain aid if I add [3.7 with sigh] *a problem that eh I found* when reading just this article [Rogers: Uh huh] of yours, eh, or *a problem that eh* [Buber sighs] *approached me*" (turn #126)

Buber's discourse became somewhat more provisional as the dialogue developed, as he implied that his view might be different if he were a therapist, when he referred to his own experience as a criterion, and when he talked about "what I call dialogue" (turn #92) rather than just what dialogue *is*. However, the cumulative weight of Buber's rhetorical style suggests concepts that are real and independent of anyone's conception of them, and a reality independent of individual experience. Often Rogers speaks of what he thinks, believes, feels, or has experienced; then Buber replies with what is "really" true.

The word "cannot" appropriately exemplifies the tone of certainty in Buber's discourse. We counted thirty-nine "cannots" and "can'ts" that indicated Buber's certainties, compared with just two "can'ts" from Rogers. This common word is reasonable in many contexts, of course. When a speaker chooses it this often, however, and uses it to demonstrate not just what is permissible but indeed, what is or is not true or real, it begins to sound like a clue to Buber's definition of his relationship with Rogers. Conversation partners may at times need to be told when they cannot do something (by one of higher status or knowledge), but surely few are likely to feel confirmed by statements suggesting that what we think or feel "cannot" be valid. Thus, the *rhetoric of cannot*, far from a rhetoric of invitation, is more likely to be heard as a request to acquiesce to authority. As this is not what Buber believed to be a hallmark of dialogue, we can only assume that he was unaware of the presence or of the potential effects of such a conversational style.

Stance on terminology. Buber relies on conceptual precision far more than Rogers, whose use of terms was occasionally fuzzy during his career. Several examples show their divergent styles for discussing basic principles with contingent human language.

Rogers had suggested the possibility of inner meeting and surprise—that is, that different facets of a person's existence might "meet" in a moment of insight that is similar to dialogue. But he admitted that his point might depend on a difference in how he and Buber use the word. Such a statement can serve a metacommunicational function in which the speaker might soften a claim, back off from a literal interpretation, or open a conversational door for the other to disagree. Of course, Rogers may have meant none of this. However, the statement is consistent enough with his normal rhetorical style to be taken at face value as an expression of an informal belief about communication.. He was suggesting that in any linguistic interchange, there may be underlying agreement despite differing usage of terms as referents—or underlying disagreement despite utilizing similar terms. Mediators are very aware of both situations and often specifically test or challenge the parties' understandings of specific basic terms as they are used. Rogers asked his question, Buber replied, and Rogers responded when Buber interrupted:

> And you see, may I add a *technical* matter? [Rogers: Uh hmm] . . . I have learned in the course of my life to appreciate terms. [Rogers: Uh hum] . . . And I think that modern psychology . . . does it not in sufficient measure. . . . When I . . . find something that is essentially different from another thing, I want a new term. (turn #96)

Buber is, in one sense, responsive to Rogers, and in another sense somewhat unresponsive. He responds on a literal plane with an observation about the necessity of different terms to distinguish different constructs (with which Rogers predictably agrees in his next turn). Other implications ride with this comment as baggage, however. We have already shown how talk becomes coherent through "conversational implicature" (Grice, 1975) quite apart from its literal references; this is the assumptive glue that holds people together in their understandings, the things that communicators understand to be true without ever having been said. Buber's statement could also be interpreted as an expression of an underlying informal philosophy of communication and a statement of his relationship to Rogers. Understood in this way, Buber's comment also implies: (1) the different terms are rooted in "essential differences" in reality, rather than in people's experiences or interpretations, (2) that terminological divergence cannot and does not reflect similar experiences, and (3) taken as a direct reply to Rogers, and without excepting him explicitly, the indictment of "modern psychology" can be understood to include Rogers (even if unintentionally), and might function as a slight.

An additional example is found in our earlier analysis of the acceptance/confirmation colloquy. Buber insisted that his notion of *confirmation* must be distinguished from how Rogers uses *acceptance*. He thought confirming subsumed acceptance, but went beyond it to a fully engaged acknowledgment of a person's potentiality; in confirmation, he believed, we might confront and struggle with the other, going beyond a passive acceptance. In his reply, Rogers agrees, allowing that he has "put it differently" (turn #115). "Acceptance" for Rogers is far from passive, and *includes* accepting and confirming a client's potentiality; he further claimed that therapy is such an intervention. But Buber merely reasserted his distinction without acknowledging that Rogers has basically agreed with him, while applying a different umbrella term. Helping a person struggle against self is possible, Buber said, "and this I can only do if I . . . distinguish between 'accepting' and 'confirming'" (turn #116). One possible interpretation here is that Buber was so focused on his own distinction that he failed to listen carefully to Rogers's actual point. By 1957, Rogers had had decades of experience in helping clients "struggle against self," expressing an active, congruent, and empathic acceptance. What was Rogers to make of this incident? He evidently felt somewhat misunderstood (Rogers & Russell, 1991); if Buber's distinction was the "only" route to effective helping, Rogers might have reasoned, why had his own therapy—which by then had been researched as thoroughly as any branch of psychotherapy—been so effective for over two decades? In the next question, he does not argue the point, but implicitly reminds Buber not to group him with the Freudians; indeed, Rogers might have felt that he wasn't being responded to as himself, but as a more generic representative of a larger group of psychologists.

The participants highlight another terminological issue in the concluding minutes of the dialogue, illustrating how fundamentally Buber was concerned with how words are tied with ideas. Friedman asked Buber and Rogers to clarify their differences relative to his own impression that Buber locates values "more in 'the between'" (turn #124) than does Rogers. Rogers replies with a clarification of what he called the "process which we *are*" (turn #125), referring either to the therapist-client relationship or to the human tendency toward becoming. Buber's final contribution to the dialogue, however, is the terminological distinction between the concepts of "individual" and "person," which we discussed earlier in this chapter. Although Buber's point may have placed different emphasis on some particulars, here, as elsewhere, he chose to emphasize the distinctions, differences, and distance between his perspectives and those of Rogers, minimizing how his philosophy paralleled Rogers's praxis.

CONCLUSION

The Buber–Rogers meeting was a significant intellectual event, not only for the audience but for the participants themselves. Both men were changed by the dialogue: Buber came to believe, contrary to his former position, that a public occasion could also be a dialogic one. The new and revealing postscript to *I and Thou* that Buber wrote shortly after the dialogue appears to have been influenced by the tone and content of this conversation as well. Rogers subsequently infused his writing with more references to Buber's philosophy, particularly in terms of confirmation and the centrality of relationship in his conception of self, and Friedman has argued that Rogers's own positions on several issues moved toward Buber's following their dialogue (Friedman, 1986, pp. 428, 431–433).

The dialogue was significant also in that scholars continue to consider it a rich intellectual source many decades later, and it continues to attract fresh readers. The text of the dialogue contains excellent clues to the intellectual lives of these two men, and in some places shows how they developed ideas collaboratively that evening that were at best implicitly developed in their other work. The dialogue serves a historical function, too, in locating their thought relative to philosophical concepts and the professional experience of psychotherapy. In the language of some group consultants, the dialogue was a critical incident that continues to influence how we define communication and aspire to communicate in the twenty-first century.

Although the dialogue is clearly involving at an intellectual level, it has another fundamental attraction for students of interaction. Communication was their focus, and communication was their process. They were attempting a dialogue about dialogue, conversing about conversation, meeting to discuss meeting, relating with each other to try to sort out the problematic of relation. Thus the process of their talk and the conversational styles with which they interacted became interesting and revealing as well. Theirs was rhetorical talk, talk that was at times consistent with and at times inconsistent with broadly defined expectations, principles, and criteria of dialogue.

We believe a case study can reveal much about dialogue itself as a theoretical and practical possibility and, in a different sense, reveal much about Buber and Rogers as practitioners of dialogue. Although their conversation was freighted with characteristics not normally associated with a high quality of dialogue (e.g., public forum, nonparticipant onlookers, and the enfolded conversational roles that made the participants assume unequal footing), dialogue evidently did develop in many moments that evening.

This close reading of the transcript shows that dialogue is much more than an "ideal possibility seldom realized," to borrow R. D. Laing's (1969, p. 98) characterization of confirmation. Dialogue is a concretely realizable, and above all, a practical accomplishment. If it can emerge on this occasion, it can emerge in interviews between persons of unequal status or prestige. If dialogue can emerge here, it can also develop within heated arguments between persons of radically divergent goals—if they are willing to commit to bring themselves in all their genuine particularities, clear a space for talk, and listen with active confirmation. Some skeptics might say, "Of course, these two famous men can develop dialogue; surely they know how to do it." But we reach almost the converse conclusion. Not even these two can know *how* to do dialogue prior to an actual meeting with its own unique surprises. These two famous and intelligent persons were in fact constrained that night by extraordinarily difficult conditions and also might have been constrained in some ways by their own reputations.

Rogers had earned a reputation as a facilitator and expert listener. His designated questioning and maintenance roles, along with his reliance on them, limited the expansion of his own ideas and may have kept him from disagreeing more overtly with Buber. He was "supposed" to be a facilitator, and so he encouraged the spotlight to fall on his partner, even at times when his own ideas were left appearing shallow and even when confronting Buber might have stimulated cleaner descriptions or more vivid examples. Indeed, some of Rogers's positions were fuzzy at best, while others were merely abandoned. In some places he spoke solidly of his concepts, while in others he perhaps overstressed how he "felt." Buber's rhetorical style with Rogers was not always a reliable model for dialogical exploration either. Consistent with some other assessments of his conversational style, Buber appeared to relish the expert professor role here, and was more ready to correct terminology than to be open to his partner's practical experience as a therapist.

The role of expert professor was richly deserved; Buber was, after all, the century's foremost philosopher of dialogue. But Buber himself so often cautioned that dialogue partners should be open to each other as listeners that it's hard to overlook the dismissiveness of his own listening style. Indeed, Buber's rhetoric of cannot may have discouraged active exploration of ideas, if its central message was that he was already certain of the nature of dialogic reality, and that through this conversation, he was expected to teach the correct conceptual distinctions.

Yet, through all the difficulties of audience, role, and interpersonal style, Buber and Rogers spoke and listened well enough to coauthor fresh, exciting, and thoughtful dialogue. Both men evidently felt confirmed, and left with fresh insights. In the process, the viability of dialogue itself was confirmed.

CHAPTER SEVEN

Theorizing Dialogic Moments

> Dialogue must be understood as something taking part
> in the very historical nature of human beings. . . .
> Dialogue is a moment where humans meet to reflect
> on their reality as they make and remake it. Something
> else: To the extent that we are communicative beings
> who communicate to each other as we become more
> able to transform our reality, we are able *to know that
> we know*, which is something *more* than just knowing.
> . . . Knowing is a social event with nevertheless an
> individual dimension. What is dialogue in this moment
> of communication, knowing and social transformation?
> Dialogue seals the relationship between the cognitive
> subjects, the subjects who know, and who try to know.
> —Paulo Freire, *A Pedagogy for Liberation*

For the Brazilian educator Paulo Freire, dialogue is a hinge concept, one that potentially connects scientific with humanistic knowledge, theory with practice, and human nature with human behavior. As such, it invites multiple methodologies, both quantitative and qualitative, although the essence of dialogue will always remain elusive.

Freire understood that dialogue is a relation of co-constituted mutuality that exists in highly charged and experientially significant moments. Although dialogue necessarily involves unique persons, it is not an individualistic process. Although its moments are experienced immediately, they cannot be ahistorical. And although the moments are transitory, they are reality-defining, even world-making, for participants.

Despite the occasional misunderstandings in the Buber–Rogers dialogue, this meeting produced an emergent agreement—what we will

173

term the Buber–Rogers position on dialogic moments—that is consistent with Freire's insight. Dialogue is an awakening of other-awareness that occurs in, and through, a moment of meeting. This has surprisingly broad implications for human communication:

1. *Dialogue is constitutive.* Through its impact, human nature is developed, enacted, and changed. What Buber called a philosophical anthropology, his study of the nature of humanity, must be concerned with persons' experience of dialogue. This is not an atomistic experience. It does not, in other words, happen *within individuals*—in their psyches, souls, hearts, or minds—but *between persons* willing to seek mutual engagement in constantly shifting ways. What "is" is found to be active and processual rather than static or structural in dialogue. Indeed, change and the potential for being changed seem to be at the core of most coherent conceptions of dialogue. As Witherell and Noddings (1991) note, "It is dialogue that allows the negotiation of meanings through which the self in relation to other selves and to one's cultural communities is constituted" (p. 7).

2. *Dialogue's change is focused in moments of meeting.* Thus, dialogue cannot be sought as an ongoing state of full mutuality. Dialogic change is not progressive, not a constant, but the result of often surprising and even epiphanous or sporadic insight. The essentially momentary and fleeting character of dialogue mitigates any cynicism that asserts dialogue cannot develop between persons of unequal role, status, or prestige, and it softens the equally daunting fear that dialogue is unlikely between cultural groups that do not share significant worldviews, values, or conceptual linguistic patterns. Dialogue does not demand full understanding, complete mutuality, or pervasive cultural immersion; instead, it depends on sparks of recognition across the gap of strangeness. The dialogic characteristic of strange otherness should not imply that different persons or cultures will be forever alienated from each other as perpetual strangers, but it opens the possibility for momentary epiphanies of recognition from which each side learns in fresh ways what it is to be "other." This can be comforting, but as the philosopher Alphonso Lingis (1994) observed, it can be threatening as well:

> To affirm something is not simply to make oneself the momentary source of a formulation whose abstractness makes it equivalent of what any interlocutor does or can issue and receive; it is to present something to someone for . . . judgment, . . . confirmation or contestation. . . .

To question someone is not simply to make oneself a receptor for information which one will soon reissue; it is to appeal to another for what is not available to oneself.

To address someone is not simply to address a source of information; it is to address one who will answer and answer for his or her answer.

To enter into conversation with another is to lay down one's arms and one's defenses; to throw open the gates of one's own positions; to expose oneself to the other, the outsider; and to lay oneself open to surprises, contestation, and inculpation. It is to risk what one found or produced in common. To enter into conversation is to struggle against the noise, the interference, and the vested interests, the big brothers and the little Hitlers always listening in—in order to expose oneself to the alien, the Balinese and the Aztec, the victims and the excluded, the Palestinians and the Quechuas and the Crow Indians, the dreamers, the mystics, the mad, the tortured, and the birds and the frogs. One enters into conversation in order to become an other for the other. (pp. 86–88)

Lingis's statement of the otherness-moments of conversation critiques an information transmission model of communication, but in doing so also points to the genuine public risk of opening the self to surprise.

3. *Dialogue is facilitated by structuring potentially dialogic spaces, both geographic and attitudinal, and not by arranging or mandating dialogue itself.* Moments of meeting cannot be forced, but they need not be found merely by accident either. Key persons and groups will enhance the potential for dialogic moments by careful attention to the quality of public forums and by creating an inviting public commons in which citizen/theorists are more likely to try out ideas than to "hold" and "defend" them. Dialogue depends less than people often think on *what is said* (there is not a magic verbal strategy or technique to mandate or unleash dialogue) and more than we think on the quality of *where the saying happens, and with what attitude* (there are many approaches that can lead to a dialogic "destination") and how space helps to shape speaking and listening. The organizational consultant William N. Isaacs (1993a, 1993b, 1999) has specialized in such work as a member of the Massachusetts Institute of Technology Dialogue Project. He has discovered that although suspending defensiveness and exploring reasons for change are important, these cannot be his goals as a

facilitator. Rather, he writes, the "central purpose" of a dialogue session "is simply to establish a field of genuine meeting and inquiry (which we call a container)—a setting in which people can allow a free flow of meaning and vigorous exploration of the collective background of their thought, their personal predispositions, the nature of their shared attention, and the rigid features of their individual and collective assumptions" (p. 25). Earlier in this book we used the metaphor of *the clearing* to illustrate a similar idea.

    4. *Social knowledge develops as metadialogic interaction.* Persons are both individualized and socially enmeshed simultaneously as they communicate about their communication. Humans become more open for learning as they become open to engaging others about learning. This knowledge-building process is risky, as Lingis assumed. Beneath a surface of risk, however, is a dialectic of knowing—a movement similar to the "hermeneutic circle" in which generalized knowledge informs how we interpret specifics but specifics must simultaneously help us build a model of the general. Buber (1965b) referred to the necessity of both "distance" and "relation" in the experience of dialogue, and a subtle appreciation of how they exist together. The sociologist Z. D. Gurevitch (1988) also has captured this movement well. In dialogue, he believes, we move between moments of "making the other strange" on the one hand and moments of attempted familiarization:

> The otherness of the other person emerges through a process of defamiliarization, which I prefer to call "making the other strange." This experience of the other as close and present yet also distant and strange is usually threatening and thus tends to be very short in duration—sometimes lasting only a fleeting moment. Then again, the need to understand, to interpret the other in terms of "my world," resurfaces. At this stage, there can occur either regression to a denial of strangeness or a progression into a *new* quest for knowledge, while one deems previous conceptions of the other as irrelevant or unsatisfactory. Then, of course, the freshness of insight tends to be dulled by its own familiarity, and so on. (p. 1184)

A child's visit to a parent's workplace for the first time is a prototype case for Gurevitch. This experience is disorienting for the child, as it "suddenly removes the certainty" of the other being exclusively *my* parent (p. 1185). Whereas the parent was experienced previously only in familiar space with "total existence," now the child must imagine him or her in a new space too, a "foreign world" that nevertheless seems natural and well integrated for others. From this new perspective, the parent becomes suddenly "strange," as an other with dimensions not previously accessible to the child. In this new space a parent remains a parent for a child, but can never again be solely a parent; he or she also is realized to exist separately as someone's friend, someone's colleague, someone's subordinate, and someone else's manager. Although this moment of acknowledging otherness disorients the child, it also invites a new way of speaking to the parent based on multifaceted understanding of the familiar. Moments of imbalance and surprise—strangeness—become the basis for dialogue, how we negotiate the social knowing necessary for moving between personal and cultural worlds. Moments like these, in fact, invite metadialogue in the sense that we reflect on our own conceptions of relationship, much like Buber and Rogers did in 1957. In chapter 8 we will revisit this concept when discussing the power of *recognition*.

In the remainder of this chapter, however, we first bolster the view that a realistic general theory of public dialogue must not only account for, but focus on the concept of *dialogic moments*, as Freire suggested and as Buber and Rogers attempted to do. Second, we show how the Buber–Rogers position on dialogic moments that emerged from their dialogue—and to a lesser extent in their writings as distinct theorists—helped to prefigure and reinforce much of the currently influential postmodern cultural tenor. "Prefiguring" postmodern cultural issues, of course, is not the same thing as influencing those issues directly, nor is it equivalent to claiming that Buber and Rogers were themselves postmodern theorists. A prefiguration of a cultural trend is an earlier manifestation that foreshadows or presages aspects of that trend.

Earlier we surveyed important theoretical work that shows how dialogue can address both public and private phenomena; how it can influence cultural, political, and personal events; how it can shape interventions in organizations and communities; and how it can clarify educational, religious, and psychotherapeutic contexts. Only rarely does scholarship in this area consider dialogue's temporal dimension in depth.[1] Is dialogue an unattainable ideal that never occurs across serious issues, conflicts, or cultural differences, as some skeptics fear, or is it a common or regular state of relationships, an occasional transcendent quality, or a technique available as often as one wants or needs it, as more hopeful observers believe? Aside from Freire's approach, illustrated by our lead quotation, optimistic treatments of dialgoue tend to assume that it can be a relatively ongoing state. Perhaps those who think of dialogue as an unrealistic ideal do so in response to analyses of dialogue as a continuing state or a perpetual goal of a relationship. Despite an abundance of literature on dialogue, no contemporary account with which we are familiar thoroughly and explicitly theorizes dialogue as a momentary phenomenon and discusses its implications by relying on such a foundation.[2]

Yet the two theorists at center stage in our study have provided especially helpful clues for understanding this problem. Rogers discussed the moment of dialogue in successful face-to-face psychotherapy, despite using the term "dialogue" only rarely in formal descriptions. Buber referred specifically to "dialogic moments" (e.g., Buber, 1967, p. 692) and was particularly concerned about the *limits* of dialogue. Unfortunately, Rogers's theoretical work on moments of mutuality is neither well known nor carefully analyzed, especially by contemporary social scientists, and treatments of Buber have tended to ignore his emphasis on the temporal limits of dialogue. In spite of their contributions, the literature in dialogic studies has not identified either man closely with the theoretical importance of dialogic moments.

DIALOGUE AS MOMENTS OF MEETING

More important than Buber's and Rogers's separate discussions of dialogic moments is their only public conversation, where the temporal limits of dialogue were explored thoroughly (see chapter 6). And as we have seen, many discussions of the Buber–Rogers dialogue portray them as *disagreeing*, sometimes dramatically, on a number of issues—for example, when Rogers was said to have insisted that full mutuality is possible throughout psychotherapy and Buber responded that full mutuality in psychotherapy is impossible. Therefore, many readers over the years have developed the impression that Rogers argued that the therapeutic relationship was fully equal and mutual, presumably in an ongoing way, and therefore that this relationship as a whole was dialogic. In this view, the 1957 dialogue supposedly shows an older and wiser scholar exposing a younger, naïve scholar to an unexpected lesson on such normative limits of dialogue as how the unequal roles of client and helper keep such mutuality and equality from developing. It's no wonder that some scholars have thus characterized this as a debate, a debate that history has largely ceded to Buber at least on this issue. However, in reconsidering and retranscribing their actual conversation in appropriate historical context, we discovered that Buber and Rogers were in substantial if not complete *agreement* regarding the momentary nature of therapeutic mutuality.

Chapter 6 traced the details of their interchange on the point of equal or unequal mutuality. We return to this matter of equality, this time in the specific context of theorizing the importance of dialogic moments. The question of whether dialogue could be considered primarily as moments of meeting springs from the central issue of the Buber–Rogers event, which occupied about half of their conversation. Rogers had asked Buber to compare Rogers's description of the effective moments in the therapeutic relationship with Buber's own concept of the I-Thou relationship. Rogers thought an "effective moment" in psychotherapy might have "some resemblance" to the I-Thou relationship, while he stipulated that there might be differences, too. He then sketched his understanding of the qualities present in those moments, briefly describing transparency or congruence, acceptance, empathy, and the client sensing something of such attitudes in the therapist. But Buber, although acknowledging Rogers had given a "very good example for a certain mode of dialogic existence," decided to focus on a point he thought Rogers had misunderstood, one that Friedman (1985, 1991, 1992) has called the "problematic of mutuality."

Mutuality matters in a therapeutic relationship, because, as Friedman (1976) quotes Buber, "Help without mutuality is presumptuousness" (p. 120). "To be fully real," Friedman writes, "the I-Thou relation must be mutual" (p. 61). Mutuality is not to be confused with unity or identity, but involves a turning to the other and experiencing the relationship, as much as possible, as it is experienced by the other (see Buber, 1965b, pp. 85–88), while at the same time remaining aware of one's own ground.

Mutuality can develop even when persons' roles are unequal. Once equality is defined, realistically and broadly enough, to include sociocultural factors, it is clear that conditions of inequality are experienced virtually everywhere and often in ways that seem unfair at best. Jokes at the watercooler are "funnier" when the boss tells them. Women executives in corporations may feel special pressure not to disagree as openly with a male colleague as men would. People of color usually understand they are likely to be placed under special scrutiny when going for a job interview at a store in an all-white neighborhood. A teenager's complaint may be dismissed as whining too rapidly by her older sister. In a pluralistic society, one that increasingly acknowledges difference, we have not reached the point where those differences aren't translated directly into ascribed social power. Further, Kaplan's (1969) reading of Buber's dialogue distinguished between reciprocity, in which one person does something for or to another and in return the other is allowed or expected to do something for or to the first, and mutuality, "in which we do something together which neither of us can do separately" (p. 97). Although reciprocity is useful, it is mutuality, Kaplan says, that allows us to "become even more fully human" (p. 97).

Friedman (1965, pp. 21–23; 1983c, pp. 225–226; 1986; 1991; 1992, p. 368; 1994) and others (e.g., Berry, 1985; Brink, 1987; Burstow, 1987) have characterized sharp differences between Buber and Rogers regarding this issue, due to Rogers's purported focus on his "full" mutuality and fully equal relations with clients. However, where other commentators have focused primarily on the differences, contrasts, and oppositions separating their concepts of mutuality, returning to the tape recording of the dialogue itself verifies that Buber and Rogers essentially agreed about mutuality being possible only in brief moments.

The issue between Buber and Rogers was not whether a therapeutic relationship is fully mutual. Rogers agreed with Buber and Friedman that it was not, although no one fully acknowledged the agreement during the interchange. Rogers never insisted that there was total or complete mutuality or equality in any objective sense of role definition, but that a therapeutic relationship is *not totally one-sided* and that successful therapy exhibited critical *moments of mutuality* that made a decisive difference for dialogue. Just as Rogers did not assert the position that is usually attributed to him (full mutuality on every level), Buber did not assert a position entirely contrary to that of Rogers.

Although Buber and Rogers were speaking directly of the therapist-client relation as their object case, the following five principles *on which they agreed* could also be offered as propositions applicable to other role-unequal attempts at dialogue in, for example, education, organizational life, or health care:

1. *The therapist is the more active participant who creates the conditions for the relationship and, thus, for dialogic potential.*

Speaking of the therapist's dominant role, Buber says: "*You* give him something in order to make him equal to you. You *supplement* his need in his relation to you. You *make* him . . . , you give him what he wants in order to be *able* to be, just, just for this moment, so to speak, on the same . . . plane with you"; further, "And these *minutes* are made possible by you. Not at all by him" (turn #84). Rogers agrees: "That last I would thoroughly agree with" (turn #85). They agree that the therapist creates the conditions that make any mutuality possible. The "some real disagreement" that Rogers then mentions is merely a reference to Buber's metaphor of giving something, which Rogers wants to ensure is not interpreted as something tangible, but instead is an intangible sense of permission. In other words, and stated in a broader context, dialogue can be assisted by a convenor who takes special responsibility for facilitative conditions.

2. *An effective therapist provides something like permission for the other to be, rather than bestowing something on the other.*

Rogers emphasizes the importance of creating a space within which dialogic moments could be experienced: "It seems to me that . . . what I give him [2.3] is permission to be. . . . Which is . . . a little different somehow from bestowing something on him" (turn #85). And Buber then affirms Rogers's description when he replies, "I think no human being can give more than this. . . . Making . . . life possible for the other, if only for a moment. [3.3] Permission" (turn #86). Both men use "permission" to denote the space-clearing prerequisite for dialogic moments. Rogers then even notes an irony in their agreement, alluding perhaps to how Buber appeared to contradict Rogers's professional experience earlier: "If we don't look out, we'll agree" (turn #87). In other words, the goal of convening a dialogic encounter is not to force talk but to free it, opening a new space of possibility.

3. *Mutuality can develop in an unequal therapeutic relationship.*

Rogers asserts this during most of their discussion of this question, although, interestingly, this was not a premise directly addressed in Rogers's question. Recall that Buber acknowledged therapeutic mutuality was possible (see the first proposition above), but only in moments made possible by a therapist (which was all Rogers was claiming). Although Buber wonders if such equality and mutuality in such contexts can last for long (as does Rogers), he states that this co-experienced moment may be crucial in making life possible for a troubled person ("it is a tangent. It is a tangent that may not last but one moment" and "it is a situation of minutes" [turn #84]). Locating dialogue in moments, rather than in extended states or conditions, is not to diminish or restrict its significance. Saying that dialogue is a momentary phenomenon isn't in any sense a cynical observation.

4. *These periods of mutuality last only minutes or less—not for whole sessions, or hours, or throughout the relationship.*

Rogers is clear from the beginning that he is specifying a momentary phenomenon. In his initial question about mutuality, Rogers specified that it involved "the effective moment in a therapeutic relationship" and "in those moments I really am able to sense" (turn #27). Similarly, Rogers later makes it very clear that although only moments are at issue, these moments are essential to therapy: "the moments where . . . persons are most likely to change, or I even think of it as the moments in which people *do* change, . . . are the moments in which perhaps the relationship is experienced the same on *both* sides," and "in those moments . . . when real change occurred . . . , that it would be because there *had* been a real meeting of persons in which it was experienced the same from both sides" (turn #73).

Buber first uses Rogers's term "moments" in this context when he observes that Rogers's client would tell a story different from the therapist's interpretation about the *"same* moment" (turn #62). Later, Buber says there are times when dialogue with a schizophrenic cannot occur, because "at a certain moment" a wall of closure is reached (with which Rogers would surely agree) (turn #76). Finally, as we discussed earlier, Buber acknowledges with Rogers that there *can* be equal mutuality in moments, as when he referred to a client who is *"able* to be, . . . just for this moment, so to speak, on the same . . . plane with you" (turn #84). Buber continues this line in his next turn as well. Despite agreeing about the *existence* of dialogic moments, there is a notable difference in their positions; for Rogers, brief co-experienced moments of equality are the essence of dialogue itself, whereas for Buber these moments demonstrate the necessary objective limitations imposed on dialogue.

5. *When the client is able to experience a relatively full mutual relationship with the therapist—and hence, presumably, is able to experience the dialogic moments more often—the therapy is essentially complete.*

In his first response to Buber on this issue, Rogers offers as a beginning point what he thinks he and Buber agree about: "If this client comes to the point where he can experience what he is expressing, but also can experience my understanding of it and reaction to it, and so on, then really therapy is just about over" (turn #45). Buber immediately responds, "Yes. This is just what I mean" (turn #46). They established this premise at the outset, although their agreement even on this issue has been obscured for decades because the previously available flawed transcripts for some reason quoted Buber as saying that this was *not* what he meant.[3]

In addition to the five issues of agreement, there is a clearly related sixth point that Rogers proposed and to which Buber did not respond directly—appropriately, perhaps, as he was not a therapist and did not have direct experience in doing therapy.

> 6. *The moments of genuine mutuality between therapist and client are when real therapeutic change occurs.*

Rogers introduces this as a "minor point in relation to something you said that . . . struck me," but then continued by asserting and re-asserting something far from minor. Where change occurs, he'd observed, it is in the brief moments in which each side experiences a comparable awareness of the other as a real person—not the same kind of real person, but real nevertheless (turn #73). And Rogers suggested it again as the "only modification" he acknowledged in response to a question from Friedman: "Perhaps in the moments where real change takes place, then I wonder if it [the relationship] isn't reciprocal in the sense that . . . I am able to see this individual as he is in that moment . . . and he really senses my understanding and acceptance of him. And that I think is what *is* reciprocal and is perhaps what produces change" (turn #83).

Recognizing that real meeting is rare and occurs only in moments is a particularly crucial point for Rogers, one he developed initially in a conference paper presented six months before the dialogue and published in slightly revised form two years later. In different versions of this paper (1956d, 1956e, 1959a), Rogers refers to these moments variously as "moments of movement" or "molecules of therapy." These terms clarify Rogers's perspective when he talked with Buber. These are the "crucial moments" in therapy and he even calls them "existential moments." "Therapy," Rogers theorized, "is made up of a series of such molecules ["moments" in another draft], sometimes strung rather closely together, sometimes occurring at long intervals, always with periods of preparatory experiences in between" (Rogers, 1959a, p. 52). Rogers uses "moment," "moments," and "momentary" repeatedly in these papers. For example, the published version of the paper (Rogers, 1959a) uses "moments" twenty-four times and the complementary concept "molecules" ten times; in earlier versions he did not include the molecules metaphor and used moments even more often. Clearly he is developing and applying the term "moments" conceptually, not using it casually. From his clinical examples, we can infer that breakthrough moments may last anywhere from seconds to perhaps a minute or two. Similarly, during the spring of 1957 (the semester of the dialogue with Buber), Rogers began another important paper while he was a visiting professor at the University of Wisconsin (Kirschenbaum, 1979, p. 242). In "A Process Conception of Psychotherapy," Rogers continued to describe these "moments of movement" as "moments when it appears that change actually occurs" (Rogers, 1961, p. 130). In such a context, Rogers obviously did not, and could not, believe "full mutuality on every level" was possible in therapeutic dialogue; he straightforwardly notes with research examples that mutuality is possible, but *fleeting*— in moments enabled skillfully by the therapist. This insight, of course, is virtually indistinguishable from Buber's own claim.

Remember that Buber's comments during the dialogue and most of Friedman's subsequent writing on this issue indicate that they objected to seeing the *relationship* as fully mutual, and suggest that Rogers saw it that way. Buber's first response to this question (turn #28) refers to the "situation" of a person coming to a therapist for help. Friedman (1986, 1992) properly calls this a "structural" matter involving differences of "role and function" (1994, p. 53). The structure of the situation, one person asking another for help in a professional context, necessarily means that their relationship cannot be a relationship between equals, and it cannot be a fully mutual relationship. Yet Rogers was pursuing a different point: that this structural inequality didn't preclude moments of real mutuality, moments that made a decisive difference for dialogue far out of proportion to their duration. Most if not all truly challenging occasions for dialogue involve role-unequal interaction, including labor-management negotiations, police-community relations, international diplomacy, and parent-child communication.

That Rogers has been misinterpreted on this point can hardly be denied. In the accounts of previous research on the Buber–Rogers dialogue that we review in chapter 6, it is clear that many scholars suggest that Rogers just didn't get—or agree with—Buber's point, and that he argued unrealistically, instead, that therapist and client were fully equal and develop a fully mutual relation. Another example of the conventional wisdom may be instructive here. In 1962, Rogers expanded on his own research on therapeutic moments and later abridged that article in a chapter for a book with Barry Stevens, *Person to Person* (Rogers & Stevens, 1967). Friedman (1985), commenting on what this chapter disclosed about Rogers's theory, wrote: "There is no suggestion here [in 1962/1967] of full mutuality between therapist and client and there is a realism about the fact that the person-to-person meeting is often a matter of moments only *that is very close to Buber's position in his dialogue with Rogers five years earlier"* (p. 55; emphasis added). Further, according to Friedman, this position was the result of "an important *change in Rogers' teachings since his dialogue with Buber* in 1957" (p. 53; emphasis added). But the history of their dialogue shows that Rogers's emphasis on dialogic moments after meeting Buber was consistent with his prior scholarship; there was no such change. This was not a case of Rogers simply appropriating Buber's teaching. A theory of dialogic moments was not something Buber needed to convince Rogers about; plainly, although both had explored it in previous writing, it was Rogers who first mentioned this "realistic" issue in their dialogue, and he qualified almost every significant statement with it. When Buber asserted that dialogue with clients is a matter of moments only, he was not correcting Rogers, but agreeing with him.

Indeed, Rogers pursued this very theme to his last days, acknowledging with Buber, as he did in the dialogue, that, except for its crucial turning-point moments, the situation of therapy is objectively unequal and not fully mutual. A chapter coauthored with Nathaniel Raskin, under revision when Rogers died in 1987, referred to "molecule(s) of personality change," "moment(s) of movement," and "moment(s) in change" from Rogers's 1956 paper (Raskin & Rogers, 1989, pp. 178–179). In another article published shortly before his death, Rogers (1987) sounds as though he was responding directly to Buber and Friedman on stage thirty years earlier. He uses Buber's concepts of "I-Thou" relations and "the between," while suggesting that in dialogic moments (and only then) the issue of role equality, defined objectively, evaporates:

The reason I love to carry on psychotherapy is that at times I too look with awe on the incredible strength and wisdom of this vulnerable client. I participate in a miracle. At such **moments** I feel an almost ectoplasmic bond between the client and myself. It is truly an "I-Thou" relationship. At such important **moments of change** in therapy, the question of equality or inequality is *totally* irrelevant. The important thing is that two unique persons are in tune with each other in an astonishing **moment of growth and change**. Both of us are changed, although the growth may be greater in the client. Since I, as therapist, hope that I have helped this **moment** to come about, the relationship can be looked upon as an unequal one. But in the **moment** itself, all such issues disappear.[4] (p. 39; italics in original; boldface added)

As Rogers said in his 1956 "Essence of Psychotherapy" paper, written before the dialogue, as he said to Buber in 1957, as he said in the 1962/1967 passage that Friedman cited, and as he continued to say virtually to the end of his life: skillful therapists (and others) can help to create relational conditions in which "brief moments" of direct person-to-person relating happen, and that in those moments of meeting therapeutic change tends to occur (Rogers, 1967, pp. 191–192). Following the dialogue, Rogers often used Buber's phrase "I-Thou relationship" to refer to these moments of real meeting in psychotherapy. Within such moments, Rogers thought therapist and client each achieved a high-quality sensing of another's uniqueness, genuine acceptance and confirmation of the other's equal status as a human being, a certain immersive timelessness of experience, and an authentic relating that leads the communicators in unanticipated directions.

The basic character of such a dialogic moment, therefore, is the experience of inventive surprise shared by the dialogic partners as each "turns toward" the other and both mutually perceive the impact of each other's turning. It is a brief interlude of focused awareness and acceptance of otherness and difference that somehow simultaneously transcends the perception of difference itself. Maurice Friedman captured some of the importance of this concept when he wrote to Rogers late in 1957, after hearing him present a conference paper: "I particularly liked your insistence on the uniqueness of the present, of the new moment and all that implies for the approach of the therapist" (Friedman, 1957). This is probably what Rogers meant in stressing that equality is possible between such unequal roles as therapist and client, teacher and student, and in similar politically charged interpersonal situations. Such inequalities do not preclude moments of surprising mutuality in which each party experiences the present encounter in a way that transcends their roles. At that moment, and in a sense only for that moment, dialogue levels the communicative field. Such a presence, however fleeting, exhibits a potential for future change that energizes further communication.

Schrag (1969) distinguishes an existential "moment" from the chronological "instant," which is experienced as one in a series of instants. "Moment" is tied to an "apprehension of the present as a 'moment of choice,'" at the "interpenetration of present and future." To Schrag, "the present is a recent future, a recent future possibility now presented" (p. 58). Thus, the moment of immediate presence has elements of both retention and protention—it has, as Schrag (1969) says, "fringes" and is experienced as in some way "ecstatic" (p. 37). Such a "moment of movement" (to use Rogers's phrase) is almost epiphanal. It is when, as Merleau-Ponty (1973) says, the other's words "have the power of throwing me . . . toward signification that neither he nor I possessed before" (p. 142), and that such talk can, paradoxically perhaps, "at the point where we understand him and especially at the moment he withdraws from us and threatens to fall into non-sense, be capable of remaking us in his image and to open us to another meaning" (p. 143). Thus, if such dialogic moments can be described at all, they have to be understood as senses of a present that "takes us over," a present in which "I not only 'understand' the other's momentary subjective processes, I 'understand' the world in which he lives, and that world becomes my own," as Berger and Luckmann (1967, p. 130) write. Further, "we now not only understand each other's definitions of shared situations, we define them reciprocally. . . . We not only live in the same world, we participate in each other's being" (p. 130).

Buber, too, wrote about the significance of dialogic moments. His "Replies to My Critics" refers to "genuine dialogic moments" (1967, p. 692). In *I and Thou*, *Between Man and Man*, and various essays of *The Knowledge of Man*, all written before the dialogue with Rogers, he refers to the encounter of God occurring in the moment, to the transformation between I-It and I-Thou relationships occurring in moments, and even to moments of dialogue (1923/1958, pp. 63, 68–69, 151; 1965a, pp. 15, 100–101, 203–204; 1965b, pp. 85–86). In *Eclipse of God*, Buber (1952) is unequivocal about the importance of a moments concept: "The actually lived concrete is the 'moment' in its unforeseeableness and its irrecoverableness, in its undivertible character of happening but once, in its decisiveness, in its secret dialogue between that which happens and that which is willed, between fate and action, address and answer" (p. 35). In perhaps his most succinct statement, he wrote that "meaning is to be experienced in living action and suffering itself, in the unreduced immediacy of the moment" (1952, p. 35). The person who "aims at the experiencing of experience" will necessarily miss the spontaneity of such moments (p. 35), Buber thought, in a prescient early critique of contemporary self-help technologies.

In "What is Man?," written in 1938 and later published in *Between Man and Man* (1965), Buber recognized that mutuality occurs in "real" conversations, where two people "happen" to one another, even in brief moments:

> This fact can be found even in the *tiniest and most transient events* which scarcely enter the consciousness. In the deadly crush of an air-raid shelter the glance of two strangers suddenly *meet for a second in astonishing and unrelated mutuality*;

when the All Clear sounds it is forgotten; and yet it did happen,
in *a realm which existed only for that moment*. (Buber, 1965a,
p. 204; emphasis added)

Buber continued by referring to these happenings as "fleeting," ones
that "disappear in the moment of their appearance." Indeed, these nonverbal times of presence are close to what energizes the verbal realm.
The "basic presupposition of conversation," wrote Buber (1965b) in
"The Word That is Spoken," is "the moment of surprise" (p. 113).

Buber seems especially insistent about the importance of moments when describing his constellation of concepts and terms concerning the decentering or linking of one person's experience with
another's, concepts that seemed to Rogers very close to what he meant
by empathy. For example, describing what he calls "experiencing the
other side," Buber (1965a) provided this example:

> A man belabours another, who remains quite still. Then let
> us assume that the striker suddenly receives in his soul the
> blow which he strikes: the same blow; that he receives it as
> the other who remains still. *For the space of a moment* he ex-
> periences the situation from the other side. Reality imposes
> itself on him. What will he do? Either he will overwhelm the
> voice of the soul, or his impulse will be reversed. (p. 96; em-
> phasis added)

Further, this moment, although not capable of being extended or expanded, nevertheless changes everything about the relation. "I do not
in the least mean," Buber continued, "that the man who has had such
an experience would from then on have this two-sided sensation in
every such meeting—that would perhaps destroy his instinct. But the
one extreme experience makes the other person present to him for all
time. A transfusion has taken place" (pp. 96–97). When he explored
how such mutual experience of "inclusion" of the other can affect even
conflict situations, Buber also showed that this is essentially a momentary flash:

> The clearest example of this is a disputation between two
> men, thoroughly different in nature and outlook and calling,
> where *in an instant*—as by the action of a messenger as
> anonymous as he is invisible—it happens that each is aware of
> the other's full legitimacy, wearing the insignia of necessity
> and of meaning. What an illumination! (p. 99; emphasis added)

Similarly, Buber's (1965b) description of "'imagining' the real" is also presented as a momentary realization—the capacity "to hold before one's soul a reality arising *at this moment* but not able to be directly experienced. Applied to intercourse between men, 'imagining' the real means that I imagine to myself what another man is *at this very moment* wishing, feeling, perceiving, thinking, and not as a detached content but in his very reality, that is, as a living process in this man" (p. 70; emphasis added). Other such references to the significance of momentary presence dot Buber's work.

Buber's (1958) postscript to *I and Thou*, written only months after the dialogue, cites the relationship between a "genuine psychotherapist and his patient" (p. 132) as an example of an I-Thou relationship that by its very nature "may not unfold into complete mutuality" (p. 131). Indeed, Buber wrote, "full mutuality is not inherent in men's life together" (p. 131). In what almost sounds like an extension of his conversation with Rogers, Buber concludes this section with a general principle: "Every I-You relationship in a situation defined by the attempt of one partner to act on the other one so as to accomplish some goal depends on a mutuality that is condemned never to become complete" (quoted from Kaufman's 1970 translation, p. 179). This point is pivotal in one theoretical sense. For Buber, *all rhetorical relationships* are limited by incomplete mutuality, not just therapeutic relations. The issue of moments, therefore, is part of the general character of dialogue in all role- and goal-based relations, not just in therapy. That is to say, it is part of dialogic potential in all but the most trivial or transitory interactions. If such genuine moments of mutuality can happen, as Buber says, in an underground air-raid shelter or between strangers listening to Mozart in a darkened opera house (another of Buber's examples from 1965a, p. 204), surely they can happen also between therapist and client, teacher and student, parent and child, and superior and subordinate.

Perhaps it is ironic that although these two men continued to the end of their lives to articulate positions that were remarkably similar to one another and to the positions they expressed in the dialogue, the close similarity of those positions has never been recognized fully. It certainly was not pointed out that evening. The greatest dialogic theorist of the twentieth century appeared to miss much of Rogers's message, perhaps because he assumed that Rogers didn't really intend "moments" to be a conceptual term or perhaps he just listened past it. And one of the century's most famous listeners might have listened somewhat more actively and carefully in comparing the two positions. It would have been helpful if Rogers had referred less obliquely to his research on moments of movement in therapy, and, in his role as questioner and facilitator, if he had taken more opportunities for metacommunicating. With many decades of hindsight, it is easy to wish that Rogers had said something this direct to Buber at some point: "Perhaps we've misunderstood each other. Mutuality in my relationships with clients is never total or complete, and of course we communicate from unequal roles. I'm saying only that when these relations are effective, there are brief moments when we both seem to experience an unusually intense and reciprocal form of mutuality, and that this seems similar to your I-Thou relationship. Tonight it sounds like you agree that such moments exist, but still you seem to think I'm missing something. What am I missing?"

Although some commentators suggest that Buber and Rogers basically disagreed on the issue of mutuality, a reasonably coherent *Buber–Rogers position* emerged from the dialogue. This position, that mutuality in an unequal relationship can spark in moments of real meeting, becomes our foundation for considering the contributions of Buber and Rogers to a contemporary theory of human relationships. The next section explores implications of the Buber–Rogers position for prefiguring various aspects of postmodern thought.

PREFIGURING THE POSTMODERN DIALOGUE

Neither Buber nor Rogers is commonly associated with contemporary postmodernist or cultural studies approaches, and some scholars assume that their ideas have—as people say about aging uncles and aunts at the family reunion—seen better days. Nevertheless, the current intellectual interest in concepts of philosophical hermeneutics, cultural studies, deconstruction, and literary dialogism may be in part traceable to a quiet intellectual infusion of ideas earlier in the twentieth century, in the United States and elsewhere, that blended Buber's philosophical anthropology with Rogers's client-centered psychotherapy. Perhaps it is the consonance of this theory merged with postmodern cultural concerns that is stimulating a new interest in their work across various human studies disciplines. Our first chapter explained that the philosopher Buber's work is increasingly cited for its practical implications at the same time as the practitioner Rogers's work is recognized as philosophically important. What explains this curious convergence? Further, does such an explanation help clarify the general theory of dialogue?

The Buber–Rogers affinity for a certain kind of dialogue parallels in interesting and underappreciated ways the basic concerns of many currently influential thinkers of a broadly postmodern orientation. Of course, there are differences as well, and it would be misleading to suggest that Buber and Rogers were postmodernists. Equally misleading, however, would be to ignore how the Buber–Rogers dialogue presaged crucial cultural concerns that intrigue theorists associated with postmodern literary and cultural criticism and previewed certain of their concepts.

Discussions of postmodernism are made more difficult because of their definitional slippage. Those scholars who dismiss postmodernist thinking as a murky continental hoax argue that postmodernists' inability to specify the terminology of their project is evidence of its uselessness. The rebuttal is that the modernist demand for specification and definition signals its own stagnation. Postmodern theorists' disregard of definitional precision, so the argument goes, is simply a recognition that such definitions oversimplify a constantly shifting world. To pursue certainty is part of the project of modernity; in postmodern culture, supposedly, signs tend to refer only tenuously to other signs, not reliably to a concrete objective world; all meanings are said to be contingent and contextual; and something can mean simultaneously what it appears to mean and also to contradict (or undermine, or subvert) that meaning as well. Postmodern logic makes it possible for Madonna to be considered simultaneously a sex object and a feminist icon, and Michael Jackson both a secular blasphemer and a spiritual figure (e.g., Kaplan, 1988; Dyson, 1993).

When one side of a conversation insists on definitions, and the other side insists that insisting on definitions is part of the problem, the conversation, whatever its other merits or difficulties, is unlikely to proceed on the basis of great clarity. Each side has an automatic excuse for dismissing the arguments of the other, and perhaps an equally ready explanation for why the other side might not even belong in the same intellectual conversation. Yet the current intellectual climate necessitates that both—and others—indeed must sit at the same cultural table, so it might be helpful to counterpose postmodern with modernist assumptions to which they react. The purpose is not, as Mumby (1997) puts it, to "present postmodernism as a terrain of inquiry that is balkanized and separate from modernism" (p. 13), nor to reduce it to what he calls a "generic social constructionist position" (p. 23). We should note, however, those features of postmodern culture that clarify the importance of dialogic moments. Silverman (1990) stresses that understanding modernism is necessary for establishing postmodernism's conditions: "Postmodernism enframes modernism without identity or unity. It is fragmented, discontinuous, multiple, and dispersed. Where modernism asserts centering, focusing, continuity—once the break with tradition has already occurred—postmodernism decenters, enframes, discontinues, and fragments the prevalence of modernist ideals" (p. 5).

For Rosenau (1992), postmodernist thinkers in the social sciences "rearrange" the whole enterprise of intellectual investigation:

> Those of a modern conviction seek to isolate elements, specify relationships, and formulate a synthesis; post-modernists do the opposite. They offer indeterminancy rather than determinism, diversity rather than unity, difference rather than synthesis, complexity rather than simplification. They look to the unique rather than to the general, to intertextual relations rather than causality, and to the unrepeatable rather than the re-occurring, the habitual, or the routine. (p. 8)

Stewart (1991) has provided a postmodern commentary on several "traditional communication postulates." Postmodern views of communication stress language as a social process through which people co-constitute their worlds, abandon the construct of encoding, see human identity as emergent from interaction, and separate concerns for quality of communication from a simple check of fidelity (pp. 360–372). Thus, Tyler (1987) can point out how a postmodern ethnography can "foreground dialogue over monologue and [emphasize] the cooperative and collaborative nature of the ethnographic situation in contrast to the ideology of the transcendental observer" (p. 203).

A predominantly postmodern culture emphasizes the reality of surfaces rather than underlying or core essences, suggest Taylor and Saarinen (1994) in a work of postmodern communication philosophy. In that culture, pseudo-events become their own forms of reality, and to study what a philosopher calls truth is less valuable than to study the enigmas and misunderstandings of daily existence. In an obvious reference to Habermas, they write: "For those who still believe in the dream of transparent intersubjectivity or an ideal speech community of the experts who trade clear and distinct ideas, essences and concepts, misunderstanding constitutes an abiding fear. But misunderstanding can release energy. The law of the media is the law of dirty hands: you cannot be understood if you are not misunderstood" ("Media Philosophy" chapter, p. 5). The goal of science had been to formulate and test cause-effect and linear theories systematically in order to travel closer to a truth we could depend on. Instead, some versions of science have transformed it into an argumentative field on which scientists test competing rhetorical accounts. Misunderstand-

ing and prejudice, as Gadamer (1982) suggests, become productive opportunities for communication, not failed opportunities for specifying
meaning. For Taylor and Saarinen (1994), the hypertext environment
is our new cultural prototype, and dialogue our model concept: "In a
hypertextual environment, all philosophy must be interactive. Monologue becomes dialogue or, more precisely, polylogue" ("Ending the
Academy" chapter, p. 1). The new concern for dialogue concentrates,
therefore, on contingent, emergent, and discordant difficulties of
human linguistic existence rather than on proceduralist dialogue. This
is not to say that relatively orderly dialogue is impossible or unattrac-
tive in all contexts; rather, it is simply less likely to occur in neat and
tidy ways in a polyphonic or polylogic culture. Dialogue, in other
words, is more likely to be surprising, raucous, and momentary than
predictable, orderly, and sustained.

Some critics discuss the postmodern era as if it signals a fundamental break with traditions and goals of modernity. However, as cultural phenomena, the two metatheories exist together, in parallel;
postmodern theories have not supplanted as much as supplemented the
older quest for certainty with newfound skepticism about certainty itself. Continental literary and poststructuralist theories in the past several decades have upset profoundly the faith in—although not the hope
for—a stable cultural order. Change, process, appearances, surfaces, the
hyperreal, spontaneity, and multiple meanings—all these now seem increasingly meaningful, although not in a representational sense. No
wonder communication scholars have become more interested in conversation—as process, event, and metaphor—than in oratory (see King,
1992). Although King is ambivalent about many aspects of postmodernism, he points out:

> It follows that if the great orator is merely an agent of a matrix
> of dominant forces, then his or her discourse is not a unitary
> voice, but a product of group collaboration. From this point of
> view even the traditional speech loses its character as an indi-
> vidual art object, unique and unrepeatable. Rather a speech
> may be seen as a fragment of a larger dialogue between con-
> tending groups. (pp. 1–2)

The richness of the Buber–Rogers conversation becomes more obvious if we acknowledge tentatively how it resonates with much of
the tone of postmodernism. Neither man's thought is usually discussed in terms of postmodern theory, although we are not the first to
associate Rogers (Brazier, 1993b; O'Hara, 1995, 1997; Sundararajan,

1995; Teich, 1992a) and Buber (Baumann, 1992; Eisenstadt, 1992, 1997) with postmodern themes. As postmodernists advocate the near-infinite permeability of conceptual categories themselves, we can justify an exploration.

One conceptual incongruence is Buber's modernist faith in the representativeness of language. In the conversation with Rogers, Buber stresses the need to have terms defined precisely in order to distinguish between things that are essentially different, and Rogers agrees. Yet discrediting such representationalism is cited by Gergen (1994) as one of the most common concerns of postmodern social commentators.

In addition, Rogers is sometimes located within the tradition of individualism and personal, self-actualized autonomy that Gergen in another essay (1995, p. 74) terms "human agency" and disassociates from the relationally engaged agency he believes is the postmodern invitation. However, recent studies (Anderson & Cissna, 1996; Cissna & Anderson, 1990; Eisenstadt, 1992; Van Balen, 1990) have found Rogers and Buber to be largely consistent with Gergen's (1995) recasting of subjective experience as a postmodern "relational process" in which "we are no longer invited to consider our subjectivities as isolated, cut away, or alienated from others, beyond the comprehension of others. Rather, we sense ourselves as both constituted by, and constituting the other. In a certain sense, we are each other, our consciousness born of each other" (p. 78). As Schrag (1986) shows, some depictions of consciousness and self once "conceived [the ego] to be present as a monad" and "consciousness [to] function as an epistemic monologue" (p. 169). More recent descriptions have "decentered subjectivity as multidimensional and dialogical," disclosing or creating the subject as "an intersubjective event of consciousness, displaying multiple profiles, dialogical rather than monological in its hold on the world" (p. 170).

This kind of relationally sensitive shared intersubjectivity is the vector of Rogers's praxis as described in the dialogue, and the kernel of Buber's philosophy of the between as well. As Brazier (1993b) put it, "If we accept the spirit of Rogers's work, we open ourselves to the possibility that the boundaries of the person are fluid, for we are all wrapped up in one another" (p. 12). Similar conclusions led O'Hara (1995) to call Rogers an "unwitting postmodernist pioneer" (p. 47) in his development of a relational epistemology in the 1950s, and to highlight Rogers's contributions that were made possible by "the training of a positivist [and] the experience of a postmodernist" (p. 48).

Several additional issues demonstrate how Buber and Rogers prefigured much of postmodern theory without necessarily influencing it directly: conversational dialogue's suspicion of metanarratives, distrust of technique, concern for the particularities of truth, and emphasis on the unique other. With respect to each, Buber and Rogers have contributed to the increasingly congenial atmosphere in which postmodernists continue to theorize.

Suspicion of Metanarratives

One of the most influential starting points for recent continental theorizing is Lyotard's (1984) discussion of postmodernism as an "incredulity toward metanarratives" (p. xxiv). A metanarrative, as Lyotard used the term, could be thought of as a totalizing story that describes how other stories are subservient to it; metanarratives, therefore, give a culture the ways to interpret the implications of the full range of life's narratives. Metanarrative, according to Baumann (1992), serves a "legislative" function for society; it prescribes, however informally, behaviors and perceptions that are presumptively appropriate.

If a metanarrative can be conceived as an overall discursive structure explaining for significant groups "how things are"—or conceived in epistemic terms as a dominant paradigm, received view, or conventional wisdom—then it is clear why some people are satisfied with certain explanations that others find inadequate. Different groups may seem to be analyzing the same problem, but they may be listening to, and believe themselves members of, different metanarratives. Some listeners to sociocultural discussions of gays in the military, for example, are satisfied that the explanation "God condemns homosexuality" mandates their opposition to a policy because they know God is a sufficiently powerful authority to decide human affairs. Religion provides a master story, therefore, whose authority renders smaller plots intelligible. Few persons of faith would argue that premise, although thoughtful commentators might be led further to another level of questioning that builds on a postmodern theme: Who has the authority to interpret God's authority relative to sexuality? Who gets to tell the rest of us what counts as God's will, and what gives their story explanatory power? This process, which critical theorists call legitimation, is observed when people say such things as "my country, right or wrong," "I'll always be a Democrat because my party speaks for the common citizen," or — to use an apt example here—"scientific inquiry must always be objective and value-free." Why do some claims become legitimate and ideologized, reaching the status of propositions, while others do not? A postmodern critic could certainly be attuned to the existence of authority structures interpreting the metanarratives, and would presumably want to inquire regarding how these authorities came to be socially influenced, came to be taken as authorities in the first place, and how they have become interpreted in certain authoritative ways.

When postmodern theorists distrust metanarratives, this does not mean they necessarily renounce all of what those narratives claim; they merely cast doubt on the authority structures that legitimize the claims, and therefore can point out how contingent those claims may be. Narrative authority becomes radically dispersed in postmodern thinking, in other words, and the very processes of suspicion, questioning, contradiction, and multiplicity are held to be more appropriate than a search for consistency, unity, and conceptual closure.

Few commentators on the Buber–Rogers intellectual relationship or on their dialogue have noted how deeply Rogers was engaged in the mid-1950s with another professional dialogue that was more ongoing, and within which he expressed incredulity toward the prevailing dual metanarratives in his profession: (1) logical positivism in the behavioral sciences, and, in particular, a behaviorism within psychology that Rogers thought emphasized manipulation and behavior control, and (2) Freudian psychoanalysis as an assumptive base for psychotherapy, which characterized humanity as essentially evil and which tended to elevate analysts into experts whose diagnoses of "patients" were derived more from preexisting theories than from immediate human experience. Despite their widespread acceptance and popularity, Rogers thought both systems ignored a basic dilemma: how can we help persons to become more human if we objectify them in the very process of helping them? This concern, he thought, reflected the essence of Buber's fear of overemphasizing "I-It" tendencies.

As chapter 5 illustrated, Rogers framed his meeting with Buber in the larger context of his mistrust of the behaviorist metanarrative. His 5 x 8 note cards with typed quotations from a 1950 edition of Buber's *I and Thou* also contained this note to himself (Rogers, nd-c): "Reading Buber after Skinner is like stepping into another world. Control to the former seems to be something essentially irreconcilable with his poetic claim to retain human personhood in our modern world. Manipulation transforms a Thou to an It and thus violates the most basic value he can think of."

In the 1950s, just when therapists had won a measure of hard-earned respect in the intellectual world, Rogers renounced technique and explicitly decentered the therapist in the process of therapy. By doing so, he decentered psychology from its place at the control panel of the process of communication. Cognitive accounts, and even behaviors, were not systematic markers of who people were or what they were capable of becoming in relationships. Neither could measurement tell us all of what we want to know, although Rogers explicitly supported quantitative research and in many ways believed deeply in the rationality of science. This is why no one could reasonably claim that Rogers's system discounts the scientific method by advancing a meaningless relativism, but it is also why many postmodernists would be loathe to claim him as their own.

Understanding the need to study human nature in a wider, more inclusive context, Rogers expanded his theorizing beyond counseling, psychology, or psychotherapy to the broader cultural system of communication, and welcomed newer interpretive and experiential approaches to the philosophy of science, such as that of Polanyi (1962), and newer, more dialogic accounts of scientific knowing, such as Prigogine's (1978). Yet early in his career, Rogers asked that the psychotherapist be removed from a diagnostic pedestal and become primarily a listener to the real experts who spoke neither as theorists nor as conceptual legislators (Baumann, 1992), those clients who spoke of their own dilemmas and problems. It was this faith in persons, not in expert systems or metanarratives, that stimulated Rogers. He came to believe that reality was not unitary but multiple, and that meanings were not even potentially stable but necessarily fluctuating and contingent on the vagaries of experience (1978). Such fluctuation demanded attention to moments of unique meeting.

For example, when Rogers empathized with a client who seemed desperate, he did not assume he knew how that despair was experienced or felt by the client, but instead assumed the opposite: he could never be certain about it. "Despair" is not to be discussed from the standpoint of essentialism, as though despair has an essence that simply expresses itself differently in different clients; rather, despair to Rogers was heard as a way a particular client talked about her or his life. This concept was not basically representational at all—a term like "despair" could not stand for anything beyond the client's tentative choice of it, perhaps, in a conversation with a trusted other. With such scant contextualizations, the client-centered therapist creates conditions in which clients can explore the unique and irreproducible meanings of personal life by explicitly not presuming prior knowledge about what the client meant, but by focusing on *momentary* knowledge forms. Thus traditional therapies were turned on their heads: the very person most therapists least trusted was the only person Rogers deemed ultimately trustworthy in this conversation. Rogers understood, as did Gadamer (1982), that we generally don't converse to express things we already know, or to plant knowledge in others, but that we talk in response to questions that involve at deep levels the perplexities and uncertainties of understanding itself.

Rogers did not remove the therapist from the textual equation. Empathizing, Rogers believed, is not a projection into another's mind, leaving one's ground. Rather, it is an act of engaged imagination, an attempt to imagine another's experience as if it were one's own, but without losing the "as if" (e.g., Rogers, 1975). Despite the attempts of some of Rogers's students to manufacture a method or technique out of Rogers's empathic responses, there is no method here—only a constantly shifting sensitivity to flux, to difference, and to changes of the moment. Here is nothing of the presumption that the therapist knows best; the therapist becomes in effect the student of the client's teaching. When Buber told Rogers in the dialogue that the therapeutic relationship was necessarily unequal, he was evidently unaware that Rogers tended to see the supposed inequality the other way around—that it was the therapist, in a sense, who served, by renouncing authority. Empathy is how the therapist tentatively requests feedback in a situation of confused, perhaps contested, and certainly contexted, meanings. When Buber and Rogers talked about the moments of dialogue that sparked across the inequality, two vectors of inequality were being played out.

Postmodernist thinkers note the blurring of intellectual and academic disciplines (see Lyotard, 1984, p. 39), and this is precisely what Rogers's and Buber's rhetorics, separately and in their dialogue, together, have encouraged. Lyotard (1984) links this blurring with Buber and a "delegitimation" of the mystique of "science":

> If this "delegitimation" is pursued in the slightest and if its scope is widened (as Wittgenstein does in his own way, and thinkers such as Martin Buber and Emmanuel Levinas in theirs) the road is then open for an important current of post-modernity: science plays its own game; it is incapable of legitimating the other language games. The game of prescription, for example, escapes it. But above all, it is incapable of legitimating itself, as speculation assumed it could. (p. 40)

Eisenstadt (1992), Buber's successor as chair of sociology at Hebrew University and an influential interpreter of Buber's work in the social sciences, finds it

> not surprising that the importance of Buber's contributions has become even more visible in the so-called "postmodern" era, in which there has taken place a far-reaching decharisma-

tization of large social formations like nation, state, and ideological parties . . . and of such cultural domains as science. These processes of decharismatization gave rise in large parts of the contemporary discourse to the denial of the search for truth and of the validity of any absolute values. (p. 21)

Buber was concerned with "more dispersed and less central situations" and "in this sense he seemingly was a 'postmodern' fully aware of the multiplicity of the authentic forms of life and of social interaction" (Eisenstadt, 1992, p. 21), even though he continued in other ways his search for more basic values. "Buber was one of very few thinkers to have attempted to combine what we now call deconstruction with a continuing search for ultmate values. . . . For Buber, the fluidity of our era was an important, potentially creative component of the contemporary situation" (Eisenstadt, 1997, p. 56). If, for Lyotard and Eisenstadt, Buber assisted in delegitimizing the mystique of science, paving the way for postmodernist speculations, we might extend the observation: Rogers's work provided an analogous function within psychology, freeing psychology for newer constructionist, existential, and experientialist epistemologies that relied far less on assumptions of rationalized modernity.

Conversation, Dialogue, and the Suspicion of Technique

Buber and Rogers foreshadowed the contemporary interest in conversation as an access metaphor for communication, and thus both theorists contributed to a philosophical understanding of interpersonal communication. Of course, Dewey (1927), Mead (1934), Burke (1957), and, more recently, Rorty (1989), among others, have been their intellectual compatriots in this move; but it seems particularly significant when one of the most famous psychologists of his time meets the world's foremost proponent of dialogical philosophy, and both agree that genuine human reality is found in the moments of immersion in the "between"—that region in which no individual is seen, understood, or manipulated as an object.

Only with difficulty can today's scholars imagine or sufficiently credit the radical nature of this move for Rogers; he was advocating that psychology need not start with cognitive events (relational reality was his bedrock), but, beyond that, he was renouncing simultaneously two other entrenched psychological practices: the psychologist's reliance on diagnosing (legitimating or legislating definitions) through an expertness-based role, and a briefcase of techniques that therapists might use on clients. In fact, as we have seen, Rogers popularized the substitution of "client" for "patient" (Kirschenbaum, 1979, pp. 115–117), another quietly revolutionary move too easy to underestimate in today's intellectual climate. To imagine a conversation partner as "patient," as in the psychoanalytic tradition, is to define the other as deficient or sick, to objectify the person, and, in effect, to monologize significant portions of interpersonal talk. Buber also reacted against this tradition when he studied psychiatry early in his life (as he described briefly early in their dialogue).

To Rogers and Buber, communication could not be understood as a sequence of planned and deliberate acts. Instead, each utterance, each interchange, sets the stage for new surprises in ensuing moments of meeting. Both men, therefore, stressed *listening* to an extent previously unheard of in either philosophy or psychology. Buber understood listening as a "turning toward" the unpredictable and mysterious other, and for him listening became an attitude of "inclusion" and "imagining the real" of the other life as it is lived. The basis for self could not be psychological, because one discovered self through living relations. To "psychologize" (assuming mental reality was foundational) or to mind-read was never Buber's intent, therefore, and Rogers, despite reservations expressed by Buber and Friedman, appeared to agree. Rogers's goal in therapy was to create a safe space in relationship for the client to feel comfortable in exploring the unknown. Although the space could never be fully, or equally, mutual in an ongoing sense, Rogers's responses were not external interpretations or analyses, but probes he hoped would convince the other that personal clarifications were possible. There was a certain individualistic cast to Rogers's early therapeutic theory because individuals, after all, presented themselves to him for therapy. But it was always individualism in soft focus (except in the parodies that came from his detractors), an individualism in service of relational interdependence.

Polarities of Human Nature and Particularities of Truth

The dominant paradigm of traditional philosophy of science, derived from Enlightenment thought, sought to discover a truth that, in some sense, would stand still. The elusiveness of such a truth and even its inaccessibility was not thought to be a function of its flux, its constant movement. Truth was, in other words, neither a moving target nor a near one; nor was there much doubt about whether progress would lead to truth. Science needed to "advance" toward an accurate depiction of reality and science needed better tools or methods with which to observe. Science, with its faith in method, would be the vehicle for such discovery. Finding answers in such a paradigm meant that a seeker needed to move closer in order to examine distant mysteries, making them less mysterious.

The Buber–Rogers dialogic moments position could not ratify this linear view of progress, and substituted instead a more conversation-based assumption. Although Buber was in many ways a traditionalist who would reject much of contemporary postmodernism, and although Rogers for most of his life trusted the scientific method to provide solid data necessary to test theories, certain aspects of their blend approach to dialogue held scientific progress in essential tension with human understanding. Buber and Rogers argue for a dialogic truth that is near, dialectical, fluctuating, interpersonal, immediate, and momentary. This is neither a denial of the possibility of truth nor a simplistic relativism. From the Buber–Rogers perspective, truth is just not singular, normative, or imposed, nor can it be fully discernible. But neither is it a distant goal. Rather, dialogic theory presumes an elemental human truth that emerges only in the meeting of person with person, in the moments of I meeting Thou with the serendipity of reply. Within postmodern cultural assumptions, dialogic truth is not a matter of propositions but of presence, and it is not available to be examined propositionally, but conversationally (Shotter, 1993a; 1993b, pp. 19–35).

Reconsider, for example, the issue of polarity in human nature that emerged in the 1957 dialogue. On one level, the two men apparently disagreed, with Rogers seeming to suggest a basically positive vector for human nature, and Buber replying that it is instead polar. Rogers believed that the therapist did not have to make a case for why the client should or could develop better interpersonal relations, need not "persuade" the client to be communicative and to seek positive encounters with others. Rogers's experience taught him that human nature is characterized by an "actualizing tendency" that tends toward growth and development when the organism perceives ways to grow (and not that persons were inherently or always "good"). Because of interpersonal dilemmas, however, many clients cannot perceive their own opportunities, and therefore often fail to take them. Buber replied that human nature instead is essentially polar, and that the poles are not the opposing forces of good and evil, but the interdependent tendencies of "yes" and "no"—"acceptance" and "refusal"—and that the yes/acceptance response is the sense of direction that one person can help another reinforce. Rogers then reaffirmed this suggestion of interpersonal assistance and did not deny that human nature indeed exhibited these poles. The Buber–Rogers position that emerged thus seemed to be that human nature is neither glowingly good (as some critics of Rogers characterize his position) nor essentially negative or evil (as in some psychoanalytic theory), but polar. Human nature provides simultaneous and opposed choices of direction and directionlessness—a theme that resonates with postmodern implications. Each moment's decisions are born of such a dialectic.

In an important essay, Buber (1965a) relates polarity to this concept of "moments." In discussing the need for simultaneity and presence rather than the imposition of strict norms and maxims, he writes:

> In spite of all similarities every living situation has, like a newborn child, a new face, that has never before been and will never come again. It demands presence, responsibility; it demands you. . . . Good and evil are not each other's opposites like right and left. The evil approaches us as a whirlwind, the good as a direction. There is a direction, a "yes," a command hidden even in a prohibition, which is revealed to us in *moments like these.* In *moments like these* the command addresses us really in the second person, and the Thou in it is no one else but one's own self. Maxims command only the third person, the each and the none. (p. 114; emphasis added)

It seems that Buber is interested in the moments of inner life that acompany the interhuman. In this regard, another of Buber's responses to Rogers remains somewhat puzzling. Rogers, you will recall, had offered for Buber's consideration what he thought was a congenial claim: "in therapy . . . there are some very vivid moments in which the individual is meeting . . . some aspect of himself, a feeling he has never recognized before, . . . something of a meaning in himself that he has never known before" (turns #89, 91). Buber disapproved of this description of inner or self-meeting, asserting that it lacks the essential dialogic element of surprise. Yet it is difficult to see how Rogers's self-meeting analogy differs much from Buber's own prior position: a self addresses itself as a Thou in moments of (inner) meeting that provide human direction. Considering all the evidence, it seems reasonable to conclude that both men acknowledge that the concept of dialogic moments can be extended to an inner encounter, out of which direction for the person emerges. But this inner encounter is a form of immediate presence, both men believe, that can be assisted from without. The form of that help, however, cannot be a command or even an external motivation. It cannot, in other words, be someone else's imposed truth.

When David Bakan (1966) considered the differences between the tendencies he called agency and communion in *The Duality of Human Existence: Isolation and Communion in Western Man*, he found Rogers to be the contemporary "healer" most aware of that duality. In contrast to the controlling agency imposed by most therapists of his time, Rogers understood the risk of being vulnerable himself, the risk of having the faith that his attempt to understand the other's experience will help clients develop a sense of direction that they need—which is not the same thing as giving a sense of direction (Bakan, 1966, pp. 96–101). Bakan thought that in Rogers's healing, "Understanding of the person by the healer is the model and beginning for opening understanding within the individual" (p. 101). *Agency* (in Bakan's sense) is the mode of modernity—making things happen, controlling variables, mandating precision. *Communion* suggests more of a postmodern temper—risking oneself into relations of ambiguity, contingency, unspecifiability. Communion is the challenge of inviting what you can't predict, not the comfort of knowing ahead of time how you'll react in the next moment. In fact, the impulse toward communion once got Rogers deeply immersed in a confusing and toxic therapist-client relationship that he could not fathom and from which he escaped for several months of vacation only through the grace of a younger colleague's willingness to take over the case (Kirschenbaum, 1979, pp. 191–194). If Buber had tried to explain how Rogers could get himself into such a fix, he might have noted, as he stressed in their meeting, that dialogue partners must be willing to be surprised by what happens in the next moment, not attempt to control it fully. Ironically, Rogers's dilemma sprang in part from his effectiveness in Buber's style of dialogue, not from his incompetence.

Because of the unpredictability of dialogue, neither Buber nor Rogers believed they could aim for a single truth about human nature, a single narrative to describe it, or a single technique to control it; both theorists basically trusted the directions persons can take in building truths when they find themselves in genuine relation. Rogers was perhaps somewhat more optimistic about persons' inclination toward affirming the "yes," and both recognized that this was an interpersonal process. Through the polarities of yes and no, existing simultaneously for persons in relation, we create a constantly shifting sense out of tension, contradiction, and opposition. "The mass of contradictions," Buber said in a speech to teachers in 1939, "can be met and conquered only by the rebirth of personal unity," by which he did "not mean a static unit of the uniform, but the great dynamic unity of the multiform in which multiformity is formed into unity of character" (1965a, p. 116).

Buber's multiform conception of human experience is quite close to Mikhail Bakhtin's polyphonic sense of understanding language and literature and to his dialogic and social understanding of human experience (see Bakhtin, 1986; Holquist, 1990). In fact, Buber's work influenced Bakhtin while the latter was still a student (Clark & Holquist, 1984, p. 27). Bakhtin, who with Derrida is the literary critic perhaps most commonly cited among today's postmodern thinkers, became fascinated with the conditions of otherness by reading Buber and other philosophers. Todorov (1984, pp. 116–117) reports that Bakhtin knew Buber, esteemed his work, and used "polyphony" and "philosophical anthropology" in senses similar to Buber. Bakhtin called Buber "the greatest philosopher of the twentieth century, and perhaps the sole philosopher on the scene" (quoted in Kepnes, 1992, p. 62). Mirroring Buber's central contribution, Bakhtin also assumed that the I and the Thou were not separate entities, but that the I emerged from an ever-ambiguous social encounter with otherness. "I-Thou" is a *primary word*, Buber reminds us, that must be "said" before there can be an I (Buber, 1923/1958). Buber's contribution is clear in justifying how unity must be, as he put it, multiform.

In Kepnes's (1992) analysis of Buber's narratives in the essay "Dialogue," we can see Buber's reluctance to clarify the moments of multiform reality in traditional ways. Buber, Kepnes believes, emphasized the *middles* of his plots rather than their endings or beginnings, and this strategy served to introduce ambiguity, contingency, conflict, and a radical need for interpretation. Far from desiring an "aha!" moment of clarity and recognition, Buber wanted his readers to experience the I-Thou concept in an analogous way to how communicators themselves discover a dialogic relation—in surprise and even obscurity or unspecifiability. As Kepnes (1992) shows, "Buber's narratives clarify his philosophy in the very fact of their unclarity. What the I-Thou narratives do is to present that mix of order and disorder, of illumination and doubt, of abiding question and surprise that is at the heart of the I-Thou encounter. It is precisely in their ambiguity, their obscurity, their openness to a variety of interpretations, that the tales shed light on I-Thou" (p. 102).

Listening as Celebration of the Other

The common concern of the philosopher Buber and the psychotherapist Rogers as they conversed at mid-century turns out to be essentially the same challenge that confronts postmodern communication theory according to Barnett Pearce (1993): *how to turn toward, address, and respect otherness.* Lingis's (1994) philosophy positions the other less as an audience than as a part of a community to which all speakers and listeners already potentially belong, and with that membership comes a resonance to which we can tune ourselves. This does not mean persons are potentially the same, or even variant versions of each other; they will be different in ways that must be respected and in ways that generate real responsibility. Although for more than two thousand years communication models have emphasized the significance and the skills of effective speaking, postmodernism shifts focus from an "elite speaker" to the rhetoric of what might be called "emerging," "muted," or "subaltern" voices (King, 1992, p. 1). Sampson (1993) observed that the dialogic or postmodern turn must deemphasize a "possessive" or "contained" self in order to "take conversations seriously" (p. 97), as Buber and Rogers always did. They recognized in unprecedented ways the importance of careful and responsible listening. Their projects show a profound interest and faith in the other and a willingness to engage others on their terms, all without relinquishing one's own ground. This results in an emphasis on the small, silent voices "who are struggling to speak" (King, 1992, p. 2). Such voices, if heard at all, do not emerge in monologic soliloquies but in moments of dialogic surprise and uncertainty.

Rogers wrote about listening per se largely in practical terms for lay audiences, and aligned it most closely, as we have seen, with empathy or empathic understanding. For Rogers, empathy means perceiving and appreciating the other's internal frame of reference accurately, understanding another life from the other's perspective, while not relinquishing one's own identity. Empathy implies communion, while not foregoing agency. It recognizes that the feeling of being understood by another is a powerful stimulus for deepening a relationship, making moments of dialogue more possible. Buber, too, gave priority to being sensitively attuned to the other person. He called it *inclusion, experiencing the other side,* or, as he told Rogers in their dialogue, *"imagining the real."* Although Buber used the term "empathy" differently, to mean relinquishing one's own side (see Buber, 1965a, pp. 97) and "transposing oneself into the dynamic structure" of an other (Friedman, 1976, p. 88), empathy for Rogers and inclusion for Buber both actively acknowledge the reality of the other without forfeiting one's own.[5] Buber wanted to ensure that his concept of inclusion validated the between, and had no sense of bringing the other inside a perceiver's soul or experience. He stressed this kind

of warning more than Rogers. For example, in a critique of Jung's psychology, Buber (1952) wrote:

> The actual other who meets me meets me in such a way that
> my soul comes in contact with his as with something that it is
> not and that it cannot become. My soul does not and cannot
> include the other, and yet can nonetheless approach the other
> in this most real contact. . . . All beings existing over against
> me who become "included" in my self are possessed by it in
> this inclusion as an It. Only then when, having become aware
> of the unincludable otherness of a being, I renounce all claim
> to incorporating it in any way within me or making it a part of
> my soul, does it truly become Thou for me. (pp. 88–89)

Buber feared that psycholologists might take others' experiences and
use them "as contents" (p. 88), renouncing real relation by objectifying the other. Buber's notion of inclusion (and Rogers's empathy as he
defines it) cannot be a path to diagnostic certainty or precision, but instead is a move clearing the way for the contact of souls or selves. His
"unincludable otherness" is a powerful reminder that listening must
not be a passive reception. It explores a valued but unknown territory
of the between. Rogers was probably the American psychologist of the
time whose therapy was most aligned with this assessment. Despite
subtle differences in emphasis, it's hard to imagine explanations of a
concept that come from different disciplines and ways of knowing
being any more similar than this. And, of course, being able to listen
thoughtfully, attentively, and nonpossessively is freeing and powerful
not just in psychotherapy, but in any genuine relationship (Thorne,
1992, p. 99). This insight, deepened and informed by his contact with
thinkers like Buber and Polanyi, encouraged Rogers to broaden his system from "client-centered therapy" to the interpersonal and intercultural applications of the later "person-centered approach."

CONCLUSION

The Buber–Rogers conversation exemplifies a unified if not entirely
consistent position on several theoretical issues, most significantly that
mutuality and, by extension, dialogue involve moments of meeting.
Certainly the impact of dialogue is not restricted to its briefest moments; but it is a momentary phenomenon, one that appears often unexpectedly, perhaps serendipitously, and leaves before we are ready. The

Buber–Rogers position on dialogic moments has been underscored by Shotter (1993a). Therapeutic communication, he wrote, "must be . . . 'rooted' in certain 'special moments': moments in which therapists share with their clients, not so much understandings as *feelings*, thus to establish with them something of a common ground, a shared . . . basis in terms of which *both* can intelligibly contribute in their different ways to the joint authorship of a (new) biographical account of the significance of just those very feelings" (p. 120).

Interestingly, in the context of discussing such moments, Buber and Rogers prefigured or laid intellectual groundwork for important aspects of postmodern theory. The Buber–Rogers position justifies taking dialogic moments more seriously in public and mediated settings, such as we take up in the next chapter. It helped to decenter and make more fluid a monological self, made problematic the prevailing metanarratives of psychology and science, emphasized an emergent and relational reality, valued a "multiform" truth that emerges from conversation, and enacted a profound respect for difference and otherness. Although not postmodernists themselves, Buber and Rogers helped to shape an intellectual climate in which key postmodern themes could flourish.

CHAPTER EIGHT

Conversations of Democracy

Participation is by its very nature public activity whose
aim is to produce publicity or public-mindedness.
Participation is participating in public discourse
(finding discourse that is public) and participating in
public action (action possible only when actors act
together) in the name of creating public things (*res
publica*). The language of consent is *me* language: "*I*
agree" or "*I* disagree." The language of participation is
we language: "Can we?" or "Is that good for us?"
    —Benjamin Barber, "Liberal Democracy
        and the Costs of Consent"

The transformation of "I" into "we" brought about
through political deliberation can easily mask subtle
forms of control. Even the language people use as they
reason together usually favors one way of seeing things
and discourages others. Subordinate groups sometimes
cannot find the right voice or words to express their
thoughts, and when they do, they discover they are
not heard. [They] are silenced, encouraged to keep
their wants inchoate, and heard to say "yes" when
what they have said is "no."
    —Jane Mansbridge, "Feminism and Democracy"

Fr. Walter Ong (1982) has distinguished "primary orality," an era of direct personal speech that characterized human language before the ad-
vent of writing and reading, from later eras of "literacy" and
"secondary orality." The invention of literacy made possible linear

209

logic, science, and the recording of history, changing human life forever. We now live in a third great era in which orality has made a comeback. Our contemporary experience is a secondary orality, a time of radio, television, and rapid access to the speech of others across gulfs of space and time. It, too, is changing us, subtly but irrevocably.

The contemporary cultural immersion in secondary orality means that many people who need to, want to, or ought to be talking with each other will have to do so through highly public and mediated channels rather than in primary orality's direct but restricted face-to-face speech situations or literacy's linear logic. And increasingly the media of this secondary orality, infused with computer technologies, generate new forms of presence Buber and Rogers would not have anticipated in 1957, such as virtual reality, e-mail, computer chat rooms, and entire online support communities of people who experience close bonds despite never having met, as we say, "in person." In addition, the electronic media of television and radio with which these teachers were familiar, often termed "mass" media, offer newer forms of mediated representation in lieu of direct face-to-face democratic action. Many of them are described as appropriate ways to sustain interpersonal-quality communication even when people cannot be in each other's immediate physical presence.

However, because Buber was especially skeptical of technologically mediated dialogue, and suspicious of dialogue attempted with a nonparticipating audience, we want to pose a basic question: is dialogue still viable as a *public* concept or goal, given newer forms of presence? In responding to it, we can also address others: can persons become citizens by moving from blatantly "I" language to inclusively "we" language when a wide variety of other people are listening? Further, if we can, is this something we want?

We hope to address such questions in ways these two spokespersons of dialogue would have appreciated. Although they focused more often on interpersonal face-to-face presence, both also imagined interpersonal life in wider social, cultural, and political contexts.

THE DEMOCRATIC IMPULSE OF DIALOGUE

Five years before his meeting with Martin Buber, Carl Rogers offered a seminar at the University of Chicago on the topic of "Client-Centered Therapy in Relation to Current Philosophical Thinking." The course syllabus announced to students his interest in whether the effective interpersonal relationship of therapy was "parallel" to Buber's I-Thou conception. Rogers asked pointedly, "Would Buber's thinking enrich our own?" (1952, p. 1). His answer, to judge by the readings, must have been "yes."

Yet something else about the syllabus is also interesting, and probably a bit surprising for his psychology graduate students who might have expected to explore only issues related to face-to-face therapies. Rogers wanted the class to consider how therapeutic experiences and insights could enhance a wider political and social dialogue: "In therapy it often seems to me," he wrote to the students, "that we are *discovering a basic psychology of democracy*. I would find it fruitful to consider our experience in therapy as it is related to the philosophical basis of democracy, anarchy, communism, and the like" (1952, p. 1; emphasis added).

Rogers was not only right about several important connections between client-centered therapy and Buber's philosophy of dialogue, but the psychologist's curiosity about connections between personal and political relations in democracy also paralleled Buber's speculation about the relations between the social and the political. In an essay originally published in 1951, the year Rogers first circulated this syllabus, Buber was grappling with how a state can maintain a vigorous form of "social spontaneity" among its contending "societies, groups, circles, unions, co-operative bodies, and communities varying very widely in type, form, scope, and dynamics" (1957c, p. 173). He thought what he called "Society" could not by itself quell unnecessary conflicts and harmonize various groups. Instead, he believed that such facilitation of harmony was a viable role of the "State." Yet a state cannot just "govern"; it must rely on social practices of *administration* for its directions—practices that pivot around certain people's expertise in structuring solutions. For Buber, administration was not a technical or mundane activity; when done well, it transforms social practices, making them more human and dialogic. While government relies on edict, administration is, in a sense, a problem of how to structure public occasions. Buber believed the social principle (which represented diversity and spontaneity) and the political principle (which represented a governable cultural unity) existed in dialectical relation to each other. Earlier, we developed the similar notions of play and ploy, which also exist in dialectial tension with each other. The problem for Buber's politics became, then, a question of how to make political decisions reflect *administration* more and *government* less.

Not surprisingly, Buber believed—as did Rogers in his own way—that this problem could be addressed fruitfully in the sphere of education. Buber (1957c) argued that there is "a way for Society . . . to prepare the ground for improving the relations between itself and the political principle":

> That way is Education, the education of a generation with a truly social outlook and a truly social will. Education is the great implement which is more or less under the control of Society; Society does not, however, know how to utilize it. Social education is the exact reverse of political propaganda. Such propaganda, whether spread by a government or by a party, seeks to "suggest" a ready-made will to the members of the society, i.e., to implant in their minds the notion that such a will derives from their own, their innermost being. Social education, on the other hand, seeks to arouse and to develop in the minds of its pupils the spontaneity of fellowship which is innate in all unravaged human souls and which harmonizes very well with the development of personal existence and personal thought. This can be accomplished only by the complete overthrow of the political trend which nowadays dominates education throughout the world. True education for citizenship in a State is education for the effectuation of Society. (p. 176)

Phrased in more contemporary terms, Buber seemed to say: although we have to rely on the state in many aspects of our lives, we must not trust it to impose solutions to social problems on us. If we want to respond to the complex moral conflicts inherent in multiculturalism, politicized identities, distrust of government, and similar problems, we must develop ways to structure—"administer"—places and moments of public meeting in which difficult issues of mutual concern can be addressed spontaneously and engaged immediately. Government cannot, or should not, force this to happen, but a different and more dialogic philosophy of social education could facilitate such communication. If this is not quite Rogers's "basic psychology of democracy," it is a basic social pedagogy of democracy whose impulse toward dialogic learning flowed from many of the same sources.

Buber, however, had another fear, in addition to worrying about government imposition on the social realm. He was intensely suspicious of the ever-widening influence of mass media. Buber's (1949) *Paths in*

Utopia had expressed his concern with modernity's "great link-up" in an essay published more than a decade before the dialogue with Rogers:

> The modern city has no agora and the modern man has no time for negotiations of which his elected representatives can very well relieve him. The pressure of numbers and the forms of organization have destroyed any real togetherness. . . . We have no use for "immediacy." The collectivity is not a warm, friendly gathering but a great link-up of economic and political forces . . . only understandable in terms of quantity, expressing itself in actions and effects. (p. 136)

Then, in 1953, when presented with the Peace Prize of the German Book Trade, Buber expressed the fear that in conducting a "non-war," "debates between statesmen which the radio conveys to us no longer have anything in common with a human conversation: the diplomats do not address one another but the faceless public" (1957c, p. 237). A technical age invites "propagandists" who don't even believe their own causes because their messages must be entrusted to "special methods" and techniques that Buber associates with mass media—this person's "symbols are the loudspeaker and the television advertisement" (1965b, p. 83).

Here we want to explore the extent to which Buber's skepticism about public dialogue was warranted, and whether his own philosophical approach to dialogue can help public dialogue flourish even in a media age. Blending Buber's philosophical approach with Rogers's concrete praxis of communication can energize a democratic discourse and in this conversation the public might rediscover its own vitality. Similar to how Buber was able to change his mind after the Ann Arbor conversation on stage with Rogers (about his prior assumption that public dialogue was impossible), citizens and politicians must be challenged to examine implicit presumptions that dialogue is impossible, impractical, trivial, or counterproductive in a mediated democracy.

After examining the need for public dialogue and analyzing the models, difficulties, and dilemmas of contemporary dialogic attempts, we explore several important contemporary experiments in facilitating it. We then examine Buber's and Rogers's suggestions about facilitating dialogue. Finally, we nominate and reinforce several institutional means for creating public discursive space for dialogue. These suggested sites and catalysts for dialogue, we will see, follow Buber's own advice about administering without governing, and are consistent with Buber's and Rogers's positions on education for a multiform reality.

WHY TALK IN PUBLIC?

What makes a public situation public? Why should people desire more public talk? And who should be the talkers—and who the listeners?

Consider what makes human action "public." Such acts are counterposed to what we consider to be the "private" or protected realms of everyday life by the simple fact that public acts are observable. This means not only that they are available for others—often unanticipated others—to perceive, but that in being available they also invite judgment, recollection, and representation outside the control of the actor. Public acts must presume far greater opportunities for differential interpretation, and thus far greater dangers of misinterpretation or misunderstanding. Further, public acts form, or at least are capable of forming, a record that could be expected to commit an actor to a future position. Another way of saying this is that a public context presumes conditions of audience in ways that a private context will never exhibit. Although private talk, such as sharing secrets, can be relatively consummatory, guarded, and self-contained, public talk is protensive; that is, it has a "beyond itself" character and is presumed to stimulate further talk. Public talk, in an interesting and sometimes frightening way, becomes uniquely textualizable; it can be used for purposes never realized by speakers at the moment of utterance. It can be taken out of context without our knowledge by strangers, and thus becomes intensely threatening.

Public participation is both a bane and a boon for communicators. Hannah Arendt (1959) believed that two basic and interrelated functional characteristics make situations "public." Although she chooses different language, we could call them, broadly speaking, the *world-making* and the *coordinating* functions. First, public life constructs a human *world*. When things are seen and heard by many others in a wide audience, a kind of identity-shaping and reality-affirmation occurs that does not seem to characterize what she terms the "intimate sphere"; she wrote that

> the presence of others who see what we see and hear what we hear assures us of the reality of the world and ourselves, and while the intimacy of a fully developed private life, such as had never been known before the rise of the modern age and the concomitant decline of the public realm, will always greatly intensify and enrich the whole scale of subjective emotions and private feelings, this intensification will always come to pass at the expense of the assurance of the reality of the world and men. (p. 46)

Rogers might observe that this sense of public participation is, at least in a broad sense, therapeutic for people in that it reaffirms an appropriate sense of our own ability to make a difference in the world. Buber might observe that public participation contributes at least potentially to confirmation.

Second, public life coordinates human diversity. Arendt believed the term "public" signifies what we have in common, and builds on it creatively. A public participation helps us to manage and order artifacts and define our common reliance on each other: "The public realm, as the common world, gathers us together and yet prevents our falling over each other, so to speak" (p. 48). Another way of saying this is that public situations are those that structure systematic opportunities for communication with others who are not necessarily similar to ourselves. It is not only individual existence that seems worthy after public participation, but a commitment to public participation communitizes individual life, broadening and deepening persons' appreciation for the fit or balance between autonomy and coordinated action. Beyond this, public talk vividly demonstrates the systemic nature of communities and how those communities must reflect vigorous diversity. Without public participation of some sort, without some action that commits one in the public gaze, citizens risk paying a price in terms of identity ("who am I as an effectual being?") and in terms of coordinative actions ("how do I participate with others, perhaps even cultural strangers, in constructing a coherent social order?"). In the absence of routine public participation—or, as Buber would remind us, at least a *willingness* to engage in public dialogue (Buber, 1965b)—people risk the incestualization of already-agreed-to ideas and mores.

But we should move this point to a more concrete level. It is simply daunting for many to take public positions, and to risk their ideas and feelings in an open forum. Many sincere citizens habitually forswear, or at least fear and try to avoid, public conversation (Eliasoph, 1996; Mansbridge, 1980, pp. 149–162), and there are in fact persuasive reasons for them to do so. Some believe that public talk is unproductive, because the real political work goes on in backstage regions. Others don't like the anger they experience in public, and are afraid of what they might say when highly emotional. People who like to be liked must deal with the possibility of being disliked or criticized in open forums if they speak up strongly to support a position.

Still others are uncomfortable with the contemporary tendency to nominate hard-liners to speak most strongly for a given position. Those who fear the extremism of transforming preferences into demands might prefer to work actively but in low-key ways for change rather than participating in what they believe is a public rhetoric of spokespersonship. "In the new, politically charged environment," Hugh Heclo (1999) observed, "activists abound, but in their crusading zeal, they are very different from average citizens. The activists are seldom satisfied with moderate, nondoctrinaire solutions to public problems, . . . [but instead are] pursuing their own ideological agendas" (p. 64). This kind of headbutting public drama is reinforced by the media trend toward using experts to represent and dramatize wide ranges of political thought. The public, while watching *Nightline* and other interview shows invite the same "experts" month after month, may get the impression that one would have to be either famous, inflexible, or both to express opinions openly. Celebrities certainly do often hog the public's center stage, convincing ordinary people that their own opinions are marginal or meaningless—or at least less important than George Will's or Cokie Roberts's. Then there's the "what's the use?" factor: certain people and groups have become resigned to the fact that theirs are minority positions that can never get a full public hearing. Perhaps Elisabeth Noelle-Neumann's (1984) reasoning behind her theory of the spiral of silence helps explain why unpopular positions are perceived as even less influential than they really are, and therefore are expressed less and less often. Thus, potentially forceful ideas are squandered because advocates acquiesce to their own mental models of popularity and unpopularity whereby the powerful tend to be heard and minorities become increasingly silent.

Finally, too, we see a reduced faith in public dialogue from a variety of politicized groups and institutions. Their skepticism, although in some ways regrettable, is not wholly unrealistic—as Jane Mansbridge reminds us in the quotation heading this chapter. For example, marginalized or oppressed groups might understand ahead of time that their access to sites of public conversation has been restricted. Although they might remain politically active, they have little faith that open dialogue will produce a fair hearing for their concerns. To the contrary, some groups such as labor unions, civil rights groups, and Native Americans, who are convinced they are in power-shy, oppressive relations with stronger cultural or political groups, might suspect that dialogue would dilute their valid claims. Dominant hegemonic groups might renounce or neglect dialogue for different reasons—to engage in public dialogue might advertise that their positions are negotiable, that they are open to change, that their strength is wavering, that their cultural or political opponents might actually be able to make a potent case after all. In the contemporary cultural moment in the United States, identity-concerned politicized groups are suspicious about endorsing dialogue wholeheartedly because their voices have already been marginalized. These include racial and ethnic minorities, gay and lesbian organizations, feminists, environmentalists, and others. On the other hand, politicized groups such as the pro-life movement, cultural conservatives aligned against multiculturalist educational reform, some fundamentalist Christian and fundamentalist Islamic groups, and militias distrustful of so-called Big Government become suspicious about dialogue because their positions are deemed morally non-negotiable. It is worth noting that many of this latter group experience society as marginalizing them as well. Interestingly, some conservative political spokespersons have criticized the concept of dialogue itself as a kind of multiculturalist plot (e.g., Burd, 1995).

Whatever the commonly expressed reservations about public dialogue in a mass society, it remains clear that certain advantages are secured by a naturalized participation in open public talk about social, cultural, and political problems. If democratic theory holds, it should be the norm rather than an anomaly when distinctive opinions are compared and tested with audiences. It should be the norm rather than an anomaly when everyday citizens participate in such conversations, not just expert or celebrity representatives of predetermined positions. The media system is well positioned to enable more of this broader assisted dialogue, but the question of whether the cultural system is equally prepared is a vexing one. Despite the guidance of fresh theorizing about the public sphere, many attempts at public dialogue now seem to have a regrettably experimental character to them—almost as if acts associated with dialogue are weird and radical notions that threaten the social order rather than confirming its vitality and political essence. Before considering self-conscious efforts to facilitate dialogue, we will consider four common models of public conversation dominated more by the appearance, rather than the spirit, of dialogue.

MEDIA MODELS MIMICKING PUBLIC DIALOGUE

We have no shortage of people talking with each other on radio and television, and in computer chat rooms. Generally, these conversations, which are designed to fulfill both informational and entertainment functions, satisfy some communication needs of audiences while subverting others. We do not present them as illustrations of some basic underlying process, or as long-term answers to any basic question of dialogue, but as demonstrations of the somewhat truncated level of public discourse that some observers may mistake for dialogic attempts. Four models are most prevalent; we'll label them the *Moyers Model*, the *McLaughlin Group Model*, the *Political Debate Model*, and the *Interactive Broadcast Model*. We don't intend to attack or condone them inherently; we merely suggest they are not appropriate substitutes for more genuine conversational forms of public dialogue.

The Moyers Model. In PBS series and elsewhere, we hear taped interviews and explorations of topics in which an intelligent and informed questioner attempts to elicit information and perspective from an expert commentator by asking questions about which both interviewer and interviewee already know the answers. Bill Moyers's interviews are exemplary in this genre, including his popular conversations with Joseph Campbell and his interviews with a stunning range of poets in *The Language of Life*, interspersed with tapes of the poets' public readings (see the collections in Moyers, 1995a, 1995b). Moyers works hard to link insiders—working poets, for example—to the kind of language that outsiders would appreciate, and his intense and skillful preparation is strikingly transparent as he opens out and explores his interviewees' expertise. Moyers knows the answers to many of the questions he raises, but asks them anyway because he's trying to invite responses fitted to the audience's listening, not to his own. Because he doesn't tightly plan or script the interviews, the result has the flow and surprise of dialogue, while it is always clear that the interviewer functions more as a representative of a distant audience than as a fully present participant.

The McLaughlin Group Model. In *Breaking the News*, James Fallows (1996) highlights PBS's "The McLaughlin Group" as a particularly interesting turning point in televised attempts at "dialogue." At the urging of the host, a group of journalists fling strong opinions about public issues toward each other, typically in challenging and blunt ways. McLaughlin (and now a raft of local, regional, and national imitators) not only introduces the topics, but encourages bipolar arguments and analyses of issues. McLaughlin conducts the discussion like a maestro, and if the entertainment value lags a bit or journalists swerve toward an accidental nuanced position, he inserts a forced-choice issue by making participants take sides. His most famous pronouncement, "WRONG!," alerts viewers that he is about to correct someone's incompetent reasoning in a sentence or two. Less education than political agon, the show makes little pretense of teaching an audience anything new about these issues; instead, the dialogue is between what Buber called "conversational duelists" who aren't interested in learning anything new. The audience participates symbolically in neatly staged pseudoconflicts, but is unlikely to be more thoughtful or discerning after viewing the show.

The Political Debate Model. When networks televise candidates debating each other in front of invited audiences, many people would like to think that public dialogue is the result. Unfortunately, however, each candidate usually prepares and rehearses discrete packages of argument to be recited after questions from designated news representatives or, at times, from everyday voters in town hall-type meetings. It seems out of bounds for candidates to question or challenge each other directly and spontaneously, as they are expected to wait for others' questions. Although such debates sometimes produce entertaining and surprising results, these serendipities usually have to do with whether the performers do "better than expected" or worse, according to critics or polls. Typically, the participants seek to represent, rather than to present and consider, positions. They don't—and, in some ways, can't—speak genuinely with each other, in fact, but must address the unseen audience using the thin presence of an opponent largely as a foil. It would be truly risky for a political debater to appear persuaded in any significant way by an opponent's argument, and it's possible that this format also models issue entrenchment for audiences as well.

The Interactive Broadcast Model. Radio and television talk shows implement a different style of public conversation, one that attempts to involve an audience for entertainment and edification. Most successful examples, such as Rush Limbaugh's radio show, sustain a form of interaction through a host's ideological assertions stimulating either outrage or (usually) assent among audience members. The audience speaks up, calls in, faxes, or e-mails opinions or questions on cultural or political issues, to which the host responds with pithy commentary designed to stimulate interest further. Although the celebrity host may interview guests, the ideological turn of the talk, and the rightness of the host, is for all practical purposes foreordained.

These contemporary models and their various mutations encourage many types of communicative response, but rarely do they approach Buber's conception of dialogue. Despite their differences, they share several characteristics that would appear to deflect or even preclude dialogue:

- Participants try to decide beforehand what they will say and how it will be performed.
- Participants try to represent a wide range of positions that are not necessarily their own; their goal is to hold, not to consider or even to present ideas; they "tend" ideas for audiences as shepherds tend flocks, but often whether they

live or own those ideas personally is treated as incidental by their audiences.

- Participants speak *to* or *at* each other but not particularly *for* each other (here we use "for" in the sense of consciously intending a message for an addressee); they know that public rhetoric will not persuade other spokespersons or experts, so they strategize to use such occasions as platforms to persuade or entertain distant audiences.

- Participants may be politically honest and responsible as individual rhetors, but many learn they do not need to be immediately "response-able" within the situation; they abide, in other words, by what philosopher Stephen Claflin (1979) calls "The Rules"—a set of implicit monologic understandings that guide public media discussions. Although public media and their audiences want influential persons to speak their opinions, "The Rules" mandate that they should not be pressed by other influential spokespersons for replies, nor should they necessarily have to provide concrete examples on the spot, nor should they be criticized too openly for sidestepping difficult questions, nor is it expected that they even need to listen closely to each other's comments in such appearances.

DIFFICULTIES AND DILEMMAS OF
CONTEMPORARY PUBLIC DIALOGUE

Many of our challenges do not directly involve media formats at all, but are matters of social expectation. Four especially serious social challenges that restrain the potential of public dialogue are: a naïve communitarianism, a presumption of exclusivist identities, a longing for narrative closure and simplistic dramatism, and a recognition that dialogue can diminish already oppressed groups. These are not exactly problems in the sense that they must be, or even can be, solved; rather, they are conditions within which we must coordinate public acts.

Naïve Communitarianism

Communitarian thinking is an important antidote to radically individualistic views of human nature that overlook much of what is distinctive about human experience. In fact, the individualism it critiques is similar in some ways to what Buber criticized as psychologism. At its best, communitarian thinking reminds us of how experience necessarily is grounded in group relations, shared narratives, ongoing tradition, and moral responsibilities that must transcend individual rights. Important thinkers contributing to this movement have included philosopher Alasdair MacIntyre (1984), political theorists Michael Sandel (1982) and Mary Ann Glendon (1991), sociologist Robert Bellah and his colleagues (1985), and social communitarianism's most aggressive spokesperson and marketer, sociologist Amitai Etzioni (1993). Others, including the influential Canadian philosopher Charles Taylor (1985, 1989), have been linked with communitarian ideas through their emphases on the dialogic constitution of selves and society. In the communication discipline, the most prominent communitarian text is Christians, Ferré, and Fackler's (1993) analysis of journalistic values, *Good News*. Yet if the critique of a radicalized individualism is culturally coherent, and we believe it is, this doesn't necessarily mean that overgeneralized communitarianism should be immune from criticism. By using the term "naïve," we certainly don't suggest that communitarian social critics are themselves naïve, ignorant, or untrained, but that some rhetorical constructions of communitarian thought might invite a blanket assent from readers and supporters that is as simplistic as the radical individualism they seem to counter. Because the critique of liberal individualism appears to be gathering momentum, reasserting the dialectic between person and society might require that we think twice before accepting all so-called communitarian assumptions.

Derek Phillips's (1993) sociohistorical communication analysis, for example, has tested the typical communitarian assumption that solid homogeneous cultural values guided us effectively in the past, before recent cultural forces of postmodernism and multiculturalism led us astray. Examining the historical record, he finds that earlier supposed "golden ages" of community were far from the stable, cooperative, predictable, family-based, and uncontentious experiences that communitarian thinkers sometimes suggest were typical. Before we jettison multiculturalism or attack individual rights simply because implementing them can be contentious and divisive, we should ask whether any type of calm communitarianism of the type imagined by adherents has ever characterized complex societies, and whether societies based on electronic media for information, relational development, and problem solving ever could take for granted a cultural consensus.

Although communitarian thought has defined useful goals, such as an increased sensitivity to the power of social support and ethical values, its potential for co-optation by politicized agenda-setters—

along with the implicit denial of a multiplicity of voices and a mistrust of conflict—can reduce communitarian thinking to a counting mentality, a "we outvote you" approach to public life that can severely strain forums for dialogue. Haiman (1991) warned that a communitarian label or philosophy is sometimes applied merely as a trendier term for what used to be called "majoritarian" arguments for a community restricting individual speech freedoms or limiting the public voice of unpopular groups or causes.

When life gets complicated, people hope for a mechanism of consensus that can lead us out of turmoil. Dialogue can seem to provide that doorway: "If we only could engage in genuine dialogue, then we could see what we have in common and all will be well." Although his understanding of the dynamic of power is certainly more sophisticated than this, Jürgen Habermas's (e.g., 1990) description of the characteristics of an *ideal speech situation* offers such a dialogic hope. To Habermas, dialogue partners have equal access to the discourse, they are equally able to assert positions and question others, and they attempt to reach consensus by crediting the "force of the better argument." Another theorist, political scientist Bruce Ackerman (1980), advocates a public form of dialogue in which "conversational restraint" takes the form of a presumed neutrality. The differences between Ackerman and Habermas need not concern us here, but each has assumed at least that society might reach a public consensus on issues through a rationalized form of public dialogue.

Yet some critics (e.g., Barber, 1988; Young, 1990) who consider themselves equally dialogic point out that the Habermas and Ackerman models may be too rationalized, too linear, and too oriented toward consensus to be able to accommodate multiple cultural voices. The critique is persuasive at least in questioning the goals of dialogue; it is only a certain kind of dialogue that hopes for consensus, trying to establish procedures for its implementation. It is only a certain kind of dialogue that asks people with deep investments of identity and feeling in their political positions to express them in utterances that are "neutral." Perhaps it is not eloquence leading to consensus that is necessary; this privileges already powerful groups that have fully articulated and rationalized their goals, and have even institutionalized their own definitions of eloquent argumentation and why it should be a prevailing criterion for dialogue (i.e., in Western thought, men, whites, the wealthy). Critics of communitarianism, Habermas's discourse ethic, and Ackerman's dialogic neutralism all implicitly question the consensus assumption in dialogue. We don't necessarily communicate in order to submerge our differences in agreement, they argue; we often communicate to co-create understandings of how different we are. For this dialogue, which can be just as revolutionary, society needs what Buber called "administration," which amounts to public forums in which different voices can be listened to, and not just ventilated, even when they are nonprocedurally or ineloquently articulated.

Presuming Exclusivist Positions

An important challenge for dialogue comes from a distinctly noncommunitarian direction; it is the contemporary tendency to presume that positions taken on social issues should be determined by an exclusive allegiance to group identity. If communitarianism presumes too readily that everyone hopes for consensus, identity politics might assume too readily that consensus or common ground can never be possible between deeply committed but deeply divergent persons or groups.

Dialogue relies on the capacity of being surprised, of finding yourself open to change, and perhaps finding yourself persuaded, even in public, of that with which you've never agreed before. The power of recognizing otherness relies on granting to different persons the full depth and nuance of genuine personal experience that each of us assumes for ourselves.

One contemporary social trend, however, tends to undermine this potential resource for dialogic understanding. Its employment, whether sincere or cynical, encourages people caught in the middle of controversy simply to give up, to quit listening, to retreat into previous positions, or to choose sides artificially. We refer to the increasing reliance, similar to what some philosophers call "essentialism," on the claim that "I'm different. You can't possibly understand me." As with the communitarian position, this expresses a nugget of truth; communication research does teach that persons can never experience another's experience, or fully understand another culture as a native would. We are right to be suspicious when Jewish speakers claim they fully understand African-American anger at being stereotyped in certain ways, or when Irish-Americans claim they understand anti-Semitism because they, too, were once discriminated against. Experience is culturally inflected and particularized. But we should be suspicious primarily of the clarity claimed for the understanding, not its motivation. Communities are not well served when we deny that there may be a deeper reservoir of human compassion and mutual responsibility from which persons can all draw imaginatively to empathize with others' lives, while not renouncing their own positions. What is needed is not metaphors of separateness, but the notion of dialogic conversation, as advanced by Henry Louis Gates Jr. (1992): "Mayor Dinkins' metaphor about New York as a 'gorgeous mosaic' is catchy but unhelpful, if it means that each culture is fixed in place and separated by grout. Perhaps we should try to think of American culture as a conversation among different voices—even if it's a conversation that some of us weren't able to join until recently" (p. 175).

In a series of analyses of the recent U.S. cultural scene, communication scholar Mark McPhail (1991, 1997, 1998; Flores & McPhail, 1997) has critiqued such forms of essentialism as antidialogic forces. Even in the understandable assertion by marginalized groups of particularized and positive identities, McPhail finds the potential for a dangerous essentialism that contributes to the very dualistic, simplistic thinking that presumably oppresses them. While praising the impulse and genesis of of some Afrocentric philosophies, for example, he interrogates how their proponents dismiss the ability of non-African groups to understand Afrocentric styles of speaking and thinking. In his "complicity theory," McPhail suggests the irony that if oppressed groups maintain their essentialist identities, they may be culturally complicit in strengthening the very groups they oppose.

A Longing for Narrative Closure

The third challenge for dialogue is concerned with what kind of audience we have become for public messages and what we expect those messages to provide for us. Media audiences naturally seek resolutions to the plots of public drama. When there is a debate, we want to know who wins. When groups demand social change, we want to know how and when they are successful. Unfortunately (or perhaps, fortunately), life often turns out to be messier than our expectations for it. Real debates are much more open-ended, and social changes much more ambiguous, ambivalent, and gradual, than we'd sometimes would like them to be. But at least in our narratives about those debates and changes, we can superimpose a rhetorical order. We can tell stories of victories and defeats, of reputations gained and lost, of turning points in life after which nothing can be the same.

One of our narrative devices for closure is a voting mentality that often trumps suggestions for dialogue at school board meetings, parish counsels, committees, and academic departments all across the country. Dialogue, it is argued, just takes too long, and "we have to make a decision today," or "we've talked long enough about this," or "Jan, you're always trying to slow us down when the rest of us are ready to make a decision." Dialogue, for all its advantages, will probably not be accused of being efficient, at least in the short run. Dialogue can frustrate a desire for closure because it encourages exploration, the fleshing out of positions, fuller opportunities for reply, and even the teasing out of nuances of opposition. But these subtleties are largely out of favor these days, as we want to know "right now" who's guilty and who's innocent, who's popular and who's not.

Robert Entman (1989) explains such phenomena by calling our attention to the dramatistic *production biases* of mass media: simplification, personalization, and symbolization. *Simplification* is the tendency to report the stories that are most easily reportable; *personalization* is the tendency to oversimplify complex processes by referring primarily to individual action and individuals in conflict. *Symbolization* is the bias by which media reduce complexities to easily grasped symbols and stereotypes that ultimately convince audiences they understand the complexities because they recognize the symbols chosen to stand for the complexities. For example, during the Gulf War, most American reporters focused on stories derived from government-sponsored news briefings, accounts with plenty of details about U.S. successes but few about Iraqi successes; this *simplification* dramatized the war by framing it as a struggle between an effective "good" side versus an inept "bad" side. Iraq's leader, Saddam Hussein, came to stand for the force the United States was countering in the same way that Generals Colin Powell and Norman Schwartzkopf became *personalized* as U.S. leaders of integrity. Finally, the media made the process more accessible by invoking stereotypes. Such *symbolization* comforted American audiences with allusions to Hitler-like aggression and cruelty, the supposed power of Iraq's army, the innocence of the invaded Kuwait, and U.S. technological precision through the use of "surgical strikes" and "smart bombs." Entman's production biases suggest that dialogic practices will often swim against the current of institutional journalism, in part because dialogue subverts the kind of simplistic symbolic drama we have come to expect. CNN reporter Peter Arnett experienced just this kind of disorientation as the only U.S. journalist broadcasting from Baghdad for a time. Instead of being congratulated for adding more voices and more nuance to the news mix, Arnett found himself reviled by many as "anti-American" and a Saddam Hussein sympathizer. In much the same way, former Attorney General Ramsey Clark was verbally attacked by many everyday citizens and news people after a visit to Baghdad, where he reported that U.S. bombing was causing widespread sickness and death among women, children, and elderly citizens, as it produced (whether by design or not) contaminated water supplies and other nonmilitary damage.

Diminishing the Already-Diminished

Dialogue is an excellent opportunity to achieve some goals, such as exploring subtle positions, attempting to find areas of hidden commonality, or establishing a basis for empathy or identification across sterotypical boundaries. However, some social groups have been concerned—realistically—with how dialogue could function perhaps inadvertently as a political tool against them.

Dialogical theorists in the Habermas tradition at times seem to presume that power relations either are, or could become, relatively egalitarian. A symmetrical relation, rather than a complementary one, appears to be our major model for ethical relations, and thus becomes a presumptive dialogic paradigm. Yet this denies the everyday experience of attempting dialogue when we are not at all equal in power to others with whom we must speak and listen. As the political philosopher Nancy Fraser (1993) points out, "Insofar as the bracketing of social inequalities in deliberation means proceeding as if they do not exist when they do, this does not foster participatory parity. On the contrary, such bracketing usually works to the advantage of dominant groups in society and to the disadvantage of subordinates" (p. 11). Further, she argues, "We should question whether it is possible even in principle for interlocutors to deliberate as if they were social peers in specially designated discursive arenas, when these discursive arenas are situated in a larger societal context that is pervaded by structural relations of dominance and subordination" (p. 12). The realistic question cannot always be "how can we become more equal here?" Sometimes we must confront a situation of "We're not equal, nor will we be in the forseeable future. Now, nevertheless, how can we talk effectively to resolve this particular problem: a new labor contract, a grade change, or a new vacation leave policy at work?"

When power is asymmetrically distributed, and when some parties are either mean-spirited or blind to the existence or effects of their own power, setting up contexts for dialogue could undermine the hard-won strength of already-marginalized and exploited minorities. This is especially true when journalists and others automatically interpret a willingness to talk as a softening of positions. Further, some committed participants within exploited groups have found that to negotiate openly with those in power will in fact legitimize the power structure *unless* the exploited group states its positions as demands. As the psychologist and colleague of Rogers, Richard Farson (1978), observes, dialogue still can have heavy political baggage: "We risk [a] problem every time we attempt to 'improve communication' between men and women, parents and children, Blacks and whites, administrators and students. When there exists a marked differential in power between two or more parties, increasing or opening communication may reinforce, even exaggerate the existing power relationships" (p. 21). Farson suggests that although a society might want to encourage dialogue generally, some groups who support valuable social reform won't be enthusiastic about dialogue's strategic desirability. Especially in hegemonic relations, an exploited group may at some moments need to nurture its anger and promote internal solidarity more than it needs to imagine how real the other's position might be to them.

THE RESURGENCE OF DIALOGUE AS REALISTIC DEMOCRATIC RESPONSE: LOCAL, NATIONAL, AND GLOBAL PROJECTS

Although dialogue might not always be seen as a practical solution to a well-defined crisis, it is increasingly being proposed as a practical move for diagnosing potential problems, exploring imaginative alternatives, averting a crisis mentality, acknowledging the valid identities of multiple voices within a larger community, providing important information and sensitivities for later decision making, and creating a symbolic environment that reinforces the notion that change within complex and interlocking communities is possible. One term that suggests all these possibilities is that public dialogue at its best is capable of becoming *deliberative*. The potential for a genuinely deliberative democracy to replace both interest group liberalism and a wistful conservatism rests on the willingness of diverse groups and communities to take public dialogue seriously, not rejecting it out of hand.

This seems to be happening, at least to some extent. At local, national, and even global levels, many experiments in dialogue are energizing public decision making. We now will survey only a few of the more prominent recent explorations of public dialogue; even a cursory glance, however, shows that we participate in an age that is curious about dialogue in ways unimagined just a few decades ago and, further, is willing to explore its possibilities. Many of the projects have been motivated by dissatisfaction not with life in general, but with the quality of what we could call public life—not only with the character of government and its decision making, but with the process through which democratic decisions are made. Many groups, discouraged at the loss of community and the absence of "free spaces" for conversation (Evans & Boyte, 1992), are now trying to structure organized dialogue projects in public discourse. They aren't chasing romantic ideals, but are creating real and practical possibilities that can make a difference in everyday lives.

Community and Organizational Dialogue Projects

Many promising projects have recently placed dialogue at the center of community life. Among them are:

The Utne Reader *Neighborhood Salon Association.* The *Utne Reader*, which has called itself "American's fast-growing general interest magazine" (General Utne, nd, p. 1), thought its readers might be eager to do something more than merely subscribe to and read the magazine, that they might be receptive to exploring opportunities for conversation and dialogue in their own communities. The cover story for its March/April 1991 issue concerned "Salon," and was subtitled "How to Revive the Endangered Art of Conversation and Start a Revolution in Your Living Room." Articles described something of the history of salons, explained the Native American concept of "Council," described an electronic "virtual" salon, and included excerpts from two essays on dialogue by David Bohm. The issue concluded with a short advertisement titled "Shall We Salon?" that invited interested readers to return a clipout coupon. With over 8,000 responses, Neighborhood Salon Association was born. By 1995, there were over 300 community-based salons, with over 20,000 Neighborhood Salon Association members (It's Time to Meet, nd; The Salon-Keeper's Companion, nd; Sandra, 1997).

The *Utne Reader* conceives salon dialogue as something that has to be initiated and facilitated, and ultimately as a process to be entrusted to the participants and members themselves. The conveners and facilitators play important roles, but limited ones, and even those roles can be and typically are shared among many of the participants. They seem to believe that, provided with only minimal guidance, people are capable themselves of engaging in dialogic conversation.

The Public Dialogue Consortium. The Public Dialogue Consortium involves various communication teachers, practitioners, and researchers who want to improve the quality of communication in public disputes (Walters, nd). Through "Kaleidoscopes," workshops, and seminars, they seek to teach "new and better ways of communicating . . . in a complex, dynamic, and diverse society" (p. 2). They utilize a systemic approach for understanding problems, looking for patterns, connections, and context (Pearce & Walters, 1997a, 1997b) by bringing people with different backgrounds and goals in contact with each other.

The Consortium starts with the assumption that most public talk about controversial issues unproductively focuses on "deficit language" and negativity: "what people lack (rather than on what they possess), problems to be solved (rather than opportunities to be taken advantage of), and things people don't like (rather than their highest hopes and dreams)" (Pearce, 1998, p. 277). To counteract this, workshop participants engage in learning and teaching skills of "appreciative" language and inquiry that are aimed more at including of multiple voices within a conversational system than at problem-resolution (Pearce & Pearce, 2001).

The most prominent Consortium project has involved the central California city of Cupertino. Through a series of community focus groups, training sessions, intergenerational community interviews, dialogue meetings, public discussions, and a two-day workshop on dialogue skills, facilitators have helped residents develop "new patterns of communication within the city about public issues" (Pearce & Walters, 1997a, p. 6). The Cupertino project is an excellent example of how a practical application of dialogue, in this case of sustained community self-awareness and community building, can be at the same time theoretically informed—in this case by the theory known as the *coordinated management of meaning* (see Pearce, 1989; Pearce & Cronen, 1980; Pearce & Pearce, 2000). As Pearce (1998) reports of one initiative:

> We facilitated a Town Hall Meeting with about 150 residents who heard and told their stories about cultural richness. All the while, we felt the tension between this way of dealing with the issue and those who preferred or were more accustomed to confrontational styles of communication. Some criticized us for not getting at the "real issues," which we understood to mean that we did not elaborate the narrative structures of "problem-opponent-strategy-solution" or "accusation-guilt-confession-resolution." Others felt undercut; without enemies, they did not know whom to fight and, in the absence of fighting, what else to do. We took the responsibility of working with these persons, to take advantage of their energy and commitment while redirecting them in the forms of communication in which they engaged. Some of these people have subsequently become central players in the project. (p. 277)

The Public Conversations Project. A group of therapists affiliated with the Family Institute of Cambridge began in 1989 to explore whether their skill as therapists could be applied to intractable public controversies (Chasin et al., 1996; Roth et al., 1992). Polarized public conversations, the therapists observed, had many of the same attributes as the polarized and conflictual conversations between family members: the conversations are highly predictable, genuine questions are rarely asked, partisans exalt their own side and think the other side dismissable, they listen to each other only to find negative attributes and rarely to deepen their understanding of the others' concerns (Becker et al., 1995a, 1995b).

These therapists accepted a significant challenge: to attempt to facilitate dialogue on the issue of abortion between and among advocates of pro-choice and pro-life positions, perhaps the most difficult and divisive issue in our society. Subsequently, they have applied their approach to other controversies (e.g., the future of forests in the Northeast and preparations for a U.N. conference on population and development) (Chasin et al., 1996), and they are offering workshops on dialogue at sites around the United States.

Several factors seem to have contributed to the success of the Public Conversations Project approach (Roth et al., 1992, p. 8):

1. Careful preparation and clear ground rules have been more important than any elaborate family therapy techniques.
2. Creating a context of safety and respect has allowed people to express the complexity of their thoughts and feelings and doubts, and to be open to those of others.
3. Getting participants voluntarily to restrain their behavior by following the ground rules provides an opportunity for growth as they begin to listen to the other.

Bolstering the effectiveness of their model are two dynamics that transform a destructive debate mentality into a dialogic one (Roth et al., 1992, pp. 9–10). The first is that they offer participants an alternative villain to the one they have, a villain most of them hadn't thought about before. Implicitly, the whole of the process suggests that polarization is an evil, and it becomes the new enemy to connection, understanding, and communication about the issue. But it is an enemy common to *all* sides. Second, their dialogic context encourages feelings of safety that allow for expressing one's self and respect that increases acceptance of the other.

The MIT Dialogue Project. William Isaacs (1993a, 1993b, 1999), Peter Senge (1990; Kofman & Senge, 1993), and colleagues (see Schein, 1993), at the Massachusetts Institute of Technology (MIT) Dialogue

Project often draw from the work of the theoretical physicist and dialogic theorist David Bohm (1990, 1996), as do Ellinor and Gerard (1998) in a related book. Their primary application has been within organizations, primarily for-profit businesses. For them, "dialogue is not merely a strategy for helping people talk together," but "often leads to new levels of coordinated action" without requiring agreement. Aligned actions are the result of a participation in a "pool of shared meaning" (Isaacs, 1993a, p. 1). Their guidelines for dialogue include suspending certainties, listening to one's own listening, slowing down the inquiry, becoming aware of thought, and maintaining peripheral attention (Isaacs, 1993a, p. 3). Although operating typically as consultants for organizations, they have also offered "Foundations for Dialogue" seminars open to interested individuals (Isaacs, 1993b).

Peter Senge's best-selling book *The Fifth Discipline* is probably the most widely influential text of the MIT Dialogue Project, and since its publication in 1990 it has stimulated a vigorous cottage industry of workshops, articles, offshoot books, and even copycat works. The image-metaphor of the *learning organization* has struck a deep chord with organizational managers who are rightly suspicious of quick-fix solutions and new prescriptive systems for what to do for ailing corporations. Instead, Senge and his colleagues ask decision makers to forego prescriptions entirely, and rather than adopting systems generated by others, they are urged to adopt a new way of thinking: to think of their own organizations as systems of creative communication. Organizations will learn to adapt to new challenges as they foster dialogue. Three conditions of dialogue, adapted from Bohm's work, are crucial: participants must suspend assumptions, they must regard each other as "colleagues," and they must find a facilitator who "holds the context" of dialogue (Senge, 1990, pp. 243–247). As time goes on, the need for a facilitator begins to evaporate as organizations and learning teams become acclimated to maintaining their own systemic contexts; this is an example of what the MIT group calls the *discipline* of learning and dialogue.

National and International Dialogue Projects

Other dialogue projects focus less on face-to-face community building in neighborhoods, towns, or organizations, and more on a wider conception of a deliberative public sphere.

The Public/Civic Journalism Movement. A recent evaluation of journalism's cultural dilemmas stated that "The prime role of journalism . . . , and the only way by which it can survive as a viable institution in the public arena, is to take the responsibility to stimulate public dialogue on issues of common concern to a democratic public" (Anderson, Dardenne, & Killenberg, 1994, p. xx). One of the most divisive issues within journalism in the past several years has been a vigorous movement that reflects a similarly dialogic philosophy. Variously termed public journalism, civic journalism, communitarian journalism, or conversational journalism (Gunaratne, 1998), its advocates chart a course that is more ambitious and proactive than institutional journalism's traditional task of reporting news. Without sacrificing traditional journalistic values of objectivity and fairness, argues Jay Rosen (Rosen, 1994a, 1994b, 1999; Rosen & Merritt, 1994), the movement's primary theorist, newspapers and other media can and should sponsor the kind of public spaces in which citizen dialogue can flourish.

Journalism professor Edmund Lambeth (1998) recently sought to distill a definition of public journalism from existing commentaries and research, finding that five basic features characterized the movement. Public journalism, in this implicit operational definition, is the attempt by traditional news and media organizations to:

1. listen systematically to the stories and ideas of citizens even while protecting its freedom to choose what to cover;
2. examine alternative ways to frame stories on important community issues;
3. choose frames that stand the best chance to stimulate citizen deliberation and build public understanding of issues;
4. take the initiative to report on major public problems in a way that advances public knowledge of possible solutions and the values served by alternative courses of action;
5. pay continuing and systematic attention to how well and how credibly it is communicating with the public. (p. 17)

Some public journalism projects have involved citizen forums, participatory forms of community polling, a more active role of everyday people in the practices of the daily paper in the form of citizen councils or citizen consultants, and a more interactive relationship—often involving electronic links—with its audience.

Arthur Charity (1995) provides several examples of how dialogue figures into public journalism projects:

- In North Carolina, the *Charlotte Observer* focuses its attention for six weeks at a stretch on a single high-crime neighborhood, reporting on the reasons for the area's problems and drawing help and suggestions from across the entire city. The paper's community liaison helps volunteers and local organizations coordinate efforts to bring the neighborhood back.

- Borrowing an idea pioneered in Charlotte, the Hyannis Mass. *Cape Cod Times* consulted a panel of representative citizens to set priorities in covering the 1992 campaigns. After election day, the panel proposed setting a permanent agenda for Cape Cod. So the paper surveyed its readership, promised long-term coverage of their six areas of greatest concern, and drew 600 people to public meetings on these issues. . . .

- The *Wisconsin State Journal* in Madison created "grand juries" and "mock legislatures" composed entirely of citizens to deliberate over a property tax plan, the national budget, and health care reform, and then reported on the deliberations to spur wider public talk. (p. 13)

Critics of public journalism fear that it renounces straightforward news reporting and becomes too entangled in the thicket of community political advocacy, thus demeaning the role of newspapers as a neutral medium. According to critics, public journalism sacrifices traditionally valuable watchdog functions as journalism becomes a more active player in the civic life of communities (for reviews of some critiques, see Black, 1997; Gunaratne, 1998; Lambeth, Meyer, & Thorson, 1998). At the same time, few cultural institutions are better positioned than newspapers to promote accessible public dialogue across a wide range of community interests. Further, Rosen and others reply, journalism does not need to forego its traditional mission of news reporting in order to enhance civic dialogue and deliberation. They see no reason why "news" cannot encompass the stories and aspirations of everyday citizens as well as the interests of celebrities and politicians.

The National Endowment for the Humanities' National Conversation Project. Sheldon Hackney began his term as the chairman of the National Endowment for the Humanities (NEH) with a speech to the National Press Club in November 1993, followed by a point of view article in *The Chronicle of Higher Education* (Hackney, 1994), and numerous other speeches and interviews (including a lengthy stint on "The MacNeil/Lehrer News Hour" ["Interview With," 1994]). Hackney faults our existing conversation on national and public issues on numerous grounds, and he argues that we need to engage in a "national conversation" about what it means to be an American.

NEH promoted two primary projects designed to foster a conversational sensibility on a national scale. It developed and circulated a "conversation starter kit" (National Endowment for the Humanities, 1995) "to help Americans get their own conversations started without a grant" (p. 1). In addition, NEH funded a series of projects through a special competition in its Division of Public Programs that were explicitly designed to promote and foster a national conversation.

The NEH (1995) conversation kit's "Handbook of Tips" envisioned "thousands of small-group discussions across the country conducted by Americans from many backgrounds who come together for frank and open exchanges about our differences as well as our common ground" (inside front cover). NEH anticipated that these conversations would build on the experience and knowledge of the people involved, stress cooperation and participation, and affirm that every viewpoint is important. The kit includes a handbook of tips for creating a conversation, significant founding documents of the country, a series of brief essays written by eminent American scholars especially for this kit, a set of conversation starters (quotations, excerpts, background information) to spark reaction and get a conversation going, and a list of suggested readings and films.

In addition, NEH funded a number of special projects designed to facilitate conversations in particular communities. We examined the six successful proposals from the first round of NEH funding of these National Conversation proposals. They go well beyond what we ordinarily think of as a group engaged in dialogue. For example, to consider the most expansive (and expensive) case, the Great Books Foundation proposed to convene 259 conversations over a 6-month period in Philadelphia, Chicago, and San Francisco. The project would be launched with 93 one-day conversation events held simultaneously in those cities over a 3-day period; 166 additional conversations would be convened in those cities over the following 6 months. Finally, they would invite over 20,000 high school teachers and librarians, all trained Great Books discussion leaders, to conduct conversations on their own in schools and libraries throughout the country.

The NEH conversations are diverse. All of them assume conversations need to be "started," and the leadership of these conversations will be more directive than might be typical in encounters we usually think of as dialogic. Many will utilize established formats—Great Books' shared inquiry method, study circles for adult education, Socratic seminars, Kettering's National Issues Forums (see below)—and several seem to emphasize learning from the texts more than learning from one another or arriving at something new together. Others are less specific about the characteristics or training of their facilitators. Virtually all see dialogue as involving face-to-face meetings, although one or two incorporated kick-off or closing events that were mediated, and one will use e-mail but only as a way for the staff and leaders to stay in touch.

The Kettering Foundation National Issues Forums. In 1982, the Kettering Foundation began a program to bring people together to talk about public issues. In libraries and churches, in schools and civic groups, and in a wide variety of other organizations and institutions, Kettering has been creating a contemporary version of the American town meeting. Kettering is attempting to involve people in deliberative discussions, which it sees as the essential ingredient in a healthy democracy.

The National Issues Forum model has developed into a network of more than 5,000 groups meeting regularly to discuss and deliberate on such public issues as the future of schools, immigration policy, juvenile violence, poverty, the federal debt, racial inequality, abortion, day care, the environment, and many others. David Mathews, president of Kettering and author of *Politics for People* (1994b), distinguishes between "deliberative dialogue" and other kinds of talk: "Dialogue . . . refers to a particular type of talk that promotes the reasoning required for making choices" (1994a, p. 68). It is a "serious and intense interaction among people, one so intense that it changes the participants and produces new insights." It is neither casual discussion nor debate. It is exploratory and reflective, where "listening carefully to one another is more important than speaking eloquently."

These appear to be highly structured conversations, orchestrated to ensure that each person will select one of four positions on each issue. We do not know whether participants find these choices constraining or liberating. The goal is that participants learn to listen in new ways, that they come to form more mature political beliefs, and that something of a group position develops on each issue, based not as much on the preexisting positions of the participants as on their dialogue together.

The Fishkin Deliberative Democracy Project. Political theorist James Fishkin has advocated, developed, and, working with a variety of groups in the United States and England, implemented a particularly intriguing innovation in deliberative democracy. Fishkin wants citizens to participate more in the democratic dialogue, but he understands that this does not happen naturally and neither will it develop within a media system that saturates the public with reports based on the omnipresent "public opinion" poll as it is used today. Merely asking citizens one by one what they think, according to Fishkin (1991), can never approximate genuinely *public* opinion processes. Private opinions, summed and analyzed, are not the same thing as opinions developed and tested in a public crucible of dialogue. Thus, Fishkin is interested more in what he calls *deliberative polling*, which attempts to avoid the prime failing of normal polls (they aggregate data from both informed and [very often] uninformed citizens). In fact, Fishkin believes that by continually asking isolated individuals their opinion, the media actually encourage them to be, in Fishkin's terms (1995) *rationally ignorant*— that is, to decide that it is personally reasonable for each individual not to make much effort to become informed, and, given the unlikelihood of being able to influence others, it is rational and efficient not to invest much personal energy in public sphere activities. Thus "public opinion" becomes little more than a snapshot of a basket of whims. Fishkin asks, though: Would it be better to discover what a random sampling of citizens *would* think about the issues central to their political choices if they *actually were brought together* with the expectation that they will talk their ideas out with each other and listen to information and interpretations they never knew existed?

Such *National Issues Conventions* (NIC), although some observers find them idealistic, nevertheless have constituted one of the most tangible attempts to bring public dialogue into the political arena. Organizers bring a citizen sample to a face-to-face forum with small group and plenary sessions, together with a series of content experts whose role is to clarify factual issues. Notable early experiments were in Britain in 1994 and 1995, and in the United States at the University of Texas at Austin in January 1996 (moderated by noted broadcast journalist Jim Lehrer and televised in part on PBS). Fishkin (1995) says of the deliberative polling process:

> Deliberative polling creates a social context where it becomes reasonable for ordinary people to overcome "rational ignorance," and to behave more in the way we would like ideal citizens to behave. We may not be able to get the entire citizenry engaged with the issues. But, with deliberative polling, we can conduct the experiment and broadcast the results to the whole country—making the conclusions of an engaged microcosm available to everyone else. (p. 1)

Participants' opinion shifts were tracked by the National Opinion Research Center of the University of Chicago. Researchers found statistically significant changes on a number of issues of taxation, welfare, and foreign aid and intervention. Following the Texas NIC, news programs reported that after dialogue the 459 citizen-delegates had grown dramatically more positive about spending on education, increased state support of welfare programs, and military cooperation with other nations in responding to "trouble spots" around the world, among other issues. On the other hand, the group's initially favorable response to a suggested flat tax diminished dramatically after deliberation.

Ideally, of course, the importance of each NIC transcends its own occurrence; by being reported as a media event (see Dayan & Katz, 1992), the effects could be expected to ripple outward into a wider dialogue in the free public spaces of everyday political discourse. The fact that ordinary citizens can, through speaking and listening, be open to argument and change their minds should make news and encourage others to participate more fully in the political dialogue.

Now that we have surveyed a representative terrain of current dialogic prospects that reflect our media tendencies and cultural assumptions, we have to ask if the lofty goal of dialogue is just too lofty, too impractical.

REVISITING BUBER AND ROGERS: VECTORS OF DIALOGUE

In chapter 1, we discussed how the work of Buber, Rogers, and other thinkers seems to rely on some basic elements in defining dialogue. To review, dialogue appears to emerge in conditions of:

- *Immediacy*: Dialogue partners are present for each other, both in the *now* and in the *here* senses of "present." The condition of immediacy emphasizes that although dialogue can be disciplined and even prepared for, it is—at its best—unscripted and unrehearsed.
- *Emergent surprise*: Dialogue partners find themselves open to unanticipated consequences of their encounter. If they hold goals, they hold them flexibly and are ready to revise, to improvise, and to reframe their interpretations. Dialogue is a form of mystery.
- *Strange otherness*: Dialogue partners assume that the other is not only another person, but that he or she is a person whose depth cannot be understood fully from outside. Dialogue partners, in other words, are also uniquely mysterious. In order to confirm or accept them, we must notice how different they are from ourselves. Dialogue doesn't develop when participants believe the other is just another, perhaps differently informed, "me." In this sense, consensus, as it is usually understood, is neither a prerequisite nor a necessarily admirable goal for dialogue.

- *Collaborative orientation*: Dialogue partners assume that communication is not something done to others, but is a meeting of one's own ground with the unique ground of the other. Buber's concept of "the between" means, in practical terms, that causality is complex; communication outcomes arise from "we" issues rather than "me" issues. I don't communicate anything *to* you; we communicate *in* collaboration. Dialogue doesn't develop when participants believe the other is thoroughly alien and unapproachable.
- *Vulnerability*: Dialogue partners are willing to be changed by the experience. Thus, dialogic contexts are perceived as risky by many people. To be truly open to the experience and arguments of the other—whether that openness is termed empathy and positive regard (Rogers) or inclusion, imagining the real, or personal making present (Buber)—may mean that one risks making previously solid ground a little shaky.
- *Mutual implication*: Dialogue partners interdepend for their senses of self, each constructing self, other, and relationship all at the same time. Each person becomes incorporated into the other's talk as it is spoken. Even when one voice seems to predominate, other voices resonate within it in a kind of polyphony, and resound within the silences as well.
- *Temporal flow*: Dialogue partners realize that history matters. Spontaneity in a dialogic moment, often experienced as immersive by participants, is facilitated by a sensitivity to relational history, with the anticipation of an open future.
- *Genuineness*: Dialogue partners trust that others speak from a moral stance of honesty, and that their speaking is not fundamentally strategic or tactical. Dialogue is typically experienced as moments in which participants are released from having to "think over" what should be said in order to maintain a persona or an artificial allegiance. Buber expressed this as a difference between *seeming* and *being* as modes of interpersonal existence.

Each characteristic points to a slightly different possibility for public talk, and implicates somewhat different criteria by which that talk might be evaluated. Although few occasions of public talk can (or need to) satisfy them all, we might find that the challenges and problems of creating sites for public dialogue seem less intimidating if such criteria were taken more seriously. The Buber–Rogers dialogue was intellectually significant because it convinced participants that even under pragmatically difficult conditions (on stage, with assigned asymmetrical roles and not terribly compatible conversational styles, in front of a tape recorder and large audience, and at the end of a tiring day for both men), moments of real dialogic insight are possible. It should be obvious that dialogue cannot be ordered or enforced; nor can it be a state of ongoing communication satisfaction; nor can it be "taught," at least in the traditional sense of teaching and learning. Instead, dialogue merely can be enabled by facilitative communicators in contexts where there aren't too many impediments.

Many of the contemporary dialogic experiments we survey are especially promising precisely because they are realistic about seeking dialogue within difficult conditions. They make few promises, and risk much. The embarrassing potential for failure is never far away, as the recently resigned NEH Chair Sheldon Hackney found when his "National Conversation" project was attacked by conservative critics for being "politically correct" and wasting money. Dialogue never should imply a soft expressionism that avoids or band-aids conflict. And public dialogue fails if it tries to be a "let's all hug and be friends" occasion, because conflict, contention, and the risks of position-taking are all in its lifeblood. Dialogue is not, in other words, appropriately conceived as a crisis management technique, but as basic communication maintenance. Therefore, to structure dialogue is to structure conditions within which people are more likely to feel a part of decisions. Yet some people will still feel better than others, some will still retain or regain more power than others, some will still find themselves more influential than others, some will still wield power in haughty and arrogant ways. Dialogue does not guarantee equality or calm; it merely makes mutuality and reasonable accommodation more likely.

Therefore, Buber and Rogers, if we read them accurately, would have us approach dialogic situations realistically. It appears that most attempts at dialogue require at least some structural facilitation and a reasonably well marked space or clearing for talk. After groups become more familiar with disciplines of dialogue and its inherent surprises, the need for facilitation might recede, but beginnings are challenging in a practical sense. Certain warnings are particularly helpful for dialogicians, as we will see by consulting the philosophies of Buber and Rogers alongside the lessons from their meeting.

1. Dialogue is more difficult if conducted in front of audiences, and if technologized by electronic media. Buber feared that speakers would play to audiences more than talking with each other. He must have foreseen "The McLaughlin Group" and contemporary talk shows. Yet, Buber and Rogers also proved that public dialogue is not impossible or even impractical, even though the audience influenced their interaction (Anderson & Cissna, 1996; Cissna & Anderson, 1996). After their meeting, remember, Buber had his editor remove a statement about the impossibility of dialogue from an upcoming chapter. As his 1952 syllabus showed, Rogers had long suspected that his client-centered therapy, dependent as it was on a form of dialogic acceptance, was relevant for democratic theory in the public arena. After Rogers left the University of Wisconsin in the late 1960s, he increasingly devoted his professional life to facilitating dialogue in large public groups, in cross-cultural groups, in politically and racially charged environments in the public spotlight and in the popular media. *Whoever structures public dialogue sites must anticipate how the presence of an audience might mitigate the criterion of immediacy.*

2. Dialogue cannot be forced, as it is not an ongoing state or a sustained outcome but a series of moments of insight that can be quite ephemeral and mysterious. Yet occasions in which it can develop may be structured. *Whoever structures public dialogue sites must consider the criterion of surprise, and the potential for new information to arise.* Richard Farson, who moderated Rogers's dialogue with anthropologist Gregory Bateson, reported that he asked Bateson before the event how they'll know whether they'd "done their job" that night. Bateson replied, "if either Carl or I say something that we haven't said before, we'll know that it's a success" (Kirschenbaum & Henderson, 1989a, p. 185).

3. Dialogue is more difficult if its environment does not explicitly encourage listening, although dialogue is often associated more with talk in the public imagination. However, public dialogue cannot be conceived as an opportunity for talk unless it is structured equally as a responsibility to listen. *Whoever structures public dialogue sites must emphasize the criteria of both strange otherness and vulnerability— how listeners can be changed by careful attention to an other they know they don't yet fully understand.*

4. Dialogue is more difficult if participants are rewarded for expressing certainties. Strong positions are natural. But non-negotiable demands, edicts, and pronouncements by fiat stifle dissent and discourage listeners. *Whoever structures public dialogue must be concerned with the criterion of vulnerability; dialogue partners must somehow be able to say, "I'm not really sure—what do you think?"*

5. Dialogue is more difficult when roles are clearly unequal. Buber told Rogers not to expect fully mutual dialogue with his clients. Although the therapist could see the situation from his side and from the client's side, their objective roles and the problematic of the therapy situation made it impossible for the client to see from the therapist's side (at least, until therapy is almost over). Public dialogue can exacerbate role differences, making interaction more risky for many participants. *Whoever structures public dialogue sites must anticipate the criterion of vulnerability in both its positive and its negative consequences, as well as the criteria of mutual implication and collaborative orientation.*

6. Dialogue is more difficult if participants are rewarded for withholding information or for playing phony roles. *Whoever structures public dialogue sites must consider the criterion of genuineness and how to limit deception and the human tendency to want to impress others.* No one wants to look bad while losing an argument in front of voters, consumers, friends, or critics. But if we are skillful enough at creating spaces for public dialogue, we might be able to set norms that make exploration of ideas more common than competitions with winners and losers. For example, some "inauthentic" public discourse develops from sincere attempts to represent others' points of view, as a lawyer or political candidate might. This speaker doesn't speak as an explorer of ideas in the immediate moment, but represents previously decided positions packaged to represent disembodied others in a contest of ideas.

CONCLUSION

After a recent public lecture, one of the authors was confronted by two questioners who vigorously defended the position that dialogue in public is little more than idealistic pie-in-the-sky thinking. Although deeply committed friends may engage in intimate dialogue, they implied, or some small groups might even engage in dialogic styles of problem-solving in controlled settings, the potential for a large-scale public dialogue worthy of the label is virtually nonexistent. Modern media and postmodern attitudes about them have distanced us too much ever to expect a dialogic public sphere. A truly conversational or deliberative democratic process, a truly public journalism, a truly genuine and open cultural discussion of race or abortion—all these were held to be "nice" goals but not particularly worthy of serious discussion.

Contemporary media models that structure public discourse are, in fact, serious compromises of many of the criteria of dialogue. This seems natural, even obvious, because dialogue has long been thought to apply primarily to interpersonal, face-to-face contexts. The presence of an audience, especially an electronically mediated mass audience, creates (at least to some critics) insurmountable obstacles. Yet, are the obstacles truly insurmountable, or has our definition of dialogue simply not been realistic enough?

Our own investigations of dialogue have integrated confirmation theory, dialogic philosophy, and applied communication practices with family communication, organizational and professional interviewing, therapeutic communication, and the emerging projects of public or civic journalism. At the center of our work, we've placed the intellectual relationship of a foremost theorist of dialogue, Martin Buber, and a foremost practitioner of a similar model of dialogue, psychotherapist Carl Rogers. Constructing a sustained case study from their 1957 dialogue, we identify and describe useful criteria that could guide future public dialogue projects.

Democracy divorced from dialogue only simulates a truly public sphere. We have examined why even sophisticated critics such as Buber can mistrust the promises of public dialogue. To counter such skepticism, we offer Buber's own experience and compare a promising group of recent public dialogue experiments with contemporary media models that supposedly approximate a participatory discourse, but without generating genuinely creative dialogue. Finally, we revisit Buber and Rogers to develop a series of reminders for those who would structure sites and spaces for realistic public dialogue in a media age. Next, in our final chapter, we summarize this project and speculate on what the next voices of public dialogue might say.

CHAPTER NINE

The Next Voices

What can we do with a philosophy of dialogue if it
is not able to be reconnected with the discipline
of the human sciences, if it is merely a face-to-face
relationship, and if it cannot provide us with, if it
cannot structure, an epistemology?
—Paul Ricoeur, "The Conflict of Interpretations"

Dialogue is messy and difficult. Nobody can make it work, which is
not to say it doesn't work. It just will not work predictably, on cue,
with a scriptwriter's precision, or according to a director's timetable. It
is not product but process.

We like its outcomes, or we don't. But dialogue is not a particularly good goal, however paradoxical this seems to hopeful communicators. Straining toward the goal almost always means that it eludes
our grasp, in the same ways as struggling to become a self almost always means the development of an artificial if not awkward sense of
self. As Friedman wrote (1992) about groups in the human potential
movement:

> the deepest feelings arise not when we are focusing on our
> own feelings but when we are really responding to someone
> else. . . . If instead we focus on having experiences of touching
> or on having feelings, we cut off our contact with real other-
> ness and isolate ourselves still more. . . .
>
> We can grow in the strength to be there for another, really
> there, so that we are not at all concerned at that moment
> about whether we are realizing our selves or our potentiality.
> All great self-realization is a by-product of being really present

in the situation in which we are involved. . . . [The concern
for] How may I grow through this? or, What can I get out of it?
. . . will stand in the way of our really being spontaneously and
unselfconsciously present for the other members of the group.
Carried far enough, we will miss the trip entirely; for the
present will be seen only as a means to the end, the future, and
the group event will never seem real enough to call us out in
our wholeness. (p. 33)

Friedman warns us against "aiming at the self" in attempting to improve our lives (pp. 15–34), and this reminder is equally insightful and
appropriate for those who hope to increase the chances for dialogue in
the public sphere. Singleminded devotion to making self-improvement
a goal objectifies and undercuts the process. Attempts to improve dialogic relations present similar temptations, and are characterized by approximately the same dynamic: the more you aim at them, need them,
will them, even itch for them, the less likely they become.

   In this final chapter, we connect the study of dialogue tangibly to
the human sciences disciplines, first, by revisiting the notion of technique we developed in chapter 2. With a suspicion of technique and
template as context, we then turn our attention to anticipating a future
for public dialogue. In order to be fully realized, that future, we believe,
will feature certain core "rhetorics," ways of talking and thinking
about social communication itself. These rhetorics largely reflect the
Buber–Rogers position on the importance of dialogue but extend the
pragmatic scope of that appreciation.

TECHNIQUES, TECHNOLOGIES, AND KUDZU

Buber was not concerned simply about the social effects of monologic
manipulation. He also was worried about the pale imitations that sometimes masquerade as dialogue. Something that looks and sounds like dialogue but has been concocted by technique or procedure is likely to be
little more than misleading sham. Because dialogue so directly depends
on an attitude of confirmation, and because the basic movement of dialogue is what Buber calls a "turning toward" another person in all of his
or her uniqueness, "technical dialogue" (Buber, 1965a, pp. 19, 22)—the
alternation of speaking turns—will not substitute for the real thing.
Communication attempts that are fundamentally procedural are unlikely to lead to dialogue, at least in Buber's sense of "genuine dialogue." Techniques, even those that mandate two-way speech, will not

produce dialogue because their structure precludes two-way listening and open becoming. Similarly, seemingly dialogic situations in which participants want to win or score points fit Buber's criteria for "propaganda" more closely than his criteria for dialogue.

Perhaps the most trenchant critiques of the technique ethic since Buber have come from Jacques Ellul (1964, 1985) and William Barrett (1979). The sociologist Ellul urges an ingrained skepticism toward contemporary society's tendency to reduce difficult human dilemmas to problems of efficiency. In this set of assumptions, which he critiques as nearly omnipresent, human living is removed from the realm of values, nuance, and creative application and moved to a newer realm of technique—prepackaged answers, images, and sets of responses that are fit to already-defined conditions someone labels as "problems." Ellul believed the technical tendency has two essential characteristics, rationality and artificiality (1964, pp. 78–79). By *rationality* he refers to how the society rewards turning complex problems ideally into automatic and mechanical systems of decisions. We resist the spontaneous or unique in favor of "systematization, division of labor, creation of standards, production norms, and the like" (p. 79). Further, in his discussion of *artificiality* Ellul bemoans that "technique is opposed to nature" in that our technologies affect the natural world in ways we do not and cannot understand. Presumably, people talking with each other in natural settings will find their talk radically undermined by the imposition of mass-mediated technique, and this problem is made worse by the fact that the technical world absorbs the natural little by little.

Ellul in fact expands on this fear and explores its theological facets in his book *The Humiliation of the Word* (1985). He claims, in unannounced resonance with Dewey's thought, that the visual image predominates the culture of technique; the more people think in terms of technical solutions, the more they move into a mode of image-thinking that devalues the word. However, it is auditory thinking—conversational thinking, in a sense—that connects humans to each other and ultimately, he believed, to God. And it is this that we renounce or give up in favor of the supposed comforts of predictability and efficiency. Ellul (1985) understands modern living enough to know that technique is not all bad, but he wants to explore our obsession with it (which he notes by capitalizing the term):

> Technique never grasps anything but space. That is why the famous time-travel machine is a dream of science fiction: the machine is localized. It acts on a given space and has absolutely nothing to do with time. It is even the negation of

time in the sense that it always reproduces the same motion. The thousandth time, the product that comes out of a machine or the motion of a piston are identical — no time has passed. The machine follows a pattern of rigorous similarity, because it deals entirely with immediacy and space.

Technique permits a taking over of space, but as far as time is concerned, Technique can only reject and deny it. By the same token, visualization is apprehension of reality *as* Technique—or a machine—apprehends it. Techniques can teach us to see a thousand times better, a thousand times more. They enable us to see new universes, or an unexpected detail in a familiar face. But space is always involved. Techniques do not teach us to listen or to hear. They never enable us to penetrate meaning. . . .

An object can have innumerable meanings. Only language, something auditory, can unravel them. (p. 226)

Technique is not evil but imperialistic. It is necessary, but as it overspreads in human institutions it acts like a behavioral kudzu, crowding out other forms of being. Thus, as we eliminate or, in his terms, "humiliate," the word in favor of the objectified image and an objectified technique, we lose something dear and irretrievable. We lose the engagement of dialogue. Buber, of course, based his I-Thou/I-It distinction on similar premises; although an I-It dimension to human life is inevitable and even productive and necessary in many ways, elevation of its premises alone means that dialogue in any genuine sense becomes impossible and human life diminished. Dialogue grows out of a willingness to hear each other anew and its brand of making is a constant, surprising, shapeshifting, mutualized remaking. Dialogue is not, he would say, a seeing, but a hearing/speaking phenomenon that resists becoming technologized.

"A technique," wrote William Barrett (1979), is a "standard method that can be taught. It is a recipe that can be fully conveyed from one person to another. A recipe always lays down a certain number of steps which, if followed to the letter, ought to lead invariably to the end desired. The logicians call this a decision procedure" (p. 22). Barrett explored the overreliance on technique from different and often more philosophical angles than Ellul's, yet his affinity for conversational knowing was equally well developed. If a technique is a recipe that is capable of full conveyance from person to person, then its existence fashions an implicit communication model that is unilinear, a kind of "internal thought transferred to internal thought" presumption. Drawing on the later work of Wittgenstein among others, however, Barrett argues against a simple toolbox or procedural approach to language: "Language opens into the world more abruptly and extensively than any set of tools" (p. 185). "What we understand by a conversation," Barrett suggests in his notion of a dialogic and nontechnologized human existence, is

> the situation in which two people are genuinely interested in a topic, become absorbed in exploring it, and are held together in the unity of their talk. The conversation, in short, is *between* A and B and *within* language. Notice we emphasize the prepositions here. If we are to take language seriously, we have to give the prepositions their due, for they are in fact indispensable. Without them we cannot assemble the isolated ingredients of minds and bodies into a conversation. That is why neither dualism nor behaviorism really permit us to talk as we do in life. A conversation does not take place inside each other's heads alternately, nor at the surfaces of our bodies in their overt behavior; it is really in the region between the speakers that the conversation takes place. (p. 184)

Here Barrett grounds his critique of technique not only in Buber's assumptions of the vital between, but in the same mistrust of behaviorist and psychological technique that motivated Rogers to treat each client as a new opportunity to listen, a new and irreproducible voice.

This is why Rogers not only fundamentally mistrusted technique-centered therapies, but was disturbed when he found that his own had been transformed into one by some therapists. It is difficult to believe you have a significant insight into one of the foundations of human behavior, as Rogers believed he had, and not try to package an explanation and application of it in a tidy system; indeed, early in his career, he lapsed at times into a shorthand discussion of his therapy in technique-dependent ways. Yet, in the 1950s, beginning perhaps with *Client-Centered Therapy* (1951) and continuing with the essays that would appear in *On Becoming a Person* (1961), of which several were directly and indirectly referenced in the dialogue with Buber, Rogers increasingly described client-centered therapy as a broader, nonprescriptive process of communication. Later he labeled this more general set of guiding notions the *person-centered approach*, and the word "approach" was apt. Rogers was concerned with how people thought and spoke about their relationships, because these things affected how they approached new relations. Approach is a rhetorical term that is based in a metaphor of

relational/spatial movement—one approaches another *from* some-
where, with that different unique perspective. In Rogers's theoretical
system, congruence, regard, and empathy were more attitudes than behaviors, and although they could be learned and internalized, they
could not be "taught" in the sense of conveyance that is sometimes intended by that word. They were aspects of an integrated *approach*. Late
in life, Rogers also referred to his ideas as "a way of being"; this phrase
is similarly metaphorical if "way" is understood in the Taoist sense of
a path that permits a variety of styles of approaching a goal.

Rogers and Buber, therefore, would support Farson (1978) and
Friedman (1992), who warned professionals and the public about self-
help psychologies that turn troubled persons into desperate consumers
by convincing them that experts have ready-made, automatic answers
for their problems. During his lifetime Rogers believed that a major
threat of a technique-centered culture was that large-scale institutions
like the state or its schools could shape and control persons in a version
of the behaviorist agenda he attributed to B. F. Skinner; the issue of
freedom versus control became for him an intellectual hook on which
to hang his thinking. Later it was not institutional control of techniques but the very proliferation of self-help technologies available for
individuals' free use—and manipulation—that began to concern him,
especially when such thinking threatened to co-opt his own suggestions for better person-to-person communication.

The term "self-help" ironically became oxymoronic in that con-
sumerist psychologies created a technique dependence or a guru mentality. It's not the literal notion of "self-help" that's the problem here.
All help to Rogers and Buber must rely fundamentally on decisions and
experiences of the person-in-relationship. But the surprisingly contradictory implication of many of these systems is that individuals are deficient and must depend on a set of techniques that are discovered by
experts and dispensed to needy consumers. Such help is *not* fundamentally based on a processual or a conversationalized self that is capable
of constructing creative responses to life's relationships. Dialogue is not
an outcome of these technical systems because dialogue resists specification; in Barrett's terms it can never be a "decision procedure." It is
hard to specify how (or how often, or how well) it "works." With dialogue there can be no money-back guarantee.

Rogers was not an uncritical advocate of the human potential
movement, strongly criticizing some self-help technologies (1977a).
Barrett's (1979) *The Illusion of Technique* provides a particularly vivid
example of how seductive it is to technologize self-help. While writing
this book, Barrett decided to give up alcohol because it sapped too

much of his energy and time. He was motivated partly by his topic— the book was "about" human freedom and how we are more than con- sumers of others' techniques. Ironically, he reported, he was so successful at his personal discipline that he became seriously tempted to write a manual on "How to Give up Drinking." Only later did he re- alize how the manual, offering help to passive consumers, would con- tradict the premise of his own book on human technologies: "there is no automatic technique that would be valid for everyone. What works for one person may not work for another. In the business of changing ourselves, each of us is ultimately on his own. . . . We touch again on our old question of the relation of technique to the individual and prob- lematic situations with which experience confronts us" (p. 333).

Such concerns help us clarify what we've learned and, more im- portant, what we hope to contribute to a broader conversation about a democratic public. It feels somehow incomplete not to consolidate a coherent description of dialogue to cap this book, even if we urge no concurrent action plan. This is practical; practicality is more than the ability to give instructions. Our goal, while less precise, is, we be- lieve, more realistic: to describe ways of thinking and defining inter- human problems that can orient thoughtful citizens toward a more dialogic future.

Like Barrett, we suspect we don't have a reliable formula for dia- logue, however tempting it would be to offer one. Neither do we have a grand theory of public discourse that we'd like to advertise. Our preten- sions have always been slighter—more mundane and and more immedi- ate. We set out to see where we would be led if we listened carefully and comprehensively to one uniquely effective conversation between partic- ipants who wanted to talk about dialogue. We wanted to circle that con- versation as much as historical listeners can: to hear and sense it from different angles, to get behind it and in front of it, to ask it questions, to sketch its biography, and to try out its ideas in contexts neither of the participants might have expected. We emerge from this process less with a system than with a fresher sense of dialogue than we had before. Maybe we have added just a little to the connections the philosopher Paul Ri- coeur wanted between the study of dialogue and a disciplined epistemol- ogy of the human sciences (see the opening quotation of this chapter).

This chapter turns toward the next voices of dialogue to hear where they might take us in a complex and pluralistic global culture. Rather than prescribing or predicting what those voices should sound like, we have decided to discuss ways of thinking that seem dialogically inviting in troubled times—and to discuss some of the caveats and dangers that accompany them. Older and more static feel-good versions of dialogue just won't do any more, as they are not supple enough to withstand the rigors of challenge. And if there is any given in our future, it is that public discourse will be challenging.

If the next voices of dialogue will necessarily confront pluralistic disorder, and therefore inevitably will test society's understanding of the roles of communicative stability, then citizens should at least talk together about what they desire. This is the premise of such institutional dialogue programs as deliberative democracy and public journalism. Structured programs of formulas and techniques (procedures for how we should *talk about our thinking*) are not needed as much as an orientation toward how we might more inclusively *think about our talking*. What kind of thinking and what kind of assumptions it entails will become orienting issues for the coming culturally pluralized century. Without wishing to prescribe, we can at least describe some of the productive and less productive ways of thought this study has discovered.

DIALOGUE-PRODUCTIVE RHETORICS

The emergent Buber–Rogers position stressed how crucial and central dialogic moments are to communicators. In this way it signals important clues to a communication style more applicable to the demands of multicultural and pluralistic social organizations. Dialogue is not a distant hope. It is an immediate, if fleeting, potential in all relations. Those who dismiss it as unrealistic and those who desperately desire it as an ongoing state are both missing the essential point Buber and Rogers articulate for us. Dialogue is possible, but it is hard-won in the moment, actually achieved in moments of surprise made possible by open listening and contingent speaking. It does not sprout just anywhere, but grows where the soil of communication has been cleared and cultivated, without guarantees, for it.

If Buber and Rogers are right, the cynics will always have plenty of evidence to point to in their quest to prove, in any given context, that dialogue is either impossible or unlikely. At any time, dialogue as a phenomenon is not likely to be obvious. Someone isn't listening, or has dug in heels refusing to be moved by a better argument, or is acting haughty or just plain snotty, or has put down a partner unintentionally, or is running a manipulative game on someone else. Or a leader may have become so deeply and publicly committed to a "just cause" that the prospect of dialogic communication could seem fearfully close to a kind of capitulation. Participants and observers alike would need a wider, deeper, more historical, and more protensive perspective to hear the possibility dialogue offers. One would need to be as aware of what is *not* happening as what is. What might that perspective entail? We have come to believe that such a perspective can be described in terms of a series of *facilitating rhetorics*.

Rhetorics in this sense are patterns of talking and thinking about ongoing communication challenges. Such rhetorics are similar to speech habits if we think of speech, as Buber did, as the elemental, existential way humans constitute themselves in and for the world. For example, there is in some circles a "rhetoric" of so-called American individualism that embeds in our talk the view that rights are individually possessed and useful in pressing individuals' claims against others within an inherently competitive social framework. Another rhetoric, as a way of talking about society, commonly assumes that voting and majority rule are the fundamental tenets of democracy that always trump other goals and interests. As we hope our study has shown, many cultural signs indicate there is a gathering momentum of alternative dialogic rhetorics in institutions both small and large, and these rhetorics are not premised on individualism, competition, rights, or majoritarian assumptions. If enough people collaborate to talk and think within the vocabularies and grammar of these rhetorics, dialogic moments will be far more common.

How we speak matters, as does how we think about how we speak. Humans not only *have* conversations; as Buber stressed in a variety of ways, humans in their fundamental being *are* conversations.

The obvious interdependence of various rhetorics suggests this is not a "to-do" list; rather it becomes a holistic pattern of speaking, thinking, and doing in which all the elements are fully implied in and by each of them, much like a hologram.

Commons Rhetoric

A commons, considered historically and culturally, is a gathering place suffused with a sense of common ownership, stake, or participation. A commons is not controlled by one person or group and offered to others for their use. Rather, it is a publicly maintained and shared space— "ours." A rhetoric of the commons will not naïvely assume that bringing people together will cause good things to happen, but rather offers only ongoing opportunity. It presumes, at the least:

- If people don't find themselves often in situations of common presence with others, they are unlikely to

       understand either the commonalities or the divergences
       of their concerns.

- Common presence does not happen automatically. Even
  when people find themselves in proximity with each
  other, they may be experientially divorced from each other
  by habit or fear such as in many airports, urban apartment
  complexes, and college classrooms.

- Common presence must be facilitated, and common
  spaces created, by those willing to take responsibility for
  structuring public dialogue.

The attempt to create a dialogic commons does not presuppose that
those who inhabit it will always agree; in fact, Buber and Rogers would
urge the converse. So would the activist political dialogician Paulo
Freire (Horton & Freire, 1990), who once remarked that conflict is the
"midwife of consciousness" (p. 187). Opposition and contention form
the lifeblood of an organically conceived public forum for talk. Without
it, what would be the point of statement, of assertion, of speaking up
for oneself? Attempts to create a dialogic means of learning in public
have to start from what Friedman (1974) called an "organic base":

> It must build on social reality and find its roots in the com-
> munity already there. It must be concerned about real com-
> munication with the people whom it approaches. For the
> distinction between propaganda and education does not lie in
> whether one is a communist or a pacifist but in whether one
> approaches another wishing to impose one's truth on him or
> whether one cares enough for him to enter into dialogue with
> him, see the situation from his point of view, and communi-
> cate what truth one has to communicate to him within that
> dialogue. Sometimes that dialogue can only mean standing
> one's ground in opposition to him, witnessing for what one be-
> lieves in the face of his hostile rejection of it. Yet it can never
> mean being unconcerned for how he sees it or careless of the
> validity of his standing where he does. We must confirm him
> even as we oppose him, not in his error but in his right to op-
> pose us, in his existence as a human being whom we value
> even in opposing. (p. 284)

Commons rhetoric as the rhetoric of community, therefore, presumes
inclusion. By "community," Buber never had in mind the bounded
drawing together of likeminded and culturally homogeneous groups,

for it is the confrontation with other ways and other ideas that teaches us most profoundly who we are and who we might desire instead to become.

The next voices of dialogue may explore further the fresh forms of commons rhetoric that are heard in online culture. Barnett Pearce (1993) perceptively argued that new electronic media have constituted a new kind of social "place" (p. 67), a conclusion reinforced by Bird's (1999) study of on-line community. Howard Rheingold's (1993) sentiments are clear even when he couches his description in contingencies. Although cyberspace communities like the WELL (an early "virtual community" on the Internet) may not meet all of people's needs for social gatherings, and although they obviously forego some cues of interpersonal presence, they nevertheless can fill a dialogic niche:

> Some people—many people—don't do well in spontaneous spoken interaction, but turn out to have valuable contributions to make in a conversation in which they have time to think about what to say. These people, who might constitute a significant proportion of the population, can find written communication more authentic than the face-to-face kind. Who is to say that this preference for one mode of communication—informal written text—is somehow less authentically human than audible speech? . . . Most of what goes on in the Parenting conference and most virtual communities is informal conversation and downright chitchat. The model of the WELL and other social clusters in cyberspace as "places" is one that naturally emerges whenever people who use this medium discuss the nature of the medium. (p. 24)

Rheingold's balanced analysis of such communities clarifies what dialogic community can be in a new online culture. Although he has been an enthusiastic participant, he recognizes the dangers, too. Communicators in computer-mediated communities may adopt inauthentic personae to deceive and manipulate others, and some may become so immersed in them that they lose their grip on IRL relationships, as online regulars say ("in real life"). Still, the sense of community often is real enough for students of dialogue to imagine this form of commons and to take it seriously. Rheingold plants an option and a task immediately in front of anyone who desires a vital public sphere: "Perhaps cyberspace is one of the informal public places where people can rebuild the aspects of community that were lost when the malt shop became a mall. Or perhaps cyberspace is precisely the *wrong* place to look for the rebirth of community, offering not a tool for conviviality but a life-denying simulacrum of real passion and true commitment to one another. In either case, we need to find out soon" (p. 26). Is this a kind of commons in which mutuality can flourish within diversity, or is it a glitzy pseudoworld offering higher-tech versions of anonymity?

Mutuality Rhetoric

When Buber and Rogers discussed mutuality in psychotherapeutic relationships in 1957, Buber mused: "Let me say . . . that I could talk to him, to your patient, too. I would, of course, hear from him . . . a very different tale about this *same* moment" (turn #62). Mutuality rhetoric is that way of talking about experience that reclaims it from the individualized and psychologized forms that Buber so effectively critiqued. What Buber means, at least in part, is that human narration is not just any story; it is a story told by someone about something to someone with an anticipation of response, and the very opportunity to tell it to another changes the content that is told. The audience helps to shape the story, and thus each audience hears a different story. The "very different tale" Buber would hear is a tale of a situated relational moment, not simply of that client.

At the same time, Buber was clearly interested in normative limits of mutuality. Many relationships, according to Buber, are not fully mutual even though they can exhibit essentially dialogic moments. Teachers and students, for example, and therapists and clients can never have fully equal relationships because teachers and therapists can reasonably expect to be able to imagine both sides of the meeting but students and clients usually cannot. Indeed, it is the professional's skill at imagining the other side that probably draws many people who want to learn or grow to initiate the relationship in the first place. As Friedman (1991) summarized, "There is mutuality of contact and mutuality of trust and *some* sense on both sides of where the other is coming from. But the responsibility and concern is focused by both partners on the education or healing of the one who is helped and not on that of the helper" (p. 369).

Of course, few if any human relationships would be characterized by full equality in this sense. Numerous relations in which we aspire to dialogue are typically experienced as socially, culturally, or organizationally hierarchical: employer-employee, parent-child, wealthy-poor, powerful-powershy, even—as we have increasingly understood—communication across many gender, sexual preference, and racial differences in which white heterosexual men have predominated traditionally in Western culture. Mutuality rhetoric can run deeper than literal equality in this sense, however, and can even mandate the ultimate thinness of such equality as a concept to guide us. If potential dialogue partners wait for equality, many will wait forever.

A deeper rhetoric of mutuality will characterize the next voices of dialogue. They will invite fuller understanding not by asking what something *is*, nor by asking "what does it look like?" or "what does it do?" Thinking mutualistically involves, for example, asking, "How can we understand anything without understanding how it exists in relation to other processes, ideas, and things?" It asks, "How does the existence and communication of one person interdepend with others in his or her sphere?" It asks, "How can it be that words coming out of my mouth are not, in a sense, mine alone, but ours?"

Moments Rhetoric

The Swiss physician Paul Tournier's unfortunately neglected book of essays about dialogue and personhood was first published in 1957, the year Buber and Rogers met at Michigan. In *The Meaning of Persons* (1973), he observed that

> In the life of each of us there are decisive hours that tell us more about the person than all the rest of our lives put together. Do I say hours? Minutes, seconds, rather; moments which are to determine the whole course of our lives thereafter. . . . Now the crossroads is this moment of true dialogue, of personal encounter with another person, which obliges us to take up a position with regard to him, to commit ourselves. Even to run away is to make some sort of decision, choosing a side road in order to evade the dialogue. (p. 128).

In a similar vein, Buber (1965a) once wrote:

> Each of us is encased in an armour which we soon, out of familiarity, no longer notice. There are only moments which penetrate it and stir the soul to sensibility. And when such a moment has imposed itself on us and we then take notice and ask ourselves, "has anything particular taken place? Was it not of the kind I meet every day?" then we may reply to ourselves, "Nothing particular, indeed, it is like this every day, only we are not there every day.

> The signs of address are not something extraordinary,
> something that steps out of the order of things, they are just
> what goes on time and again. . . . Most of the time we have
> turned off our receivers. (pp. 10–11)

If dialogue occurs in moments, then we must revise our customary
ways of perceiving and referring to dialogue that in effect set up unrealistic expectations for it. Buber is suggesting that although dialogue
exists in these penetrative moments, we can become more attuned to
them, more able to "be there" and be ready for them.

Although there are different senses and meanings for the word "dialogue" than we have developed here, a moments rhetoric will *not* be
likely to refer primarily (except perhaps metaphorically) to:

- An ongoing or constant "state" or "condition" of dialogue;
- An inherently "dialogic person";
- A persistent or all-encompassing "goal of dialogue"; or
- A precise technique of "dialoguing" with others.

Since writing our essay on dialogic moments (1998), we have been
surprised how the moments perspective can so thoroughly redefine the
spirit and task of dialogic scholarship, but at the same time how subtly
inherent it has always been in the scholarly conversation. This idea of
genuine or powerful dialogue existing in moments rather than states or
conditions was mentioned by Buber, but primarily in the context of
other ideas. Perhaps it was even more explicit in the attempts of Rogers,
begun in the months before his meeting with Buber, to describe what he
called the "molecules" of therapy—those moments experienced between client and therapist that are characterized by a sense of breakthrough, of intense mutual understanding, or movement in the client's
ability to sense the relationship itself. Curiously, though, scholars of
Buber and Rogers have largely overlooked this insight. Among contemporary dialogic scholars in communication, philosophy, and psychology,
John Shotter (e.g., 1993a, pp. 53, 120; 1993b, pp. 135, 229) appears most
ready to analyze the moments issue conceptually, although his insightful comments about it occur primarily in the context of other issues
that seem larger to him.

Yet, the Buber–Rogers dialogue, as we show in chapters 6 and 7,
was tinged with this notion throughout. It is how Rogers premises each
of his important inquiries leading to their discussions of mutuality/
equality and acceptance/confirmation, and even when Buber at times
seems not to respond fully to the moments issue, clearly he considers

this as a good description of the normative limits of mutuality; dialogue in helping contexts can happen, but participants must not expect it to persist. It happens in moments or minutes, and, because of the necessary role distinctions, it is "made possible" by the therapist or counselor, not by the person being helped. Interestingly, this one conversation may actually be our best available text in either the Buber or the Rogers corpus for examining moments rhetoric.

In moments rhetoric we construct the best response to cynics who might argue that dialogue is an impossible or frivolous dream. Their cynicism, though, is not unjustified. It reflects the *reasonable* suspicion that dialogue cannot be a normal state of affairs, "business as usual." Their cynicism is reasonable when deriding the pollyanna-ish assumption that two groups with mutually exclusive goals can patch up their differences and enter sustained dialogue with each other as a result of just changing their attitudes or coming together with a skilled facilitator. Cynics are reasonable to think that dialogue is unattainable—but only if dialogue is defined as a blissful state of transcendent understanding.

The next voices of dialogue will be voices that, like Martin Luther King's, increase our readiness to listen rather than increasing our control over situations. Evidently the facilitators of the Public Conversations Project (e.g., Becker, et al., 1995a, 1995b) or the Public Dialogue Consortium (Pearce & Walters, 1997a, 1997b) use something like moments rhetoric when they bring groups together *not* for the purpose of mutually coordinated action or consensus-building, *not* primarily for skill-building or agreement, and *not* necessarily to reduce the psychic distance between persons (Buber knew that distance and difference, honestly perceived, are allies of genuine dialogue), but to allow for or invite spontaneously charged moments of shared concern. Then those moments, if or when they occur, become the bases for people to build on in enhancing communication.

Vulnerability Rhetoric

No communicators can hope for moments of dialogue in the public forum if they are not willing to allow others' speech to change them somehow. Some politicians and political audiences, however, have decided that it's enough for dialogue that spokespersons merely compare their different immutable positions, or that they simply debate the relative merits of the positions. Comparisons, debates, and even some deliberations may exhibit the back-and-forth character we associate with dialogue.

Yet debate, as we have seen, generates different expectations than dialogic experience (Tannen, 1998). Part of the reason for this is that public audiences hear talk from leaders and spokespersons as essentially dramaturgical occasions, through which the audiences become a part of larger symbolic processes. That is, audiences associate causes and issues with specific public advocates, and this helps them clarify the public sphere, if occasionally artificially or erroneously. Complex issues are made to seem more manageable as they become thus dramatized. This is not to say that no moments of dialogue are possible in debating contexts, but that debate structure makes them rare and minimizes their effect. Debates tend to dualize and polarize positions; debates involve forced choices between this and that, and as such the gap between the positions can be made to appear so insurmountable that winners and losers, "good" positions and "bad" ones, inevitably emerge. Public advocates in debate contexts become invested in, and defined by, their public positions so much that to change one's mind is to adopt a different kind of life identity. Politicians understand this better than most, as opponents so often look for instances of "waffling" or inconsistency about issues. The politicians who change their minds on important issues, especially as a result of striking encounters or experiences, sacrifice a certain image of strength or power.

Some might assume that this kind of situation would lock leaders into walled cubicles of unchanging positions. Some sociologists and critics of political symbolism (Edelman, 1964, 1988; Klapp, 1964, 1969), however, suggest that the threat of being too ideologically identifiable has also encouraged a strategic ambiguity that dilutes a wide range of public moral and practical discourse. Instead of being locked into positions and being invulnerable to meaningful dialogue, public leaders also can be dialogically closed by crafting public statements that are so ambiguous that precise positions cannot be identified. Audiences find only dramatic distinctiveness between symbolic leaders (this one seems "vigorous and youthful," that one "stable and oriented to family values").

Another aspect of this rhetoric is less commonly discussed, but equally important. To understand it, pay less attention to what leaders say and more to how listeners identify with public rhetoric. We discussed earlier how Rogers stressed the value of empathy, and Buber encouraged us to "imagine the real" of the other. In each process, to employ something like Buber's language, we inhabit the realm of the between, the place where the psychological realm is supplemented with the more relational knowing that comes with actively imagining the experience of the other while not renouncing personal experience.

But the more effectively a person empathizes, the more personal beliefs or values are placed at risk. Few commentators have captured this vulnerability as vividly as Charles Hampden-Turner (1971):

> Suppose that I am trying to convey to a friend the value I see in a new social policy. In order to comprehend how it is impinging upon his needs and interests I must temporarily suspend the structure of meanings that it has for me and imagine myself in his place. I must do this in spite of the frightening consequences for myself. The risk I undertake is permitting my structure to crumble, with the knowledge that a new element supplied by him may prevent the logical restructuring of my beloved ideas. I risk being ridiculed by him at a moment when my competence is not firmly in my grasp. By investing my undefended worth I am risking the verdict that I am worthless. I tell him something which shows that I value his judgment but leave him free to disconfirm and devalue my judgment and so alter the definition of our relationship. I do this because I am seeking confirmation from him and the expansion of my ideas—*yet I cannot gain these without temporarily "surrendering" and risking permanent loss.* (p. 48)

Hampden-Turner dramatizes how vulnerability can become an interpersonal asset, but only if it entails what Buber called a genuine "turning toward" the other. Through empathic processes we discover others who are successful, perhaps while renouncing the very thing we "knew" was indispensable to our own success. We must change somehow when this happens. We encounter others who seem to be failures, even though they are embracing the very things we "knew" would guarantee success. We must somehow revise our way of evaluating existence when this happens. We encounter still others whose moral systems, however alien to us, clearly suit them well. We must be changed once we see *their* challenges from *over there*, not from here.

In terms of dialogue, taking public positions creates vulnerability, but so does successfully imagining private ones. Despite the ways these things threaten us, there is no other way dialogue can reach us. The next voices of dialogue and dialogic community leadership may come from those persons who rely less on consistency and conventional power bases. The voices may be from people who can describe how they've been affected by strangers and enemies who are not remotely like themselves—how, for example, they have been affected by the disaffected.

Praxis Rhetoric

Most dialogic theorists go to great lengths to answer the criticism that dialogue belongs to a realm of flighty impracticality. Buber (1965a), for instance, addressed his reader:

> You are really able. The life of dialogue is no privilege of intellectual activity like dialectic. It does not begin in the upper story of humanity. It begins no higher than where humanity begins. . . .
> You put before me the man taken up with duty and business. Yes, precisely him I mean, him in the factory, in the shop, in the office, in the mine, on the tractor, at the printing-press; man. I do not seek for men. I do not seek men out for myself, I accept those who are there, I have them, I have him, in mind, the yoked, the wheel-treading, the conditioned. Dialogue is not an affair of spiritual luxury and spiritual luxuriousness, it is a matter of creation, of the creature, and he is that, the man of whom I speak, he is a creature, trivial and irreplaceable. (p. 35)

A praxis rhetoric is a style of talking and thinking about human life that is not primarily "theoretical" at the expense of being "practical." Neither is it a pragmatic action system that disdains theory. It must be both.

It makes a theoretical difference to assert that outside pathology, all meaningful personal action is collaboratively or jointly undertaken: people in their everyday concreteness responding to what others say or do and being open themselves to responses. Both Buber and Rogers sustained this view of "personal," that to become a person is a form of constitutive human achievement. Nothing human is or can be wholly individual. We act to enact roles or accomplish ends relative to self and other. We speak or write or demonstrate, but only in anticipation of another who can or will, we presume, audit, take note of, and respond to, our messages. Being human, ontologically speaking and from this overtly constructionist rhetoric, means that "the primary human reality is conversational or responsively relational, that one's 'person-world' dimension of interaction or being exists within a whole melee of 'self-other' relationships or dimensions of interaction" (Shotter, 1993b, p. 161).

Social constructionism makes a difference for how we talk about learning, and where we look for research opportunities. Essentialist rhetorics take as their goal to search for personality traits, for example. Or they want to imagine that African peoples, or Germanic, or Asian, or women or men for that matter, act as they do by drawing from a well of behavioral dispositions to which each has special access. Another aspect of essentialist rhetoric is that one has to be _____ [fill in the blank here with desired cultural designator] to understand the issues of _____ [fill in variant of same cultural term]. Unless you are African-American, you are forever walled off from understanding the blues. Only women can direct feminist films. Although essentialist thinking does preserve a viable reminder of unique experience, it misses what we might call *the potent with*. Relational being means that talk, which can sound like a noun, is always a verb at heart: talking is a *doing* that is constantly shifting, a conversational process-meeting with someone else.

The word "research" can inform the next voices of dialogue about the importance of change. As we speak it, the "re-" becomes our constant reminder that searching always must happen over and over again, shifting to accommodate new relations in living practice that is both concrete and everyday, on the one hand, and can be abstracted and patterned on the other. The resemblance to Rogers's own research program is striking. When we said in chapter 4 that he had developed a philosophical praxis of dialogue, it was to this insight that we referred. Rogers gathered data incessantly from immediate relationships with clients. When he feared that all this was dependent on his own unique relational presence, he enlisted others to check whether the phenomenon was in fact more general. When he studied specific types of therapeutic cases more intensively (institutionalized schizophrenics, for example, after he went to Wisconsin), he readily questioned some of his earlier premises.

Recognition Rhetoric

Simone Weil once observed: "Someone who does not see a pane of glass does not know that he does not see it. Someone who, being placed differently, does see it, does not know the other does not see it" (quoted in Young, 1990, p. 39). Without talk, the glass is either visible or invisible, depending on perspective, but it cannot be understood as a potentially mutual or divisive issue. Such is the problem of recognition. It is forever intertwined with situatedness. One basic characteristic of dialogue, as we have stressed throughout, is the encounter with strange otherness. We learn and change when we confront what is not-us and imagine what can be seen and heard from that place. We do not automatically attempt to change it, deny it, possess it, assimilate it, explain it away, or dilute its power. If dialogue is desired, it demands a vigorous discipline of recognition that can be heard in talk.

Staying open to dialogue means that communicators recognize how others are successful in meeting their own goals in ways different from our own. Yet think of two alternate senses of recognition and how they might be relevant here. To "recognize" someone means that you perceive her or him as who that person truly is (in a perhaps too-concrete example: "Oh. That's the woman I met at the diner the other day. That's Marty's friend"). There is an element of Buber's confirmation inherent in such a sense of the word; when minority groups are told that they (whoever "they" may be) "all look alike," or if one becomes as in Ralph Ellison's novel, "invisible," this denotes a recognition problem at this first level. To be recognized means to have your presence noted. Yet there is an additional layer of meaning that can help enrich a concept of dialogic recognition; to "recognize" someone means also that you not only perceive persons as who they are, but go beyond acknowledging presence to acknowledge their worth, their contributions or achievement, their essential validity (one might say: "Did you know Marguerite got this year's Community Builders Award? She was recognized for her work with teens"). This second conceptual form of recognition may still represent a kind of confirmation, but it goes beyond it, too, to something more like affirmation. Carl Rogers occasionally used the word "prizing" to refer to this phenomenon.

Neither confirmation nor affirmation preclude conflict or disdain. I see you; but I might also see that I don't like your behavior and must tell you so. I appreciate the depth of your contribution to our organization; but I also sincerely believe you are the wrong type of leader to help us move to a higher quality of work. I hold your intelligence in high regard; for that reason in part I am drawn to tell you how wrong I believe you are. If you didn't matter to me, I might be less likely even to try to alter the relation. Buber and Prime Minister Ben-Gurion of Israel were sometimes bitter political opponents over that country's policies toward the Arab world. On Buber's 80th birthday, however, he received a letter from Ben-Gurion that came "in love and veneration." In part, the letter read:

> Your deep and original philosophy, your faithful participation in the work of the rebirth of Israel from your youth to the present day, your deep ideal and existential relationship to the vision that the prophets of Israel had of national and universal redemption and a reign of righteousness, peace, and brotherhood in the world, the total agreement between your strivings and demands and the conduct of your life—for all these you are entitled to praise and fame in the history of our people and our time. (Friedman, 1983c, p. 345)

Friedman reports that Buber was very happy to have received this letter, and replied that his feelings about Ben-Gurion were similar. However— and this is crucial—Buber also used this moment to reassert a previous disagreement with his friend, admirer, and opponent (Friedman, 1991, p. 427). A sick man, whose cause Buber had represented previously to the prime minister, ought to be pardoned from his prison sentence. Ben-Gurion refused. In a sense, the conflict between them was *personal*, but not, because of the kind of recognition that characterized their relation, *personalized*. Something similar can be glimpsed in the relationship of Rogers with his intellectual adversary, the behavioral psychologist B. F. Skinner. Because Rogers believed Skinner's philosophy dehumanized people, turning them into automatons, he was eager to engage the Harvard psychologist in a series of public dialogues. This was much on his mind around the time of the Buber dialogue as well. Yet, as we show in chapter 5, although Rogers and Skinner were perceived in the public mind as conceptual arch-enemies, their personal relationship was respectful, friendly, even warm. They cooperated, in essence, in testing each other's claims.

The next voices of dialogue are likely to face even greater challenges than did Buber or Rogers, as the power of pluralistic conceptions of culture grows and the space that used to divide diverse groups shrinks. Cultural critics and theorists Gloria Anzaldúa (1987) and Renato Rosaldo (1989) are among those who believe that a new phenomenon has begun to develop, one that has powerful implications for dialogue in the coming century. Anzaldúa's term for the concept is the *borderlands*; by this she means that the old cultural borders that divided groups no longer apply as they once did. Borders were clear separations between "us" and "them." However, most people's lives in postmodern society are lived in zones of interdependence and cultural interdefinition where "us" and "them" (while they undeniably remain potent psychological categories) are in flux. People's identities, says Anzaldúa (1987) are more complex than that; the borderlands are the spaces of living where people are defined by new zones of cultural identity that are not insulated from each other. Borderlands thinking describes how people may live in the vicinity of a cultural border, and therefore be affected by cultural practices on both sides of that border simultaneously. Latino culture in the United States, for example, does not inscribe a border of homogeneous lifestyle that may or may not be crossed, but a vast space of merged cultural influences. Some influences are clearly imported from Spanish-speaking cultures, some from Native American, some from Anglo or African-American life. Yet this leads to what Rosaldo (1989) calls "new forms of polyglot cultural creativity"; he describes how "such cultural border zones are always in motion, not frozen for inspection" (p. 217).

Anzaldúa and Rosaldo do not exactly *advocate* a borderland; they simply describe the cultural changes they feel and see. Racial, ethnic, and cultural identities are valuable in their distinctness, yet increasing numbers of us live blended lives in which it's not immediately clear from outward appearances how culturally different, how "other," the other is. Such borderlands are zones of necessary listening and speaking, and zones that will test our best attempts at recognition rhetoric. Recognition thinking usefully reframes the problem of otherness from an essentialist understanding ("What are white people like?", "What are only women able to understand?") to a contextualist/spatial understanding ("From what vantage point does she perceive me?", "How are his cultural influences situated in our talk?").

CONCLUSION

Thus we have come full circle. Our intensive and microscopic look at a particular mid-twentieth-century case has stimulated an extensive and macroscopic examination of perhaps the most pervasive challenges of twenty-first-century life.

That, at least, is what we have intended. What we have *not* intended to do may be equally important to mention. We have not tried to critique the poor quality of public dialogue in our age. That has been done admirably in many articles and books. Neither have we attempted to chronicle all the ways a more public dialogue is necessary in the new century, because that would involve better crystal-ball gazing than we could possibly accomplish.

At the very least, we hope to have established that Martin Buber and Carl Rogers are not only relevant thinkers for our time, but that their thought can be understood as far more intertwined than other scholars have believed. Although most commentaries stress their differences, we have shown that a remarkably consistent position emerged from their talk. Their dialogue about dialogue—often successful, occasionally disappointing, like most human conversation—demonstrated their intellectual convergence in ways that perhaps even Buber and Rogers failed to appreciate.

Again imagine yourself in the audience on 18 April 1957, as we asked you to do in the beginning of the book. After about an hour and a half of two men talking, your listening remains focused. Buber and Rogers have explored timeless issues: the challenge of inviting dialogue, the problem of regarding other persons as mutual partners in complex human relationships, the limits of a psychological conception of self, the potential for genuine faith in human nature, the complications of accepting and confirming others who are radically different from yourself, and finally the very nature of a dialogical definition of personness. Twice it sounded as though they might stop, only to have another question extend their encounter. But now there's been a slight lull, a silence of seconds. You and others perhaps shift positions in your seats. Maurice Friedman, in his role as moderator, then sums up the evening with comments that might apply equally well to our larger study. "We have reason to be deeply indebted to Dr. Rogers and Dr. Buber," he said, for "a unique dialogue. It is certainly unique in *my* experience: . . . because it is a *real* dialogue, taking place in front of an audience" (turn #128). Friedman went on to observe that this real dialogic relation could not only be attributed to what Buber and Rogers were willing to give, but also to what the audience gave through its own participation.

We are all indebted to Buber and Rogers for a conversation that provided moments of utterly unique dialogic insights available nowhere else, while at other moments we recognize particularly incisive statements of ideas the two had developed separately. They agreed some and disagreed some. They understood each other well, and at times missed each other's intentions. They were open, and and at times ego-involved. Yet as we sit through it all as responsive listeners, we achieve a clearer view of ourselves-as-audience. We think about our ability to talk in new ways in a common forum, generating more to say, considering ideas we hadn't considered before, and recognizing an ever-wider range of listeners.

That is the potential for public dialogue. That is why it matters that we are here, with each other.

Notes

CHAPTER ONE. DIALOGUE IN PUBLIC SPACE

1. Hereafter, quotations from the Buber–Rogers dialogue will be cited by a turn number, keyed to the Anderson and Cissna (1997) transcript and commentary.

2. A series of scholarly and general trade books have appeared in recent years. For example, trade books include Isaacs's (1999) *Dialogue and the Art of Thinking Together*, Tannen's (1998) *The Argument Culture: Moving from Debate to Dialogue*, Ellinor and Gerard's (1998) *Dialogue: Rediscover the Transforming Power of Conversation*, Saunders's (1999) *A Public Peace Process: Sustained Dialogue to Transform Racial and Ethnic Conflicts*, Ross's (1998) *A Tao of Dialogue: A Manual of Dialogic Communication*, Stone, Patton, and Heen's (199) *Difficult Conversations: How to Discuss What Matters Most*, and Yankelovich's (1999) *The Magic of Dialogue: Transforming Conflict into Cooperation*. Recent scholarly books in communication include Bergman's (1991) *Dialogical Philosophy from Kierkegaard to Buber*, Swidler, Cobb, Knitter, and Hellwig's (1990) *Death or Dialogue?*, Wold's (1992) *The Dialogic Alternative*, Arnett and Arneson's (1999) *Dialogic Civility in a Cynical Age: Community, Hope, and Interpersonal Relationships*, Pearce and Littlejohn's (1997) *Moral Conflict: When Social Worlds Collide*, Baxter and Montgomery's (1996) *Relating: Dialogues and Dialectics*, Anderson and Cissna's (1997) *The Martin Buber–Carl Rogers Dialogue: A New Transcript with Commentary*, Anderson, Cissna, and Arnett's (1994) edited collection *The Reach of Dialogue: Confirmation, Voice, and Community*, and McNamee and Gergen's (1999) *Relational Responsibility: Resources for Sustainable Dialogue*, as well as a double issue of the *Southern Communication Journal* devoted to "Studies in Dialogue" (Cissna, 2000). For a brief and

now somewhat dated discussion of the emerging interdisciplinary scholarly literature on dialogue, see Cissna and Anderson (1998); for a brief overview focused on the dialogic literature in the communication field, see Anderson and Cissna (2001).

CHAPTER THREE. BUBER AND
THE PHILOSOPHY OF DIALOGUE

1. For expanded discussions of Buber's cross-disciplinary influence, see Agassi (1999), Breslauer (1990), Eisenstadt (1992), Friedman (1969), Mendes-Flohr (1989), and Schilpp and Friedman (1967).

2. See also the forty-page bibliography included with *The Philosophy of Martin Buber* (Schilpp & Friedman, 1967, pp. 747–786) and Moonan's (1981) *Martin Buber and his Critics: An Annotated Bibliography of Writings in English Through 1978.*

3. We have not cluttered the biographical sections of this chapter with all of the citations necessary to indicate the various sources we relied on. The best and most complete biographies of Buber are Friedman's three-volume (1981, 1983b, 1983c) and one-volume (1991) works. Schaeder is also very helpful—both her biographical volume (1973a) and her sixty-page "biographical sketch" that introduces the English edition of Buber's letters (1991). *The Letters of Martin Buber* (Glatzer & Mendes-Flohr, 1991) and Buber's own "Autobiographical Fragments" (1973) were invaluable. Other sources we found useful in understanding Buber's life include Avnon (1998), Breslauer (1990), Gordon (1988), Hodes (1971), Kaufmann (1980), Manheim (1974), Moore (1974), Panko (1976), Schmidt (1995), Simon (1974), Smith (1967), Vermes (1988), and Wood (1969). Finally, Maurice Friedman read this chapter in draft form and kindly clarified several issues that had confused us.

4. "Adele Buber ran away with an army officer to Russia without divorce or even notice of any kind. Buber's father Carl had to get special permission from a rabbi to remarry" (M. Friedman, personal communication, 18 March 2000).

5. Buber was an active correspondent his whole life. For most of it, he wrote his letters by hand, sometimes in multiple drafts. He wrote letters, he said, only when a face-to-face conversation was not possible. He sought in his letters, as he did in conversation, to establish "a direct relationship with the other person," yet Simon (1991) reports that "this did not come easily to him," in person or in writing. Simon believes that Buber eventually became more practiced in achieving such a relationship in letters, "so much so that his method of achieving that relationship

was in danger of congealing into a mechanical technique" (p. xi). For a partial collection in English of his letters and of others' letters to him, see Glatzer and Mendes-Flohr (1991); a more complete three-volume German edition is also available (Schaeder, 1972, 1973b, 1975).

6. The commentary on the *Chuang Tzu* is readily available in English translation as "The Teaching of the Tao" in *Pointing the Way*, a collection of Buber's more important early essays (Buber, 1957c, pp. 31–58). Jonathan Herman's *I and Tao* (1996) includes an English translation of Buber's German translation of the Chinese folktales and his own translation of Buber's commentary. One might wonder how Buber produced German translations of Chinese texts, as he had no more than casual familiarity with the Chinese language. Herman suggests that Buber relied primarily on extant translations of *Chuang Tzu* as well as on the help of a Chinese friend to produce the volume of Taoist wisdom.

7. We discuss Taoism and the *wu-wei* again in the next chapter, as Carl Rogers was also influenced by this ancient Chinese philosophy.

8. For a careful and fascinating study of the development of Buber's *I and Thou* from early outline to final publication, see Horwitz (1988). She shows that *I and Thou* was not written, as Kaufmann suggests, quickly and without revision. In "Replies to my Critics" (Schilpp & Friedman, 1967), Buber indicates that he wrote under an inspiration and that he would not, forty years later, revise the text, "even for the sake of exactness" (p. 706). He does not say, however, that he made no changes to the text as he was writing it, and Horwitz shows that the book underwent extensive revision.

9. Translation is always a difficult and vexing problem, one about which Buber himself wrote in connection with his work both on the Hasidic tales and on the Bible. Kaufmann, most prominently, prefers to translate Buber's *Ich-Du* into the English "I-You," rather than the "I-Thou" first used by Ronald Gregor Smith in his 1937 edition of *I and Thou* published in Edinburgh. Actually, neither "you" nor "thou" is an ideal translation of *du*. "You" fails to suggest the close, personal relationship of the German *du*, and "thou" carries strong religious connotations that *du* does not (see Friedman, 1981, pp. 428–429, for a discussion of the two translations, including this issue). We continue to use "thou" partly because, as Friedman notes, there is a long history of both scholarly and general usage invested in it, and also because Buber approved Smith's translations of *I and Thou* in 1937 and in the 1957 postscript added to the second edition. If Buber had preferred "you" to "thou," surely he would have said so (by 1957 he was a fluent speaker of English himself).

10. Gendlin is a prominent psychotherapist. Although he didn't know Rogers at the time, they later became colleagues and Gendlin

extended Rogers's client-centered and person-centered work into new realms of phenomenology, existential philosophy, and a dialogic approach he termed "focusing."

11. In the last ten years of his life, Buber had three interesting opportunities in print to answer questions about his thought and respond to his intellectual critics. Buber's postscript to the second edition (1958) of *I and Thou* was based on a list of questions Friedman provided (Friedman 1983b, p. 252; Kaufmann's 1970 translation calls it an afterword). In *The Philosophy of Martin Buber* (Schilpp & Friedman, 1967), thirty noted philosophers provided critical essays, followed by Buber's "Replies to my Critics." In addition, the process that culminated in the book *Philosophical Interrogations* (Rome & Rome, 1964) allowed Buber to establish something of a dialogue in responding to questions posed by noted philosophers and others. All these forums provide important clarifications of Buber's thinking.

12. We are indebted to John Stewart (1994) for his thoughtful explication of the opening stanzas of *I and Thou* in his foreword to our book with Ronald C. Arnett, *The Reach of Dialogue* (Anderson, Cissna, & Arnett, 1994, pp. viii–xx).

CHAPTER FOUR. ROGERS AND THE PRAXIS OF DIALOGUE

1. Rogers himself contributed to some misunderstandings. He published many "talks" in his collected books, and frequently wrote and spoke for lay audiences. Thus the language of his published work is more casual than that of a more pure philosopher or theorist. But this language also helped him have an immediate impact on the lives of a great many people. He was, as we will argue, both a thoughtful philosopher of praxis and a concerned clinician and activist. Further, like many great thinkers and prolific writers, Rogers is probably cited more than he is read, and generally the citations are to a very few works (primarily *Client-Centered Therapy* [1951] and *On Becoming a Person* [1961], and only rarely are specific pages or even chapters noted). Finally, although he may have done too little to correct either honest misinterpretations or overzealous adherents or missionaries, Rogers should not be impeached for the loose and even naïve interpretations of others.

2. Rogers discussed Buber, the Tao, and *wu-wei* in an "intellectual autobiographical" chapter in *A Way of Being* (1980, pp. 41–42).

3. Rogers qualified the "not a scholar" comment by adding the nonrestrictive clause following scholar, "gaining my ideas from the writing of others" (1980, p. 63).

4. It is difficult to understand some of the critiques of Rogers because of their indirection. Some prominent ones are addressed, not at Rogers, but at "humanistic psychology" (Franzwa, 1973; Hart & Burks, 1972; Phillips, 1976). None of these three mention Rogers often, although all implied significant critique. For example, Hart and Burks mention Rogers only twice. The first time they allow that he "makes the point with more sophistication" (p. 78) when, in our judgment, the point was not only far more sophisticated but also was rather different from the one Hart and Burks describe. The second time they actually cite Rogers to support their argument (p. 80). Even Bochner (1982), himself a critic of the humanistic approach to interpersonal communication, describes Hart and Burks's critique as presenting a "baffling extrapolation" (pp. 110–111). Carl Rogers might hardly have recognized himself as a humanistic psychologist within the context of these articles and surely he was not a proponent of a simplistic "expressive view." We agree with much of the responses written by Sillars (1974) and Gaw (1978), in particular, that the critiques were directed largely at humanistic psychology "straw men," rather than at scholars, such as Rogers, with particular views. We are also puzzled by one presentation of "Rogers's Theory of Congruence" (Littlejohn, 1983, pp. 195–196), an umbrella phrase we are not aware of Rogers using. Although some of his writing emphasizes congruence over the other relationship conditions, other work explicitly denies this priority. The overall label "theory of congruence" seems inconsistent with the general shape of Rogers's published work for the reasons discussed in this chapter. To be fair, we note that recent editions of the book in which this label appeared do not repeat it, but its initial appearance may have resulted at least in part from the impression that Rogers advocated complete honesty in relationships.

5. Rogers rarely gave advice, at least in print. Still, he preferred congruence in himself, and we think that the corpus of his work, including the implications of himself as a model, suggests that people are generally better off moving toward rather than away from congruence.

6. Arnett also (see 1986, pp. 53, 63–64, 182–183 [notes 2 and 13]; Arnett & Nakagawa, 1983, p. 373) has observed that Rogers was often not well represented by others' presentations of his concepts, especially of empathy.

7. Identifying Rogers with "active listening" techniques is common, especially in texts in the helping professions and communication. As far as we can determine, Rogers published the phrase only once, in the booklet written with Farson (Rogers & Farson, 1957) to accompany training with business supervisors. In an interview with us, Farson (personal communication, 12 August 1993) mentioned that he had

drafted the text of this essay, perhaps further distancing Rogers from some of its terminology. Still, making active listening into a technique contradicts the Rogers and Farson concept. They envisioned active listening as a fundamental attitude that "genuinely respects the potential worth of the individual, which considers his rights and trusts his capacity for self-direction" (Rogers & Farson, 1957, p. 3), and which, if used as a mere technique, "will be empty and sterile and our associates will be quick to recognize this" (p. 3).

8. We accept Arnett's (1989) "generic notion of dialogue" and concur both that multiple approaches to dialogue are possible and that Rogers and Buber differ in several significant respects. We cannot agree with Arnett, however, that Rogers stood for an "individualized" conception of dialogue. People typically approached his therapy sessions and his groups as individuals, but to the extent that they heard his message, they built with him a relationship that became mutualized and dialogic. His conception of dialogue was never individualistic or individualized in contrast to Buber's; it was the nature of Rogers's praxis that he found he must "individualize" (that is, make unique) his responses in dialogue to each separate person who came to him for help. This is the way Buber's writings would have it too, as we each are called to treat the other "as the very one he is" (1965b, p. 79), concretely in the moment, not as some abstract category or objectification.

CHAPTER FIVE. HISTORICAL CONTEXT AND THE BUBER–ROGERS MEETING

1. Rogers's notes and preparations for the later 1962 dialogue with Skinner at the University of Minnesota at Duluth similarly cite Buber's concepts to buttress his objections to Skinner's behaviorism (see Rogers, nd-b).

2. Buber not only had read Friedman's dissertation but had worked with him to convert it into a book, and even attempted to help Friedman secure a publisher. It is a fair assumption that he had read Friedman's assessment of the similarities between himself and Rogers.

3. We have quoted the 1960 edition of *Martin Buber: The Life of Dialogue* because it presented Friedman his best opportunity after the Buber–Rogers dialogue to revise his analysis of conceptual similarities and differences if he had wanted to do so. His recognition of fundamental Buber–Rogers agreement remains intact, as these quotations demonstrate. However, see also p. 197 for added material.

CHAPTER SIX. INTERHUMAN MEETING

1. This chapter includes numerous quotations from the dialogue. As in previous chapters, they are marked with turn numbers keyed to our earlier book (Anderson & Cissna, 1997), the most definitive text to date. However, referring to it constantly would be awkward here. Readers interested in a fuller context for the statements, or in verifying them for some other purpose, should consult that work. Here we have used ellipses sparingly, only to remove a speaker's repetitions and vocalized pauses, or introjections from the listener.

2. Significant pauses (2.5 seconds or more) are noted in brackets.

3. The major published transcripts in English that contain this passage report that Buber said "certain moment" rather than "certain mode" of dialogic existence. Because Buber's accent is relatively heavy, it is possible he meant "mood" instead, but assuming he said "mode," we think, credits Buber with better semantic clarity. Perhaps Buber misunderstood Rogers and was echoing the word ("mode") he thought Rogers had used, whereas the earlier transcriber[s] misheard Buber, perhaps assuming he had echoed Rogers's actual word, "moment." If Buber did not hear Rogers say "moment" in the question, it would influence significantly how we would interpret the implications of his later responses, and influence significantly how at least this section of the dialogue should be understood.

4. In published transcripts before our 1997 work, this statement erroneously appeared as "Yes. This is not what I mean" (the original typescript) or "Yes. But this is not what I mean" (the transcript in Buber's *The Knowledge of Man*; Friedman, as editor, must have added the "but" to clarify what he thought Buber meant). These mistakes attributed to Buber a meaning nearly opposite from what he actually said. The transcriber[s] apparently misunderstood "just" as "not." Buber clearly says: "Yes. This is just what I mean." He is agreeing with Rogers about therapy being about over if these conditions applied. He makes the same point in the postscript to a new edition of *I and Thou*, written six months after the dialogue with Rogers (in October 1957; see Buber, 1958, p. 133).

5. Friedman (e.g., 1983c) has presented this exchange in a way that surprises us: "Buber asked Rogers whether he had ever worked with schizophrenics and paranoiacs and was not surprised when Rogers answered in the negative" (p. 226). Rogers definitely did not answer "in the negative." Further, Buber did not ask Rogers whether he had "ever worked with schizophrenics and paranoiacs," but whether he had "much to do" or "to do" with them—the questions

are not quite the same. In addition, the way in which Buber phrased his questions ("You have certainly much to do with schizophrenics. Is it true?") seems to indicate that he expected the verification he did receive rather than the negative response Friedman indicated he expected. We analyze this interesting question about Rogers's work with schizophrenics in more detail elsewhere (Anderson & Cissna, 1997, pp. 48–50). In some accounts of the dialogue, Buber is said to have made a telling point because Rogers *hadn't* worked with these intensely disturbed clients, and so couldn't have sensed the special problems and limits on equal relations with them. Yet, as we have shown, Rogers's experience did include such clients (as he told Buber), and he was in professional transition at this time to an appointment at the University of Wisconsin for the express purpose of arranging even more work and research with hospitalized schizophrenics.

    6. In his most recent presentation of this quotation, we note that Friedman adds the phrase "in this Buber and Rogers would agree" (p. 368).

CHAPTER SEVEN. THEORIZING DIALOGIC MOMENTS

    1. Johannesen's (1971) influential article in the *Quarterly Journal of Speech* notes that dialogue usually requires "a great amount of time" (p. 381). Stewart (1978), in discussing dialogue as focusing on transaction, the between, or relationship, provides no indication that dialogue is limited temporally. Arnett (1989) defines dialogue as "meeting the other as a person" (p. 47), and implies that such meetings can last quite some time. Baxter and her colleagues are more sensitive to issues of time than most dialogically oriented writers (see Werner & Baxter, 1994), but still note that in dialogue all participants share a responsibility for "keeping the conversation going" (Baxter & Montgomery, 1996, p. 237)—dialogue isn't momentary but exists over time and potentially throughout a conversation. David Bohm (1996) describes dialogue as "a stream of meaning flowing among and through us and between us. This will make possible a flow of meaning in the whole group, out of which may emerge some new understanding. . . . And this shared meaning is the 'glue' or 'cement' that holds people and societies together" (p. 6). "Stream" and "flow of meaning" also suggest ongoingness. Finally, even our own description, offered not many years ago, is limited in this respect. Dialogue, we had said, "implies more than a simple back-and-forthness of messages in interaction; it points to a particular process and quality of communication in which the participants 'meet,' which allows for changing and being changed" (Cissna & An-

derson, 1994a, p. 10). We implied, as many dialogic theorists do, that dialogue exists—or can exist—throughout the course of a relationship.

2. Kramer (1989) recently described psychotherapy as "moments of engagement," although he did not pursue this idea very far theoretically. Shotter (1993a, pp. 118–131), we believe, could hardly have agreed more fully with Rogers regarding dialogue and psychotherapy involving "special moments" (p. 120), although his interest seems to be more in narrative than in a theory of dialogic moments.

3. As we clarified in chapter 6, the initial transcription of this turn was unfortunate, as it completely reversed what Buber actually said: his clear statement, "Yes. This is *just* what I mean," became in the transcripts "Yes. This is *not* what I mean." Then, in a later and more often-cited transcript published in Buber's *The Knowledge of Man*, the same statement becomes "Yes. *But* this is *not* what I mean" (emphasis added).

4. This passage continues to make the claim about moments, and does so in language remarkably similar to that of the dialogue. For example: (1) in this passage Rogers mentions an "I-Thou relationship" and in the dialogue he referred to Buber's "I-Thou relationship" and to "the world of 'I-It'"; (2) in this passage he refers to both parties in a therapeutic relationship being changed, while allowing that "the growth may be greater for the client," and in the dialogue he says, "I think sometimes the client is changed more than I am, but I think both of us are changed in that kind of . . . an experience"; (3) in this passage Rogers says that a relationship in psychotherapy "can be looked upon as an unequal one," and to Buber in 1957 he said that it "could be seen as a very unequal relationship."

5. In a fascinating account of empathy and psychotherapy, John Shlien (1997) provides a different interpretation of the difference between Buber and Rogers. He reads Buber's inclusion as an attempt to dissolve the boundaries between self and other, while Rogers, with his famous "as if" clause (experiencing the other's frame of reference *as if* one is the other, but "without ever losing the 'as if' condition" [Rogers, 1959b, p. 210]), wished to preserve those boundaries and keep clients at some distance (Shlien, 1997). Shlien also provides an interesting history of Rogers's development of the concept of empathy from the late 1940s through his dialogue with Buber. Although we do not endorse his characterization of Buber's inclusion or his description of differences between Buber and Rogers, we share Shlien's view that their work had many theoretical similarities.

References

Ackerman, B. A. (1980). *Social justice in the liberal state*. New Haven, CT: Yale University Press.

Agassi, J. B. (Ed.). (1999). *Martin Buber on psychology and psychotherapy: Essays, letters, and dialogue*. Syracuse, NY: Syracuse University Press.

American Psychological Association Distinguished Scientific Contribution Awards for 1956. (1957). *American Psychologist, 12,* 125–133.

Anderson, H. (1997). *Conversation, language, and possibilities: A postmodern approach to therapy*. New York: Basic Books.

Anderson, R. (1982). Phenomenological dialogue, humanistic psychology and pseudo-walls: A response and extension. *Western Journal of Speech Communication, 46,* 344–357.

Anderson, R. (1984). Response to the symposium "Empathic Listening," ed. by John Stewart. *Communication Education, 33,* 195–196.

Anderson, R., & Cissna, K. N. (1996). Criticism and conversational texts: Rhetorical bases of role, audience, and style in the Buber–Rogers dialogue. *Human Studies, 19,* 85–118.

Anderson, R., & Cissna, K. N. (1997). *The Martin Buber–Carl Rogers dialogue: A new transcript with commentary*. Albany: State University of New York Press.

Anderson, R., & Cissna, K. N. (2001). *The future of dialogic scholarship in communication*. Unpublished manuscript.

Anderson, R., Cissna, K. N., & Arnett, R. C. (Eds.). (1994). *The reach of dialogue: Confirmation, voice, and community*. Cresskill, NJ: Hampton Press.

Anderson, R., Dardenne, R., & Killenberg, G. M. (1994). *The conversation of journalism: Communication, community, and news*. Westport, CT: Praeger.

277

Anderson, R. E. (1963). Kierkegaard's theory of communication. *Speech Monographs, 30,* 1–14.

Anzaldúa, G. (1987). *Borderlands/La frontera: The new mestiza.* San Francisco: Spinsters/Aunt Lute.

Arendt, H. (1959). *The human condition.* New York: Anchor.

Arnett, R. C. (1981). Toward a phenomenological dialogue. *Western Journal of Speech Communication, 45,* 201–212.

Arnett, R. C. (1982). Rogers and Buber: Similarities, yet fundamental differences. *Western Journal of Speech Communication, 46,* 358–372.

Arnett, R. C. (1986). *Communication and community: Implications of Martin Buber's dialogue.* Carbondale: Southern Illinois University Press.

Arnett, R. C. (1989). What is dialogic communication?: Friedman's contribution and clarification. *Person-Centered Review, 4,* 42–60.

Arnett, R. C. (1993). *Dialogic education: Conversation about ideas and between persons.* Carbondale: Southern Illinois University Press.

Arnett, R. C., & Arneson, P. (1999). *Dialogic civility in a cynical age: Community, hope, and interpersonal relationships.* Albany: State University of New York Press.

Arnett, R. C., & Nakagawa, G. (1983). The assumptive roots of empathic listening: A critique. *Communication Education, 32,* 368–378.

Attendence [sic] at the Martin Buber Conference. (1957). Michigan Historical Collections, Bentley Historical Library, University of Michigan.

Avnon, D. (1998). *Martin Buber: The hidden dialogue.* Lanham, MD: Rowman & Littlefield.

Ayres, J. (1984). Four approaches to interpersonal communication. *Western Journal of Speech Communication, 48,* 408–440.

Bakan, D. (1966). *The duality of human existence: Isolation and communion in western man.* Boston: Beacon Press.

Bakhtin, M. M. (1981). *The dialogic imagination: Four essays* (M. Holquist, Ed.; C. Emerson & M. Holquist, Trans.). Austin: University of Texas Press.

Bakhtin, M. M. (1984). *Problems of Dostoevsky's poetics* (C. Emerson, Ed. & Trans.) Minneapolis, MN: University of Minnesota Press.

Bakhtin, M. M. (1986). *Speech genres and other late essays* (C. Emerson & M. Holquist, Eds.; V. W. McGee, Trans.). Austin: University of Texas Press.

Bakhtin, M. M. (1993). *Toward a philosophy of the act* (V. Liapunov & M. Holquist, Eds.; V. Liapunov, Trans.). Austin: University of Texas Press.

Baldwin, D. (1957a). Baldwin to Buber, 11 January 1957. Unpublished letter from the Martin Buber Archives, Jewish National & University Library, Arc. Ms. Var. 350/836d:2.

Baldwin, D. (1957b). Baldwin to Buber, 11 February 1957. Unpublished letter from the Martin Buber Archives, Jewish National & University Library, Arc. Ms. Var. 350/836d:5.

Baldwin, D. (1957c). Baldwin to Buber, 8 April 1957. Unpublished letter from the Martin Buber Archives, Jewish National & University Library, Arc. Ms. Var. 350/836d:8.

Baldwin, D. (1957d). Baldwin to Rogers, 8 April 1957. Unpublished letter from the Carl R. Rogers Collection, Collections of the Manuscript Division, Library of Congress, Washington, DC (box 80, folder 13).

Barber, B. (1988). *The conquest of politics: Liberal philosophy in democratic times.* Princeton, NJ: Princeton University Press.

Barber, B. R. (1989). Liberal democracy and the costs of consent. In N. L. Rosenblum (Ed.), *Liberalism and the moral life* (pp. 54–68). Cambridge, MA: Harvard University Press.

Barge, J. K., & Little, M. (in press). Dialogical wisdom, communicative practice, and organizational life. *Communication Theory.*

Barrett, W. (1979). *The illusion of technique.* Garden City, NY: Anchor.

Barrett-Lennard, G. T. (1998). *Carl Rogers' helping system: Journal and substance.* London: Sage.

Bateson, G. (1951). Information and codification: A philosophical approach. In J. Ruesch & G. Bateson, *Communication: The social matrix of psychiatry* (pp. 21–49). New York: Norton.

Baumann, Z. (1992). *Intimations of postmodernity.* London: Routledge.

Baxter, L. A., & Montgomery, B. M. (1996). *Relating: Dialogues and dialectics.* New York: Guilford Press.

Becker, C., Chasin, L., Chasin, R., Herzig, M., & Roth, S. (1995a). From stuck debate to new conversation on controversial issues: A report from the Public Conversations Project. In K. Weingarten (Ed.), *Cultural resistance: Challenging beliefs about men, women, and therapy* (pp. 143–163). New York: Harrington Park Press.

Becker, C., Chasin, L., Chasin, R., Herzig, M., & Roth, S. (1995b). From stuck debate to new conversation on controversial issues: A report from the Public Conversations Project. *Journal of Feminist Family Therapy, 7,* 143–163.

Bellah, R. N., Madsen, R., Sullivan, W. M., Swidler, A., & Tipton, S. M. (1985). *Habits of the heart: Individualism and commitment in American life.* Berkeley: University of California Press.

Berger, P., & Luckmann, T. (1967). *The social construction of reality: A treatise in the sociology of knowledge.* New York: Anchor Books.

Berger, P., Berger, B., & Kellner, H. (1974). *The homeless mind: Modernization and consciousness.* New York: Vintage Books.

Bergman, S. H. (1991). *Dialogical philosophy from Kierkegaard to Buber* (A. A. Gerstein, Trans.). Albany: State University of New York Press.

Berry, D. L. (1985). *Mutuality: The vision of Martin Buber.* Albany: State University of New York Press.

Bird, S. E. (1999). Chatting on Cynthia's porch: Creating community in an e-mail fan group. *Southern Communication Journal, 65,* 49–65.

Black, J. (Ed.). (1997). *Mixed news: The public/civic/communitarian journalism debate.* Matwah, NJ: Erlbaum.

Blumer, H. (1969). *Symbolic interactionism: Perspective and method.* Englewood Cliffs, NJ: Prentice-Hall.

Bochner, A. P. (1982). On the efficacy of openness in close relationships. In M. Burgoon (Ed.), *Communication Yearbook 5* (pp. 109–124). New Brunswick, NJ: International Communication Association and Transaction Books.

Bohart, A. C., & Greenberg, L. S. (Eds.). (1997). *Empathy reconsidered: New directions in psychotherapy.* Washington, DC: American Psychological Association.

Bohm, D. (1990). *On dialogue.* Ojai, CA: David Bohm Seminars.

Bohm, D. (1996). *On dialogue* (L. Nichol, Ed.). London: Routledge.

Bowen, M. C. V.-B. (1986). Personality differences and person-centered supervision. *Person–Centered Review, 1,* 291–309.

Bozarth, J. (1993). Not necessarily sufficient. In D. Brazier (Ed.), *Beyond Carl Rogers* (pp. 92–105). London: Constable.

Brace, K. (1992). I and thou in interpersonal psychotherapy. *Humanistic Psychologist, 20,* 41–57.

Branham, R. J., & Pearce, W. B. (1996). The conversational frame in public address. *Communication Quarterly, 44,* 423–439.

Brazier, D. (Ed.). (1993a). *Beyond Carl Rogers.* London: Constable.

Brazier, D. (1993b). Introduction. In D. Brazier (Ed.), *Beyond Carl Rogers* (pp. 7–13). London: Constable.

Breslauer, S. D. (1990). *Martin Buber on myth: An introduction.* New York: Garland.

Brink, D. D. (1987). The issues of equality and control in the client- or person-centered approach. *Journal of Humanistic Psychology, 27,* 27–37.

Brown, R. H. (1987). *Society as text: Essays on rhetoric, reason, and reality.* Chicago: University of Chicago Press.

Bruneau, T. (1989). Empathy and listening: A conceptual review and theoretical directions. *Journal of the International Listening Association, 3,* 1–20.

Buber, M. (1949). *Paths in utopia.* New York: Macmillan.

Buber, M. (1952). *Eclipse of God: Studies in the relation between religion and philosophy.* New York: Harper.

Buber, M. (1955). *The legend of the Baal-Shem* (M. S. Friedman, Trans.). New York: Harper & Brothers.

Buber, M. (1956). *The tales of Rabbi Nachman* (M. S. Friedman, Trans.). New York: Horizon Press.

Buber, M. (1957a). Buber to Friedman, 19 February 1957. Unpublished letter from the Martin Buber Archives, Jewish National & University Library, Arc. Ms. Var. 217a/458.

Buber, M. (1957b). Elements of the interhuman. *Psychiatry, 20,* 105–113.

Buber, M. (1957c). *Pointing the way* (M. Friedman, Ed. & Trans.). New York: Harper & Row.

Buber, M. (1958). *I and thou* (2nd ed.; R. G. Smith, Trans.). New York: Scribner. (Original work published 1923)

Buber, M. (1965a). *Between man and man* (R. G. Smith, Trans.). New York: Macmillan. (Original work published 1947)

Buber, M. (1965b). *The knowledge of man: A philosophy of the interhuman* (M. Friedman, Ed. & Intro.; M. Friedman & R. G. Smith, Trans.). New York: Harper & Row.

Buber, M. (1967). Replies to my critics. In P. A. Schilpp & M. Friedman (Eds.), *The philosophy of Martin Buber* (pp. 689–744). La Salle, IL: Open Court.

Buber, M. (1970). *I and thou* (W. Kaufmann, Trans.). New York: Charles Scribner's Sons. (Original work published 1923)

Buber, M. (1973). *Meetings* (M. Friedman, Ed. & Trans.). La Salle, IL: Open Court.

Buber, M. (1991a). Buber to Farber, 19 February 1957. In N. N. Glatzer & P. Mendes-Flohr (Eds.), *The letters of Martin Buber: A life of dialogue* (No. 665). New York: Schocken Books.

Buber, M. (1991b). Buber to Rosenzweig, 28 September 1922. In N. N. Glatzer & P. Mendes-Flohr (Eds.), *The letters of Martin Buber: A life of dialogue* (No. 281). New York: Schocken Books.

Burd, S. (1995, 10 March). Republican senators take humanities endowment to task. *Chronicle of Higher Education,* p. 26.

Burke, K. (1957). *The philosophy of literary form.* New York: Vintage.

Burke, K. (1969). *The rhetoric of motives.* Berkeley: University of California Press.

Burstow, B. (1987). Humanistic psychotherapy and the issue of equality. *Journal of Humanistic Psychology, 27,* 9–25.

Cain, D. J. (1996). Rogers and Sylvia: An intimate and affirming encounter. In B. A. Farber, D. C. Brink, & P. M. Raskin (Eds.),

The psychotherapy of Carl Rogers: Cases and commentary (pp. 275–283). New York: Guilford.

Carey, J. W. (1989). *Communication as culture: Essays on media and society.* Boston: Unwin Hyman.

Carl Rogers—The Man and His Ideas [Special issue]. (1995). *Journal of Humanistic Psychology, 35*(4).

Charity, A. (1995). *Doing public journalism.* New York: Guilford.

Chasin, R., & Herzig, M. (1993). Creating systemic interventions for the sociopolitical arena. In B. Berger-Gould & D. H. DeMuth (Eds.), *The global family therapist: Integrating the personal, professional, and political* (pp. 141–192). Needham, MA: Allyn and Bacon.

Chasin, R., Herzig, M., Roth, S., Chasin, L., Becker, C., & Stains, R. R. (1996). From diatribe to dialogue on divisive public issues: Approaches drawn from family therapy. *Mediation Quarterly, 13,* 323–344.

Chevigny, P. (1988). *More speech: Dialogue rights and modern liberty.* Philadelphia: Temple University Press.

Christians, C. G., Ferré, J. P., & Fackler, P. M. (1993). *Good news: Social ethics and the press.* New York: Oxford University Press.

Cissna, K. N. (Ed.). (2000). Studies in dialogue [Special issue]. *Southern Communication Journal, 65*(2 & 3).

Cissna, K. N., & Anderson, R. (1990). The contributions of Carl Rogers to a philosophical praxis of dialogue. *Western Journal of Speech Communication, 54,* 125–147.

Cissna, K. N., & Anderson, R. (1994a). Communication and the ground of dialogue. In R. Anderson, K. N. Cissna, & R. C. Arnett (Eds.), *The reach of dialogue: Confirmation, voice, and community* (pp. 9–30). Cresskill, NJ: Hampton.

Cissna, K. N., & Anderson, R. (1994b). The 1957 Martin Buber–Carl Rogers dialogue, as dialogue. *Journal of Humanistic Psychology, 34,* 11–45.

Cissna, K. N., & Anderson, R. (1996). Dialogue in public: Looking critically at the Buber–Rogers dialogue. In M. Friedman (Ed.), *Martin Buber and the human sciences* (pp. 191–206). Albany: State University of New York Press.

Cissna, K. N., & Anderson, R. (1998). Theorizing about dialogic moments: The Buber–Rogers position and postmodern themes. *Communication Theory, 8,* 63–104.

Cissna, K. N. L., & Keating, S., Sr. (1979). Speech communication antecedents of perceived confirmation. *Western Journal of Speech Communication, 43,* 48–60.

Claflin, S. T. (1979). *A radical proposal for full use of free speech.* New York: Philosophical Library.

Clark, G. (1990). *Dialogue, dialectic, and conversation: A social perspective on the function of writing.* Carbondale: Southern Illinois University Press.

Clark, K., & Holquist, M. (1984). *Mikhail Bakhtin.* Cambridge, MA: Harvard University Press.

Clarke, A. C. (1993). *2001: A space odyssey.* New York: American Library.

Cohn, M., & Buber, R. (1980). *Martin Buber: A bibliography of his writings 1897–1978.* Jerusalem and Munich: Magnes Press and K. G. Saur.

Collins, P. H. (1990). *Black feminist thought: Knowledge, consciousness, and the politics of empowerment.* Boston: Unwin Hyman.

Crapanzano, V. (1990). On dialogue. In T. Maranhao (Ed.), *The interpretation of dialogue* (pp. 269–291). Chicago: University of Chicago Press.

Crapanzano, V. (1992). *Hermes' dilemma and Hamlet's desire: On the epistemology of interpretation.* Cambridge, MA: Harvard University Press.

Cushman, P. (1995). *Constructing the self, constructing America.* Reading, MA: Addison-Wesley.

Czubaroff, J. (2000). Dialogical rhetoric: An application of Martin Buber's philosophy of dialogue. *Quarterly Journal of Speech, 86,* 168–189.

Dayan, D., & Katz, E. (1992). *Media events: The live broadcasting of history.* Cambridge, MA: Harvard University Press.

Denzin, N. K. (1992). *Symbolic interactionism and cultural studies: The politics of interpretation.* Oxford: Blackwell.

De Ryck, P. (1982). Observations on Rogers as therapist. *Journey: An International Notebook, I (1),* 6–7.

DeVito, J. A. (1986). *The communication handbook: A dictionary.* New York: Harper & Row.

Dewey, J. (1916). *Democracy and education.* New York: Macmillan.

Dewey, J. (1927). *The public and its problems.* Denver, CO: Swallow.

Dewey, J., & Bentley, A. F. (1949). *Knowing and the known.* Boston: Beacon Press.

Dialogue [Special issue]. (1994). *Journal of Humanistic Psychology, 34*(1).

Dialogue between Martin Buber and Carl Rogers. (nd). Unpublished typescript, the Carl R. Rogers Collection, Collections of the Manuscript Division, Library of Congress, Washington, DC (box 80, folder 13), and the Carl Rogers Memorial Library, Center for Studies of the Person, La Jolla, CA.

Dialogue between Martin Buber and Carl Rogers. (1960). *Psychologia,* 3, 208–221.

Dyson, M. E. (1993). *Reflecting black: African-American cultural criticism.* Minneapolis: University of Minnesota Press.

Edelman, M. (1964). *The symbolic uses of politics.* Urbana: University of Illinois Press.

Edelman, M. (1988). *Constructing the political spectacle.* Chicago: University of Chicago Press.

Edwards, P. (1970). *Buber and Buberism: A critical evaluation.* Lawrence: Department of Philosophy, University of Kansas.

Eisenstadt, S. N. (1992). Introduction: Intersubjectivity, dialogue, discourse, and cultural creativity in the work of Martin Buber. In M. Buber, *On intersubjectivity and cultural creativity* (S. N. Eisenstadt, Ed.) (pp. 1–22). Chicago: University of Chicago Press.

Eisenstadt, S. N. (1997). Martin Buber in the postmodern age. *Society,* 34, 51–56.

Eliasoph, N. (1996). Making a fragile public: A talk-centered study of citizenship and power. *Sociological Theory, 14,* 262–289.

Ellinor, L., & Gerard, G. (1998). *Dialogue: Rediscover the transforming power of conversation.* New York: Wiley.

Ellul, J. (1964). *The technological society* (J. Wilkinson, Trans.). New York: Vintage.

Ellul, J. (1985). *The humiliation of the word* (J. M. Hanks, Trans.). Grand Rapids, MI: William B. Eerdmans.

Entman, R. M. (1989). *Democracy without citizens.* New York: Oxford University Press.

Etzioni, A. (1993). *The spirit of community: Rights, responsibilities, and the communitarian agenda.* New York: Crown.

Evans, R. D. (1975). *Carl Rogers: The man and his ideas.* New York: Dutton.

Evans, S. M., & Boyte, H. C. (1992). *Free spaces: The sources of democratic change in America* (Rev. ed.). Chicago: University of Chicago Press.

Fallows, J. M. (1996). *Breaking the news: How the media undermine American democracy.* New York: Pantheon Books.

Farber, B. A., Brink, D. C., & Raskin, P. M. (Eds.). (1996). *The psychotherapy of Carl Rogers: Cases and commentary.* New York: Guilford.

Farber, L. H. (1991). Farber to Buber, 9 April 1956. In N. N. Glatzer & P. Mendes-Flohr (Eds.), *The letters of Martin Buber: A life of dialogue* (No. 656). New York: Schocken Books.

Farrell, T. B. (1983). Aspects of coherence in conversation and rhetoric. In R. T. Craig & K. Tracy (Eds.), *Conversational coherence: Form, structure, and strategy* (pp. 259–284). Beverly Hills, CA: Sage.

Farson, R. (1975). Carl Rogers, quiet revolutionary. In R. I. Evans, *Carl Rogers: The man and his ideas* (pp. xxviii–xliii). New York: Dutton.

Farson, R. (1978). The technology of humanism. *Journal of Humanistic Psychology, 18,* 5–35.

Farson, R. (1996). *Management of the absurd: Paradoxes in leadership.* New York: Touchstone.

Ferrarotti, F. (1988). *The end of conversation: The impact of mass media on modern society.* New York: Greenwood.

Fishkin, J. S. (1991). *Democracy and deliberation: New directions for democratic reform.* New Haven, CT: Yale University Press.

Fishkin, J. S. (1992). *The dialogue of justice: Toward a self-reflective society.* New Haven, CT: Yale University Press.

Fishkin, J. S. (1995, July 17). Creating the ideal citizen [On line]. Available: http://wwwl.pbs.org/nic/poll_articles.html

Flick, D. L. (1998). *From debate to dialogue: Using the understanding process to transform our conversations.* Boulder, CO: Orchard.

Flores, L. A., & McPhail, M. L. (1997). From black and white to *Living Color*: A dialogic exposition into the social (re)construction of race, gender, and crime. *Critical Studies in Mass Communication, 14,* 106–112.

Foss, K. A., & Foss, S. K. (1991). *Women speak: The eloquence of women's lives.* Prospect Heights, IL: Waveland.

Foss, S. K., & Griffin, L. L. (1995). Beyond persuasion: A proposal for an invitational rhetoric. *Communication Monographs, 62,* 2–18.

Franzwa, H. H. (1973). Limitations in applying humanistic psychology in the classroom. *Today's Speech, 21,* 31–36.

Fraser, N. (1993). Rethinking the public sphere: A contribution to the critique of actually existing democracy. In B. Robbins (Ed.), *The phantom public sphere* (pp. 1–32). Minneapolis: University of Minnesota Press.

Freire, P. (1970). *Pedagogy of the oppressed* (M. B. Ramos, Trans.). New York: Seabury Press.

Friedman, M. S. (1955). *Martin Buber: The life of dialogue.* Chicago: University of Chicago Press.

Friedman, M. S. (1957). Friedman to Rogers, 6 October 1957. Unpublished letter from the Carl R. Rogers Collection, Collections of the Manuscript Division, Library of Congress, Washington, DC (box 6, folder 1).

Friedman, M. S. (1960). *Martin Buber: The life of dialogue* (2nd ed.). New York: Harper & Row.

Friedman, M. (Ed.). (1964). *Worlds of existentialism: A critical reader.* New York: Random House.

Friedman, M. S. (1965). Introductory essay. In M. Buber, *The knowledge of man: A philosophy of the interhuman* (pp. 11–58). New York: Harper & Row.

Friedman, M. S. (1969). Martin Buber and the theatre. In M. Buber, *Martin Buber and the theatre* (M. Friedman, Ed. & Trans.) (pp. 3–25). New York: Funk & Wagnalls.

Friedman, M. (1973). Introduction. In M. Buber, *Meetings* (M. Friedman, Ed. & Trans.) (pp. 1–13). La Salle, IL: Open Court.

Friedman, M. S. (1974). *Touchstones of reality: Existential trust and the commmunity of peace.* New York: E. P. Dutton.

Friedman, M. S. (1976). *Martin Buber: The life of dialogue* (3rd ed.). New York: Harper & Row.

Friedman, M. S. (1981). *Martin Buber's life and work: The early years—1878–1923.* New York: E. P. Dutton.

Friedman, M. S. (1982). Comment on the Rogers–May discussion of evil. *Journal of Humanistic Psychology, 12,* 93–96.

Friedman, M. S. (1983a). *The confirmation of otherness: In family, community, and society.* New York: Pilgrim Press.

Friedman, M. S. (1983b). *Martin Buber's life and work: The middle years—1923–1945.* New York: E. P. Dutton.

Friedman, M. S. (1983c). *Martin Buber's life and work: The later years—1945–1965.* New York: E. P. Dutton.

Friedman, M. (1985). *The healing dialogue in psychotherapy.* New York: Jason Aronson.

Friedman, M. S. (1986). Carl Rogers and Martin Buber: Self-actualization and dialogue. *Person-Centered Review, 1,* 409–435.

Friedman, M. S. (1987). Reminiscences of Carl Rogers. *Person-Centered Review, 2,* 392–395.

Friedman, M. (1991). *Encounter on the narrow ridge: A life of Martin Buber.* New York: Paragon House.

Friedman, M. (1992). *Dialogue and the human image: Beyond humanistic psychology.* Newbury Park, CA: Sage.

Friedman, M. S. (1994). Reflections on the Buber–Rogers dialogue. *Journal of Humanistic Psychology, 34,* 46–65.

Friedman, M. (1996a). Being aware: A dialogical approach to consciousness. *Humanistic Psychologist, 24,* 203–220.

Friedman, M. (Ed.). (1996b). *Martin Buber and the human sciences.* Albany: State University of New York Press.

Friedman, M. (1996c). Martin Buber's "narrow ridge" and the human sciences. In M. Friedman (Ed.), *Martin Buber and the human sciences* (pp. 3–25). Albany: State University of New York Press.

Friedman, M. (1996d). Reflections on the Buber–Rogers dialogue: Thirty-five years after. In M. Friedman (Ed.), *Martin Buber and the human sciences* (pp. 357–370). Albany: State University of New York Press.

Gadamer, H.-G. (1976). *Philosophical hermeneutics* (D. E. Linge, Trans.). Berkeley: University of California Press.

Gadamer, H-G. (1982). *Truth and method* (G. Barden & J. Cumming, Trans.). New York: Crossroad.

Gadamer, H.-G. (1989). Text and interpretation (D. J. Schmidt & R. Palmer, Trans.). In D. P. Michelfelder & R. E. Palmer (Eds.), *Dialogue and deconstruction: The Gadamer-Derrida encounter* (pp. 21–51). Albany: State University of New York Press.

Gadamer, H.-G., & Ricoeur, P. (1982). The conflict of interpretations. In R. Bruzina & B. Wilshire (Eds.), *Phenomenology: Dialogues and bridges* (pp. 299–320). Albany: State University of New York Press.

Galati, M. (1969). A rhetoric for the subjectivist in a world of untruth: The tasks and strategies of Søren Kierkegaard. *Quarterly Journal of Speech, 55,* 372–380.

Gates, H. L., Jr. (1992). *Loose canons: Notes on the culture wars.* New York: Oxford University Press.

Gaw, B. A. (1978). "Rhetoric and its alternatives as bases for examination of intimate communication": A humanist response. *Communication Quarterly, 26,* 13–20.

Geller, L. (1982). The failure of self-actualization theory: A critique of Carl Rogers and Abraham Maslow. *Journal of Humanistic Psychology, 22,* 56–73.

Gendlin, E. T. (1974). Client-centered and experiential psychotherapy. In D. A. Wexler & L. N. Rice (Eds.), *Innovations in client-centered therapy* (pp. 211–246). New York: Wiley.

Gendlin, E. T. (1988). Carl Rogers (1902–1987). *American Psychologist, 43,* 127–128.

General Utne email salon announcement (ver. 2.0). *Utne Reader* Internet E-mail Salons. (Received 31 March 1995)

Gergen, K. J. (1994). Exploring the postmodern: Perils or potentials. *American Psychologist, 49,* 412–416.

Gergen, K. J. (1995). Postmodernism as a humanism. *Humanistic Psychologist, 23,* 71–82.

Glaser, S. R., & Frank, D. A. (1982). Rhetorcal criticism of interpersonal discourse: An exploratory study. *Communication Quarterly, 30,* 353–358.

Glatzer, N. N., & Mendes-Flohr, P. (Eds.). (1991). *The letters of Martin Buber: A life of dialogue.* New York: Schocken.

Glendon, M. A. (1991). *Rights talk: The impoverishment of political discourse.* New York: Macmillan.

Goffman, E. (1974). *Frame analysis: An essay on the organization of experience.* New York: Harper & Row.

Goffman, E. (1981). *Forms of talk.* Philadelphia: University of Pennsylvania Press.

Goodall, H. L., Jr. (1991). *Living in the rock n roll mystery: Reading context, self, and others as clues.* Carbondale: Southern Illinois University Press.

Gordon, H. (1988). *The other Martin Buber: Recollections of his contemporaries.* Columbus: University of Ohio Press.

Greatbatch, D. (1988). A turn-taking system for British news interviews. *Language in Society, 17,* 401–430.

Greenberg, L. S. (1996). The power of empathic exploration: A process-experiential/Gestalt perspective on the case of Jim Brown. In B. A. Farber, D. C. Brink, & P. M. Raskin (Eds.), *The psychotherapy of Carl Rogers: Cases and commentary* (pp. 251–260). New York: Guilford.

Greenberg, L. S., Rice, L. N., & Elliott, R. (1993). *Facilitating emotional change: The moment-by-moment process.* New York: Guilford.

Grice, H. P. (1975). Logic and conversation. In P. Cole & J. L. Morgan (Eds.), *Syntax and semantics: Vol. 3. Speech acts.* New York: Academic Press.

Griffin, E. (1994). *A first look at communication theory* (2nd ed.). New York: McGraw-Hill.

Grudin, R. (1996). *On dialogue: An essay in free thought.* Boston: Houghton Mifflin.

Grummon, D. L. (1979). Client-centered theory. In H. M. Burks Jr. & B. Stefflre (Eds.), *Theories of counseling* (2nd ed.) (pp. 28–90). New York: McGraw-Hill.

Gunaratne, S. A. (1998). Old wine in a new bottle: Public journalism, developmental journalism, and social responsibility. In M. L. Roloff (Ed.), *Communication Yearbook 21* (pp. 277–321). Newbury Park, CA: Sage.

Gunn, G. (1987). *The culture of criticism and the criticism of culture.* New York: Oxford University Press.

Gurevitch, Z. D. (1988). The other side of dialogue: On making the other strange and the experience of otherness. *American Journal of Sociology, 93,* 1179–1199.

Gurevitch, Z. D. (1990). The dialogic connection and the ethics of dialogue. *British Journal of Sociology, 41,* 181–196.

Gurman, A. S. (1977). The patient's perception of the therapeutic relationship. In A. S. Gurman & A. M. Razin (Eds.), *Effective psy-*

chotherapy: A handbook of research (pp. 503–543). New York: Pergamon.

Gutmann, A., & Thompson, D. (1996). *Democracy and disagreement.* Cambridge, MA: Harvard University Press.

Habermas, J. (1990). *Moral consciousness and communicative action* (C. Lenhardt & W. Nicholsen, Trans.). Cambridge, MA: MIT Press.

Habermas, J. (1992). *Autonomy and solidarity: Interviews with Jürgen Habermas* (P. Dews, Ed.). London: Verso.

Hackney, S. (1994, 20 April). Organizing a national conversation. *Chronicle of Higher Education,* p. A56.

Hackney, S. (1997). *One America indivisible: A national conversation on American pluralism and identity.* Washington, DC: National Endowment for the Humanities.

Haiman, F. S. (1991). Majorities versus the first amendment: Rationality on trial. *Communication Monographs, 58,* 327–335.

Haley, J. (1963). *Strategies of psychotherapy.* New York: Grune and Stratton.

Halling, S., & Leifer, M. (1991). The theory and practice of dialogal research. *Journal of Phenomenological Psychology, 22,* 1–15.

Hampden-Turner, C. (1971). *Radical man: The process of psycho-social development.* Garden City, NY: Anchor Books.

Hart, R. P. (1986). Contemporary scholarship in public address: A research editorial. *Western Journal of Speech Communication, 50,* 283–295.

Hart, R. P., & Burks, D. M. (1972). Rhetorical sensitivity and social interaction. *Speech Monographs, 39,* 75–91.

Havens, L. (1986). *Making contact: Uses of language in psychotherapy.* Cambridge, MA: Harvard University Press.

Heclo, H. (1999, Winter). Hyperdemocracy. *Wilson Quarterly,* pp. 62–71.

Heisenberg, W. (1930). *The physical principles of quantum theory* (C. Eckart & F. C. Hoyt, Trans.). New York: Dover.

Heritage, J. (1985). Analyzing news interviews: Aspects of the production of talk for an overhearing audience. In T. A. van Dijk (Ed.), *Handbook of discourse analysis:* Vol. 3. *Discourse and dialogue* (pp. 95–117). London: Academic Press.

Herman, J. R. (1996). *I and Tao: Martin Buber's encounter with Chuang Tzu.* Albany: State University of New York Press.

Hodes, A. (1971). *Martin Buber: An intimate portrait.* New York: Viking Press.

Holquist, M. (1990). *Dialogism: Bakhtin and his world.* London: Routledge.

hooks, b. (1994). *Teaching to transgress: Education as the practice of freedom*. New York: Routledge.

Horton, M., & Freire, P. (1990). *We make the road by walking: Conversations on education and social change*. Philadelphia: Temple University Press.

Horwitz, R. (1988). *Buber's way to "I and Thou": The development of Martin Buber's thought and his "Religion as Presence" lectures*. Philadelphia: Jewish Publication Society.

Hutterer, R., Pawlowsky, G., Schmid, P. F., & Stipsits, R. (Eds.). (1996). *Client-centered and experiential psychotherapy: A paradigm in motion:* Frankfurt: Peter Lang.

Hycner, R. (1991). *Between person and person: Toward a dialogical psychotherapy*. Highland, NY: The Gestalt Journal Press.

Interview with Sheldon Hackney. (1994, 10 March). The MacNeil/Lehrer News Hour (PBS).

Isaacs, W. (1993a, April). Dialogue: The power of collective thinking. *The Systems Thinker, 4*(3).

Isaacs, W. N. (1993b). Taking flight: Dialogue, collective thinking, and organizational learning. *Organizational Dynamics, 22*, 24–39.

Isaacs, W. (1999). *Dialogue and the art of thinking together.* New York: Doubleday.

It's time to meet your neighbors. (nd). One page announcement from the *Utne Reader* Neighborhood Salon Association. (Available from *Utne Reader*, 1624 Harmon Place, Minneapolis, MN 55403)

Johannesen, R. L. (1971). The emerging concept of communication as dialogue. *Quarterly Journal of Speech, 57*, 373–382.

Johannesen, R. L. (1996). *Ethics in human communication* (4th ed.). Prospect Heights, IL: Waveland.

Jorgensen, J. (1992). Communication, rapport, and the interview: A social perspective. *Communication Theory, 2*, 148–156.

Kahn, H. (1978). *On thermonuclear war* (2nd ed.). Westport, CT: Greenwood.

Kahn, M. D. (1997). *Between therapist and client: The new relationship* (Rev. ed.). New York: W. H. Freeman.

Kaplan, A. (1964). *The conduct of inquiry: Methodology for behavioral science.* Scranton, PA: Chandler.

Kaplan, A. (1969). The life of dialogue. In J. D. Roslansky (Ed.), *Communication: A discussion at the Nobel Conference* (pp. 87–108). Amsterdam: North-Holland.

Kaplan, E. A. (1988). Feminism/Oedipus/postmodernism: The case of MTV. In E. A. Kaplan (Ed.), *Postmodernism and its discontents: Theories, practices* (pp. 30–44). London: Verso.

Katz, R. L. (1963). *Empathy: Its nature and uses.* New York: The Free Press.

Kaufmann, W. (1970). *I and you*: A prologue. In M. Buber, *I and thou* (W. Kaufmann, Trans.) (pp. 7–48). New York: Charles Scribner's Sons.

Kaufmann, W. (1978). Buber's failures and triumph. *Revue Internationale de Philosophie, 126,* 441–459.

Kaufmann, W. (1980). *Discovering the mind:* Vol. 2. *Nietzsche, Heidegger, and Buber.* New York: McGraw-Hill.

Kepnes, S. (1992). *The text as thou: Martin Buber's dialogical hermeneutics and narrative theology.* Bloomington: Indiana University Press.

King, A. (1992). What is postmodern rhetoric? In A. King (Ed.), *Postmodern political communication: The fringe challenges the center* (pp. 1–11). Westport, CT: Praeger.

Kirschenbaum, H. (1979). *On becoming Carl Rogers.* New York: Delacorte Press.

Kirschenbaum, H. (1991). Denigrating Carl Rogers: William Coulson's last crusade. *Journal of Counseling and Development, 69,* 411–413.

Kirschenbaum, H. (1995). Carl Rogers. In M. M. Suhd (Ed.), *Positive regard: Carl Rogers and other notables he influenced* (pp. 1–90). Palo Alto, CA: Science and Behavior Books.

Kirschenbaum, H., & Henderson, V. L. (Eds.). (1989a). *Carl Rogers: Dialogues—Conversations with Martin Buber, Paul Tillich, B. F. Skinner, Gregory Bateson, Michael Polanyi, Rollo May, and others.* Boston: Houghton Mifflin.

Kirschenbaum, H., & Henderson, V. L. (Eds.). (1989b). *The Carl Rogers reader.* Boston: Houghton Mifflin.

Klapp, O. E. (1964). *Symbolic leaders: Public dramas and public men.* Chicago: Aldine.

Klapp, O. E. (1969). *Collective search for identity.* New York: Holt.

Kofman, F., & Senge, P. M. (1993). Communities of commitment: The heart of learning organizations. *Organizational Dynamics, 22,* 5–22.

Kohl, G. (1997). *The language of* I and Thou. Paper presented at the National Communication Association convention, Chicago.

Kramer, P. D. (1989). *Moments of engagement: Intimate psychotherapy in a technological age.* New York: Norton.

Kramer, P. D. (1995). Introduction. In C. Rogers, *On becoming a person* (pp. ix–xv). Boston: Houghton Mifflin.

Laing, R. D. (1969). *Self and others* (2nd ed.). Baltimore: Penguin.

Lambeth, E. B., Meyer, P. E., & Thorson, E. (Eds.). (1998). *Assessing public journalism.* Columbia: University of Missouri Press.

Lannamann, J. W. (1992). Deconstructing the person and changing the subject of interpersonal studies. *Communication Theory, 2,* 139–148.

Leeds-Hurwitz, W. (1992). Social approaches to interpersonal communication. *Communication Theory, 2,* 131–139.

Leeds-Hurwitz, W. (Ed.). (1995). *Social approaches to communication.* New York: Guilford.

Lewin, K. (1951). *Field theory in social science: Selected papers* (D. Cartwright, Ed.). New York: Harper & Row.

Lietaer, G., Rombauts, J., & Van Balen, R. (Eds.). (1990). *Client–centered and experiential psychotherapy in the nineties.* Louvain, Belgium: Leuven University Press.

Lingis, A. (1994). *The community of those who have nothing in common.* Bloomington: Indiana University Press.

Lippmann, W. (1922). *Public opinion.* New York: Macmillan.

Littlejohn, S. W. (1983). *Theories of human communication* (2nd ed.). Belmont, CA: Wadsworth.

Lyotard, J.-F. (1984). *The postmodern condition: A report on knowledge* (G. Bennington & B. Massumi, Trans.). Minneapolis: University of Minnesota Press.

MacIntyre, A. (1984). *After virtue* (2nd ed.). Notre Dame, IN: University of Notre Dame Press.

Manheim, W. (1974). *Martin Buber.* New York: Twayne.

Mansbridge, J. J. (1980). *Beyond adversary democracy.* New York: Basic Books.

Mansbridge, J. (1990, Spring). Feminism and democracy. *American Prospect, 1,* 127.

Maranhao, T. (Ed.). (1990). *The interpretation of dialogue.* Chicago: University of Chicago Press.

Marcel, G. (1967). I and thou (F. Williams, Trans.). In P. Schilpp & M. Friedman (Eds.), *The philosophy of Martin Buber* (pp. 41–48). La Salle, IL: Open Court.

Masson, J. M. (1989). *Against therapy: Emotional tyranny and the myth of psychological healing.* New York: Atheneum.

Mathews, D. (1994a, Summer). . . . afterthoughts. *Kettering Review,* pp. 67–70.

Mathews, D. F. (1994b). *Politics for people: Finding a responsible public voice.* Urbana: University of Illinois Press.

McLaughlin, M. L. (1984). *Conversation: How talk is organized.* Beverly Hills, CA: Sage.

McNamee, S., Gergen, K. J., & Associates. (1999). *Relational responsibility: Resources for sustainable dialogue.* Thousand Oaks, CA: Sage.

McPhail, M. (1991). Complicity: The theory of negative difference. *Howard Journal of Communications, 3,* 1–13.

McPhail, M. (1996). *Zen and the art of rhetoric: An inquiry into coherence.* Albany: State University of New York Press.

McPhail, M. (1997). (Re)constructing the color line: Complicity and black conservatism. *Communication Theory, 7,* 162–178.

McPhail, M. (1998). From complicity to coherence: Rereading the rhetoric of Afrocentricity. *Western Journal of Communication, 62,* 114–140.

Mead, G. H. (1934). *Mind, self, and society: From the standpoint of a social behaviorist* (C. Morris, Intro. & Ed.). Chicago: University of Chicago Press.

Mearns, D., & Thorne, B. (1988). *Person-centred counselling in action.* London: Sage.

Mendes-Flohr, P. R. (1989). *From mysticism to dialogue: Martin Buber's transformation of German social thought.* Detroit: Wayne State University Press.

Merleau-Ponty, M. (1973). *The prose of the world* (C. Lefort, Ed.; J. O'Neill, Trans.). Evanston, IL: Northwestern University Press.

Mishler, E. G. (1986). *Research interviewing: Context and narrative.* Cambridge, MA: Harvard University Press.

Moonan, W. (1981). *Martin Buber and his critics: An annotated bibliography of writings in English through 1978.* New York: Garland.

Moore, D. J. (1974). *Martin Buber: Prophet of religious secularism— The criticism of institutional religion in the writings of Martin Buber.* Philadelphia: Jewish Publication Society of America.

Morgan, E. P. (1956a). Morgan to Rogers, 8 May 1956. Unpublished letter from the Carl R. Rogers Collection, Collections of the Manuscript Division, Library of Congress, Washington, DC (box 80, folder 7).

Morgan, E. P. (1956b). Morgan to Rogers, 13 September 1956. Unpublished letter from the Carl R. Rogers Collection, Collections of the Manuscript Division, Library of Congress, Washington, DC (box 80, folder 7).

Morson, G. S., & Emerson, C. (1990). *Mikhail Bakhtin: Creation of a prosaics.* Stanford, CA: Stanford University Press.

Moyers, B. (1995a). *The language of life: A festival of poets.* New York: Doubleday.

Moyers, B. (1995b). *The language of life: A festival of poets* [Collection of 8 Audio Cassette Recordings]. New York: Bantam Doubleday Dell Audio.

Mumby, D. (1997). Modernism, postmodernism, and communication studies: A rereading of an ongoing debate. *Communication Theory, 7,* 1–28.

National Endowment for the Humanities. (1995). *A national conversation on American pluralism and identity: The conversation kit.* Washington, DC: Author.

Neighborhood salon: Birth of a salon. (1992, July/August). *Utne Reader,* pp. 49–64.

Neighborhood salon: How to start (or jump start) one. (1993, July/August). *Utne Reader,* pp. 53–57.

Neumayr, G. (1995, 19 March). Dealing in bad medicine. *National Catholic Register,* p. 2.

Noddings, N. (1984). *Caring: A feminine approach to ethics and moral education.* Berkeley: University of California Press.

Noel, J. R., & De Chenne, T. K. (1974). Three dimensions of psychotherapy: I-we-thou. In D. A. Wexler & L. N. Rice (Eds.), *Innovations in client-centered therapy* (pp. 247–257). New York: Wiley.

Noelle-Neumann, E. (1984). *The spiral of silence: Public opinion—our social skin.* Chicago: University of Chicago Press.

Nofsinger, R. E. (1991). *Everyday conversation.* Newbury Park, CA: Sage.

O'Hara, M. (1995). Carl Rogers: Scientist and mystic. *Journal of Humanistic Psychology, 35,* 40–53.

O'Hara, M. (1997). Relational empathy: Beyond modernist egocentrism to postmodern holistic contextualism. In A. C. Bohart & L. S. Greenberg (Eds.), *Empathy reconsidered: New directions in psychotherapy* (pp. 295–319). Washington, DC: American Psychological Association.

Ong, W. J. (1967). *The presence of the word: Some prolegomena for cultural and religious history.* New York: Simon and Schuster.

Ong, W. J. (1977). *Interfaces of the word: Studies in the evolution of consciousness and culture.* Ithaca, NY: Cornell University Press.

Ong, W. J. (1982). *Orality and literacy: The technologizing of the word.* London: Methuen.

Ong, W. J. (1995). Hermeneutic forever: Voice, text, digitization, and the "I." *Oral Tradition, 10,* 3–26.

Palmer, R. E. (1969). *Hermeneutics.* Evanston, IL: Northwestern University Press.

Panko, S. M. (1976). *Martin Buber.* Waco, TX: Word Books.

Patterson, C. H. (1985). *The therapeutic relationship: Foundations for an eclectic psychotherapy.* Monterey, CA: Brooks/Cole.

Pearce, K. A., & Pearce, W. B. (2001). The Public Dialogue Consortium's school-wide dialogue process: A communication approach to develop citizenship skills and enhance school climate. *Communication Theory, 11,* 105–123.

Pearce, W. B. (1989). *Communication and the human condition.* Carbondale: Southern Illinois University Press.

Pearce, W. B. (1993). Achieving dialogue with "the other" in the postmodern world. In P. Gaunt (Ed.), *Beyond agendas: New directions in communication research* (pp. 59–74). Westport, CT: Greenwood.

Pearce, W. B. (1998). On putting social justice in the discipline of communication and putting enriched concepts of communication in social justice research and practice. *Journal of Applied Communication Research, 26,* 272–278.

Pearce, W. B., & Cronen, V. E. (1980). *Communication, action and meaning: The creation of social realities.* New York: Praeger.

Pearce, W. B., & Littlejohn, S. W. (1997). *Moral conflict: When social worlds collide.* Thousand Oaks, CA: Sage.

Pearce, W. B., & Pearce, K. A. (1999). "Volverse público": el trabajo sistémico en los contextos públicos ("Going public": Working systemically in public contexts). In F. Schnitman & D. y Schnitman, J. (Eds.), *Resolución de Conflictos. Nuevos Diseños, Nuevos Contextos* (pp. 179–212). Buenos Aires: Granica.

Pearce, W. B., & Pearce, K. A. (2000). Combining passions and abilities: Toward dialogic virtuosity. *Southern Communication Journal, 65,* 161–175.

Pearce, W. B., & Pearce, K. A. (2000). Extending the theory of the coordinated management of meaning ("CMM") through a community dialogue process. *Communication Theory, 10,* 405–423.

Pearce, W. B., & Walters, K. (1997a). *Public Dialogue Consortium.* Paper presented at the Central States Communication Association convention, St. Louis.

Pearce, W. B., & Walters, K. (1997b). *Why we do the work we do, and why we work the way we work: A brief description of the beliefs and commitments of the Public Dialogue Consortium.* Paper presented at the Central States Communication Association convention, St. Louis.

Pentony, P. (1987). Some thoughts about Carl Rogers. *Person-Centered Review, 2,* 419–421.

Person-to-person. (1957, 1 July). *Time,* pp. 34–35.

Peterson, J. D. (1976). *Carl Rogers and his ways of being in interpersonal relationships.* Master's thesis, Kansas School of Religion and University of Kansas.

Phillips, D. L. (1993). *Looking backward: A critical appraisal of communitarian thought.* Princeton, NJ: Princeton University Press.

Phillips, G. M. (1976). Rhetoric and its alternatives as bases for examination of intimate communication. *Communication Quarterly, 24,* 11–23.

Polanyi, M. (1962). *Personal knowledge.* Chicago: University of Chicago Press.

Polanyi, M., & Rogers, C. R. (1968). A dialogue. In W. R. Coulson & C. R. Rogers (Eds.), *Man and the science of man* (pp. 193–201). Columbus, OH: Charles E. Merrill.

Poole, M. S., & McPhee, R. M. (1994). Methodology in interpersonal communication research. In M. L. Knapp & G. R. Miller (Eds.), *Handbook of interpersonal communication* (2nd ed.) (pp. 42–102). Thousand Oaks, CA: Sage.

Poster, M. (1990). *The mode of information: Poststructuralism and social context.* Chicago: University of Chicago Press.

Poster, M. (1995). *The second media age.* Cambridge, UK: Polity.

Postman, N. (1985). *Amusing ourselves to death: Public discourse in the age of show business.* New York: Penguin.

Poulakos, J. (1974). The components of dialogue. *Western Speech, 38,* 199–212.

Prigogine, I. (1978). *From being to becoming.* San Francisco: W. H. Freeman.

Program: Mid-West Conference with Dr. Martin Buber. (1957). Michigan Historical Collections, Bentley Historical Library, University of Michigan.

Raskin, N. J., & Rogers, C. R. (1989). Person-centered therapy. In R. J. Corsini & D. Wedding (Eds.), *Current psychotherapies* (4th ed.) (pp. 155–194). Itasca, IL: F. E. Peacock.

Rheingold, H. (1993). *The virtual community: Homesteading on the electronic frontier.* New York: HarperPerennial.

Riegel, K. F. (1979). *Foundations of dialectical psychology.* New York: Academic Press.

Roffey, J. W. (1980). *A hermeneutic critique of counseling psychology: Ricoeur and Rogers.* Doctoral dissertation, University of Kentucky.

Rogers, C. R. (nd-a). Untitled notes prepared for 1956 dialogue with B. F. Skinner at the American Psychological Association convention. From the Carl R. Rogers Collection, Collections of the

Manuscript Division, Library of Congress, Washington, DC (box 80, folder 8).

Rogers, C. R. (nd-b). Untitled notes prepared for 1962 dialogue with B. F. Skinner at the University of Minnesota, Duluth. From the Carl R. Rogers Collection, Collections of the Manuscript Division, Library of Congress, Washington, DC (box 81, folder 16).

Rogers, C. R. (nd-c). Martin Buber—*I & Thou* (Trans. by R. G. Smith, Edinburgh: Clark, 1950). Unpublished notes from the Carl R. Rogers Collection, Collections of the Manuscript Division, Library of Congress, Washington, DC (box 80, folder 13).

Rogers, C. R. (nd-d). Buber's concept of inclusion. Unpublished handout [includes quotes from the "Education" essay published in Buber's *Between Man and Man*] from the Carl R. Rogers Collection, Collections of the Manuscript Division, Library of Congress, Washington, DC (box 140, folder 8).

Rogers, C. R. (nd-e). Some issues concerning the control of human behavior. Typescript from the Carl R. Rogers Collection, Collections of the Manuscript Division, Library of Congress, Washington, DC (box 80, folder 12).

Rogers, C. R. (1939). *The clinical treatment of the problem child.* Boston: Houghton Mifflin.

Rogers, C. R. (1942a). *Counseling and psychotherapy.* Boston: Houghton Mifflin.

Rogers, C. R. (1942b). The use of electrically recorded interviews in improving psychotherapeutic techniques. *American Journal of Orthopsychiatry, 12,* 429–434.

Rogers, C. R. (1951). *Client-centered therapy: Its current practice, implications, and theory.* Boston: Houghton Mifflin.

Rogers, C. R. (1952). Psychology 450A: Client-centered therapy in relation to current philosophical thinking. Unpublished graduate course syllabus, spring quarter, 1952, University of Chicago. From the Carl R. Rogers Collection, Collections of the Manuscript Division, Library of Congress, Washington, DC (box 127, folder 7).

Rogers, C. R. (1956a). Rogers to Skinner, 14 May 1956. Unpublished letter from the Carl R. Rogers Collection, Collections of the Manuscript Division, Library of Congress, Washington, DC (box 80, folder 7).

Rogers, C. R. (1956b). Rogers to Skinner, 24 May 1956. Unpublished letter from the Carl R. Rogers Collection, Collections of the Manuscript Division, Library of Congress, Washington, DC (box 80, folder 7).

Rogers, C. R. (1956c). Rogers to Skinner, 30 July 1956. Unpublished letter from the Carl R. Rogers Collection, Collections of the Manuscript Division, Library of Congress, Washington, DC (box 80, folder 7).

Rogers, C. R. (1956d, 20 October). *The essence of psychotherapy: A client-centered view.* Paper presented at the first meeting of the American Academy of Psychotherapists, New York. From the Carl R. Rogers Collection, Collections of the Manuscript Division, Library of Congress, Washington, DC (box 126, folder 2). [Included in *Counseling Center Discussion Papers,* 2(26), 1956, University of Chicago]

Rogers, C. R. (1956e, 20 October). *The essence of psychotherapy:* Moments of movement. Draft of a paper presented at the first meeting of the American Academy of Psychotherapists, New York. From the Carl R. Rogers Memorial Library, Center for Studies of the Person, La Jolla, CA.

Rogers, C. R. (1956f). Review of Reinhold Niebuhr's *The self and the dramas of history. Chicago Theological Seminary Register, 46,* 13–14.

Rogers, C. R. (1957a). Dialogue with Martin Buber: Nature of man as revealed in interpersonal rel. Unpublished notes from the Carl R. Rogers Collection, Collections of the Manuscript Division, Library of Congress, Washington, DC (box 80, folder 13).

Rogers, C. R. (1957b). The necessary and sufficient conditions of therapeutic personality change. *Journal of Consulting Psychology, 21,* 95–103.

Rogers, C. R. (1957c). Questions not used. Unpublished notes prepared for the dialogue with Buber from the Carl R. Rogers Collection, Collections of the Manuscript Division, Library of Congress, Washington, DC (box 80, folder 13).

Rogers, C. R. (1959a). The essence of psychotherapy: A client-centered view. *Annals of Psychotherapy, 1,* 51–57.

Rogers, C. R. (1959b). A theory of therapy, personality, and interpersonal relationships, as developed in the client-centered framework. In S. Koch (Ed.), *Psychology: A study of a science:* Vol. 3. *Formulations of the person and social context* (pp. 184–256). New York: McGraw-Hill.

Rogers, C. R. (1960). Significant trends in the client-centered orientation. In L. E. Abt & B. F. Riess (Eds.), *Progress in clinical psychology* (Vol. 4) (pp. 85–99). New York: Grune & Stratton.

Rogers, C. R. (1961). *On becoming a person.* Boston: Houghton Mifflin.

Rogers, C. R. (1962). Opening remarks: Rogers–Skinner dialogue. Manuscript and notes, typed and handwritten (6/5/62), for the 1962

Rogers–Skinner dialogue at Univesity of Minnesota Duluth. From the Carl R. Rogers Collection, Collections of the Manuscript Division, Library of Congress, Washington, DC (box 81, folder 16).

Rogers, C. R. (1967). Some learnings from a study of psychotherapy with schizophrenics. In C. R. Rogers & B. Stevens (Eds.), *Person to person: The problem of being human* (pp. 181–192). Lafayette, CA: Real People Press.

Rogers, C. R. (1969). *Freedom to learn: A view of what education might become.* Columbus, OH: Charles E. Merrill.

Rogers, C. R. (1970). *Carl Rogers on encounter groups.* New York: Harper & Row.

Rogers, C. R. (1971a). The interpersonal relationship: The core of guidance. In C. R. Rogers & B. Stevens (Eds.), *Person to person: The problem of being human* (pp. 85–101). New York: Pocket Books.

Rogers, C. R. (1971b). Some learnings from a study of psychotherapy with schizophrenics. In C. R. Rogers & B. Stevens (Eds.), *Person to person. The problem of being human* (pp. 183–195). New York: Pocket Books.

Rogers, C. R. (1972a). *Becoming partners: Marriage and its alternatives.* New York: Delacorte.

Rogers, C. R. (1972b). Some social issues which concern me. *Journal of Humanistic Psychology, 12,* 45–60.

Rogers, C. R. (1975). Empathic: An unappreciated way of being. *Counseling Psychologist, 5,* 2–10.

Rogers, C. R. (1977a). *Carl Rogers on personal power.* New York: Dell.

Rogers, C. R. (1977b). Rogers to Susan Perretta [Institute for Scientific Information], 1 December 1977. Unpublished letter from the Carl R. Rogers Collection, Collections of the Manuscript Division, Library of Congress, Washington, DC (box 17, folder 6).

Rogers, C. R. (1978). Do we need "a" reality? *Dawnpoint, 1,* 6–9.

Rogers, C. R. (1980). *A way of being.* Boston: Houghton Mifflin.

Rogers, C. R. (1983). *Freedom to learn for the 80s* (Rev. ed.). Columbus, OH: Charles E. Merrill.

Rogers, C. R. (1986a). Client-centered therapy. In I. L. Kutash & A. Wolf (Eds.), *Psychotherapist's casebook: Theory and technique in the practice of modern therapies* (pp. 197–208). San Francisco: Jossey-Bass.

Rogers, C. R. (1986b). Reflection of feelings. *Person-Centered Review, 1,* 375–377.

Rogers, C. R. (1987). Comments on the issue of equality in therapy. *Journal of Humanistic Psychology, 27,* 38–40.

Rogers, C. R., & Dymond, R. F. (Eds.). (1954). *Psychotherapy and personality change.* Chicago: University of Chicago Press.

Rogers, C. R., & Farson, R. E. (1957). *Active listening.* Chicago: University of Chicago Industrial Relations Center.

Rogers, C. R., Gendlin, E. T., Kiesler, D. J., & Truax, C. B. (Eds.). (1967). *The therapeutic relationship and its impact: A study of psychotherapy with schizophrenics.* Madison: University of Wisconsin Press.

Rogers, C. R., with Russell, D. E. (1991). *The quiet revolutionary* [Draft dated 1/25/91]. Santa Barbara, CA: Library Oral History Program, University of California at Santa Barbara.

Rogers, C. R., & Stevens, B. (Eds.), (1967). *Person to person: The problem of being human.* Lafayette, CA: Real People Press.

Rome, S., & Rome, B. (Eds.). (1964). *Philosophical interrogations: Interrogations of Martin Buber, John Wild, Jean Wahl, Brand Blanshard, Paul Weiss, Charles Hartsborne, Paul Tillich.* New York: Holt, Rinehart, and Winston.

Rorty, R. (1989). *Contingency, irony, and solidarity.* Cambridge: Cambridge University Press.

Rosaldo, R. (1989). *Culture and truth: The remaking of social analysis.* Boston: Beacon.

Rosen, J. (1993). *Community connectedness: Passwords for public journalists.* St. Petersburg, FL: The Poynter Institute for Media Studies.

Rosen, J. (1994a). Making things more public: On the political responsibility of the media intellectual. *Critical Studies in Mass Communication, 11,* 363–388.

Rosen, J. (1994b, Fall). *Public journalism: A progress report.* New York: Project on Public Life and the Press, New York University.

Rosen, J. (1999). *What are journalists for?* New Haven, CT: Yale University Press.

Rosen, J., & Merritt, D., Jr. (1994). *Public journalism: Theory and practice.* Dayton, OH: Kettering Foundation.

Roseneau, P. M. (1992). *Post-modernism and the social sciences: Insights, inroads, and intrusions.* Princeton, NJ: Princeton University Press.

Rosenfield, L. W. (1974). The experience of criticism. *Quarterly Journal of Speech, 60,* 489–496.

Rosenzweig, F. (1991a). Rosenzweig to Buber, undated. In N. N. Glatzer & P. Mendes-Flohr (Eds.), *The letters of Martin Buber: A life of dialogue* (No. 274). New York: Schocken.

Rosenzweig, F. (1991b). Rosenzweig to Buber, 20 September 1922. In N. N. Glatzer & P. Mendes-Flohr (Eds.), *The letters of Martin Buber: A life of dialogue* (No. 279). New York: Schocken.

Ross, D., & Friends. (1998). *A Tao of dialogue: A manual of dialogic communication*. Blue Hill, ME: Medicine Bear.

Roth, S., Chasin, L., Chasin, R., Becker, C., & Herzig, M. (1992). From debate to dialogue: A facilitating role for family therapists in the public forum. *Dulwich Centre Newsletter, 2*, 41–48.

Rudolph, F. (1962). *The American college and university: A history.* New York: Vintage.

The salon-keeper's companion: An Utne Reader *guide to conducting salons, council and study circles.* Minneapolis, MN: Utne Reader Books.

Sampson, E. E. (1993). *Celebrating the other: A dialogic account of human nature.* Boulder, CO: Westview Press.

Sandel, M. (1982). *Liberalism and the limits of justice.* Cambridge: Cambridge University Press.

Sandra, J. N. (1997). *The joy of conversation: The complete guide to salons.* Minneapolis, MN: Utne Reader Books.

Saunders, H. H. (1999). *A public peace process: Sustained dialogue to transform racial and ethnic conflicts.* New York: St. Martin's Press.

Schaeder, G. (Ed.). (1972). *Martin Buber: Briefwechsel aus sieben jahrzehnten* (Vol. 1). Heidelberg: Verlag Lambert Schneider.

Schaeder, G. (1973a). *The Hebrew humanism of Martin Buber* (N. J. Jacobs, Trans.). Detroit: Wayne State University Press.

Schaeder, G. (Ed.). (1973b). *Martin Buber: Briefwechsel aus sieben jahrzehnten* (Vol. 2). Heidelberg: Verlag Lambert Schneider.

Schaeder, G. (Ed.). (1975). *Martin Buber: Briefwechsel aus sieben jahrzehnten* (Vol. 3). Heidelberg: Verlag Lambert Schneider.

Schaeder, G. (1991). Martin Buber: A biographical sketch. In N. N. Glatzer & P. Mendes-Flohr (Eds.), *The letters of Martin Buber: A life of dialogue* (pp. 1–62). New York: Schocken.

Schein, E. H. (1993). On dialogue, culture, and organizational learning. *Organizational Dynamics, 22*, 40–51.

Schilpp, P. A., & Friedman, M. (Eds.). (1967). *The philosophy of Martin Buber.* La Salle, IL: Open Court.

Schmidt, G. G. (1995). *Martin Buber's formative years: From German culture to Jewish renewal, 1897–1909.* Tuscaloosa: University of Alabama Press.

Schoen, S. (1994). *Presence of mind: Literary and philosophical roots of a wise psychotherapy.* Highlands, NY: The Gestalt Journal Press.

Schrag, C. O. (1969). *Experience and being.* Evanston, IL: Northwestern University Press.

Schrag, C. O. (1986). *Communicative praxis and the space of subjectivity.* Bloomington: Indiana University Press.

Schrag, C. O. (1992). *The resources of rationality: A response to the postmodern challenge.* Bloomington: Indiana University Press.

Schultz, D. (1977). *Growth psychology: Models of the healthy personality.* New York: Van Nostrand Reinhold.

Schutz, A. (1967). *The phenomenology of the social world* (G. Walsh & F. Lehnert, Trans.). Evanston, IL: Northwestern University Press.

Seckinger, D. S. (1976). The Buber–Rogers dialogue: Theory confirmed in experience. *Journal of Thought, 11,* 143–149.

Senge, P. M. (1990). *The fifth discipline.* New York: Doubleday.

Sharf, B. F. (1979). Rhetorical analysis of nonpublic discourse. *Communication Quarterly, 27,* 21–30.

Shem, S., & Surrey, J. (1998). *We have to talk: Healing dialogues between women and men.* New York: Basic Books.

Shlien, J. M (1997). Empathy in psychotherapy: A vital mechanism? Yes. Therapist's conceit? All too often. By itself enough? No. In A. C. Bohart & L. S. Greenberg (Eds.), *Empathy reconsidered: New directions in psychotherapy* (pp. 63–80). Washington, DC: American Psychological Association.

Shor, I., & Freire, P. (1987). *A pedagogy for liberation: Dialogues on transforming education.* Granby, MA: Bergin & Garvey.

Shotter, J. (1992). Bakhtin and Billig: Monological vs. dialogical practices. *American Behavioral Scientist, 36,* 8–21.

Shotter, J. (1993a). *Conversational realities: Constructing life through language.* London: Sage.

Shotter, J. (1993b). *Cultural politics of everyday life.* Toronto: University of Toronto Press.

Shotter, J. (1995). Dialogical psychology. In J. A. Smith, R. Harrè, & L. Van Langenhove (Eds.), *Rethinking psychology* (pp. 160–178). London: Sage.

Shotter, J. (2000). Inside dialogic realities: From an abstract-systemic to a participatory-wholistic understanding of communication. *Southern Communication Journal, 65,* 119–132.

Sillars, A. L. (1974). Expression and control in human interaction: Perspective on humanistic psychology. *Western Speech, 38,* 269–277.

Silverman, H. J. (1990). The philosophy of postmodernism. In H. J. Silverman (Ed.), *Postmodernism—Philosophy and the arts* (pp. 1–9). New York: Routledge.

Simon, A. E. (1974). Martin Buber. In *The new encyclopedia Britannica* (Macropedia, Vol. 3, pp. 358–361). Chicago: Encyclopedia Britannica.

Simon, E. (1991). Preface to the German edition. In N. N. Glatzer & P. Mendes-Flohr (Eds.), *The letters of Martin Buber: A life of dialogue* (pp. xi–xiii). New York: Schocken.

Simons, H. W. (Ed.). (1990). *The rhetorical turn: Invention and persuasion in the conduct of inquiry.* Chicago: University of Chicago Press.

Skinner, B. F. (1955). Skinner to Rogers, 27 December 1955. Unpublished letter from the Carl R. Rogers Collection, Collections of the Manuscript Division, Library of Congress, Washington, DC (box 80, folder 7).

Skinner, B. F. (1956a). Skinner to Rogers, 21 May 1956. Unpublished letter from the Carl R. Rogers Collection, Collections of the Manuscript Division, Library of Congress, Washington, DC (box 80, folder 7).

Skinner, B. F. (1956b). Skinner to Rogers, 20 August 1956. Unpublished letter from the Carl R. Rogers Collection, Collections of the Manuscript Division, Library of Congress, Washington, DC (box 80, folder 7).

Slack, S. (1985). Reflections on a workshop with Carl Rogers. *Journal of Humanistic Psychology, 25*, 35–42.

Smith, C. R., & Douglas, D. G. (1973). Philosophical principles in the traditional and emerging views of rhetoric. In D. G. Douglas (Ed.), *Philosophers on rhetoric: Traditional and emerging views* (pp. 15–22). Skokie, IL: National Textbook.

Smith, J. A., Harrè, R., & Langenhove, L. V. (Eds.). (1995). *Rethinking psychology.* London: Sage.

Smith, R. G. (1958). Translator's preface to second edition. In M. Buber, *I and thou* (2nd ed.) (R. G. Smith, Trans.; pp. v–xii). New York: Scribner's.

Smith, R. G. (1967). *Martin Buber.* Richmond, VA: John Knox Press.

Snyder, I. (1996). *Hypertext: The electronic labyrinth.* Melbourne: Melbourne University Press.

Stephenson, W. (1953). *The study of behavior: Q-technique and its methodology.* Chicago: University of Chicago Press.

Stewart, J. (1978). Foundations of dialogic communication. *Quarterly Journal of Speech, 64*, 183–201.

Stewart, J. (1983). Interpretive listening: An alternative to empathy. *Communication Education, 32*, 379–391.

Stewart, J. (1985). Martin Buber's central insight: Implications for his philosophy of dialogue. In M. Dascal (Ed.), *Dialogue: An interdisciplinary approach* (pp. 321–335). Amsterdam: John Benjamins.

Stewart, J. (1991). A postmodern look at traditional communication postulates. *Western Journal of Speech Communication, 55,* 354–379.

Stewart, J. (1994). Foreword. In R. Anderson, K. N. Cissna, & R. C. Arnett (Eds.), *The reach of dialogue: Confirmation, voice, and community* (pp. viii–xx). Cresskill, NJ: Hampton Press.

Stewart, J. (Ed.). (1995). *Bridges not walls: A book about interpersonal communication* (6th ed.). New York: McGraw-Hill.

Stewart, J., & Thomas, M. (1986). Dialogic listening: Sculpting mutual meanings. In J. Stewart (Ed.) *Bridges not walls: A book about interpersonal communication* (4th ed.) (pp. 180–196). New York: Random House.

Stewart, J., & Zediker, K. (2000). Dialogue as tensional, ethical practice. *Southern Communication Journal, 65,* 224–242.

Still R. D. Laing after all these years: An interview with R. D. Laing. (1992). In R. Simon (Ed.), *One on one: Conversations with the shapers of family therapy* (pp. 21–33). Washington, DC and New York: Family Therapy Institute and Guilford Press.

Stone, D., Patton, B., & Heen, S. (1999). *Difficult conversations: How to discuss what matters most.* New York: Viking.

Stubbs, M. (1983). *Discourse analysis: The sociolinguistic analysis of natural language.* Chicago: University of Chicago Press.

Suhd, M. M. (Ed.). (1995). *Positive regard: Carl Rogers and other notables he influenced.* Palo Alto, CA: Science & Behavior Books.

Sundararajan, L. (1995). Echoes after Carl Rogers: "Reflective listening" revisited. *Humanistic Psychologist, 23,* 259–271.

Swidler, L., Cobb, J. B., Knitter, P. F., & Hellwig, M. K. (1990). *Death or dialogue?: From the age of monologue to the age of dialogue.* Philadelphia: Trinity Press International.

Tannen, D. (1989). *Talking voices: Repetition, dialogue, and imagery in conversational discourse.* Cambridge: Cambridge University Press.

Tannen, D. (1998). *The argument culture: Moving from debate to dialogue.* New York: Random House.

Taylor, C. (1985). *Human agency and language: Philosophical papers 1.* Cambridge: Cambridge University Press.

Taylor, C. (1989). Cross-purposes: The liberal-communitarian debate. In N. L. Rosenblum (Ed.), *Liberalism and the moral life* (pp. 159–182). Cambridge, MA: Harvard University Press.

Taylor, C. (1991). *The ethics of authenticity.* Cambridge, MA: Harvard University Press.

Taylor, M. C., & Saarinen, E. (1994). *Imagologies: Media philosophy.* London: Routledge.

Tedlock, D. (1983). *The spoken word and the work of interpretation.* Philadelphia: University of Pennsylvania Press.

Tedlock, D., & Mannheim, B. (Eds.). (1995). *The dialogic emergence of culture.* Urbana: University of Illinois Press.

Teich, N. (1992a). General introduction. In N. Teich (Ed.), *Rogerian perspectives: Collaborative rhetoric for oral and written communication* (pp. 1–19). Norwood, NJ: Ablex.

Teich, N. (Ed.). (1992b). *Rogerian perspectives: Collaborative rhetoric for oral and written communication.* Norwood, NJ: Ablex.

Theroux, P. (Ed.). (1997). *The book of eulogies.* New York: Scribner.

Thomlison, T. D. (1982). *Toward interpersonal dialogue.* New York: Longman.

Thorne, B. (1991). *Person-centered counseling: Therapeutic and spiritual tensions.* London: Whurr.

Thorne, B. (1992). *Carl Rogers.* London: Sage.

Todorov, T. (1984). *Mikhail Bakhtin: The dialogical principle* (W. Godzich, Trans.). Minneapolis: University of Minnesota Press.

Toulmin, S. (1988). The recovery of practical philosophy. *American Scholar, 57,* 337–352.

Tournier, P. (1973). *The meaning of persons.* New York: Harper & Row Perennial Library.

Trenholm, S. (1986). *Human communication theory.* Englewood Cliffs, NJ: Prentice-Hall.

Truax, C. B., & Carkhuff, R. R. (1967). *Toward effective counseling and psychotherapy: Training and practice.* Chicago: Aldine.

Tyler, S. A. (1987). *The unspeakable: Discourse, dialogue, and rhetoric in the postmodern world.* Madison: University of Wisconsin Press.

Van Balen, R. (1990). The therapeutic relationship according to Carl Rogers: Only a climate? A dialogue? Or both? In G. Lietaer, J. Rombauts, & R. Van Balen (Eds.), *Client-centered and experiential psychotherapy in the nineties* (pp. 65–85). Leuven: Leuven University Press.

Van Belle, H. A. (1980). *Basic intent and therapeutic approach of Carl R. Rogers: A study of his view of man in relation to his view of therapy, personality and interpersonal relations.* Toronto: Wedge.

van Dijk, T. A. (1985). Introduction: Dialogue as discourse and interaction. In T. A. van Dijk (Ed.), *Handbook of discourse analysis: Vol. 3. Discourse and dialogue* (pp. 1–11). London: Academic Press.

Vermes, P. (1988). *Buber.* New York: Grove Press.

Vitz, P. C. (1994). *Psychology as religion: The cult of self-worship* (2nd ed.). Grand Rapids, MI: William B. Eerdmans.

Waley, A. (1958). *The way and its power: A study of the Tao te Ching and its place in Chinese thought.* New York: Grove Press.

Wallach, M. A., & Wallach, L. (1983). *Psychology's sanction for selfishness: The error of egoism in theory and therapy.* San Francisco: W. H. Freeman.

Walters, K. A. (nd). *Public Dispute Consortium: Making communication work well in a complex world.* Cupertino, CA: Public Dispute Consortium.

Walzer, M. (1988). *The company of critics: Social criticism and political commitment in the twentieth century.* New York: Basic Books.

Warnke, G. (1987). *Gadamer: Hermeneutics, tradition, and reason.* Stanford, CA: Stanford University Press.

Watson, N. (1984). The empirical status of Rogers's hypotheses of the necessary and sufficient condition for effective psychotherapy. In R. Levant & J. M. Shlien (Eds.), *Client-centered therapy and the person-centered approach: New directions in theory, research, and practice* (pp. 17–40). New York: Praeger.

Watts, A. (1975). *Tao: The watercourse way.* New York: Pantheon.

Watzlawick, P., Beavin, J. H., & Jackson, D. D. (1967). *Pragmatics of human communication.* New York: Norton.

Werner, C. M., & Baxter, L. A. (1994). Temporal qualities of relationships: Organismic, transactional, and dialectical views. In M. L. Knapp & G. R. Miller (Eds.), *Handbook of interpersonal communication* (2nd ed.) (pp. 323–379). Thousand Oaks, CA: Sage.

Williams, R. (1985). *Keywords: A vocabulary of culture and society* (Rev. ed.). New York: Oxford University Press.

Witherell, C., & Noddings, N. (1991). Prologue: An invitation to our readers. In C. Witherell & N. Noddings (Eds.), *Stories lives tell: Narrative and dialogue in education* (pp. 1–12). New York: Teachers College Press.

Wold, A. H. (1992). *The dialogical alternative: Towards a theory of language and mind.* London: Scandinavian University Press.

Wood, J. K. (1988). Roundtable discussion. *Person-Centered Review, 3,* 382–388.

Wood, R. E. (1969). *Martin Buber's ontology: An analysis of* I and Thou. Evanston, IL: Northwestern University Press.

Yalom, I. D. (1995). Introduction. In C. Rogers, *A way of being* (pp. vii–xiii). Boston: Houghton Mifflin.

Yankelovich, D. (1999). *The magic of dialogue: Transforming conflict into cooperation.* New York: Simon and Schuster.

Yoshida, A. (1994). Beyond the alternative of "compulsion" or "freedom": Reflections on the Buber–Rogers dialogue. In D. M. Bethel & R. Miller (Eds.), *Compulsory schooling and human learning: The moral failure of public education in America and Japan* (pp. 89–102). San Francisco: Caddo Gap Press.

Young, I. M. (1990). *Justice and the politics of difference.* Princeton, NJ: Princeton University Press.

Zappan, J. P. (1980). Carl R. Rogers and political rhetoric. *Pre/Text, 1,* 95–113.

About the Authors

Kenneth N. Cissna is professor in the Department of Communication at the University of South Florida, and **Rob Anderson** is professor of Communication and professor of International Studies at Saint Louis University. Their collaborative work in the philosophy and practice of dialogue includes numerous articles and two previous books, *The Martin Buber–Carl Rogers Dialogue: A New Transcript with Commentary* (State University of New York Press, 1997), and the anthology *The Reach of Dialogue: Confirmation, Voice, and Community* (with Ronald C. Arnett) (Hampton, 1994).

Cissna is a former editor of the *Journal of Applied Communication Research* and *Southern Communication Journal* and of an award-winning collection, *Applied Communication in the 21st Century* (Lawrence Erlbaum, 1995). He is well known in the communication discipline for his contributions to confirmation theory within interpersonal communication, and to applied communication.

Anderson is the author, coauthor, or coeditor of nine previous books in communication theory, education, media studies, interviewing, and communication skills, including a dialogic exploration of contemporary journalism, *The Conversation of Journalism: Communication, Community, and News* (Praeger, 1994).

Barnett Pearce is co-principal, Pearce Associates—Specialists in Dialogic Communication; consultant, Public Dialogue Consortium; and member of the Faculty, Human and Organizational Development Program, The Fielding Institute. Dr. Pearce co-developed "coordinated management of meaning" theory, one of the most influential theories of communication in recent decades, and is the author or coauthor of many important books on communication, dialogue, and social constructionist perspectives on meaning, including *Moral Conflict: When Social Worlds Collide, Communication and the Human Condition*, and *Interpersonal Communication: Making Social Worlds*.

Author Index

Ackerman, Bruce A., 222
Agassi, Judith Buber, 268n. 1
Anderson, Harlene, 14, 65
Anderson, Rob, x, xxii, xxiv–xxv,
    9–11, 13, 26, 31, 68, 80, 85, 89,
    135, 148, 152, 158, 194, 232,
    240, 267nn. 1, 2, 268n. 2,
    270n. 12, 273n. 1, 274n. 5,
    274–275n. 1
Anderson, Raymond E., 74
Anzaldúa, Gloria, 263
Arendt, Hannah, 214, 215
Arneson, Pat, vii, 71, 267n. 2
Arnett, Ronald C., vii, 18, 26, 71, 84,
    93, 96, 97, 267n. 2, 270n. 12,
    271n. 6, 272n. 8, 274n. 1
Austin, Grey, 126
Avnon, Dan, 268n. 3
Ayres, Joe, 123

Bakan, David, 203
Bakhtin, Mikhail M., ix, 10, 19, 27,
    32, 204
Baldwin, Rev. DeWitt C., 3, 125
Barber, Benjamin B., 14, 209, 222
Barge, J. Kevin, ix
Barrett, William, 245, 246, 247,
    248–249
Barrett-Lennard, Godfrey T., 67
Bateson, Gregory, 161, 240
Baumann, Zygmunt, 194, 195, 197

Baxter, Leslie A., 148, 267n. 2,
    274n. 1
Beavin, Janet H., 161
Becker, Carol, 230, 257
Bellah, Robert N., 7, 68–69, 221
Bentley, Arthur F., 10, 75
Berger, Brigitte, 7
Berger, Peter, 7, 65, 187
Bergman, Shmuel Hugo, 267n. 2
Berry, Donald L., 180
Bird, S. Elizabeth, 12
Black, Jay, 233
Blumer, Herbert, 20
Bochner, Arthur P., 271n. 4
Bohart, Arthur C., 68
Bohm, David, vii, ix, 12, 228, 231,
    274n. 1
Bowen, Maria C. Villas-Boas, 94
Boyte, Harry C., 228
Bozarth, Jerold, 83
Brace, Kerry, 26
Branham, Robert James, 16
Brazier, David, 68, 193, 194
Breslauer, S. Daniel, 268nn. 1, 3
Brink, Debora D., 26, 64, 68, 130,
    134, 145, 180
Brown, Richard H., 20
Bruneau, Thomas, 91
Buber, Martin, xv, 1, 2, 3, 4, 5–6, 10,
    26, 29, 31, 37, 39, 40, 41, 43,
    44, 48, 49, 50–51, 52, 53, 54,

311

Buber, Martin (*cont.*), 87, 90, 95–96, 101, 102, 103, 104, 105, 106, 107, 109, 120, 124, 127, 130, 135, 136, 150, 154, 160, 161, 163, 169, 176, 178, 179, 187, 188, 189, 196, 202, 204, 205, 206, 211, 212, 213, 215, 244, 255–256, 260, 268n. 3, 269nn. 6, 8, 9, 270n. 11, 272n. 8, 273n. 4, 275n. 3
Buber, Rafael, 36
Burd, Stephen, 217
Burke, Kenneth, 20, 199
Burks, Don M., 71, 84, 86, 271n. 4
Burstow, Bonnie, 26, 130, 180

Cain, David J., 94
Carey, James W., 8–9
Carkhuff, Robert R., 95
Charity, Arthur, 13, 232
Chasin, Laura, 230, 257
Chasin, Richard, 230, 257
Chevigny, Paul, 14
Christians, Clifford, 221
Cissna, Kenneth N., x, xxii, xxiv–xxv, 9–11, 26, 31, 68, 80, 95, 135, 148, 152, 158, 194, 240, 267nn. 1, 2, 268n. 2, 270n. 12, 273n. 1, 274n. 5, 274–275n. 1
Claflin, Stephen T., 220
Clark, Gregory, 13
Clark, Katerina, 19, 204
Clarke, Arthur C., xiii
Cobb, John B., 267n. 2
Cohn, Margot, 36
Collins, Patricia Hill, 14
Crapanzano, Vincent, 14, 24
Cronen, Vernon, 229
Cushman, Phillip, 14, 67
Czubaroff, Jeanine, 18, 19

Dardenne, Robert., 13, 232
Dayan, Daniel, 237
De Chenne, Timothy K., 95
Denzin, Norman K., 20

De Ryck, Philippe, 76
Descartes, Rene, 39
DeVito, Joseph A., 86
Dewey, John, 8, 10, 20, 75, 108, 199
Douglas, Donald G., 18
Dymond, Rosalind F., 60, 81
Dyson, Michael E., 191

Edelman, Murray, 258
Edwards, Paul, 45, 46, 121
Eisenstadt, Shmuel N., 194, 198, 199, 268n. 1
Eliasoph, Nina, 215
Ellinor, Linda, vii, ix, 231, 267n. 2
Elliott, Robert, 68
Ellison, Ralph, 262
Ellul, Jacques, 7, 245–246
Emerson, Caryl, 19, 27
Entman, Robert M., 225
Etzioni, Amitai, 221
Evans, Richard D., 72, 74, 76
Evans, Sara M., 228

Fackler, P. Mark, 221
Fallows, James M., 218
Farber, Barry A., 64, 68
Farber, Leslie H., 105, 106
Farrell, Thomas B., 16
Farson, Richard E., 59, 66, 67, 76, 91, 96, 118, 119, 227, 240, 248, 271–272n. 7
Ferrarotti, Franco, 7
Ferré, John P., 221
Fishkin, James S., 13, 235–236
Flick, Deborah Lynn, vii
Flores, Lisa A., 224
Foss, Karen A., 16
Foss, Sonja K., 16, 19
Frank, David A., 16
Franzwa, Helen H., 271n. 4
Fraser, Nancy, 226
Freire, Paulo, 173, 252
Friedman, Maurice, xxii–xxiii, 2, 4, 26, 33, 36, 38, 39, 40, 41, 42, 45, 46, 48, 50, 51, 55, 56,

74–75, 79,80, 89, 92, 96, 99,
100, 102, 105, 106, 107, 108,
110, 116, 117, 121, 123, 124,
125, 126, 127, 128, 135, 136,
138, 144, 148, 150, 151, 155,
169, 179, 180, 184–185, 186,
205, 243, 244, 248, 252, 254,
262, 263, 268nn. 1, 2, 3, 4,
269nn. 8, 9, 270n. 11, 272n. 3,
273n. 4, 273–274n. 5, 274n. 6

Gadamer, Hans-Georg, 18, 23, 93,
193, 197
Galati, Michael, 74
Gates, Henry Louis, Jr., 224
Gaw, Beverly A., 80, 271n. 4
Geller, Leonard, 68
Gendlin, Eugene T., 48, 62, 63–66,
67, 82, 87
Gerard, Glenna, vii, ix, 231, 267n. 2
Gergen, Kenneth J., 24, 194, 267n. 2
Glaser, Susan R., 16
Glatzer, Nahum N., 44, 268n. 3,
269n. 5
Glendon, Mary Ann, 221
Goffman, Erving, 137, 155, 156,
161
Goodall, H. Loyd, Jr., 16, 29, 32
Gordon, Haim, 46–47, 121, 268n. 3
Greatbatch, David, 159
Greenberg, Leslie S., 68, 87–88
Grice, H. Paul, 137, 167
Griffin, Em, 70–71
Griffin, Leland L., 19
Grudin, Robert, 1
Grummon, Donald L., 82
Gunaratne, Sheldon A., 233
Gunn, Giles, 23
Gurevitch, Z. D., 99, 176
Gurman, Alan S., 83
Gutmann, Amy, 14

Habermas, Jürgen, 13, 222
Hackney, Sheldon, 233
Haiman, Franklyn S., 222

Haley, Jay, 162
Halling, Steen, 24
Hampden-Turner, Charles, 259
Harré, Rom, 14
Hart, Roderick P., 23, 71,84, 86,
271n. 4
Havens, Leston L., 91
Heclo, Hugh, 216
Heen, Sheila, vii, 267n. 2
Heisenberg, Werner, 29
Hellwig, Monika K., 267n. 2
Henderson, Valerie, 26, 31, 67, 77,
127, 135, 148, 240
Heritage, John, 154
Herman, Jonathan R., 269n. 6
Herzig, Margaret, 230, 257
Hodes, Aubrey, 35, 38, 46, 47, 156,
268n. 3
Holquist, Michael, 19, 204
hooks, bell, 14
Horton, Myles, 252
Horwitz, Rivka, 269n. 8
Hutterer, Robert, 67, 68
Hycner, Richard, 105

Isaacs, William N., vii, ix, 13,
175–176, 230, 231, 267n. 2

Jackson, Don D., 161
Johannesen, Richard L., 80, 274n. 1
Jorgenson, Jane, 24

Kahn, Herman, xiii
Kahn, Michael D., 59
Kaplan, Abraham, 23, 96, 179
Kaplan, E. Ann, 191
Katz, Elihu, 237
Katz, Robert L., 91
Kaufmann, Walter, 44, 45, 230, 268n.
3, 269nn. 8, 9
Keating, Suzanne, 95
Kellner, Hansfried, 7
Kepnes, Steven, 204
Kiesler, Donald J., 82, 87
Killenberg, George M., 13, 232

King, Andrew, 193, 205
Kirschenbaum, Howard, 26, 31, 67,
    70, 74, 76, 77, 80, 81, 89, 127,
    130, 135, 148, 184, 200, 203,
    240
Klapp, Orrin E., 258
Knitter, Paul F., 267n. 2
Kofman, Fred, 230
Kramer, Peter D., 67, 275n. 2

Laing, R. D., 129, 170
Lambeth, Edward B., 232, 233
Langenhove, Luk Van, 14
Lannamann, John W., 24
Lao Tzu, 39
Leeds-Hurwitz, Wendy, 24
Leifer, Michael, 24
Lewin, Kurt, 74
Lietaer, Germain, 68
Lingis, Alphonso, 174–175, 205
Lippman, Walter, 7–8
Little, Martin, ix
Littlejohn, Stephen W.,70, 86, 267n.
    2, 271n. 4
Luckmann, Thomas, 65, 187
Lyotard, Jean-Francois, 195, 198, 199

MacIntyre, Alasdair, 221
Madsen, Richard, 7, 69, 221
Manheim, Werner, 268n. 3
Mannheim, Bruce, 14
Mansbridge, Jane, 209, 215
Maranhao, Tullio, 24
Marcel, Gabriel, 36
Masson, Jeffrey Moussaieff, 69
Mathews, David F., 235
McLaughlin, Margaret L., 16
McNamee, Sheila, 267n. 2
McPhail, Mark, 13, 224
McPhee, Robert M., 123
Mead, George Herbert, 20, 199
Mearns, Dave, 67
Mendes-Flohr, Paul, 44, 268nn. 1, 3,
    269n. 5
Merleau-Ponty, Maurice, 187
Merritt, Davis, Jr., 13, 232

Meyer, Philip E., 233
Mischler, Elliot George, 30
Montgomery, Barbara M., 148, 267n.
    2, 274n. 1
Moonan, Willard, 268n. 2
Moore, Donald J., 268n. 3
Morgan, Edward P., 112
Morson, Gary S., 19, 27
Moyers, Bill, 218
Mumby, Dennis, 191

Nakagawa, Gordon, 71, 93, 271n. 6
Neumayr, G., 70
Niebuhr, Rheinhold, 121
Noddings, Nel, 174
Noel, Joseph R., 95
Noelle-Neumann, Elisabeth, 216
Nofsinger, Robert E., 157, 159

O'Hara, Maureen, 193, 194
Ong, Walter J., 19, 20–22, 155, 209

Palmer, Richard E., 18
Panko, Stephen M., 268n. 3
Patterson, Cecil H., 82
Patton, Bruce, vii, 267n. 2
Pawlowsky, Gerhard, 67, 68
Pearce, Kimberly A., viii, xi, 228,
    229, 257
Pearce, W. Barnett, viii, xi, 16, 24,
    205, 229, 253, 257, 267n. 2
Pentony, Patrick, 4, 124, 126
Peterson, Jean D., 26
Phillips, Derek L., 221
Phillips, Gerald M., 71, 271n. 4
Polanyi, Michael, 78, 197
Poole, Marshall Scott, 123
Poster, Mark, 14
Postman, Neil, 7, 156
Poulakos, John, 96
Prigogine, Ilya, 197

Raskin, Nathaniel J., 185
Raskin, Patricia M., 64, 68
Rheingold, Howard, 12, 253
Rice, Laura N., 68

Ricoeur, Paul, 243
Riegel, Klaus F., 17
Roffey, John W., 26
Rogers, Carl R., xv, 60, 67, 72, 74,
    75–76, 77, 78, 79, 80, 81, 82,
    83–84, 84, 85, 86, 87, 88, 89, 90,
    91, 92, 94, 95, 102, 105, 109,
    111, 113, 114, 115, 117, 118,
    119, 120, 121, 125, 133, 141,
    149, 150, 152, 157, 164, 168,
    183, 184, 185, 186, 196, 197,
    198, 211, 247, 270nn. 1, 2, 3,
    271–272n. 7, 272n. 1 (ch. 5),
    275n. 5
Rombauts, J., 68
Rome, Beatrice, 270n. 11
Rome, Sydney, 270n. 11
Rorty, Richard, 199
Rosaldo, Renato, 263–264
Rosen, Jay, 13, 232, 233
Rosenau, Pauline M., 192
Rosenfield, Lawrence W., 23
Rosenzweig, Franz, 44
Ross, Doug, 267n. 2
Roth, Sallyann, 257
Rudolph, Frederick, 110
Russell, David E., 105, 125, 133, 168

Saarinen, Esa., 14, 192, 193
Sampson, Edward E., ix, 93, 205
Sandel, Michael, 221
Sandra, Jaida N'ha, 228
Saunders, Harold H., vii, 267n. 2
Schaeder, Grete, 47, 101, 128, 269n. 5
Schein, Edgar H., 230
Schilpp, Paul A., 39, 40, 268nn. 1,2,
    269n. 8, 270n. 11
Schmid, Peter F., 67, 68
Schmidt, Gilya G., 268n. 3
Schoen, Stephen, 47
Schrag, Calvin O., 19, 186, 194
Schultz, Duane, 68
Schutz, Alfred, 65
Seckinger, Donald S., 26, 128
Senge, Peter M., 13, 230, 231
Sharf, Barbara F., 16

Shem, Samuel, 12
Shlien, John M., 110–111, 275n. 5
Shor, Ira, 173
Shotter, John, ix, 13, 14, 15, 24, 201,
    207, 256, 260, 275n. 2
Sillars, Alan L., 80, 271n. 4
Silverman, Hugh J., 191
Simon, Akiba Ernest, 268n. 3
Simons, Herbert W., 19
Skinner, B. F., 112, 113, 114
Slack, Sylvia, 76
Smith, Craig R., 18
Smith, Jonathan A., 14
Smith, Ronald Gregor, 43, 268n. 3,
    269n. 9
Snyder, Ilana, 14
Stains, Robert R., Jr., 230
Stephenson, William, 81
Stevens, Barry, 184
Stewart, John, ix, 18, 71, 92, 93, 94,
    192, 270n. 12, 274n. 1
Stipsits, Reinhold, 67, 68
Stone, Douglas, vii, 267n. 2
Stubbs, Michael, 30
Suhd, Melvin M., 68
Sullivan, William, 7, 69, 221
Sundararajan, Louise, 193–194
Surrey, Janet, 12
Swidler, Ann, 7, 69, 221
Swidler, Leonard, 267n. 2

Tannen, Deborah, vii, 258, 267n. 2
Taylor, Charles, 221
Taylor, Mark C., 14, 192, 193
Tedlock, Dennis, 14, 24
Teich, Nathaniel, 68, 194
Theroux, Phyllis, 57
Thomas, Milt, 92, 93, 94
Thomlison, T. Dean, 80
Thompson, Dennis, 14
Thorne, Brian, 26, 64, 67, 68, 80, 117,
    131, 206
Thorson, Esther, 233
Tipton, Steven M., 7, 69, 221
Todorov, Tzvetan, 19, 204
Toulmin, Stephen, 73

Tournier, Paul, 255
Trenholm, Sarah, 70, 86
Truax, Charles B., 82, 87, 95
Tyler, Stephen A., 24, 192

Van Balen, Richard, 26, 68, 117, 121,
    131, 194
Van Belle, Harry A., 80
van Dijk, Teun A., 99
Vermes, Pamela, 268n. 3
Vitz, Paul, 69

Waley, Arthur, 40
Wallach, Lise, 69
Wallach, Michael A., 69
Walters, Kimberly A. *See* Pearce,
    Kimberly A.
Walzer, Michael, 45–46
Warnke, Georgia, 18

Watson, Neill, 83
Watts, Alan, 75
Watzlawick, Paul, 161
Weil, Simone, 261
Werner, Carol M., 274n. 1
Williams, Raymond, 73
Witherell, Carol, 174
Wold, Astri H., 267n. 2
Wood, John K., 97
Wood, Robert E., 268n. 3

Yalom, Irvin D., 62, 67
Yankelovich, Daniel, vii, xiii,
    267n. 2
Yoshida, Atsuhiko, 26, 132
Young, Iris M., 14, 222, 261

Zappan, James P., 74
Zediker, Karen, ix

Subject Index

acceptance. *See also* confirmation; regard: x, 33, 56, 88–89, 103, 116, 149–152, 168, 179
as factor making for personal change, 149
actualizing tendency, 148, 201
Afrocentric philosophies, 224
Agassi, Judith Buber, xxiv, 126
audience. *See* dialogue, audience in
authenticity. *See* genuineness

Bakhtin, Mikhail, ix, 18–20, 27, 204
assessment of Buber, 204
Baldwin, Rev. DeWitt C., 125, 154
Bateson, Gregory, 240
becoming, process of, 152, 168–169
Ben-Gurion, David, 38, 104, 262–263
between, the sphere of, 32, 50, 51, 57, 152, 168, 174, 258
Between Man and Man, 44, 187
Bohm Dialogue Groups, 12
borderlands, 263–264
Buber and Rogers, comparison of thought of, 54–56, 75, 88, 90–91, 95–96, 115–117, 150–152, 168–169, 272n. 8, 275n. 5
Buber, Martin. *See also* Buber and Rogers, comparison of thought of; postmodernism and Buber; psychologism, Buber's critique

of; psychology, Buber's view of; psychotherapy, Buber's contributions to; public dialogue, Buber's skepticism about; Washington School of Psychiatry, Buber's lectures and seminars at; *specific book titles*
as communicator (*see also* interpersonal style), 46–49
biographical information, xvi, 36–45, 46, 56–57, 136–137, 268n. 4
autobiographical fragments, 40–41, 268n. 3
awards and honors, 38–39, 103
concept of moments, 187–189
contributions to human studies, 36, 49, 101
criticisms of, 44–49
Buber's response to, 270n. 11
dialogue (*see* dialogue, Buber's concept of)
facility with languages, 37
grounding in experience, 135–136
influence on Carl Rogers, 74
influences on thought of, 39–42
interpersonal style (*see also* interpersonal style; Buber, Martin, rhetoric of cannot), 46–49, 121, 145, 163–168

Buber, Martin (*cont.*),
　knowledge of Rogers's work,
　　116–117
　letters, 48, 268n. 5
　misunderstandings of, 270n. 1
　philosophical anthropology, 50–51,
　　52–53
　propoganda, concept of, 212–213
　relationship with Carl Rogers (*see*
　　Buber-Rogers relationship)
　reluctance to be filmed or
　　recorded, 3, 126
　rhetoric of cannot, 121, 165–167
　sources of learning regarding dia-
　　logue, 37, 39–42, 137, 159
　tours of United States, 1, 101–102,
　　104, 125
Buber, Paula, 37–38, 126
Buber-Rogers dialogue (*see also* dia-
　　logue, as moments of meeting,
　　Buber-Rogers position; Farber,
　　Leslie, objections of Buber-
　　Rogers dialogue occurring), xvii
　arrangements for, 1–2, 125, 126,
　　264–265
　as interview, 154, 155, 159, 160–162
　as dialogue, 124, 265
　audiotape of, making, 3, 126
　Buber's comments on, 4, 124
　　changing his mind about, 4, 11
　Buber's expectations for, 100
　commentaries on, problems with
　　other, 127–134
　dialogue, as topic of (*see also* psy-
　　chotherapy, as topic of Buber-
　　Rogers dialogue), xix, 124,
　　169–170
　interactional features of, 135–144,
　　157, 158, 273n. 2
　audience, 155–158
　humor, 137, 138–139, 141, 142,
　　143, 156
　laughter, 137, 142
　moderator, role of (*see* Friedman,
　　Maurice, role as moderator)
　Rogers's comments on, 133–134

Rogers's preparation for (*see*
　　Rogers, Carl, preparation for
　　Buber-Rogers dialogue)
　significance of, 26
　transcripts of, 26, 126, 127
　errors in previous, 134–135, 150,
　　273nn. 2, 3, 4, 275n. 3
　our new version, xxv, 31, 135,
　　273n. 1
Buber-Rogers relationship, xvii, xix,
　　47, 100, 102

Center for Studies of the Person,
　　xxiii, 61, 69, 97
Civic journalism. *See* public journal-
　　ism
Client-Centered Therapy, 60, 111,
　　247, 270n. 1
coauthorship. *See* methodology,
　　coauthorship, importance of
collaborative orientation, as charac-
　　teristic of dialogue (*see also* di-
　　alogue, characteristics of) 10,
　　238, 241
commons, as space for dialogue,
　　251–254
communication. *See also* Rogers,
　　Carl, theory of communication
　as transaction, 10
　expressive view of, 6, 271n. 4
　relationship level of, 161
　social approaches to, 24
communitarianism, 220–222
confirmation. *See also* acceptance:
　　xix, 5, 3354–56, 57, 87, 88–89,
　　116, 128, 149–152, 168, 170,
　　244, 262
conflict, 55–56, 103, 239
congruence, 80, 84–86, 95, 139, 151,
　　179, 248, 271nn. 5, 6
consensus, 222, 223
conversation analysis. *See also*
　　methodology: 15, 16, 30
Coulson, William, 69–70
criticism. *See* rhetorical criticism;
　　methodology

debate, distinguished from dialogue, xvi, 257–258
Deliberative Democracy Project, 235–236
deliberative opinion polls, 13, 236
democracy, 4, 209, 211–212
Descrates, Rene, 39, 50
Dewey, John. *See also* Lippmann-Dewey diagreement: 8–9, 60, 73, 74, 109, 111, 121, 245
dialectics. *See also* person, polar nature of: 28, 148, 260
dialogue. *See also* Buber-Rogers dialogue; psychotherapy, as dialogic existence
  as moments of meeting (*see also* psychotherapy as moments of meeting), ix–x, xii, xviii, 174, 178–190, 255–257
    Buber-Rogers position regarding, 33, 44, 173–174, 178–190, 202, 206–207, 244
    change focused in, 174–175, 182–186
  as rhetoric, 17–22, 28
  as technique, critique of (*see also* psychotherapy, Rogers's approach to technique, 199–200, 244–250, 268n. 5, 272n. 7
  audience in, xii, 153–158, 240, 258
  Buber's concept of, xvi, 5–7, 17–18, 49–57, 95–96, 160–161, 244–245
    as momentary, 187–189, 250
    examples, 51–52, 189
    grand, proposal for, 107–108
    limits to, 178
  characteristics of (*see also* collaborative orientaiton; dialogue, Buber's concept of; genuineness; immediacy; mutual orientation; strange otherness; surprise; temporal orientation; vulnerability), viii–xi, 9–11, 17, 94–96, 174–178, 237–238

difficulty of (*see also* public dialogue, Buber's skepticism about), 7, 240, 243
  when forced, x, 175, 240, 243
  when recorded, xi, 156, 240
  with audience, xi, 2, 154, 240
facilitating, 175, 250–264
importance of to society, xiii, 244
impediments to, 52–53
interdisciplinary interest in, 11, 13–14, 267–268n. 2
mediated, 12, 210, 253
power and, 226–227, 239, 259
public (*see* public dialogue)
relationship as key to, xix
research on, 123–124
structuring, 175–176, 239, 240–241
temporal nature of, 256, 274n. 1
discourse analysis. *See also* methodology: 15, 16

empathy, x, 69, 81, 89–94, 95, 115, 139, 157, 188, 197–198, 198, 205–206, 248, 259, 271n. 6, 275n. 5
equality. *See* mutuality
essentialism, 223
ethnography. *See also* methodology: 15

Farber, Leslie, 3, 104–106
  objections to Buber-Rogers dialogue occurring, 2, 4
Friedman, Maurice, xxii–xxiii, 125
  relationship with Buber, 270n. 11, 272n. 2
  relationship with Rogers, 138–139
  role as moderator of Buber-Rogers dialogue, 26, 124, 126–127, 143, 148, 163, 265
Freud, Sigmund. *See* psychology, Freudian

Gadamer, Hans-Georg, 14, 18, 19–20
  hermeneutic rhetoric of, 18
Gendlin, Eugene, 269–270n. 10

genuineness, as characteristic of dia-
    logue. *See also* congruence; di-
    alogue, characteristics of: 11,
    53, 57, 120, 238, 241

Habermas, Jurgen, 192, 222, 226
heteroglossia, 19
human nature, 103, 147, 200–203
Humanistic Psychology Archive, xxiii
Hutchins, Robert Maynard, 38, 108,
    110

I and Thou, xv, 37, 39, 44, 50, 101,
    107, 169, 187, 189, 196. 269n.
    9, 270nn 11, 12, 273n. 4
    Postscript to, 107, 130
    writing of, 43–44, 269n. 8
imagining the real, 42, 54, 57, 90,
    189, 200, 205
immediacy, as characteristic of dia-
    logue. *See also* dialogue, char-
    acteristics of: 9, 237, 240
inclusion. *See also* empathy; making
    present: 53–55, 57, 90, 115, 140,
    188, 200, 205–206, 252, 275n. 5
inner meeting, 145–147, 202
interhuman, realm of. *See* Buber,
    Martin, philosophical anthro-
    pology
interpersonal communication, quali-
    ties of, 80ff
interpersonal perception, 53–54
interpersonal style. *See also* Buber,
    Martin, interpersonal style;
    Rogers, Carl, interpersonal
    style: 6, 162–169
I-Thou, as primary word, 10, 43, 44
I-Thou relationship, 50, 87, 115, 129,
    133, 139, 204

journalism, public. *See* public jour-
    nalism
Jung, Carl. *See* psychology, Jungian

Kant, Immanuel, 39
Kierkegaard, Soren, 39, 74

Kirschenbaum, Howard, xxiv
The Knowledge of Man, 4, 44, 104,
    120 150, 187, 275n. 3

Landauer, Gustav, 42, 136
language, 18, 20, 247
    gendered use of, xx–xxi
law of the instrument, 23
learning organization, 13
Levinas, Emmanuel, 14, 198
Library of Congress, Carl R. Rogers
    Collection, xxiii
Limbaugh, Rush, 219
Lippmann-Dewey disagreement. *See
    also* Lippmann, Walter;
    Dewey, John: 7–9, 11, 108
Lippman, Walter. *See also* Lippmann-
    Dewey disagreement: 7–8
listening, xii, xix, 18, 52, 91–94, 120,
    189, 197, 200, 204–206, 240,
    244, 250, 257
    active, 91, 118–119, 271n. 7

making present. *See* inclusion
Martin Buber Archives, xxiii
McLaughlin Group, 218, 240
media
    concern for influence of, 212–213
    production biases of, 225
methodology. *See also* rhetorical criti-
    cism; conversation analysis;
    discourse analysis; ethnography
    avoiding templates for (*see also*
    law of the instrument), 22–24,
    25, 26–27
    coauthorship, importance of, 25,
    32–33
    for dialogic research, xvi, 16,
    24–33, 123
    of this book, xxi–xxiii, 26–34
Mid-West Conference on Martin
    Buber, 1, 104, 106, 122,
    125–127, 160
    participants in, 125
MIT Dialogue Project, ix, 13, 175,
    230–231

moments. *See* dialogue, as moments of meeting; psychotherapy, as moments of meeting; psychotherapy, effective moments in
Moyers, Bill, 218
mutual implication, as characteristic of dialogue (*see also* dialogue, characteristics of; mutuality), 10, 178–190, 238, 241
mutuality (*see also* mutual implication, as characteristic of dialogue), x, 33, 128, 130, 131, 139–145, 174, 182, 189–190, 254–255

National Conversation Project, 12, 233–234, 239
National Issues Forums, xii, 12, 235
National Issues Conventions, 236–237
Niebuhr, Reinhold, 38, 57, 121–122

On Becoming a Person, xv, 60, 67, 109, 152, 247, 270n. 1
Oprah Winfey show, 12
openness to experience, 79, 223
orality, secondary, 209–210
otherness (*see also* strange otherness, as characteristic of dialogue), 33, 86, 93, 102, 176–177, 205
recognition of key to dialogue, xix, 6

paranoiacs, relationships with, 142, 273n. 5
person
as distinct from individual, 152–153
polar nature of (*see also* human nature), 147–149, 201–202
person-centered approach, ix, 247
Person-Centered Journal, 68
Polanyi, Michael, 74, 77–78
postive regard. *See* regard
postmodernism, 190–207, 263
and Buber, 194–195

and communication, 192
and dialogue, 193
and Rogers, 193–195
suspicion of metanarratives, 195–199
suspicion of technique, 199–200
power. *See* dialogue, power and
praxis, 73, 260–261
psychologism, Buber's critique of, 17, 51, 92–93, 105
psychology, 114
behaviorist, 106–107, 115–116, 119, 196
Buber's view of, 104–107
Freudian, 105, 106–107, 116, 119, 166, 146, 147, 196
Jungian, 105, 106, 206
psychotherapy, 2
as moments of meeting (*see also* dialogue, as moments of meeting; psychotherapy, effective moments of), 118, 180–184, 186, 275nn. 2, 4
source of real change, 143, 149, 182, 183, 186
as topic of Buber-Rogers dialogue (*see also* Buber-Rogers dialogue, dialogue, as topic of), 4, 125, 126, 135
Buber's contributions to, 47, 132
dialogical, 105, 117
effective moments in, 87–88, 118, 139–145, 182
importance of relationship in, 116
limits of, 106
Rogers's approach to (*see also* acceptance; empathy; genuineness; regard), 1, 77, 87, 111–112, 118–120, 139, 183–184, 200
as technique (*see also* dialogue, as technique), 198
research support for, 64, 70–71, 81–83, 168
role differences in, 129

public dialogue, vii–viii, x–xii,
xv–xvi, 108, 114, 177, 216–217
Buber's skepticism about (*see also*
dialogue, Buber's concept of),
4, 109, 154, 210, 213
challenges to, 220–227
experiments in (*see also* Bohm Dialogue Groups; deliberative
opinion polls; MIT Dialogue
Project; National Conversation Project; National Issues
Forums; Public Conversations
Project; Public Dialogue Consortium; public journalism;
Utne Reader Salon), 12–14,
227–237
facilitating. *See* dialogue, facilitating
limited attempts at, 217–220
mediated, xii
possibility of, 4
structuring. *See* dialogue, structuring
public life, 5, 8–9, 109, 211–217
features of, xi–xii
functions of, 214–215
Public Conversations Project, xii, 12,
229–230, 257
Public Dialogue Consortium, vii, 12,
228–229, 257
public journalism, xii, 13, 231–233

recognition, importance to dialogue
of, 261–264
regard, 69, 80, 86–89, 95, 139, 248,
262
rhetorical criticism. *See also*
methodology: 15–16, 29–30,
32, 33
of conversation, 23–24, 27, 28, 30
rhetorical sensitivity, 86
rhetorics, productive of dialogue. *See*
dialogue, facilitating
Rogers, Carl. *See also* Buber and
Rogers, comparison of thought

of; postmodernism and Rogers;
psychotherapy, Rogers's approach to; *specific book titles*
biographical information, 60–61,
76, 89, 210–211
awards and honors, 61, 82,
111–112, 120
commitment to research, 63–64,
70–71, 76–77, 81–83
concept of moments, 183–186, 256
conception of self, 68–69, 71–72,
74–75, 78
contributions of,
to human studies, 61–62, 67
to psychology and psychotherapy, 62–67, 68
criticisms of, 61, 62, 68, 72, 90–94,
271n. 4
by communication scholars,
70–71, 84–86, 92–94
distrust of technique, 247–248
emphasis on communication, 78,
79–80
grounding in experience, 76–79,
135–136
influences on, 74–77
interpersonal style, 145, 163–168
knowledge of Buber's work, 90,
116–117, 120, 160, 210–211
misunderstandings of, 91–92,
184–185, 270n. 1
preparation for Buber-Rogers dialogue, 100, 157–158
praxis of dialogue, xvii, 72–74,
76–77, 94–96
recording therapy sessions, 3,
76–77
relationship with Martin Buber
(*see* Buber-Rogers relationship)
skill as facilitator, 119, 170
Skinner, B. F., relationship with
(*see also* Skinner, B. F.),
112–117, 196, 263
sources of learning regarding psychotherapy, 74–76

theory of communication, 72, 79–96
roles. *See also* psychotherapy, role differences in, 84–85, 179
differences, impact on dialogue, x, 158–162, 241
differences, impact on psychotherapy, 106, 120
enfolded, 160–162
Rorty, Richard, 14
Rosenzweig, Franz, 39, 43, 44

schizophrenics, 105, 130–131, 142, 261, 273–274n. 5
possibilities for relationships with, 106, 118, 129–130, 142
self-disclosure, 85
Skinner, B. F. *See also* Rogers, Carl, Skinner, B. F., relationship with: 112–117, 263, 272n. 1 (chap. 5)
social contructionism, 24, 260
strange otherness, as characteristic of dialogue (*see also* dialogue, characteristics of), 10, 174, 223, 237, 240, 261
surprise,
as characteristic of dialogue (*see also* dialogue, characteristics of), 6, 10, 20, 145–146, 223, 237, 240
in psychotherapy, 145–146
Rogers's willingness to feel, 78–79, 87

Taoism, 14, 39, 75–76, 147, 248, 269nn. 6, 7, 270n. 2
Taylor, Charles, 14
technique. *See* dialogue, as technique
temporal flow, as characteristic of dialogue. *See also* dialogue, characteristics of), 11, 177, 238
Tillich, Paul, 38, 57
transcripts. *See also* Buber-Rogers dialogue, transcripts of

accuracy of, 30
limits of, 28–29, 30–31
translation,
Buber's, 269n. 6
of Buber's work, 269n. 9
transparency. *See* congruence
truth, 200–204
dialogic, 201

uncertainty principle, Heisenberg's, 29
unconditional positive regard. *See* acceptance; regard
University of Chicago, 1, 101, 104, 110–111, 210, 236
Counseling Center, 60, 66, 112
University of Michigan. *See also* Mid-West Conference on Martin Buber: 1, 160
archives, xxiii
University of Wisconsin, 60, 117–118, 184, 240, 261, 274n. 5
Utne Reader Salon, 12, 228

value, locus of, 152, 168
vulnerability, as characteristic of dialogue. *See also* dialogue, characteristics of: 10, 203, 238, 240, 241, 257–259

Washington School of Psychiatry, 2, 6, 105
Buber's lectures and seminars at, 5, 6, 104
A Way of Being, 67
William Alanson White Memorial Lectures. *See* Washington School of Psychiatry, Buber's lectures and seminars at
Wittgenstein, Ludwig, xi, xii, 198, 247
World War I, 36, 42, 43, 136
World War II, 36, 101, 103, 110
wu-wei, 39–40, 75, 270n. 2